Entrepreneurs and the Transformation of the Global Economy

To my Wife, Christa

Entrepreneurs and the Transformation of the Global Economy

Anthony P. Ellison

Edward Elgar
Cheltenham, UK • Northampton, MA, USA

Published by
Edward Elgar Publishing Limited
Glensanda House
Montpellier Parade
Cheltenham
Glos GL50 1UA
UK

Edward Elgar Publishing, Inc.
136 West Street
Suite 202
Northampton
Massachusetts 01060
USA

A catalogue record for this book
is available from the British Library

ISBN 1 84064 819 8

Printed and bound in Great Britain by Biddles Ltd, *www.biddles.co.uk*

Contents

Preface

My interest in the effects of regulation and of its antithesis, deregulation, was awakened in the mid-1970s when I co-authored a book that sought to explain the order cycle in the world's airline industry. Like almost everyone else in my profession, I had been schooled in the tradition of neo-classical economics, and the book fell within the same model-testing and predicting tradition with which I was familiar.[1]

When, afterwards, I became part of a research team assembled by the Regulation Reference of the Economic Council of Canada, a Federal Government agency, charged with examining the effects of regulation on economic activity and with providing reasoned policy alternatives, I found myself among economists whose skills and perceptions had also been honed in the same neo-classical tradition. The method applied by the team accorded fully with this tradition. The inhibiting effects of protective regulation on productivity were measured and the predicted gains from exchanging through the market were provided, whereupon they were used to support both the reform and deregulation of markets in Canada. The resultant document made a substantial contribution to the debate then being conducted in Canada on the implications for Canada's transport system of the ongoing reform, and deregulation of the transport sector of the United States.

Continuing my sojourn in the realm of regulation, my next move took me into a unit within the Treasury Board, a central department of the Federal Government, whose express task was to initiate regulatory reform from within the Federal Government. In 1984, I assisted Counsel to the Minister of Transport at hearings into regulatory reform of the air transport industry, conducted through the regulatory agency, the Canadian Transport Commission.

These inter-related experiences and their outcomes, some of which are reflected in this study, brought it home to me that policies formulated from concepts, approaches and ideas, the very stuff of the neo-classical approach, are always destined to remain inert and never to serve as a stimulus to action unless they are taken up by an active proponent of change - the entrepreneur - willing and able to charge them with his passion and emotion.

---

[1] Ellison, Anthony P. and E. M. Stafford (1974), *The Dynamics of the Civil Aviation Industry*, Westmead and Lexington: Saxon House, Lexington Books.

Preface

These conclusions and the implications that they have for my understanding of economics, are based on the detailed analysis that I present in this study. The key to my thinking lies in the quest that I undertook to find an explanation for the entry and exit of regulation in the transport and communication sectors and the impact of these measures on trade and on financial regimes. In this quest, I discovered that the individual actor in economic life is not an automaton, a passive entity or an ideal type, but a responsive, purposeful human being who holds beliefs, fosters preferences and expectations and who, above all, is in possession of knowledge. It is such human qualities, along with the elements of uncertainty and ignorance and institutionally-shaped incentives, which combine to shape the conditions under which individual entrepreneurs make decisions which ultimately determine the trade and financial regimes that govern economic life.

I thank Mrs A. Fine and Ms Caroline Blochlinger for typing earlier drafts, and Professor Brian Bayliss and Professor Mark Blaug for their support for the project. My editor, Dr Colin Vale, not only knocked the manuscript into shape but has been a constant support and friend.

Above all, I owe an enormous debt of gratitude to my wife, Christa, for her encouragement and patience in waiting for this project to come to fruition.

A. P. ELLISON

Miami, Florida
15 August 2001

Acknowledgements

The author and publisher wish to thank the following who have kindly given permission for the use of copyright material.

American Economic Association for the articles: 'US Industry Adjustment to Economic Deregulation,' with Clifford Winston, *Journal of Economic Perspectives*, 1998, **12**(3) Summer, p.92. 'The Private Uses of Private Interests: Incentives and Institutions,' with Joseph Stiglitz, *Journal of Economic Perspectives*, 1998, **12** (2), Spring, p.21.

Council on Foreign Relations for the article, 'The Capital Myth', with Jadish Bhagwati, *Foreign Affairs*, **77**(3), 1999, p.12. Copyright 2002 by the *Council on Foreign Relations, Inc.*

Duke Law Publications for the article, 'Revisionism Revised? Airline Deregulation and the Public Interest,' with Michael E. Livine, *Law & Contemporary Problems*, 1981, **44** (1), p. 194.

Economic Strategy Institute for the quote from the testimony of Clyde V. Prestowitz, House of Representatives Aviation Subcommittee, 15 June 2000.

George Mason Law Review for the article 'Incentives versus Regulation: The Case for Airport Noise Charges,' with Roy A. Nierenberg, *George Mason University Law Review*, **2**(2), 1978, p.169.

ITU for the Paper presented by Dr. Pekka Tarjanne, former ITU Secretary-General, at *Forum ITA '97*, 'Telecommunications and World Development: Forecasts, Technologies and Services,' Moscow, 5 February 1997.

MIT Press for the quotation from *Pop Internationalism* with Paul Krugman, 1998, p.83.

MIT Press Journals for the articles: 'Some Fallacies in The Interpretation of Social Cost,' with Frank H. Knight, *The Quarterly Journal of Economics*, **38** (4), August 1924, pp. 586-587, 605. 'The International Telecommunications Regime,' with Peter Cowhey, *International Organization*, 1990, **44**(2), pp. 198-199.

Acknowledgements

The Brookings Institution for the articles: 'The Economic Theory of Regulation after a decade of Deregulation,' with Sam Peltzman, *Brookings Papers on Economic Activity, Microeconomics*, 1989, p. 59, and 'Enhancing the Performance of the Deregulated Air Transportation System,' with Elizabeth E. Bailey, Steven A. Morrison and Clifford Winston, *Brookings Papers on Economic Activity, Microeconomics*, 1989,p. 61, 84, 85 and 113; and 'You Can't Get There from Here. Government Failure in U.S. Transportation,' *Brookings Review,* **17**(3), 1999, Summer, p. 37, pp. 45-46.

The National Academies for the article 'Airports Under Deregulation: Congestion, Saturation and New Technology,' with Roy J. Pulsifer, *TR Circular 286*, Transportation Research Board, National Research Council, Washington DC, 1984.

The New Republic for the article 'The Insider,' with Joseph Stiglitz, *The New Republic*, 17 and 24 April 2000, pp.58 and 60.

The University of Chicago as publisher and the *Journal of Law and Economics* for the articles: 'The Problem of Social Cost', with R.H.Coase, (3 *J.Law & Econ* 1 1960), p. 43. Copyright 1960 by *The University of Chicago*. All rights reserved. And 'Landing Fees and the Transformation of the Global Economy,' with Michael E. Levine, (*12 J.Law & Econ*. 79, 1969), pp. 91 and 100. Copyright 1969 by *The University of Chicago*. All rights reserved.

University of Toronto Press Incorporated for the quotation from *The Bias of Communication* (Reprinted 1991) with Harold A. Innis, p. 90.

Every effort has been made to trace all the copyright holders but if any have been inadvertently overlooked the publishers will be pleased to make the necessary arrangements at the first opportunity.

Introduction

This book examines the causes and consequences both of regulating and of deregulating transport, telecommunication, trade and financial regimes. Its aim, simply stated, is to review methodologies appropriate for a practising political economist in general, and for a transport economist in particular.

However, the writing of it has taken me, unexpectedly, into many fields which I might once have considered remote from, or at best peripheral to, transport economics, and an unexpected unity has emerged among the several disciplines which interest me, revealing the underlying unity in human thought and endeavour.

As a professional economist, I initially set out to explain the deregulation of the transport modes in North America. The task appeared to be almost routine: another cataloguing of sequential events leading inevitably to a known conclusion. But, as I wrote, an unexpected dialectic emerged from the conditions of regulation and deregulation. The word 'regulation', as unremarkable at first as 'obedience' or 'law-abiding', began to take on a more significant, if not ominous, character. It slowly became apparent that, for these antithetical terms to be in any sense comprehensive, explanations had to address the question as to why, in the first place, regulation had occurred.

It seemed to me that the right to movement is as central to the concept of human freedom as are the right to think or the right to act. Freedom, in the truest sense, can only exist in the absence of regulatory restraint on movement. Therefore, a free man may be defined, not only as one who can think what he likes, do what he likes (within the law), but also as one who can go wherever he wishes, taking, if he so chooses, his goods with him. Indeed, to be free to move is to be as free as it is possible for a man to be. Every form of freedom, including freedom to trade, depends, therefore, on the freedom of movement.

But there is yet another dimension to the freedom of movement - the dimension of self-realisation, the liberation of the spirit into the varied and abundant realms of human experience. For many, movement that takes the form of travel is the most sublime of pleasures and experiences. Travel conjures memorable images and sensations whether the familiar or unfamiliar is glimpsed, perhaps breathlessly, in a blur through the windscreens of fast cars or lovingly surveyed through the carriage windows of slow steam locomotives. Travel is spatially liberating, life-affirming and life-enhancing.

While the movement of the individual is expressive of spatial liberation, commodities move in response to market exchanges. The movement of both people and of commodities has been influenced by attitudes towards the perceived effects of individual liberty, as well as by the perceived effects of the market process. There is an historical dimension to these notions. The vision and daring of the railroad entrepreneurs made them the true exemplars of the age of *laissez-faire*. However, their exercise of unrestricted power was short-lived. Their opposition came from the proponents in the inherent conflict as to the efficacy and resulting distributive justice of unrestricted trading through the market process by business organisations. The resultant regulation of the railroads, which was to last about a century, signifies a divide between the dynamic era of *laissez-faire*, from which the railroads emerged and were shaped, and the start of the era of mass industrial order that was steered by the state.

With these thoughts in mind, I re-defined my objectives. The task became that of considering explanations for the regulation and deregulation of transport modes in North America. This exercise involved outlining various hypotheses of regulatory change and then evaluating them by pitting their explanations against the observed historical events.

But observing historical events has consequences, for patterns emerge from such observation and stretch from era to era across decades, centuries and continents. I realised that the deregulation of domestic transport systems and the liberation of the international regulatory regimes were part of a shift towards what came to be described as globalisation. This process has attracted fierce debate and has sparked violent confrontations between the elites that are seen to be promoting this process and the protest movements that are themselves, thanks to the Internet, organised on a global scale.

Hugely disparate groups oppose globalisation. Some opponents see markets as encouraging selfishness and soul-destroying materialism. The market's cycles of creative destruction wipe out tradition and engender economic and social instabilities, while the uncoordinated pursuit of personal gain results in increasing commodification, reprehensible practices and tawdry societies. The removal of national barriers extends the reach of the market in such a way that communities are being linked, not by a supranational democratic process, but by market forces. The market is not democratic, for all folks don't have the same dollars to 'vote' with. Some are, accordingly, more equal than others. Furthermore, these market forces are allegedly destroying the environment, causing social unrest (as immigrants clash with indigenous groups), and exploiting the lives of countless millions. The political elites are the target of the protestors because it is they who are seen to be tearing down their nations' remaining protective borders against the all-powerful, profit-driven, intrusive market process. These elites are deemed to be traitors to their own peoples, for they are responsive not to the needs and wants of the people they purport to represent but, it is claimed, to the captains of global capitalism. Indeed, to the protestors, it is a far from proven case that the majority of the world's voters actually want to be subjected to a rampant, materialistic, market order.

These are important and diverting issues that are examined in Chapter 3.

The immediate task to hand, however, was to explain the liberation of the international regulatory regimes of all those activities that were to constitute the global market-trade, telecommunications and finance. Again, hypotheses purporting to explain regulation and deregulation of international regimes were evaluated against the facts of history. Telecommunications, impacting on costs and the penetration of information, have greatly enhanced the co-ordinating capability of the global market.

It soon became clear to me that the hypotheses I had been examining were, in essence, explanations of the nature of the market process (or of capitalism) in its various forms or stages. The changes that I was studying constituted the transformation from what are sometimes described as mass industrial to post-industrial orders.

This led me to evaluate some of the theories of transformational change. Here I returned to the Newtonian universe of the neo-classical paradigm, to which I refer in the Preface, and found it wanting. History is predictable in this Newtonian world, for the return to equilibrium is inevitable. However, this is not so if the economy is complex, process-dependent, organic and evolving rather than deterministic and predictable.[1] The 'mutations' of history could spin the system into chaos. I was reminded of Hick's observation, 'As economics pushes on beyond 'static,' it becomes less like science, and more like history.'[2]

History and economics share a common subject matter and attempt to explain phenomena of human action within the context of societal interaction and the material world. If regularity in the examined phenomena cannot be expected in the near future, the two at least examine the same phenomena within the same time zone, the past. Historians, economists and physicists encounter the same difficulties in observing directly the phenomena under investigation. All three have deployed empirical testing. The implications of the posed theory are deducted and are interpreted as an explanation of the phenomena for which it is difficult, usually impossible, to account. Extending meaning to the correspondence between the tested phenomena and the actual manifestations of the phenomena has meant using the process of verification, i.e. confirmation by empirical observation of 'facts.' Stating the implied tenet differently, if the hypotheses were invalid, then the explanation provided by the tests would not be confirmed. Hence, of necessity, if not of choice, historians and economists have engaged in validation rather than falsification of their explanations.[3]

Schumpeter draws the line on candidate theories of economics in saying: '...when we succeed in finding a causal relation between two phenomena ...the one which plays the 'causal' role is non-economic.'[4]

When economic hypotheses hit the economic bedrock identified by Schumpeter, they have to address the non-economic explanations of the four delineated exogenous parameters of tastes, technologies, endowments and rule structures. Put simply, the issues are: which, what form and to what extent are these parameters to be treated as endogenous? (The candidate hypotheses are introduced and compared in the first part of Chapter 4.)

In pursuing explanations, I journeyed backwards in time and into social as well as economic areas of enquiry. Here is a route guide:

Chapter 1 presents an interpretation of the role of transport in the economic development of the United States and Canada. The chapter focuses on the differences between the policies and institutions within which the transport systems of the respective countries in which they operated. It charts the entry and exit of transport regulation in the two countries by examining the regulatory changes that occurred. It provides, also, information on transport institutions and policies. The time frame of this chapter is the modern era, when the market order came to shape the emerging economies of North America.

The first part of Chapter 2 explores the formation of ideologies within the transforming, modernising societies of Western Europe and North America. These are then related, in the second part, to the containment and release of the market process and, in particular, to the formation and later disintegration of domestic and international regulatory regimes in transport, tele-communications, trade and finance. The emerging contemporary global economic system is described.

Kenneth Arrow, writing almost forty years ago about what could be described as the mass industrial economy of the United States with its orders of market exchanges, coercive collectivities and affirmative relationships, postulated an adaptive hypothesis. He suggested that when the market order fails, 'society will recognise the gap, and non-market social institutions will arise attempting to bridge it.'[5] Some have inferred that the global market is guided by the propensity for adaptation of the constituent societies. Others disagree, and suggest that this process is unstable and destructive.

Chapter 3 describes the results of deregulating the market constraining domestic and international regulatory regimes. The computerised and electronic communications systems have formed a set of interlocking markets that have enabled almost instantaneous movement of information around the globe. The chapter proceeds to explore the contesting analyses concerning the stability or instability of this global market process and the various alternatives that have been proposed to contain the ensuing instabilities.

Chapter 4 reviews the contesting hypotheses concerning the stability or otherwise of the global market process, and subjects them to evaluations. At issue is the compatibility or otherwise of open international regimes. In part two, explanations of transformational or large-scale historical change are presented. In the third part, I examine the various contending theories of regulation while the fourth part contains an evaluation of explanations of the opening of international regulatory regimes that have contributed to the globalisation of the market process.

In the four Chapters that follow, I explore two approaches to transport economics, the engineering and the neo-institutional approach. The neo-classical price-engineering and the neo-institutional price theory shapes the engineering policies that are recommended for the transport sector. The engineer specifies the prices and quantities, as they would emerge under conditions of equilibrium, and then proceeds to appraise and implement policies according to the effect they allegedly elicit in equilibrium situations.

From these exercises emerge the often implicit forms of idealised orders. The neo-institutional approach is built upon a conceptualisation of property rights. The property regimes in the respective institutions are seen as providing individuals with incentives to discover, generate, exchange and act upon information. Individuals in institutions cannot be assumed, as they are in the neo-classical approach, to readily accept prices and taxes that purport to maximise welfare. Nor can the structure of institutions be changed without any regard to unintended effects.

Chapter 5 situates the respective transport policy prescriptions by high-lighting their conceptual origins. In the first part of the chapter, the Pigouvian, or engineering approach to the 'transport problem' is examined. The concept of contestable markets is treated in part three, while parts four and five describe the comparative, neo-institutional approach. Chapters 6, 7 and 8 explore the implications of these varied approaches.

In Chapter 6 there is a comparison of the way in which the active deregulators of the US transportation system conceptualised the deregulatory process, and of the way in which they, and other analysts, have measured and interpreted the performance of the deregulated airline industry.

Chapter 7 examines and evaluates the prescriptions put forward to correct for the resource misallocation in the US air transportation system, while Chapter 8 examines the formation of policies with respect to the Canadian aviation system.

Chapter 9 compares and contrasts the engineering and the neo-institutional approaches that have been examined in the three previous chapters. The appropriateness - or otherwise - of contending approaches and theories were tested according to their explanatory powers.

The results of this quest are outlined in the concluding Chapter 10.

Notes

1. Kauffman, for instance, has conceptualised the economy as a 'web of transformation of products and services among economic agents' that harbour 'internal endogenous forces which tend to autocatalystically drive an increase in the number of tasks, goods and services which fit into the growing web.' *The Economy as an Evolving Complex System*, Santa Fe Institute Studies in the Science of Complexity, **5**, Redwood City, CA, p.126. Richard Day, in his review states that: 'Kauffman shows the beginnings of a theory that can illustrate economic evolution, its driving propensity to create new forms and to evolve ever more intricate interconnectivities through specialisation and exchange.' Day, Richard (1991), Book Review, *Journal of Economic Liberation*, **29**(March), p.79.
2. Hicks, John R. (1979), *Causality in Economics*, New York: Basic Books, p.xi
3. Hamouta, O. F. and Price, B. (1991), *Verification in Economics*, London: Routledge.
4. Schumpeter, J. A. (1911), *The Theory of Economic Development. An Inquiry into Projects, Capital, Credit, Interest, and the Business Cycle*, translated by R.Opie (1965), London and New York: Oxford University Press, 1961, pp.4-5
5. Arrow, Kenneth J. (1963), 'Uncertainty and the Welfare Economics of Medical Care,' *American Economic Review*, **53**(December), p.967.

1. Transport's Punctuated Precession in North America

INTRODUCTION

The early French explorers in the North American wilderness named the majestic, but awesome river they first encountered, the St. Laurentius to honour a courageous third-century martyr. To their insignificant settlement in the vastness of the new continent, they gave the name Montreal, and, perhaps hopeful of an early breakthrough in their quest for the Northwest Passage, the major rapids guarding one of the gateways to the Appalachian barrier, they called Lachine.

It was not China they had entered, however, but a gargantuan drainage basin covering over 270 thousand square miles, encompassing a quintet of Great Lakes comprising an area of some 9500 square miles, the threshold of the country that was to become Canada.

Further exploration by Marquette and LaSalle located portages between the St. Lawrence uniting, under French control, the great river of the central plains, the Mississippi, with the mighty St. Lawrence.

Prior to 1713, France held the vast area west of the Great Lakes and down the Mississippi to New Orleans. At that time Britain's colonies were confined primarily to the eastern seaboard. That was to change in 1713, when, in terms of the Treaty of Utrecht, the Spanish possessions east of the Mississippi became British. When, in 1763, St. Lawrence also came under British control, the French possessions were divided and the formerly united St. Lawrence and Mississippi basins were separated politically.

When, in 1776, these states gained independence they quickly broke into civil factions, with the seaboard states establishing port fees that were profitable but hardly encouraging to the trade of the upriver states. The Commerce Clause of the Constitution granted to the US Congress the exclusive power to regulate interstate commerce. In 1787, a statute was approved that provided for freedom of navigation. According to one commentator, the guiding principle of freedom of navigation emerged as a prerequisite, '…holding and defending the Trans-Appalachian West against the depredations of foreign powers and the splintering tendencies of the remote frontier.'[1]

The Gallatin Report, in 1808, proposed a system of nation-wide canals and river improvements to be undertaken at US federal expense. In 1824, Congress passed the *General Seaway Act* that empowered the President to employ civil engineers and Officers of the Corps of Congress to produce survey plans and prepare estimates for the building of roads. The 1826 *Rivers and Harbours Act* became the prototype of enabling legislation for the improvement programme upon which the Corps embarked.

For over a decade, starting in 1824, federal appropriations for river and harbour improvements were stepped up, averaging $702,000 per annum in the 1820s and $1.3 million during the 1830s, under the Jackson Presidency. In parallel, by establishing private monopolies,[2] the state provided support for local projects conducted by the Corps.

The movement westward intensified and, operating behind a high tariff wall, industries grew, and trade between the industrialising East and the Midwest expanded. In 1812 the US tried and failed to capture the St. Lawrence. Five years later the Erie Canal was started in an attempt to lure away from Montreal the trade of the upper Mississippi Valley. The Erie was a public works project of the state of New York, linking the tide water at New York City, by way of the Hudson River, with a canal along the Mohawk Valley and entering Lake Erie at Buffalo.

After the opening of the Erie Canal, New York controlled a route that was more economical than the improved St. Lawrence waterway. In 1825, a canal route around the Niagara peninsula, known as the Welland Canal, was completed. Further improvements to the St. Lawrence were made with government support. The Rideau Canal was completed in 1832, the Cornwall Canal in 1842, and the St. Lawrence Canals between 1845 and 1847. By 1855, with the building of a canal by the Americans at Sault St. Marie, the navigable waterways spanned a third of the Continent.

By this time, however, the railways had superseded the canals in importance. The first railroad in the United States was chartered in 1827. By 1840, there were as many miles of rail-track as of canals. The strategy of the British colony during the first half of the nineteenth century was to attract, down the corridor of the St. Lawrence, the trade of the American mid-west. Commenting, in the late 1950s, on the strategies of the British in Canada, the economic historian, H.G.J. Aitken, argued that throughout its history, Canadian development expansion had been defensive in character. 'Each phase of expansion in Canada has been a tactical move designed to forestall, counteract, or restrain the northward extension of American economic and political influence.'[3]

The size of the Canadian state relative to the British Empire and its neighbour the United States understandably led Aitken to identify the forces to which the Canadian state responded as emanating from the existence of these two powerful influences. However, he interprets the self-preserving Canadian state's responses to perceived external threats, not as that of a militaristic, extractive tax collector and as requisitioner of resources from the domestic, but as that of a state mobilising resources, stimulating economic growth and creating economically efficient property rights. The innovative corporate form, for instance, established initially by individual statute (and later by general statute), was a response to the needs of larger, risk-taking transport, manufacturing and banking interests.[4]

During the middle period of the century, the settlement and westward expansion of the United States was undertaken largely by private ventures. The railroads enjoyed freedom from government regulation. Some, such as the transcontinental railroads, received generous subsidies in the form of land grants. Between 1850 and 1880, some 10-20 per cent of the Gross Domestic Product was invested in the railroads.[5] By 1882, the Pennsylvania Railroad was the largest private business in the world. Its 30,000 employees exceeded the number in the employ of the federal government. The railroads were the exemplars of America's age of *laissez-faire*.

This changed in 1887 with the passing of the *Interstate Commerce Act* which established the first independent regulatory commission (the ICC) in the United States. The ICC was set up to attempt to regulate the activities of the railroad entrepreneurs. The passing of the *Act* constitutes the divide between the dynamic era of *laissez-faire*, from which the railroads emerged and which they, in turn, shaped, and the start of the mass industrial order that was to be steered by the state well into the future.

At this point in the narration a word of caution is in order. Robert Fogel, in his celebrated 1964 counter-factual book, '*Railroads and American Economic Growth: Essays in Econometric History,*'[6] attempted to quantify the claims of those who credited the railroads with an inordinately large but imprecise contribution to America's economic growth. He approached this task by 'removing' the railroads from history and estimating how the American economy's transport 'needs' might have been accommodated by means such as the canals. His estimates go some way towards muting the trumpeting of contemporary railroad enthusiasts and boosters. The railroads, he observes, did absorb a sizeable share of investment, and private returns, particularly in the last decade of the nineteenth century, were modest. However, the expenditure on the railroads was arguably justified by their social rate of return. In other words, the railroads had multi-dimensional impacts and any economic history of America must address them.

Prior to the start of the New Deal era in 1933, only railroads, pipelines and water carriers were subject to direct federal economic regulation. Within a decade, the ICC had regulated entry into and had set the minimum rates of the interstate motor carriers, barge lines and freight forwarders. The Civil Aviation Authority, for its part, regulated interstate freight and passenger carriers. The transportation sector was central to the public work programmes that were designed to create employment, while 'public utility' regulation was introduced into carrier markets considered to be subject to disorder and uncertainty.

The building of the 'railway bridge' between the two settled parts of Canada is held up as the buckle in the belt that bound the newly-founded Confederation, and which prevented the annexation of the West by the United States. Requisitioning resources and the imposition of protective tariffs in 1878 constituted an attempt to encourage the development of manufacturing in central Canada and to stimulate traffic along the east-west transport route. This was known as the National Policy.[7] These were extractive policies, directed, not at accruing military might, but at establishing and sustaining complementary agricultural and industrial economies.

In this way, the strategic approach that was to last a century was launched. The state of Canada deployed all modes of transport and later tele-communications and broadcasting in implementing its grand strategy, which was aimed at accomplishing the almost impossible task of simultaneously maintaining equilibrium between the shifting regional economies of the Confederation and of buttressing the perceived notions of Canadian regional and national social identities against the powerful undertow of the American economy and culture to the south.

In the United States, the protective economic system remained in place until the eighth decade of the twentieth century. Then, regulatory policies changed rapidly. Under pressures that were generated by the financial failure of the railroads, breaches were made in the regulatory regime of the railroads. The air transport industry was subject to a phased deregulation in 1978. While policy changes occurred as early as the 1970s, effective legislative change only took effect in 1976 with the railroads *4-R Act*, ending with the *Motor Carriers Act* of 1980.

A substantial part of the Canadian transport industry was deregulated between the early 1960s and the end of the 1980s. During that time, the national flag carrier, Air Canada, was privatised. The signing of a Free Trade Agreement with the United States meant that Canada entered the tenth decade of the century with much of its trade in goods and services traversing across a substantially, liberated domestic market. With the launching of the North

American Free Trade Agreement (NAFTA) in 1993, this trade traversed the American and Mexican markets as well.

These two periods, one that marked the entry of regulation into the US transportation industry and the other its exit, were turning points in the economic history of the United States. In the 1880s, the shift was away from *laissez-faire* to regulation by 'scientific government' of independent commissions. Almost a century later, there was a rejection of scientific government and protective regulations and a move towards *laissez-faire*. The regulatory reform and deregulation of the US transportation system profoundly affected Canada. In moving from protectionism to free trade, from regulation and state ownership to deregulation and privatisation, from extractive to mobilising policies, Canada was not returning to a state of *laissez-faire*. It was embracing an ideology that governments of Canada since the founding of the nation a hundred-and-thirty years earlier had repeatedly rejected.

Canada's Constitution had established a parliamentary democracy, a system of government distinctly different from the separation of judicial legislative and executive powers which was enshrined in the Constitution of the United States. This difference, in part, accounted for the deployment of regulation under federal direction in Canada rather than through independent regulatory agencies as happened in the United States. Unlike the governments of the United States, which supported railroad development but left ownership in the hands of private interests, the governments of Canada engaged in railway building, nationalising when the private roads went bankrupt. Other differences were also evident. While the Canadian provinces did not accept Federal regulation of inter-provincial trucking, in the United States federal regulation of civil aviation was confined to interstate movement. Moreover, state regulation in the US and provincial regulation in Canada differed from federally regulated aviation and trucking respectively. These differences opened up the opportunity for the development of comparative case studies that were to play a part in shaping the course of regulatory reform.

In this chapter the following aspects of the regulatory regimes in both Canada and the US are discussed:

First, under the subhead, Railroads, Railways and Regulation, as well as the regulation and formation of the government supported rail cartels.

The second part describes the formation of the regulated transport sectors in the two countries, while the reform and deregulation of the US transportation sector is described in section three.

The fourth section, drawing heavily on research published by the author,[8] examines the unravelling of the Canadian transport sector. Here was a sector that had been cushioned within protective regulation and deployed as a conduit for federal subsidies but was to emerge finally as largely deregulated and privatised. The effects of trade between the two countries on Canada's regulatory structure, the distinguishing characteristics of the Canadian regulatory system and political and bureaucratic entrepreneurship are all highlighted.

RAILROADS, RAILWAYS AND REGULATION

The 1850s were years of unprecedented growth in North America. It was a decade during which the United States expanded rapidly. The state of California had gained admission to the Union in 1850 and neighbouring Oregon nine years later. The states of Iowa, Wisconsin and Minnesota were established in 1858 and, during this period, the upper Mississippi was also settled. Between these Mid-Western states and the West Coast lay the vast expanse the national territory of the United States.

Immigrants poured into the country and surged through the gateways to the prairies and beyond to California. Their passage was eased by the railroads, the first of which, stimulated by the demands of the Civil War, was undertaken by private capital under a charter, its cost subsidised by land grants.

Thereafter, the construction of railroads proceeded with furious speed during the 1850s. Philadelphia and Baltimore were linked with the Ohio Valley, Cincinnati and St. Louis with the East in 1853 and a bridge was constructed over the mighty Mississippi in 1856.

By the end of the decade, Chicago had become the main distribution point for agricultural products from the mid-west, the export of which had been stimulated by Britain's military entanglement in the Crimea.

In 1864, the Northern Pacific was granted a charter to run from the head of Lake Superior across the Northwest. To the south, the Texas and Pacific and the Atcheson, Topeka and Santa Fe lines were brought together amid much controversy over the size of the government subsidies for these two systems.

In 1869, the Union Pacific Company line met up with the eastward Central Pacific Company in Utah forming the first transcontinental railroad system in North America.

Canada, facing exclusion from the preferential trade system of the United States and with little prospect of regaining preference under Britain's policy of free trade had little option but to hasten the establishment of a transcontinental federation, linked by rail and water transport and comprising a customs union. In 1867, the *British North America Act* (BNA) joined the provinces of Canada, Nova Scotia and New Brunswick under a federal constitution.

The construction of the Intercontinental Railway between the *Maritimes* and *Riviere de Loupe* was completed in 1876. Propelled by the desire to secure the West Coast for the new confederation and supported by a protective tariff, the Canadian Pacific Railway (CPR) was built. The line, completed in 1878, traversed the barren region north of Lake Superior, providing an all-Canadian route to the Pacific. Under Clause 15, of the Act establishing the Canadian Pacific Railway, the 'monopoly clause' guaranteed that for twenty years no other line would be constructed south of its line to run within fifteen miles of latitude 49, the international boundary with the US.

The transcontinental line from Montreal to the Pacific, completed in 1866, two years after the Northern Pacific line, linked the head of the Great Lakes and the Twin Cities with Puget Sound. The CPR linked Winnipeg with the Twin Cities in 1878 and in 1893, it completed an alternative transcontinental route - 'the Soo' - by means of an extension of the Minneapolis, St. Paul and Sault St. Marie.

The Grand Trunk linked Montreal with Portland, Maine, and then moved westward. The Northern moved from Toronto to Georgia Bay. A southern route lay along the lower lake to Windsor at the border. The Great Western linked Toronto, and reached Sarnia in 1859. By 1855, the Great Western, crossing the peninsula, linked Ontario with the New York Central system. Montreal, Quebec and Chicago were linked by traffic arrangements over American lines beyond Sarnia. The Grand Trunk and the Great Western received 40-60 per cent of their gross revenue from American sources. They were also subject to rate and traffic agreements. By 1881, the Grand Trunk, had reached Chicago and was merged with the Great Western in 1882.[9]

In 1888, the Northern was added to the Great Western system. Competition for western traffic was intense. On the Canadian side, the Grand Trunk was joined in competition by the CPR, which, in 1890, was extended to Windsor. This gave the Canadian transcontinental carrier access to American railroads in Detroit. Competing on the American side were the New York Central, Erie, Pennsylvania and Baltimore and Ohio Railroads.[10]

By the 1870s, the railroads linked the United States into a single, great market. They became the dominant enterprises of the American economy by virtue of the fact that they were the exclusive providers of carriage over their own tracks. Protected by regulations, in terms of which they were incorporated and, simultaneously, enjoying monopolies over carriage, railroad companies were put in the enviable position of being able to determine rate levels as well as quality of service. Shippers, on the other hand, could rely only on competition between companies to protect their interests.

There were distinct differences between the transportation systems of the US and Canada.

The problems that emerged in the United States sprang from the exclusivity of the franchises that the railroads enjoyed and they were resolved through legal channels, particularly through the courts, which attempted to maintain the law of common carriage. In Canada, on the other hand, there was far less competition among participants than in the US. Furthermore, the Canadian government had at various times financed, controlled or had actually provided substantial transport facilities. Consequently, decisions about franchises and conditions of service were made, not by the courts, but by legislatures and by legislation.[11]

In the United States, farmers, in particular, were dissatisfied because, given low levels of competition, they were vulnerable to profiteering in their dealings with banks and railroad companies. Farming organisations appealed for government protection against high interest rates. While the frantic construction of new railroads had led to intensive rivalry over rates. Instead of reducing them it produced monopolistic agreements and practices which effectively raised rates, tilting the balance between shippers and carriers in the latter's favour. While few denied the importance of the railroads, there was resentment at the elimination of competition between railroad companies. Farmers even claimed that railroad owners and elevator operators had bribed legislators in order to achieve higher profits. There was dissatisfaction over government weakness in dealing with the railroads and owners' trusts. It was alleged that the courts were not up to the job of protecting small producers, and that the common law courts had failed to maintain the law of common carriage in the face of the power of the railroads.

The Granger Movement, which brought the question to a head, sprang from the 'National Grange of the Patrons of Husbandry,' an association of Mid-Western farmers formed, in 1867, to promote social and educational goals. From it soon emerged an organised protest movement against alleged economic abuses, principally the failure of the courts to protect farmers' interests. The onset of a recession in agriculture prompted the Movement to petition states for protective regulation.[12]

The resultant 'Granger Laws' varied from state to state. Some established state commissions with authority to set maximum rail rates and to eliminate discrimination. The response of the private railroads was to argue that, as private business undertakings, they ought not to be subjected to rate regulation. Those railroads that were interstate undertakings argued that they were subject to federal, not state authority.

The Granger cases went to the Supreme Court. In the 1877 *Munn* case, the Court upheld an Illinois law fixing minimum charges for the storage of grain in warehouses in cities of not less 100,000 inhabitants. Chief Justice Waite, speaking for the majority of the Court, used the concept of 'affected with a public interest' a concept established in a treatise written in 1670 by Lord Hale. Counsel for the elevator companies regarded it as the equivalent of police power. '(W)hen private property is affected with a public interest, it ceases to be *juris privati* only.'[13]

Despite the Court's support in the *Munn* case for the state regulation of public utilities, it was another Court decision, in 1886, the *Warbus* case , that declared that the states could not regulate an interstate business. One year later, 'An Act to Regulate Commerce', the *Interstate Commerce Act* (ICA) was promulgated.

The ICA established an independent regulatory agency, the Interstate Commerce Commission (ICC). Although subject to Congressional 'over-view,' Congress did not have the power to enforce its decisions except through legislation. Commissioners enjoyed security of tenure. The Act applied to any common carrier engaged in the transportation of property wholly by rail. Provisions in the Act showed concern over the dis-criminatory practices of the railroads. Discriminatory practices among locations and persons were prohibited, but railroads were allowed to retain their value of service rate structures. Pooling was prohibited. While the Commission, however, did not have the power to establish rates, they had to be filed with the ICC and were made public. According to Nelson, the railroads were left to take care of themselves without minimum rate regulation and lawful pooling of traffic.[14]

The federal government had asserted its power over interstate commerce. A compromise ensued, whereby private property and private projects were not to be appropriated and confiscated. The railroads were not to be broken up or nationalised. They were to be regulated by an independent commission staffed by experts rather than political appointees. Competition was not to be abandoned; it was to be regulated. In 1883, the Civil Service Commission was established with the intention of introducing the merit principle. Staffed by experts, the ICC became the prototype of scientific government. The efficacy of such action was a main tenet of a political movement that became known as the Progressive Movement. This Movement gained momentum in the 1890s, following the declines in agricultural areas. Demands were made to expand the currency based on silver. But other proposals, which were distinctly socialistic, raised opposition from conservatives. Some reformers moved into the Progressive Movement in part to stave off socialism. One of these reformers was Theodore Roosevelt who became President in 1901 following the assassination of President McKinley.

In response to over-capacity, the railroads attempted to restrict supply by forming cartels. Accounts of shipments published weekly were in some cases rendered inaccurate by members who cheated on the cartels' prices by making secret agreements. Until 1890, cartel practices such as restricting supplies were perfectly legal. This changed with the passage of the *Sherman Antitrust Act* of which Roosevelt deployed against the Northern Securities Companies, a giant trust which had been formed out of the two railway systems that had fought over the rail traffic centred on Chicago.[15]

In a ruling handed down by the Supreme Court it was held that fixing rates by traffic associations was unlawful under the 1890 *Sherman Antitrust Act*. This Act had the effect of elevating agreements among oligopolists from unenforceable contracts to a criminal conspiracy. Amendments to the regulatory legislation were introduced to strengthen further the protection offered to the shipper. The 1903 *Elkins Act* rendered every departure from a published schedule of rates *prima facie* evidence of discrimination. The 1906 *Hepburn Act* allowed the ICC to establish maximum tolls, while the juris-diction of the Commission was extended to cover industrial and private car lines. Pipelines carrying oil and other commodities were included under ICC control. The 1910 *Mann – Elkin Act* gave the Commission the right to suspend rate changes for a period of six months, during which it was to determine the reasonableness of the rates. The Commission now possessed the power effectively to regulate long and short haul rate discrimination.

The 1912 *Panama Canal Act* made it illegal for any common carrier to own, base, operate, control or have any interest in competing common carriers engaged in commerce in the United States or passing through the Panama Canal without the express permission of the ICC. The purpose of the legislation was to protect the water-borne transport industry from domination by the railroads. As integral operators of the vehicle and transport infrastructure, railroads were considered not only to have advantages over shippers, but also to be internally stronger than the emerging forms of water, pipelines, highway trucking and other modes of transport.[16]

In Canada, regulatory control over the railways has a very different history. In 1851, a regulatory body, known as the Railway Committee of the Executive Council, assumed responsibility for examining and approving the expenditure on railway construction in Canada. Its aim was to protect the public purse. In 1867, a Department of Public Works was established which was divided, in 1879, into two parts: the Department of Railways and Canals, and the Department of Public Works.[17]

In 1888, the Canadian Pacific Railway's monopoly clause was removed. This development reflected a growing awareness of the monopoly position of the railways. The 'common carrier' obligations of fair and reasonable treatment were brought into play. Shippers, as well as regional and pro-vincial organisations and governments called for equality of opportunity, which often translated into requests for preferential rates. Special statutory rates and rate regulation were the resulting means used to enhance regional equality of opportunity.

In the 1897 Crows Nest Pass Agreement and in the Manitoba Agreement of the same year, the federal government exchanged rail subsidies in return for concessionary rates. These rates were, in turn, voluntarily extended by all rail carriers to their export grain traffic. The slower, all-water routes incurred rates lower than the competing water-rail routes. Through-rates on these water-rail routes, however, were closely matched. Competitive forces were such that the Lake rates to Bay Ports plus the 'At and East' rail rates from Bay Ports to Montreal were established with reference to the Lake rate to Buffalo plus the 'At and East' rate from Buffalo to the seaboard. The 1899 Royal Commission established that the CPR had extended its monopoly power by agreeing, with any party that would build an elevator at a loading point, that it would prohibit the boarding of cars at that point either over the loading platform or through a flat warehouse. The 1900 *Manitoba Grain Act* and subsequent amendments required construction of loading platforms on the basis of local petitions, the licensing of elevators and the filing of maximum rates. The railways were forced to institute and to abide by the car order book. By 1920, two farm organisations controlled almost one-third of the terminal capacity at the head of the lakes. The 1912 *Canada Grain Act* introduced a Board of Grain Commissioners and provided for the construction and acquisition of terminals at the head of the lakes by the federal government.

Spurred by the flow of immigrants into the Prairies and the clamour for more competition for the CPR, the federal government responded by supporting the construction of another transcontinental railway. The Grand Trunk Pacific and the National Transcontinental system connected the *Maritimes* with British Columbia. The government built the line connecting Winnipeg to Moncton. The second transcontinental system, the Canadian Northern, received substantial provincial support. It was completed in 1915. After agreeing to lower rates from Manitoba to Lake Superior, the 1914 *Western Rates* case produced an order equalising rates across the Prairies. The demands of war failed to eliminate the excess capacity of Canada's railway system. Cost increases exceeded rate increases and heavy-operating losses ensued. The Grand Trunk Pacific was placed in receivership in 1917, and became part of the new government-owned railway, Canadian National (CN) in 1920. Canadian Northern was taken over by the Dominion government in 1917 and joined CN in 1923. So was born the Canadian rail duopoly.[18]

At the turn of the century, the federal government faced increasing pressure to deal with allegations of unjust discrimination. The 1903 *Railway Act* was revised, and a rail regulatory body, the Board of Railway

Commissioners, was established. The bar on pooling and the attempt to impose rate equality, in effect, prevented the formation of an effective railway cartel. However, the process requirements of rate filing and the prohibition of rebates buttressed rail rate stabilisation.

In regulating originating and terminal switching services in 1908, the rail commissioners attempted to deal with the monopoly power of terminal railways. The outcome was a demarcation of carriers' markets by rates and distance limits. Within these limits shippers were protected. At a time when there were few trucks, what was of importance were the agreements and rates established between carriers at the inter-switching points of the railway lines. While the shipper wished to have alternative routings, the carriers, desirous of achieving maximum returns on their investment, were disinclined to lose some of their captive shippers to another carrier by charging low inter-switching rates. Following complaints concerning the inter-switching parities and rates charged by railroads, the Railway Commissioners established, in Central Order No.II of 1908, rate and area limits that were to prevail for eighty years.

PROTECTIVE REGULATION AND CENTRALISED PLAN-NING

The railroads in the United States also fared badly. Subject to maximum rate controls, they incurred heavy deficits. When they were returned to private ownership after the Great War, during which they had been requisitioned, the ICC established their rates in order to enable them to earn a fair rate of return on a fair valuation of their properties. The ICC had become a planning agency, matching demand with supply in order to fulfil the general public interest.[19]

The enthusiasm for planning public work projects continued, particularly with the Secretary of Commerce, Hoover. The modern highway programme began in 1916. It aimed at a 'co-ordinated national road network to facilitate the nation's commerce.'[20] The federal aid system consisted of 170,000 miles of road in 1923, or five percent of the nation's roads.[21] The 1927 *Rivers and Harbours Act* authorised the Corps to develop what became known as the '308 reports.' They provided much of the basis for water resource development during the New Deal and the immediate post Second World War periods.

The 1909 Boundary Water Treaty guaranteed 'forever' to the inhabitants and vessels of Canada and the United States, the free and open navigation of all boundary waters. A 1921 joint report of these two countries recommended the building of a 25-foot navigation channel and the development of the electric power from the international rapids section of the St. Lawrence.

In 1918, an air mail service was inaugurated by the Army. The *Air Commerce Act* of 1926 vested jurisdiction over safety and maintenance of airways and navigational facilities in the Secretary of Commerce. Direct subsidies to the manufacturing and operating companies were eschewed but the Department of Commerce was empowered to charter the airways, maintain navigation facilities and promote air commerce. The Act contained a specific prohibition against federal participation in the construction of airports. They were considered 'local,' rather than 'national' infrastructure, analogous to ports and waterways. So came to pass the so-called 'dock' concept that remained federal policy until 1940.[22]

Under the *Water Act*, mail subsidies to US air carriers were based on plane-miles flown, rather than on mail actually carried. This favoured the carriers, who were considered 'infant,', in need of encouragement. Rigged bids along with side payments occurred. President Roosevelt was prompted to terminate all existing air mail contracts. The ensuing 1934 *Air Mail Act* placed the regulation of carriers and entry under the authority of the ICC. A competitive bidding process was instituted for allocating route authority. The carriers understood that if mail rates were bid down to levels insufficient to cover costs, the carrier could petition the ICC for subsidies or passenger rate increases. In fact, this happened, as carriers competed to reduce the mail content rates to very low levels, and then looked to the ICC to bail them out of their approaching bankruptcy. Faced with an ICC that was hesitant in responding to their requests for passenger rate increases and subsidies, the carriers pressured Congress for protective regulation.[23]

The *Civil Aeronautics Act* of 1938 transferred responsibility from the Department of Commerce, to a new regulatory Commission within the Department, the Civil Aeronautics Authority (CAA). The Authority was given regulatory authority over interstate, overseas and foreign common carriage by air. The CAA was authorised to issue operating authority to any applicant who was 'fit, willing and able.' Rates were to be published and observed. All had to be just and reasonable and not unduly discriminatory. The CAA also had the authority to prescribe minimum, maximum or the lawful rates. The Authority's power over economic regulation was to be deployed, for the best part of the next four decades, in the protection of the incumbent carriers.

In Canada, the Minister of National Defence, under the 1927 *Aeronautics Act*, was given general power to regulate and control 'aerial navigation over Canada,' subject to approval by the Cabinet. The Act, unlike the *Air Commerce Act* of the United States, included provisions for federal involvement in aerodromes. The regulatory authority, the Air Board, viewed all aerodromes (and not just those that were federally-owned) as essential to air navigation and aeronautics and, therefore, subject to the general power to regulate and control. However, since aerodromes and seaplane bases were of financial benefit to the operators and the aviation companies it was policy that the user or beneficiary should build and maintain them.

By the end of the 1920s the object of air transport policy had been to develop military defences. However, the threat of scheduled US carriers moving northwards on Canadian routes transformed the objective into one of 'defensive expansion.' According to J. A. Wilson, the Controller of Civil Aviation Division, and an active civil servant during the inter-war period, 'it was not desirable that Canadian traffic should become an adjunct to the United States airways system. It was imperative, in the national interest, that Canada should commence without further delay, the construction of the transcontinental airway.'[24]

The first vital step in building the airway was the establishment of a scheduled mail service and investment in complementary airway and aerodrome infrastructures. Airways were deemed to be similar to canals or harbours, while aerodromes – or airports as they came to be known – were likened to docks. Although the main airports of the Trans Canada Airways were subject to this 'dock' policy, the government had also ventured into the building, ownership and operation of what it was to term a 'national airport.' St. Hubert, near Montreal, was selected as the site of the first such airport and was the centrepiece of an attempt by the Canadian government to win a share of the North Atlantic air traffic from New York.

Consolidations among the carriers occurred in the late twenties. Two groups were formed, one in the east, the other in the west. Most operated services to the inaccessible northern mining communities. Encouraged by the government, the two railway companies (CN and CPR) financed the formation, in 1930, of Canadian Airways. In turn, this entity merged the two major carrier groups in the east and west. Canadian Airways was awarded mail contracts worth $1.2 million in 1930-31.[25]

But by the middle of the decade it had become obvious that Canadian Airways had failed to develop and to sustain, transcontinental-scheduled airmail and passenger services. It still comprised two separate branches, one on the Prairies and the other in Central Canada. Operating with inadequate equipment and with little or no support from its the railway companies which had brought it into being, Canadian Airways incurred losses, in 1936, of some $71,000 on operating revenues of $964,000.[26] Most significantly, the carrier failed to receive subsidies from its scheduled inter-city airmail contracts. The Post Office deployed competitive tendering and established rates that often included a mileage element. By charging the public the same rate regardless of distance, the Post Office, and not the carriers, profited on the shorter routes.[27]

The Dominion of Canada's policy was influenced by the evolution of policy in the US, particularly when it came to determining the structural characteristics of the airline industry. In the US, it was believed that the carrier industry was subjected to 'destructive competition'[28], proved by the acceptance of the airmail subsidy system by the carriers. Canadian Airways argued similarly the low bids from bush operators, which they could not meet on the northern routes, were the product of destructive competition.

The Canadian Airways' interpretation was influential in shaping the 1938 *Transport Act*. This Act established the Board of Transportation Commissioners, empowering it to grant licenses for the transport of goods and passengers by air. Carriers were to file details of their fares with the Board. The Board did not lay down fares, although 'unreasonable and discriminatory' fares were not to be authorised. Despite these powers, the Board was not an independent regulatory agency. The Cabinet could establish the routes to be licensed, while Section 6(3) of the *Department of Transport Act* placed the Board under the control and supervision of the Minister.

In the view of the carriers, control over entry - but not over rates - limited the effectiveness of the Board at a time when the industry was entering a major downturn at the onset of the war. Earlier, in 1937, the government had created a government owned monopoly carrier operating over government designated scheduled routes. The 1937 *Trans-Canada Airways Act* authorised the functions of Trans-Canada Airways (TCA) to be performed according to the terms of two contracts - one between the Corporation and the Minister of Transport, and the other, an airmail contract, between the Corporation and the Postmaster General. The statement of policy made in the debates in the House during the passage of the Bill made it clear that the Corporation was, as an instrument of national policy, to be granted exclusive operating rights over the nation's major inter-city routes. The Act also authorised the Corporation to participate in the building of the Airways infrastructure. Although TCA was the instrument of the government in maintaining all transcontinental air transport services, the Department of Transport, through the Air Services Branch, was the channel through which municipal grants passed. The Branch was responsible for the building of new airports and facilities, and, eventually, for the direct operation of the Airways' main airports.

CPR management merged many of the regional carriers. In effect, a duopoly was created. CPAL, however, pursued a policy of developing its regional routes and renounced its ambitions for a transcontinental route system. A statement by the Prime Minister, in 1943, made it clear that TCA was intended to operate all transcontinental routes and 'mainline' services as the government might, from time to time, designate.[29] On these routes, TCA was protected from competition and was expected to develop a system of internal cross-subsidisation. Privately-owned carriers were confined primarily to north-south routes. Despite the entry of CP Air (as CPAL became known) into the international market in 1949, TCA retained its monopoly on transcontinental routes. It was not until 1959, when CP Air was awarded a transcontinental route in order to connect its existing international operations at Vancouver and Montreal, that the monopoly was broken.

In the United States, the Executive met the onset of the Depression with an unprecedented intrusion into the legislative process of Congress. Interventionist planning measures were favoured as the means of ameliorating the ravages of economic decline. 'Scientific government' was again mobilised.

There were differences, however, between the New Deal and the Progressive era. During the latter period, the railroads had been regulated but competition remained alive. This now changed. The ICC and the Civil Aeronautics Board (formerly the CAA) enforced protective economic regulation. Incumbent railroads, airlines and road carriers were protected and new entrants were disallowed. Cartel agreements were generally authorised.

The 1933 *Emergency Railroad Transportation Act* attempted to encourage financial revitalisation by means of regional co-ordinating committees. More significantly, the Act contained a rule of rate-making in which the ICC was no longer required to establish a fixed return for the railroads. Specifically, the Commission was empowered to reject a rate application if it considered that the rate would divert railroad traffic to other modes. In the face of a challenge to the legality of the rate bureaux under the *Sherman Anti-Trust Act*, in 1948, Congress granted the railroads (through the *Reed-Bulwinkle Act*) exemption from the anti-trust laws. The Commission was empowered to approve rules and agreements of the bureaux and to exercise general surveillance over their activities by requesting reports and inspecting accounts.

Road transport had grown in strength during the 1920s, often behind state imposed regulation. Federal regulation arrived in 1935 with the passage of the *Motor Carrier Act*. Common and contract carriers were required to obtain certificates or permits to commence interstate operations. Private carriers and carriers transporting livestock, fish and agricultural commodities were exempt. The ICC was authorised to establish maximum and minimum rates. The approach to rate making would appear to have been based on the notion of 'fair competition' between rail and trucks.[30] Unlike the canal operations, which had faced unrestricted competition from the railroads, the latter were to be protected from trucking competition.

By 1942, the ICC's authority extended to rail inter-city traffic, interstate carriers (except bulk commodities) and inter-city truck carriers (except agricultural commodities). Exceptions to ICC regulations were granted to all private motor and water carriers and legal minimum rates were allowed for contract motor and water carriers. The CAB could prescribe maximum, minimum and actual rates for air carriers and regulate entry and exit into the industry. By the 1960s, economic commentators were describing the policies of the CAB as having established cartel fares that were 'competed away' through frequency and service quality competition.[31]

The arrival of hostilities prompted the extensive involvement of the Federal Government in airport and airway construction. The 1946 *Federal Airport Act* specifically dealt with the Federal involvement in airport development. The Act provided matching funds to encourage State and municipalities to build airports. The money came from the General Fund. The first dedicated trust fund for aviation was established in 1970,[32] following the enactment of 1970 *Airport and Airways Development Act*. Levies collected on airline tickets, taxes on general aviation fuel and other user fuels were placed in the Fund. In 1958, the Federal Aviation Agency (FAA) was established, with responsibility for the technical aspect of air traffic control and aviation safety. In 1972, Congress declared it to be unlawful for the FAA to finance any of the operating costs from the Airport Fund. The Fund was intended to pay for the modernisation of the Air Traffic Control System and the Airport Development Aid Programme (ADAP). The ADAP provided grants to assist airport operators in funding capital projects. Between 197 and 1980, $13.9 billion accrued to the Fund. Of this, $4.1 billion was invested in the airport system through ADAP grants.[33] The *Airport and Airways Development Act* expired in 1980. It was replaced by the 1982 *Airport and Airways Improvement Act*. This Act re-established the operation of the Fund, along with a revised schedule of user taxes. A new capital grants programme, which involved a formula for the distribution of airport aid and criteria for eligibility, was introduced via an 'Airport Improvement Programme.'

In Canada, at the outbreak of the war, the federal government took over municipal airports, under leases, at the onset of the war. The government realised that subsidies were required and the Department of Transport absorbed the main airports. In a statement to Parliament in 1948, the Minister laid down the 'principles' which would guide the infrastructure programme. These included the development of a 'minimum' number of international airports, the development of mainline airports to permit the utilisation of the 'most modern types' of aircraft, and the assumption of the cost of maintenance of those airports under the control of the Department of Transport.

Ten years later, in response to the growth of scheduled services, a new policy was adopted. Airports were categorised as 'mainline', 'satellite', 'local', 'remote' or 'development.' By 1970, there were 416 licensed airports in Canada, of which the Department of Transport operated 80 and others operated 336. Twenty-one of the latter received operating subsidies. [34]

By this date, air services accrued the largest share of the governments' transportation budget. Total air service expenditures quadrupled, from $3 million in 1951/2 to $150 million in 1961/2. The operating costs of annual air services tripled from $26.6 million to $75 million.[35] During 1968, the costs of civil aviation infrastructures totalled $227 million against revenues of $45 million.

The railways had not been immune from the depression. The Duff Commission's enquiry into the industry led, not to protective regulation, but to the formation of a rail cartel following the adoption of the 1932 *Canadian National - Canadian Pacific Act*.[36] In freight markets, the railways were permitted to act in a collective manner, allowed to exchange cost information and to establish common rates. The trucker's competitive threat to the railways' higher valued commodities increased as the decade of depression advanced. The 1938 *Transport Act* enhanced the railways' competitive position by permitting them to establish agreed charges. In effect, these were quantity discounts. These discounts were to be given in exchange for all (or most) of the traffic of shippers with whom the agreements were made. The Act also introduced significant protective regulations to a segment of the shipping industry.

In 1943, the Canadian Wheat Board was re-established and assumed full control of the marketing of Canadian wheat in foreign markets. Grain shipping rates were now negotiated between the Board and the lake shipping companies.

Added to the continuing Canadian interest in the capture of the grain trade by an all-Canadian water route, was the American interest in the possibilities of the waterway as a source of hydroelectric power. Such a scheme also held out the possibility of cheaply transporting iron from the Quebec/Labrador field to the Ohio steel mills. Although the 1941 'Great Lakes St. Lawrence Agreement' failed to obtain Congressional approval, a decade later the Canadian government established the St. Lawrence Seaway Authority. This Crown Corporation was authorised to construct a deep waterway between Montreal and Lake Erie. The *Wiley–Dondero Act* authorised the construction by the St. Lawrence Seaway Development Corporation, on US territory, of the facilities required to navigate around the barriers on the International Rapids. Construction was completed by April 1959 and officially opened in June of that year. Specially built vessels, carrying up to 28,000 tons, started to ply the system. The project was also unusual in another way: the two governments agreed that shippers, through the use of tolls, would repay the entire cost of the Seaway Project.

The end of the 1930s marked a sharp turnabout in transport policy. The Dominion, by means of legislation, subjected the major transport modes to planned control from the Cabinet through the newly established Department of Transport, and to regulation through the Board of Transport Commissioners. The Board was to carry out its duties 'with the object of co-ordinating and harmonising the operations of all carriers engaged in transport by railways, ships and aircraft.' Failing to secure support from the rapidly growing trucking sector, the Dominion government left the regulation of trucks and buses to the Provinces. In contrast, armed with a critical report on the commercial failures and political opportunism of harbour commissioners, the Dominion government adopted the report's recommendation by establishing, in 1936, a Central Harbours Board. This was a permanent board, located in Ottawa, with responsibility for managing the major harbours. Although, with the establishment of an Air Transport Board and a Canadian Marine Commission, regulatory control was soon shifted away from the Board, power lay with the Minister. For twelve consecutive years, through to the end of the depression, the war, and the post-war reconstruction, one Minister, D.C. Howe, alone shaped transport policy.

The system of centralised regulation, constructed and operated by Howe, functioned within the same structure for some three decades. During this period, the federal government responded to the rise of the aviation industry and motor vehicle transport modes by making massive investments in aviation and road infrastructures. Wary of permitting inter-modal competition, Ottawa was faced with two problems: the rapidly declining importance of the rail mode; and the rejection, by the regions, of the notion that transport modes be the instruments of national policy.

The railway duopoly operated within a legal and policy framework that deemed transport, and rail in particular, to be the best means of furthering the national interest by neutralising the cost of conducting business in the less advantaged regions of the country. The regulated rail cartel, with its competition in service and collusion in rate-making, was perhaps seen, not only as a means deferring the settlement of the potentially undesirable instability ensuing from unregulated competition between the two railways, but also as a means of furthering the national economic interest. This might be achieved by establishing rate-parity among the regions and among different shippers. While legislation prohibited forms of personal rate discrimination, commodity rate discrimination still occurred. The emerging rate structure was one in which shippers were treated with varying degrees of equality with respect to their size and location and offered rates on the transportation of commodities that reflected the capabilities of the commodities to bear transport charges and comparative transport demand elasticities. Such commodity rate discrimination did not go unrestricted. Statutory determinations constrained rates on export grain, a substantial portion of their traffic, and on export traffic from the Maritimes. In the mid-1950s, a form of rate equalisation was introduced.

The increasingly effective competition from road transport brought about the termination of equalised discriminations, the recognised need for (constrained) forms of competition and ended what Darling dubbed the 'Railway Age Ideology.'[37]

REFORM AND DEREGULATION

The 1961 Canadian Royal Commission on Transportation was initiated at a time when the railways were experiencing labour unrest and were urging substantial rate increases. The Commission's report recommended a radical policy. Transport modes were to be freed from regulation and competition was to be encouraged. However, owing to political caution, it took more than ten years for the new policy to be implemented.

According to the policy statement of the 1967 *National Transportation Act* competitive modes were to be the means of achieving an efficient transport system. This goal, however, was to be subject to two constraints. Competition was to be inter-modal and not intra-modal. Second, 'due regard for national policy' was also to be considered. The newly-established regulatory agency, the Canadian Transport Commission (CTC) was distinguishable from its predecessors in being a multi-modal agency with (almost) exclusive regulatory authority. Although the Ministry of Transport was left with an ambivalent policy rôle, successive Ministers of Transport proceeded to promote modal policies. The result was that the policy development that emerged from the CTC over the next twenty years evolved as a product of individual adjudiciary decisions.

A summary of the evolving regulatory policy of the first decade of the CTC's existence would be as follows:

Air: Regulatory policy served to protect the two national carriers (Air Canada and Canadian Pacific) that shared the transcontinental routes, from effective competition from regional carriers. They were confined to designated geographical areas.

Railways: Changes to the *Railway Act,* in 1967, removed the regulatory restrictions on non-statutory rates, empowering the railway duopoly to compete against trucks and water transport. As a result, the railways were able to engage in commodity rate and locality discrimination. With the major exception of the statutory crown rates, which the railways were expected to cross-subsidise from profitable freight traffic, the railways were compensated for the obligations imposed by the government.

Trucking: Failure to implement Part III of the NTA, left Canadian for-hire trucking regulation subject to ten different boards, acting under ten different sets of regulations, and procedures. While different in the severity of its application, the test of public convenience and necessity was applied to entry into intra- and extra-provincial markets. Rates were controlled by means of prescribing, or by requiring filing, or by exercising rate approval, sometimes over rates made by truckers' tariff bureaux. Entry into extra-provincial trucking was tightly regulated but there was little control of rates. Each province exempted private trucking from regulation and, sometimes, selected commodities were exempt.

In the United States, over the period 1970 to 1972, there were numerous financial railroad failures, the most conspicuous being Penn Central. The legislative response to the declining rail passenger services was the *Railway Passenger Services Act* of 1970. The Act froze the discontinuance of passenger trains for five months, took them out from under ICC regulation and instructed the Secretary of Transportation to draft a system for long-haul passenger trains. The result was the emergence of Amtrak, the National Railroad Passenger Corporation. While this corporation was owned by the private railroads, 50 per cent of its budget came from the federal government. Amtrak owns the passenger routes in the Northeast corridor and enters contracts with railroads elsewhere.

An instrument similar to Amtrak was created in the aftermath of the failure of the freight-carrying railroads in the Northeast. The *Regional Rail Reorganisation Act* (*3-R Act*) established the United States Railway Association as an 'off-budget' federally-chartered non-profit corporation, the Consolidated Rail Corporation (Conrail). The creditors of the bankrupt railroads owned it. In contrast to this trend, rate competition was encouraged. The *Railroad Civil Alignment and Regulatory Reform Act* of 1976 (4-R Act) allowed the railroads to lower their rates to the levels of variable costs without authorisation from the ICC. But the railroads were not tempted. There was very little competitive rate-making.[38]

In the fall of 1973, Arab oil producers choked off their shipments to the United States. Instead of freeing the market in energy, the federal government introduced extensive price controls and regional allocations. The state was intruding further and further into market exchanges. But inflation, unlike productivity, was not falling. Controversy swirled around those who advocated monetarist policies. Academics and researchers specialising in micro and institutional economics made two observations. One, that direct economic regulation was one of the causes of the faltering performance of the economy. Two, that regulatory bodies had been captured by the entities they regulated.

This alleged conspiracy involving the regulated and the regulators posed a major problem. The advocates of regulatory reform and deregulation showed that competing entities would encourage higher productivity, lower costs and prices that would benefit producing agents and consumers alike. But, if the regulated producers, the regulating bureaucrats and the politicians were all beneficiaries of the regulatory arrangement, who was to break this 'iron ring' and initiate deregulation?

The regulatory break-through came in the civil aviation industry. The industry had been adversely affected by the downturn in the economy following the oil embargo. The response of the CAB was to sanction capacity limitations and to impose a route moratorium.

Then in 1975, John Robson was appointed Chairman of the CAB. The route moratorium and capacity limitations were terminated. In 1977, Britain and the United States re-negotiated their air bilateral, to be known as Bermuda II. While in itself not particularly 'pro-competitive', the agreement was to launch the United States on a more liberal approach to bilateral agreements. Of greatest significance was the fact that the staff of the CAB itself produced an in-house evaluation of protective regulation. The 1975, 'Pulsifer Report' argued that the CAB's exercise of protective regulation was sufficiently detrimental to warrant deregulation.[39] This was a singular and crucial event in the regulatory reform process in the United States. The advocates of deregulation were neither academics nor consumer advocates. They were regulators bureaucrats, who were, in effect, advocating the termination of their own services. Furthermore, this report was issued prior to the arrival at the CAB of the reforming academic, Alfred Kahn.

In Show Cause Order (D-32315) of January 1977, the Board announced its intention of granting multiple entry to all fit applicants. Fares remained subject to floors and ceilings, between which carriers could establish their own fare level and structure of fares. The *Airfreight Deregulation Act* of 1977 deregulated the air freight industry. The 1978 *Airline Deregulation Act* (ADA) consisted of a series of policy measures that liberalised entry and fare regulation within the existing regulatory structure. In effect, entry de-regulation occurred before complete fare deregulation. All cities served by certified carriers on the date of passage of the ADA were guaranteed 'essential' service for the next ten years. The CAB disappeared in 1985. The Department of Justice obtained jurisdiction over domestic air carrier mergers and acquisitions.

Although the *Staggers Rail Act* of 1980 was the major legislative step in the direction of deregulation, the ICC deregulated the transport of fruit and vegetables by a rule issued in 1981. A year later, the ICC deregulated piggyback traffic which had allowed the railroads to solicit business and compete with trucks on their own lines. *Staggers* made changes that eased the railroads' rate-making powers and facilitated easier entry and exit into the industry. Railroads could establish cuts within a wide band. The variable cost level was the lower level of reasonableness. The maximum limit was imposed for those railroads that the ICC found to have market dominance. There was a maximum limit for those without market dominance. If dominance existed, rates had to be reasonable. *Staggers* codified the ICC 1979 ruling on contracts between shippers and railroads. Such contracts were to be filed with the ICC, which had to approve them in principle. Contract rates were permitted to take priority over the carrier's legal duty to serve every applicant. The carrier was exempt from the prohibition against discrimination.

In 1987, the federal government sold its ownership interest in Conrail for $1.9 billion. Then, in 1997, Conrail was sold to the CSX Corporation and Norfolk Southern Corporation for $10 billion. On 1 June 1999, the new owners divided Conrail's principal routes, giving many customers access to two railroads instead of one. In 1995, Burlington Northern took over Santa Fe Pacific Corp. for $4 billion, while a year later Union Pacific took over Southern Pacific Rail Corp.

The *Motor Carrier Act* of 1980 offered carriers the opportunity to participate in a zone of rate freedom. They could raise or lower rates by as much as 10 per cent over rates previously in effect without threat of suspension or investigation by the ICC, on the grounds that the rates were unrecoverable. The rate bureaux provisions in the Act and the subsequent ICC rule-making restricted rate bureaux practices, such as establishing collective rates, and provided incentives for individual carriers to set rates independently. Since 1984, it has been illegal for single-line carriers competing on a given route to agree upon the rate to be charged. Applicants for entry faced easier standards. Instead of showing that service was 'required' by public convenience and necessity, the onus was upon opponents to demonstrate that the new entry was 'inconsistent' with public convenience and necessity. The *Bus Regulatory Reform Act* of 1982 applied the case entry requirements of trucking, to the bus industry and, in effect, ended antitrust immunity to bus rate bureaux.

This burst of legislation occurred over two years, not under the Republicans, but under the Democratic administration of Jimmy Carter. And, as a measure of how ideology was changing, in the middle of this period there was an energy crisis caused in part by a revolution in Iran. Deregulation, not regulation, was 'sold' by administrators as a means of reducing inflation. This period was also notable for the number of professional economists who promoted reform while acting as advisers and administrators in the regulatory agencies. Alfred Kahn was Chairman of the CAB from 1977 to 1978, while Michael Levine and Elizabeth E. Bailey also held posts in the agency. At the ICC were D. Gaskins Jr. and G. Douglas. The speed and import of change were breathtaking.

The fact that the legislation removed, in part or in whole, the protective regulation of interstate carriers, had immediate and profound effects on Canada. The major deregulatory transport legislation in America resulted not only in regulatory incongruities with Canada, but in the emergence of a deregulated American transport industry that was competing for customers in trans-border and in domestic markets.

During the period of regulation, many of the regulated US industries were, in large part, immune to operations of the American antitrust laws. So were neighbouring Canadian industries. Much of their immunity, however, was removed in the *Staggers Rail Act*, the *Motor Carrier Act*, the *Airline Deregulation Act* and the *International Air Transportation Competition* Act of 1979. Such rescission of immunity meant that carriers in the air, rail and trucking industries were subject to the antitrust laws.

So, too, were Canadian carriers, for the antitrust laws of the United States are extraterritorial in their scope and are applied to action in a foreign country where the effects of the challenged activity have a direct and substantial effect on foreign commerce. Despite the highly regulated, and limited extent, to which transport services had been 'traded', the sizeable trade in goods between the two countries made it possible for the impact of Canadian carriers on US commerce to be deemed direct, and substantial. Hence, conduct that was entirely legal under Canadian law could be subject to scrutiny, either by private plaintiffs or by the government of the United States.

It was not possible to travel on an American carrier over a Canadian route, neither on a Canadian carrier over an American route. The proximity of the Canadian population to the United States border, however, was a telling factor. It was possible to travel from say Toronto to Vancouver by moving over the border to Buffalo and flying to Seattle. As a result, Canadian carriers began to experience some of the competitive impacts they would have incurred had their services been traded in a competitive market. The increasingly efficient, and less costly, transportation and communications systems in the United States attracted business from those Canadians wishing to travel, ship their goods and communicate across the continent.

The initial response of the Canadian carriers and regulators was defensive. By 1984, however, the Canadian federal government had embarked on a shift away from extensive regulatory policies towards the more efficient mobilisation of resources facilitated by exchange through less constrained markets.   The 1987 *Motor Vehicle Transport Act* and the *National Transportation Act*, effective on 1 January 1988, introduced a phased, if not fully extensive deregulation. These and other measures both in tele-communications and financial sector in particular, constituted a movement away from the defensiveness towards the embrace of the continental market which had been the federal government's posture since the establishment of the state of Canada.

This momentous change, in effect, was a defeat for most regulators and carriers. They were defeated by an epistemic community of academic and consumer groups whose interests were deftly deployed by an entrepreneurial politician in an election year. For an entrepreneurial politician, the opportunity that emerged was the chance to exchange restrictive regulations for electoral support and votes. Such an exchange required the politician to manoeuvre away from the interests of the carriers, the bureaucracy and the regulatory agencies towards alignment with the epistemic community.

The epistemic community comprised a number of interest groups. They included: academics, individuals within the federal government's Economic Council of Canada (which in 1981 published a programme of regulatory reform), the Canadian Consumers Association, the Bureau of Competition Policy, the Department of Consumer and Corporate Affairs, and, from 1981, the Office of Regulatory Reform, an agency within the Treasury Board which was a central agency of the federal government. Together, they championed the interests of the transport consumers and strengthened the forces promoting continentalism that they were to unleash. The foremost entre-preneurial politician was the Liberal Party's Lloyd Axworthy who was appointed to the post of Minister of Transport in 1983. It was his entrepreneurial moves, during the brief period from September 1983 to September 1984, that were to be decisive in undermining the regulatory superstructure created by his predecessor, C.D. Howe.

THE UNRAVELLING OF THE REGULATION OF THE CANADIAN TRANSPORT MODES

In the early 1980s, regional carriers, which were defined as the 'preferred vehicles' for the development of regional and local air services in each of the five regions of the country, were struggling. As a result, on the one hand, of a failure of the Regional Air Carrier Policy to diversify and sustain the regional revenues, and, on the other by their disadvantageous position vis-à-vis Air Canada. The state-owned carrier entered into competition from the advantageous position of being 'first among equals.'[40] The response of the policy makers was to keep the aviation map and to merely re-draw the lines.

The 1981 Domestic Air Carrier Policy was, in the words of one official, 'a regime that should increase competition within a regulated environment.'

Retrenched protectionism continued through to the fall of 1983.[41] Nordair, a regional carrier, had its proposed off-peak fares disallowed. Into this vexed situation a new Minister of Transport was precipitated, Lloyd Axworthy, who determined to chart a different course, a course designed, in an election year, to curry favour with travellers and shippers rather than concern itself with the financial well-being of the carriers and shippers. The Minister announced the banning of the use of travel passes by the staff of the Canadian Transport Commission. Prompted by the discontent aroused by the Nordair decision, he published a letter in September 1983, stating that the recent events relating to 'discount fares highlighted the need for a comprehensive discussion of the entire domestic air pricing policy.'

Stressing the importance of ensuring the broader public interest be represented at subsequent hearings, the Minister activated Section 54 if the *National Transportation Act*, and asked the Minister of Justice to appoint counsel to act as the advocate for the public interest. Two months later, in December 1983, he formed an inter-departmental task force on airline regulation. There were to be two fora, one open to public scrutiny, and the other exclusive to government officials, within which the issue of airline deregulation was to be examined. Members of this task force were instructed to circulate their comments on the drafts to the executive consultant to Air Canada.

While Canadian travellers were aware of the wide range of fares offered by deregulated US carriers, perhaps only a few were informed of the deregulatory policies being promoted by the loose coalition of Canadian academics, consumer and administrative groups. The public hearing was exposed to these deregulatory policy options. Crucial to the Minister's success in enacting regulatory change in aviation was his deployment of the directive power he possessed, as Minister of Transport, over the crown carriers and the regulatory agency. Most of the political appointees in the regulatory agency, the aviation policy makers in the Department of Transport and the major crown and privately-owned scheduled carriers, formed a powerful defence of the regulatory *status quo*. Furthermore, the Minister was in the Cabinet of a Liberal government that had yet to accept the ideology of a liberalising economic policy. The mark of his entrepreneurial achievement was to breach these opposing forces by shifting the regulatory structure in aviation from that of eroded protectionism to one of differentiated liberalisation. This in turn facilitated the privatisation of the crown carrier.

The two national carriers and the regionals expressed, through the hearings at the Air Transport Committee (ATC), their opposition to deregulation. The interdepartmental task force was supplied with draft documents, most of which devoted favourable comparisons of the Canadian as against that of the deregulated American industry. In March 1983, the Minister hit back. In Winnipeg he argued for a liberalisation of the industry. At the end of the month the directors of Air Canada instructed management to temper their criticism of the Minister's proposed policy. These directions were evidenced at the hearings. An official of Air Canada, Pierre Jeanniot, accepted in principle a phased liberalisation of protective regulation. The advocates of regulation, and in particular the air carrier organisation, the Canadian Air Transport Association (CATA), were left supporting a policy no longer requested by the carriers. The Minister announced his policy, the 'New Canadian Air Policy' to the House of Commons Standing Committee on Transport in May 1984. He argued for a two-staged process of liberation. The first phase proposed an immediate liberalisation of the industry from regulation without a change in legislation. The second phase instructed the ATC to consider the longer-term issue of deregulation. The ATC, by contrast, recommended the relaxation of regulation 'but not deregulation.'

By the end of the month the old order was changing. Jeanniot replaced the critical Claude Taylor as President and Chief Executive Officer of the crown carrier. Whether or not Air Canada was to be broken up and privatised was an issue for the second phase.[42]

In August 1984, an air agreement was signed between Canada and the United States. A zone, averaging 500-miles, traversing the border was established, within which regional and local carriers traversing the border would largely be free of regulation. The ATC, however, remained steadfast in refusing to speed up regulatory reform. The Minister dispatched a strongly worded letter encouraging enactment of reform. Although the Minister and his party lost the election in early September 1994, the ATC's 28 September notice largely acquiesced to the requests of the Minister.

The new Air Transport Policy, modified by the decisions of the ATC during the first month after the election, changed the regulatory structure from that of eroded protectionism to one of differentiated liberation. In place of a chosen instrument protected by entry restrictions was to be a liberated but differentiated regulation. There were to be two countries in one: a liberated South and an unchanged protected North. Within the liberated South there was to be differentiation. Local carriers were free of entry and fare restrictions within the 500-mile border. Furthermore, carriers operating routes to and from Mirabel Airport (Montreal) and Mount Hope airport were to enjoy greater ease of entry and fare flexibility than they were on other routes.

The airline industry responded to the new liberalism by eventually forming into a duopoly of carriers operating coast-to-coast networks structured according to hub-and-spoke systems. In 1986, CP Air was purchased by

Pacific Western Airlines, forming Canadian Airlines International (CAI), a union that also involved former regional carriers. While CAI established further affiliates for its hub at Toronto, Air Canada did likewise for its Vancouver and Toronto hubs.

In August 1988, the federal government announced its intention to sell 45 per cent of Air Canada to the public. In the fall of 1989, the federal government proceeded to sell most of its holdings in Air Canada. Twenty-five per cent was reserved for non-Canadian investors. After incurring heavy losses on its scheduled routes, Wardair, a former charter carrier was purchased by CAI in January 1989. The Competition Tribunal, established under the 1986 *Competition Act*, was called upon to determine whether the merged computer reservation system of Air Canada and CAI was anti-competitive. The Tribunal approved the Gemini merger, but Transport Canada was instructed to develop a code of conduct.

The *National Transportation Act* of 1987 (NTA) abolished the CTC and replaced it with the National Transport Agency. For southern air routes, the applicants' test of public convenience and necessity, which served to protect incumbent carriers, was replaced with a test of 'fit, willing and able.' This change allowed insured and safe carriers to enter and compete. The carriers, however, had to be seventy-five per cent Canadian owned or controlled. Carriers were able to establish rates. Regulatory authorisations were retained only for proposed increases in regular fares on 'monopoly routes.' Air services to the thinly-populated northern regions were to retain entry, exit and rate regulation.

The incoming Liberal government negotiated a bilateral air agreement and launched two initiatives: an accelerated transfer to local authorities of federal airports and a movement towards the commercialisation of the air navigation system. Under the Canada-US air bilateral, signed in February 1995, Canadian and US carriers have unlimited access to fly between any cities in both countries. Canada negotiated free access to 24 new daily slots at Chicago's O'Hare and New York's LaGuardia airports. The 'open skies' agreement enables Canadian carriers to acquire additional slots under established 'buy/sell' rules at each American slot-controlled airports. Canadian carriers continued to be protected by the limits placed on foreign ownership and by the refusal of the government to exchange *cabotage* rights. These rights allow foreign airlines to operate on domestic routes.[43]

In the rail sector, the threat to the Canadian regulatory regime grew as shippers responded to the non-competitive US railroads released by the 1980 *Staggers Rail Act*. There were shippers in some regions, such as the Prairies, who regarded the emerging discriminatory rate structures as sufficiently inimical to their region's as to support the dissolution of the cartel. The Minister's constituency was located in this region, as was his immediate successor in the incoming Conservative government. Such a conjunction of interests probably prompted the Minister to cajole a reluctant regulatory agency into recommending regulatory changes and to urge his successor to establish congruity between the Canadian and US rail regulatory regimes.

Prior to the 1980 *Staggers Rail Act,* a congruity existed in the cartel-supporting regulatory systems of Canada and the United States. For the most part, rail traffic between points in both countries and overhead traffic were subjected to international joint through- rates, which, in turn, were filed and published. Enjoying immunity from anti-trust and anti-combines legislation, joint through- rates were set collectively by the railways and at levels that preserved parity with the longer hauls in the domestic US market. The result was an equalisation of rate levels over numerous route combinations.

Staggers diminished much of the support for regulation of the US rail cartel. Exemptions from rate regulation were removed from a substantial portion of traffic. Confidential rates and rebates were permitted on much traffic and inter-modal competition was encouraged. By removing the anti-trust immunity formerly enjoyed by US carriers, *Staggers* exposed collectively established international joint rates to the *Sherman Act.*[44]

The advent of intra-carrier rail competition in the US threatened collective rate-making in the Canadian portion of the international rates and also placed pressure on collective rate agreements on domestic routes. The threat came from the lower rates offered by the US railroads to shippers of international freight and the ability, denied the Canadian carriers, to strike confidential contracts with shippers. Attractive international rates invited requests from Canadian shippers for lower domestic rates. In the meanwhile, Canadian shippers took the opportunity to use US carriers and US rail rates.

In response to the growing competitive pressure from US railroads,[45] the Minister of Transport requested the CTC to report on the implications of *Staggers.* The CTC reported in April 1984, suggesting that no changes be made to the regulations. Minister Axworthy responded by requesting a further and broader inquiry. The final report, issued in December 1984, re-commended that carriers be allowed to enter confidential contracts with shippers on the Canadian portion regarding the movement of rail traffic between the two countries. Such measures, if implemented, would have limited the cartel's power over international movements but would have left it intact in the domestic market. The Conservative Minster of Transport requested the Committee to extend the agenda by considering the implications of regulatory change on the domestic rail market.

Reporting in June 1985, the Committee recommended the extension of confidential contracts and rebates to Canadian shippers and carriers. They also supported the retention of collective rate-making, although in a modified form. In July 1985, the government issued its policy. The White Paper,

Freedom to Move, endorsed the proposals of the CTC allowing confidential contracts on domestic and international routes, but argued against retention of those regulations which enabled the carriers to exchange cost information and to establish common rates. The proposed removal of the legal supports to the rail cartel was accompanied with recommendations that were aimed at encouraging intra-modal competition and enhancing the position of the captive shipper.

The NTA, in eliminating collective rate-making, removing exemption from the *Competition Act* and permitting rebates and confidential contracts, effectively withheld the legislative protection that was afforded to the 50-year old rail cartel. The new regulatory agency, with its direction over running rights, joint-track usage and joint rates, was empowered to facilitate rather than limit intra-modal competition. If it were considered to be in the public interest, the Cabinet could request a railway to consider joint or common use of the same right of way. The inter-switching limit was increased from 4 miles to 18 miles. Within 30 miles of any interchange point, a carrier is able to exercise 'terminal running rights' by agreeing to pick up, carry and deliver over the tracks of another railway. Shippers captive to one carrier and at a distance from an interchange point would, if they could arrange a deal with a second carrier, be able to apply to the agency to establish a competitive line rate to the interchange point. Minimum rate regulations were retained.

CPR had 80 per cent of its business in the West consisting primarily of bulk commodities. This was a reason why the company re-located its headquarters to Calgary. At the same time, in 1995, CPR created an eastern subsidiary, the St. Lawrence & Hudson Railway. Its headquarters were in Montreal and it was responsible for operations in the movement of manufactured goods in containers and trailers to and from the Montreal-Toronto-Chicago corridors and throughout the north-eastern US. In 1995, the federal government repealed the *Western Grain Transportation Act* and eliminated the transportation subsidy. Rail car allocation was now the responsibility of the industry. Grain rail rates to West Coast ports, Churchill and Thunder Bay were now regulated by the federal government through the authority of the *Canada Transportation Act.*

The 1978 *Capital Revision Act* relieved Canadian National of most of its debt to the government. During the mid-1980s, the CN Corporation pared away its non-rail activities. Starting in 1992, it's workforce was reduced by one-third, and the network pruned by more than 4,300 kilometres. It was privatised in November 1995, when the issue of shares raised $2.2 billion. CN had been transformed into a main-line railway with a network that connected major production centres. CP and CN now vigorously competed over their high-capacity mainline corridors fed by highway trucks or private short lines.

The privatisation of CN was facilitated by amendments to the NTA, provision for which was contained in the 1996 *Canada Transportation Act* (CTA). The 1985 *Railway Act* was repealed, along with a number of rail-related provisions of the NTA. Subsection 27(2) of the CTA removed the leverage afforded shippers, including the extension of inter-switching and competitive line rates. In effect, power was shifted away from the shipper towards the carriers. The 1985 *Competition* Act is applicable to transportation undertakings, while the 1985 *Canada Business Corporation Act* is applicable to the corporate governance and structure of CN. The Canada Transportation Agency would henceforth be able to operate on a broader cost-recovery basis but would no longer have authority to interpret transportation policy. The public interest would no longer be a matter subject to the jurisdiction of the Act. By these measures, the government effectively deregulated the transportation sector and announced its intention to refrain from involvement in private business transactions.[46]

By the fall of 1994, the major stakeholders in the air transportation sector reached a consensus that Canada's air navigation system should be removed from Transport Canada and operated by a 'not-for-profit' private corporation. This alliance called for 100 per cent funding by user charges based on a 'fair and equitable allocation of costs to all users.' With the support of the federal government, the alliance drew up articles of incorporation and, in mid-1995, created NavCanada. Legislation was enacted a year later, and on 31 October 1996, NavCanada was sold for $1.5 billion (Cnd). This was the first private-sector company in the world to use a non-share capital structure to commercialise a government service.

The reformation of trucking regulations was not a politically attractive proposition for federal politicians. Shippers commanded less voting power than air travellers. The 'nationalist' issue of American ownership of trucking companies aroused little sentiment. Most significantly, the issue of trucking regulations had for thirty years, rested with provincial politicians. As a result, the federal Minister of Transport 'repatriated' powers over extra-provincial trucking and introduced the possibility of a more liberal regulatory regime only when it became clear that the politicians in the major provinces had failed to establish effective regulatory reform.

Until the passage of the 1980 *Motor Carrier Act*, for-hire trucking industries in the two countries were subject to similar forms of protective regulation. In Canada, trucking remained under the control of ten different regulatory boards acting under different sets of regulators. Intra-provincial trucking regulation varied. In Alberta it was largely unregulated.

But extra-provincial trucking was subject to considerable control. Although extra-provincial trucking is a federal responsibility under the *British North America Act*, the power to regulate extra-provincial trucking was passed to the provinces through the *Motor Vehicle Transport Act* (MVTA) in 1954. Under Part III of the *National Transportation Ac*t, however, the federal government had only to exempt a motor carrier from the provisions of the MVTA for the carrier to come under the jurisdiction of the CTC. The federal government faced strong provincial opposition to this provision and did not implement Part III.

It was on the trans-border traffic, particularly between Ontario and neighbouring states, that the impacts of the *Motor Carrier Act* were felt. In 1981, the US Department of Justice launched a criminal grand jury investigation into the members of the Niagara Frontier Tariff Bureau. This involved trans-border trucking between eastern Canada and the eastern US. Following this, an ICC proceeding, instituted by a notice served in 1982, was initiated. The stated purpose was to 'determine whether Canadian law and policy effectively discriminated against US motor carriers.' Legislation passed by Congress, and signed by the President, placed a two-year moratorium on applications by Canadians for US operating authority. The findings of the ICC investigation were published in October 1982. Shortly afterwards, the moratorium was lifted and the two governments established administrative guidelines for jointly resolving trans-border trucking problems.

While the competitive, deregulated US carriers continued to seek operating conditions in Canada similar to those in the US, provincial carriers petitioned regulators to maintain their protection. Such carriers perceived that, with their much deeper market and given their ability to offer leg shipments, American carriers enjoyed considerable advantages over provincial carriers who operated within the shallow Canadian market.

The volume of traffic in and out of Ontario was such that a relaxation of regulation would have a significant impact on the easing of the restrictive entry regulations that existed in the extra-provincial trucking market in Canada. Despite the erosion of the for-hire-carrier market, Ontario retained restrictive entry controls over provincial and American carriers. Instead of maintaining the test of public convenience and necessity, a special committee recommended, after two years of study, an objective but restrictive fitness test. Legislation had not been enacted when the Liberals won the Ontario provincial election in 1985. Faced with a regulatory *status quo*, American truckers switched from attempting to win operating authority on international routes towards purchasing Canadian carriers. The incoming Conservative government, in 1984, had eased the conditions of foreign ownership exercised by the Foreign Investment Review Agency (FIRA).

Moving in parallel with the proposed regulatory reforms in Ontario was an activity aimed at achieving a form of extra-provincial trucking deregulation. The federal and provincial transport ministers signed 'The

Memorandum of Understanding Expecting a Federal-Provincial-Territorial Agreement on the Economic and Administrative Regulation of Truck Transport' on 27 February 1985. A five-point programme to deregulate extra-provincial trucking over the period 1985-86 was proposed. The federal government promulgated the 1987 *Motor Vehicle Transport Act* (MVTA) which replaced the 1954 *Motor Vehicle Transport Act.*

The MVTA eliminated trucking rate regulation as of 1 January 1988 and introduced more stringent safety regulations. The Act, however, introduced a deregulation of extra-provincial trucking to be phased in over five years. The Act also opened entry into Canadian trucking. Pressure was placed on most of the provincial regulators to liberalise their procedures, but liberalisation did not occur immediately. On 1 January 1993, the reverse onus test in the 1987 MVTA was resolved. All extra provincial licensing in Canada was, henceforth, to be based upon a fitness test alone. As a result of the Canada Agreement on Internal Trade, all economic regulation of intra-provincial truck transportation ceased on 1 January 1998. Save for customs, immigration and road taxes, the US and Canadian truck transportation companies are free to provide services within and between the two countries.[47]

By the end of the 1990s, the airline duopoly had become a virtual monopoly. In 1999, Air Canada acquired the debt laden CAI. The federal government negotiated with Air Canada, the agreements of which were contained in *BillC-26.* This came into force on 5 July 2000. It gave the Competition Bureau new powers to address anti-competitive behaviour such as price gouging. The CTA was given the power to monitor prices on monopoly routes and to address a wider range of consumer complaints, such as overbooking and lost luggage. Air Canada was forced to surrender slots and airport facilities mostly to charter companies. The carrier was also forced to delay starting a discount carrier. The limit on foreign ownership was maintained at twenty-five per cent and *cabotage* rights continued to be refused.[48]

In March 1999, the US Surface Transportation Board approved CN's takeover of Illinois Central. The network includes a marketing alliance with the rail-operating unit of Kansas City Southern Industries Inc., which extends into Texas and Mexico. With 18,700 miles of track stretching from Halifax and Vancouver to Mexico City, CN is seen as attempting to capture an increasing share of the $70 billion annual value of goods shipped by rail between the three NAFTA members. The move marks a historic switch away from east-west to north-south trade. Union Pacific took over Southern Pacific Rail Corporation, while Burlington Northern acquired Santa Fe Pacific Corp. From sixty-six major carriers in 1980, there are now four large

US railroad systems: Union Pacific, Burlington Northern Santa Fe, Norfolk Southern and CSX.[49]

There was the prospect of further concentration. On 20 December 1999, the Burlington Northern Santa Fe Corp. and the Canadian National Railway Co., agreed to combine their rail systems. The combination, valued at (US)$6 billion, would create a 50,000-mile route system, extending from Los Angeles to Halifax and from the Gulf of Mexico to Vancouver. However, in March 2000, the US Surface Transformation Board imposed a moratorium on the merger. [50] This was lifted in June 2001.

There is no better illustration of the changes wrought to Canada's transportation policy than the posture of CN. Effectively bankrupt in 1995, despite receiving $17 billion (Cnd) in federal subsidies over the previous fifty years, the carrier was declared five years later to be the most efficient in North America. In 2000, officials of the burgeoning CN pressed, during the comprehensive review of the CTA, for the complete deregulation of the rail industry.

The shift from protectionism to free trade, regulation and state ownership to deregulation and privatisation, marked a shift from extractive to mobilising policies. They reflected the realities of NAFTA, as Canadian carriers engaged in fierce competition for a share of the one billion dollars a day that cross the Canada-US border by sea, air, road and rail. These changes are not yet complete. Totally free trade in transport (and telecommunication) services does not yet exist. The *Jones Act*, for instance, effectively prohibits non-US ships from taking cargo from one US port to another. Cultural 'services' are still constrained, but a profound change has nevertheless occurred. The kaleidoscopic coalition of interests, bound by implicit contracts between the regions, peoples and the two recognised Canadian nations, has been shattered. A reformulated Constitution has yet to be forged that will re-order the contracts between the two nations, regions and native peoples of Canada.

Notes

1.   Hull, William J. and Robert W. Hull (1967), *The Origins and Development of the Waterways Policy of the United States*, Washington: National Waterways Conference Inc., p.8.
2.   Taylor, George (1951), *The Transportation Revolution 1815-1860*, New York: Rinehart, p.21.
3.   Aitken, H. G. J. (ed) (1959), *The State and Economic Growth*, New York: Social Science Research Council, p.114.
4.   Risk, Brian (1973), 'The Nineteenth Century Foundation of the Business Corporation in Ontario,' *University of Toronto Law Journal*, **23**, pp.270-306.
5.   Gallman, R. E. (1966), 'Gross National Product in the United States, 1834-1909,' in *Output, Employment and Productivity in the United States after 1800*, National Bureau of Economic Research.
6.   Fogel, Robert (1964), *Railroads and American Economic Growth: Essays in Econometric History*, Baltimore: The Johns Hopkins Press.

7. Dales, J. H. (1979), 'National Policy Myths, Past and Present,' *Journal of Canadian Studies*, **14**(3).
8. Ellison, Anthony P. (1984), 'Regulatory Reform in Transport: A Canadian Perspective,' *Transportation Law Journal*, **15**(2), pp.175-243.
9. Baskerville, Peter (1981), 'Americans in Britain's Backyard: The Railway Era in Upper Canada, 1850-1880,' *Business History Review*, **55**, p.30.
10. Wilgus, W.J. (1937), *The Railway Inter-Relations of the United States and Canada*, Newhaven: Yale University Press.
11. Risk, R.C.B. (1981), 'The Law and the Economy in Mid-Nineteenth Century Ontario, A Perspective,' in Flaherty, D.H. (ed), *Essays in the History of Canadian Law*, The Osgoode Society, **I and II**(3), pp.24- 125.
12. Miller, George. H. (1971), *Railroads and the Granger Laws*, Madison: The University of Wisconsin Press, pp.2-33.
13. Munn versus Illinois (1877), 94, US 113, p.26.
14. Nelson, James, C. (1987), 'Politics and Economics in Transport Regulations and Deregulation – A Century Perspective on the ICC's Role,' *Logistics and Transportation Review*, **23**(1), pp. 5-32.
15. Campbell, A. E. (1971), *America Comes of Age, The Era of Theodore Roosevelt*, London: Library of the 20th Century, p.3, observes that Roosevelt 'demonstrated that trusts must take notice of the national interest and that they could be held to account by a sufficiently active and courageous President.'
16. Cherington, Paul and David M. Schwartz (1970), 'The Common Ownership Issue from Political Ideology to a Practical consideration of Benefits and Goals for Public Service,' *Transportation Law Journal*, **2**(1), p.2, pp.1-10.
17. The latter Department remained in existence until 1936, when the Department of Transport was established and assumed its functions.
18. Eagle, John. A. (1981), 'Monopoly or Competition: the Nationalisation of the Grand Trunk Railway,' *The Canadian Historical Review*, **61**, pp 3.-30. Lewis, Frank and Mary MacKinnon (1987), 'Government Loan Guarantees and the Failure of the Canadian Northern Railway,' *Journal of Economic History*, **48**(1), pp.75-196.
19. Nelson, James C., op.cit, p.9.
20. Congress of the United States (1983), 'Public Works Infrastructure,' *Policy Considerations for the 1980s*, Washington DC: US Govt. Printing Office, p.7.
21. ibid., p.7.
22. *Airport System Development* (1984), Washington DC: US Congress, Office of Technology Assessment, OTA-STI-231, p.1.
23. Keeler, Theodore, E. (1979), 'Domestic Trunk Airline Regulation,' Senate Government Operations Committee, Case Studies of Federal Regulation, Washington DC.
24. Wilson, J. A. (1959), 'Development of Aviation in Canada, 1877-1948,' *Articles*, Ottawa: Development of Transport, p.59.
25. McGrath, T. M. (1985), 'History of Canadian Airports,' Transport Canada Airports and Construction, TP5239E: p.771.
26. Studnicki-Gizbert, K. W. (1962), 'The Structure and Growth of the Canadian Air Transport Industry,' C.P.S.A. Conference on Statistics, Toronto: University of Toronto Press, p.228.
27. Currie, A.W. (1976), *Canadian Transportation Economics*, Toronto: University of Toronto Press, pp.547-549.
28. Currie, A.W., op.cit., p.81.
29. Corbett, David (1965), *Politics and the Airlines*, London: George Allen & Unwin, Ltd., p.163.
30. Nelson, James C., op.cit., p.12.
31. Douglas, George W. and James C. Miller III (1974), *Economic Regulation of Domestic Air Transport. Theory and Policy*, Washington DC: The Brookings Institution.
32. A Highway Trust Fund to provide finance for construction of interstate routes was started in 1936. A Trust Fund was started for waterways in 1978 and for transit in 1982.
33. Airport System Development, loc.cit., p.11.

34. McGrath, T.M., op.cit., p.84.

35. For figures on Investment in aviation infrastructure and revenue generated see D.O.T. Annual Reports (1938-48), *Canada in the Jet Age* (1962), Dept of Transport Air Services, CAIDT A 66C14.

36. Ellison, Anthony P. (1987), 'The Formation and Dissolution of the Canadian Rail Cartel,' *Transportation Law Journal*, **XV**(2), pp.175-243.

37. Darling, Howard J. (1974), 'Transport Policy in Canada: The Struggle of Ideologies versus Realities,' in K. W. Studnicki-Gizbert (ed), *Issues in Canadian Transport Policy*, Toronto: Macmillan, pp.8-9.

38. Thomas, William E. (1982), 'Clear Track for Deregulation of American Railroads, 1970-1980,' *Transportation Law Journal*, **12**(2), p.8.

39. Civil Aeronautics Board (1975), '*Regulatory Reform: Report of the CAB Special Staff,*' Washington D.C.

40. Ellison, Anthony P. (1982), '*Air Canada: The Cuckoo in Canada's Aviation Nest,*' Centre for the Study of Regulated Industries, Montreal: McGill University.

41. Ellison, Anthony P. (1986), 'The Rise and Decline of Protective Economic Airline Regulation in Canada,' *Transportation Law Journal*, **15**(1), pp.105-136.

42. Ellison, Anthony P. (1985), 'The New Air Transport Policy. Liberalisation not Deregulation,' *Regulatory Reporter*, Ottawa.

43. Dresner, Martin, Caroline Hadovic and Michael E. Tretheway (1989), 'The Canada-US Air Transport Bilateral: Will it be Freed?' *Transport Practitioner's Journal*, **56**(4), pp.393-405.

44. Ellison, Anthony P. 'The Formation and Dissolution of the Canadian Rail Cartel,' op.cit. pp.175-243.

45. Ellison, Anthony P. (1984), 'Regulatory Reform in Transport: A Canadian Perspective,' *Transportation Journal*, **23**(4), pp.19.

46. Rehner, Maria (1966), 'The Canada Transportation Act,' *Journal of Transportation Law, Logistics and Policy*, **63**(4), pp.08-513.

47. But NAFTA regulations prohibit Canadian drivers from participating in *cabotage* in the US and prohibit US drivers from participating in *cabotage* in Canada. Saul, Dean (1996), 'Deregulation of Travel Equipment *Cabotage*: A Canadian-Unite States Initiative,' *Transportation Law Journal*, **23**(3).

48. Baglole, Joel, 'Of Airlines and Air Lanes: a Quandary,' *The Wall Street Journal*, June 12.

49. Wilde Mathews, Anna and Daniel Machalaba (1999), 'US Approves Canadian National Acquisition,' *The Wall Street Journal*, 24 March.

50. Holle, Peter (2000), 'Us Regulators Jolt a US-Canadian Rail Merger Off Track,' *The Wall Street Journal*, 14 July.

2. Regulating and Deregulating the Transformations

The bourgeoisie, during its rule of scarce one hundred years, has created more massive and more colossal production forces than have all the preceding generations together.   Subjection of nature's forces to man, machinery, applications of chemistry to industry and agriculture, steam navigation, railways, electric telegraphs, clearing of whole continents for cultivation, canalisation of rivers, whole populations conjured out of the ground - what earlier century had event a presentiment that such production forces slumbered in the lap of social labour?

Karl Marx and Friedrich Engels

Improved communication has played havoc with the European system of Metternich and of the Holy Alliance. The diffusion of intelligence by the post-office and the telegraph has forced the most conservative authorities to move. The rush of travel has broken down the passport system. The extension of trade is forcing us into unity of money, weights, and measures. It has prevented each nation from settling its own problems by itself.[1]

Arthur T. Hadley

If human nature felt no temptation to take a chance, no satisfaction (profit apart) in constructing a factory, a railway, a mine or a farm, there might not be much investment merely as a result of cold calculation.[2]

John Maynard Keynes

In earlier history, wealth was measured in land, in gold, in oil, in machines. Today, the principal measure of our wealth is information: its quality, and the speed with which we acquire it and adapt it. The truth of our age is this, and must be this: open and competitive commerce will enrich us a nation. It spurs us to innovate. It forces us to compete. It connects us with new customers. It promotes global growth without which no rich country can hope to grow wealthier.[3]

US President W.J. Clinton

INTRODUCTION

The term globalisation may be of recent coinage but the constituents of globalisation -'networks of interdependencies at multi-continental distances'[4] - have been present for the last five centuries.   Indeed, the contemporary global economy has yet to attain the interdependencies engendered by the open trade and international financial regimes that operated between approximately 1850 and 1914.

The first of the quotations that preface this chapter is taken from the 1872 Communist Manifesto. Marx and Engels characterised free trade, the gold standard and the mobility of labour of this phase of globalisation as a process of 'constant revolutionising of production' and an 'endless disturbance of all social conditions.'[5]

The transport economist Arthur Hadley, from whom the second quotation is taken, outlined in his 1888 study the creative destructiveness of transport and information technologies. The third quotation is taken from Keynes' General Theory. Published in 1936, in an era characterised by exchange rate instability, competitive devaluations and protectionist trade policies, it is a reminder that open regimes do not necessarily remain so for ever.

The last of the quotations expresses the potential of contemporary information technology to transform the economic and social orders. It is taken from a speech made, in 1993, by US President Bill Clinton. The newly elected President was to continue the policies of his Republican predecessors, dubbed 'the Washington Consensus,'[6] which advocated fiscal discipline, privatisation, deregulation and the liberalisation of global trading and financial regimes.

Historical comparisons contain some surprises. The distinguishing characteristics of the contemporary global system are neither the extent of its interconnectedness nor the fact of its financial volatility. The free trade/gold standard regime of the nineteenth century, with its mobility of capital and labour, was highly interconnected and not infrequently punctuated by dislocating financial crises. The advent of the telegraph marked the major leap in communicating velocity. Indeed, the distinguishing features of the contemporary globalisation are the enormous increases of data, capital and information-intensive services and goods flowing over communication and transportation networks. These flows are, in turn, the consequence of the drastically reduced costs of communicating and transporting.

The obvious question is, what has caused these cost reductions in communications and transportation? A considered answer is that the costs of communicating have been driven downwards by what seems to be almost constantly self-transforming information technology. But they, and the reduced costs of transportation, have, in turn, been brought about by policy decisions which (selectively) removed the protective barriers to competition. In other words, it is policy decisions, not technical advances, that remove barriers to competition.

Many have expressed relief at the prospect of leaving behind the smokestacks and bureaucratisation of mass industrialisation. By contrast, others have been steadfast in the defence of the old order and some have warned that information technology will insinuate itself into culture and into leisure, thereby increasing the isolation of men, one from another, and their alienation from a sense of belonging. Indeed, the most intense controversy has swirled around the prospect of what has been variously termed 'the fully developed industrial society'[7] or the 'post-industrial order.' Opposing those who predict imminent beneficence from deregulated global markets and the spread of democratic capitalism are those who challenge the implied technological determinism and the assumed disinterest of the elite. They point to the coercive measures that the international agencies have deployed in spreading their favoured form of the Washington Consensus. They deplore the consequences of deregulating capital flows, question the motives of governments and query the role of multinational corporations. They state that without the restoration of market-contained structures and international regulatory regimes, there would be instability, accelerated regression into social decay and the destruction of the new order.

Whatever their differences, few of the protagonists would disagree that the controversies largely concern the ramifications of technical innovation. Put simply, contemporary Western economies are characterised by the silicon chip technology. This is converging with fibre optics, also largely silicon, to create an information economy in which fossil energy is being replaced with knowledge. Such technical change is accelerating the rate at which information is produced and exchanged. In doing so, it is shifting the respective levels of transaction costs. The friction-less new economy challenges the old friction-impaired economy.

Cable and satellite technologies, computers, VCRs, video cassettes, faxes, printers, copiers and enhanced telephones, have merged, combining into interactive networks from which has emerged information expressed in sounds and symbols. These are transforming the production of information, spreading its exchange and dissemination and permeating totalitarian and open societies alike. The marginal costs of using the Internet are effectively zero. Although markets are still far from frictionless, thanks to the costs of shipping over distances, the almost zero costs of search are encouraging significant substitutions. The customer and buyer are able to shop anywhere. Forced tie-ins, local monopolies, cosy oligopolies and price discrimination are under threat. As a growing number of customers have access to broadband, there is likely to be an increasing fragmentation of markets and an unbundling of services. The downscaling of the mass, homogeneous products of the industrial era is well under way. They are, in some cases, being substituted by knowledge-intense, heterogeneous and lighter commodities produced in enterprises that are distinguished by their flexibility and horizontal forms of communication. But at the same time, and by way of contrast, there are concerns that the 'info-communications sector' is being subjected to increasing market concentration.

In services that are conveyed via a channel of communication, the intangible service itself often contains, or is itself, a form of information. Transport is an input into this communication of information. The passenger at his destination, and sometimes during the trip, conveys and exchanges information. The arriving goods convey information as to their condition and quality. The postal systems deploy common and, sometimes, private and protected modes. Later, the telegraph systems operated alongside rail tracks. The efficiency of the market, in executing its co-ordinating functions in the pre-telegraph era, depended upon the efficiency, reliability and safety of the mode that carried the individual or the postal package. The telegraph was a significant invention because information could be conveyed at a faster rate than could be achieved by a person travelling by rail or by a rail-transported letter. The transatlantic cable of 1866 reduced the time of transmission of information by a factor of a thousand. By contrast, the telephone increased the velocity by only a few minutes and the Internet over the telephone by hardly any time at all. But the significance of the Internet lies with its much lower costs of communicating. As the means of communicating via telecommunications have widened, the modern telecommunication systems have acted as 'sixth modes.'

The technical processes of invention, innovation, development and transmission are continuing to change the technical infrastructure of societies, and, in particular, are changing the spatial and time dimensions of the competitive market process. The market's co-ordination of existing knowledge, its generation and dissemination of new information and the interaction between consumer and producer, is greatly enhanced by the speed, accuracy and, above all, by the reduced cost of transmission of print, sound and visual images. The penetration of interactive market exchange into increasing areas of activities and locations is, in turn, contributing to what has been described as economic, social and political transformations.

At this point, a cautionary note is appropriate. The technical progression, or 'revolution', and the emergence and technical enhancement of the market process, are not the only factors contributing to the social transformation of Western (and other) societies. As well as material forces, there are forces arising from new knowledge and forces that are the consequence of intellectual dispute. Furthermore, it has been persuasively argued that religion, non-rational elements and ideology shape a society's moral axioms and condition its constituent structures. Attitudes toward technology and the competitive market process have influenced their application, penetration and containment. Whether these are the attitudes of the few, or of the many, has mattered little, for discerning the 'collective consciousness' of the many has frequently degenerated into imputing dogma. Ideology and dogma have, in turn, influenced the scope and direction of economics, for this discipline bases its explanation on its own construction, the self-seeking economic man in the marketplace. This construction has been influenced by what is, or is not, deemed to be human, moral or immoral about economic man. Ideologies have also shaped, enhanced and, sometimes, contained social transformations by deregulating or regulating the market, suppressing the market process or substituting the dictates of government for the competitive market process.

The entry into play of intellectual history introduces the dispute as to whether mind rules matter or matter mind, whether all change is dependent on new ideas, concepts, ideology and logic or whether the social processes cause these intellectual transformations. Behind these disputes lies the quest for a complete explanation, probably a futile one at that, for it is an illusion to bring the whole complex economic, let alone social reality, within the confines of a single explanation. (These and related issues are examined in Chapter 4, in which regulatory theories are examined in the light of economic and social theory.)

The characteristics of Western societies have placed limits on the time and space of this analysis. They are characterised by the combination of scientific discovery and the systematic and large-scale application of technical innovation. In turn, they have augmented the market process and, together, have provided the most pervasive and forceful stimuli in the revolutionary process known as 'modernisation' an umbrella term, involving a number of unavoidable reductionisms. Bearing this cautionary injunction in mind, the term 'modernisation' is taken herein to mean a shift in values, knowledge and cultures that, over the last two centuries has transformed Western societies.

Within the time frame of this modern era, in this chapter, aspects of the histories of North America and Western Europe are highlighted in order to accomplish two objectives. The first is to explore the relationships between the regulation and, later, the deregulation of the transport, communications, trade and financial systems of the respective economic orders and their pervading economic and political ideologies; and the second is to chart the emergence of the contemporary global economic system. (An examination of the stability, or lack of stability, of the contemporary global order is reserved for Chapter 3)

FROM MERCANTILISM VIA *LAISSEZ-FAIRE*

During the twelfth century, medieval Europe, resplendent in its apotheosis, was a world of broad ideological zones linked by subjective beliefs held in common.[8] A divinely inspired internal order was governed by institutions of the Church that reinforced the subjective, communal vision by pitting the metaphysical against the material. Rewards were bestowed by the grace of God - not attained by man's efforts. Prices and services were determined by moral criteria. Rewards were dedicated to God's purposes. There were no institutions structured around productive assets. Exchange was limited. Settlements and villages were isolated, each struggling for self-sufficiency. Markets, that frequently took the form of fairs franchised under the monarch, served to facilitate the exchange of goods provided by entrepreneurs. Individual activities were occasional and intermittent. Those individuals who were dedicated to providing a public service were deemed to be following a 'common, or public, calling,' They undertook a duty, that of serving adequately all who applied at reasonable prices for service. Such common callings reflected the increasing division of labour and the effect of the widening market. Business regulations narrowed, as more agents sought the freedom to exchange and negotiate contracts. Spurred by quickening trade, widening markets and the increasing growing rationalisation, more common or public callings developed as distinct from the 'public interest.'

The modern age of Western civilisation is recognised as having dawned at the turn of the fifteenth century. The Renaissance, the re-birth of classical culture, coincided with other great transforming events in the history of Europe, in particular the discovery of the New World and the Reformation, and laid the foundations of the Enlightenment, with its articulation of the individual. Gutenberg's bible, printed with movable type at Mainz in 1456, started a flood of books that released new streams of communication between and among persons. Imbued with the revolutionary notions of time and space and aided by maps and chronometers, it was the adventurous individualists of Renaissance Europe who sought their liberation by conquering nature. Space, as a 'dimension' of nature, was mapped, navigated and conquered by 'shrinkage.' Time was conceptualised in linear terms.

Enlightened thought operated within Newton's paradigm of a universe of homogeneous time and space. The market process, according to the Scottish Enlightenment, contained a 'hidden hand', as it was called, that converted the actions of actors of dubious moral sentiments into outcomes advantageous to all. In constructing roads, canals and railways, systems of communication and organisation, entrepreneurial activity parcelled public lands into exchangeable private property and extended the geographic reach of the market process by reducing distances and the duration of communication.[9]

Modernisation is a revolutionary process, involving a shift in values, knowledge and culture. The market process was both a product and an agent of modernisation.

Centralised nation states emerged from the dissolution of medieval Europe. Their unabashed accrual of political and economic power found expression in the system known as mercantilism. According to mercantilist precepts, wealth was measured by bullion (and maximised by restrictive international trade policies), by the exchange of exclusive monopoly licences and subsidies and by the protective regulation between the government, in the person of the monarch, and merchant capitalists. Mercantilism was costly in its beggar-thy-neighbour trading policies, the dead-weight losses of its zero sum transfers, and the rent-seeking behaviour of its merchant capitalists. This system attained its most developed form under the centralised rule of Louis IV's government in seventeenth century France.

Increasing trade between nation states necessitated consideration of the binding principles in law concerning trade and transport. Hugo Grotius (1583-1645) initiated consideration of the universal aspects of international law. He postulated that all relationships in the world are subject to the 'rules of law' and promoted a regime of freedom of the seas.[10] While this was clearly in the interests of the Netherlands's merchant navy, the consideration of equal rights to the use of the sea, freedom of navigation, and, in territorial seas, 'innocent passage', reflected an awareness, in the face of conventional opinion, of the mutually beneficial effects of trade.

The American naval strategist, Mahan, laid stress on the military dimension of sea power.[11] He argued that the rise and fall of sea power was linked to the rise and decline of nations. The link was maintained via the commercial and military command of the sea. By deploying successful war strategies, England, according to Mahan, had retained its sea power and, in so doing, had secured its economy and colonial possessions.

In England, during the seventeenth century, the number of common callings shrank, clustering, eventually, around the transport system. Common callings drew in innkeepers and blacksmiths, as well as wharfingers, lightermen, ferrymen and bargemen. Common callings, unlike private commercial activities, imposed on their practitioners, not only a duty to serve, but also the burden of liability for all damage to or loss of goods. The special status of the constituent parts of the transport system has been ascribed, not to the tendency of the modes to monopoly, nor to the distinctions established by the legal process, but to the ability of the influential aristocracy to sustain legal protection for the carriage of their persons and transport of their effects.[12]

France became the first modern, centralised, nation state. As a means of consolidating his government's power, Louis XI seized the postal service from the cities and placed it under his national administration. The first school of civil engineers in Europe to be recognised by government, the Corps des Ponts et Chaussées, was founded in 1706. A training school, the École des Ponts et Chaussées, was added 1749. The trained economic engineers produced by these institutions, postulated, with Cartesian logic, welfare functions acceptable to the administration, and, in time, developed the tool of consumer surplus as a measure of 'maximum satisfaction.' This tool was then deployed in evaluating competing public projects. The state, rather than the private sector, as in England and the United States, planned, financed, owned and operated first the roads (the Routes Nationales in 1776), the canals (the Freycinet Plan of 1879), and the railways (the Railway Law of 1842 establishing the plan of the network). The 'Legrand Plan' leased the government-owned railways, the Nationale des Chemins de Fer Français, to private companies.

Hayek, in locating the emergence of 'scientism', has made the following point:

> (B)oth the great intellectual forces which in the course of the Nineteenth Century transformed social thought, modern socialism and that species of modern positivism, which we prefer to call scientism, spring directly from the body of professional scientists and engineers which grew up in Paris, and more particularly from the new institution which embodied the new spirits as no other, Ecole Polytechnique.[13]

Nelson, commenting on the form of economic planning in France, has observed that 'France is the only country in the world that has avowedly introduced marginal cost principles as a matter of deliberate long-term policy into transport (and public utility) rate making.'[14]

In Britain, parliament's rise to power over the monarchy and the reduced value of monopolies and cartels as a result of alternative technologies, contributed to the early demise of Britain's mercantilist policies. These factors also helped to confine more and more economic processes to voluntary associations of individuals.[15] Emergent capitalism was complemented by a liberal philosophy that promoted personal freedom and espoused a *laissez-faire* economic policy.

Such political arrangements, along with geographical and social factors, facilitated the application of a growing stock of scientific knowledge by entrepreneur-innovators, the consequence of which was the quickening of economic growth and the transformation of the economy. The technical improvements in textile manufacturing, iron and steel, refrigeration and the steam engine, were the product of entrepreneurial endeavours to lower costs, which widened markets and forced organisational change.[16]

Market-expanding transport projects laid the path of progress that led to the transformation of traditional, largely agrarian societies into the mass industrial orders of the twentieth century. The large-scale projects that pierced isthmuses and shrank continents, binding them with roads and railways, were hailed as the paving stones upon which progress travelled. The heroes of the age were the precursors of progress, the engineers and financiers, whose endeavours had diffused knowledge, accelerated economic and social intercourse and reduced isolation. Admired begrudgingly by Marx, the individualistic bourgeois entrepreneur was the exemplar of the modern age. He challenged the *status quo*, kicked open the doors of the frontier and championed the free interchange of goods and people through the emerging portals.

Technical advances in transport and communication contributed to the launch of the industrial economic order by enhancing the co-ordinating potential of the market process. The shift into fossil-based energy, the resulting stimulation to the technical application of the coal-fired steam engine, refined methods of iron and steel production and textile manufacturers, acting together, transformed an agrarian Europe and its North American colonies from rural into industrial economies - all within a mere two generations.

The application of steam and electricity to transport and communications – the telegraph was commercially viable by 1847 – facilitated a spatial flow of goods at a vastly increased speed. The railways and telegraph companies were the prototypes of industrial organisation. By subdividing their functions, they increased the velocity of services and reduced costs.[17] Their co-ordination of distribution facilitated increased throughputs and scales of operation. The visible hand of the organisation replaced the invisible hand of the market.

The mobility of capital, labour and materials increased and aggregated into large-scale production. Technical advances in printing influenced written communications. Newspapers adopted the pressing cylinder in 1814, the rotary press in the 1840s and the automatic printer in the 1860s all facilitated by the invention of the continuous roll of paper. In the 1880s, the 'linotype' machine improved typesetting, but it was to be technical developments around electricity that were to change the way individuals conveyed information, news and instructions.[18]

Owing largely due to the work of Faraday, scientific understanding of the nature of electricity and magnetism dawned in the 1830s. The first patent of the electric telegraph was taken out in 1837. Morse incorporated his famous code in 1843. The first cable across the English Channel was laid in 1851. The Transatlantic cable of 1866 and the Indian Ocean cable followed in 1872. In 1868, the electrical telegraph system in the United Kingdom was taken over by the Post Office. Alexander Bell, in 1876, registered voice on an electric current. Amplification was invented two years later and the Bell Telephone Co. was founded. The circuit-switched telephone system shrank distance for voice communications. Using the work of Maxwell and Hertz, Marconi established the first wireless or radio communication in 1901. In 1873 the Remington Co. produced the first typewriter.

At the turn of the new century, a number of major inventions and innovations revolutionised commerce and industry and public services: the telephone, typewriter, tabulating machine and cash register combined to revolutionise the office; the introduction of the use of aluminium and vulcanised rubber profoundly altered manufacturing and transport. The electric washing machine transformed domestic employment patterns and the emergence of the aeroplane, in the first decade of the new century, called up new visions of the destiny of humanity. While the large organisations generated economies of scale, the mobility of capital and labour, along with the reliability and speed of transport and communication, facilitated mass production. This mass production, through capital-intensive corporations, evolved later into mass merchandising and into mass media.

The interconnected industrial and financial orders, however, were subject to vicissitudes that engendered social instability among the dependent urban populations. Various attempts were made to restore stability. There were also issues of equity. Should government attempt to ensure universal access to telephone and electricity? Cartelisation was, in part, legitimised in Europe. But in the United States this was politically unacceptable, and, instead, anti-trust regulations, protective regulation and corporate concentration characterised the industrial order.

Central government budgets, whose main sources of revenue were trade tariffs, were kept in balance, in part, by the increased trade resulting from lower tariffs and the mid-nineteenth century trading boom. Britain's superior industrial capacity, its mobile, military naval force, developed banking and financial system, complemented by a strengthened gold standard, worked to create a trading and international payments system that enjoyed reinforcing levels of liquidity and confidence.

Adherence to the rule of the gold standard under Britain's hegemony meant that governments sacrificed the domestic stability of their growing, but still small, industrial bases. Domestic currencies were convertible into gold at a fixed official price. However, while this convertibility usually maintained a stable domestic price level, the costs, in the form of fluctuating unemployment rates, were high. Furthermore, the ruling elites encouraged the free flow of capital and labour because such mobility was deemed to enhance the prospects of their economies. Benefits were perceived to flow by allowing labour and capital to move where individuals considered them to be most productive. It was the freedom of labour and capital to move between markets (reflecting the high transport costs and limited information), that produced an important characteristic of this era, the separation of markets and the mobility of capital and labour between them. Despite such movements, the *laissez-faire* that was celebrated at the centennial of Smith's publication was the freedom from interference that allowed the impersonal 'iron laws' of scientific economics (scientism) to operate.

It has been claimed that from the end of the civil war to the middle of the 1880s the ruling ideology among legislators, jurists and others in the public life of the United States, was the *laissez-faire* doctrine. Consequently, political economy and this doctrine were virtually synonymous. However, the transformation of an economy by the market, in which labour and land entered the process, and were subjected to its vicissitudes, was to introduce qualifications to the ideology. So, too, was the alleged introduction of market monopoly by, among others, the merging railroad companies.' The *Granger Laws*, the *Interstate Commerce Act*, the *Sherman Act* and state utility legislation met the resulting demand for legislative restraint of monopolistic tendencies in industry.

The experience of the railroads had been salutary. With the judicial declaration and elaboration of the principle that 'common carriage' was affected in the public interest, transportation provided a real or fictional analogical base for declaring a variety of businesses as similarly affected. There was, as a result, less need to contend that the 'calling' in such services as grain elevators and stockyards, had been traditionally regulated.[19]

Between 1910 and 1938, the state created and protected natural monopolies.[20] They were established, in particular, in the transportation, communication and electrical utilities, all of which confer 'portability' and are part of a network. The legislation, however, considerably enlarged the regulatory obligations that had been imposed by the common law. Entrants into transport markets were subject to tests of 'public convenience and necessity.' Utilities were subjected to regulatory corollaries of rate regulation.

The 1935 *Public Utility Holding Company Act* restricted the operations of multi-state utility holding companies. Such companies could not diversify much beyond their core utility and natural gas holdings, providing a barrier, not only to utility company diversification but also to the entry of non-utility companies into the electricity business. Regulators told utilities how much they could charge for producing and distributing electricity. Utilities, in turn, earned a fixed rate of return on the capital they invested in power plants and transmission lines, provided they were reliable and operated within reasonable cost limits.

The beginning of the 1880s also saw a narrowing in free trade and the start of a hectic race between the European powers for colonial markets.

At the turn of the century, the world was unstable as two blocs vied for dominance. This instability culminated in the catastrophic Great War. Yet, in spite of the major threat to world order, the mass industrial era entered into its expansive stage. Organisations were formed to facilitate the scale production of new technologies. The motor car and the aeroplane reduced transport time and propelled the spread of the mass industrial process. The broadening of telephone ownership established a quickening and reinforcing of communications networks. Contained within protective regulation, either restricted by anti-trust legislation or by operating within sanctioned cartels, concentrated mass industrial organisations found themselves subjected to the undulations of the industrial cycle. The growth of urban, industrial populations and the dependence of more people on industrial employment forced governments into considering policies to promote domestic stability. These policies were in conflict with the economic forces set in motion by the payments deficits and gold flows under the gold standard. With Britain unable and unwilling to shoulder its responsibilities as hegemon, individual governments, in an attempt to restore the value of their currencies, pursued neo-mercantilist[21] and nationalistic policies.[22] The result was that the post-war gold exchange standard foundered in the wake of protective tariffs, disorderly capital flows, competitive devaluations and the discriminatory foreign exchange dealings of the 1930s.

In Keynes' view, uncertainty among the agents operating through the money exchange economy was the source of the instability in the real economy of investment, savings and employment. In the presence of uncertainty, agents made investment decisions that did not necessarily lead, as was claimed by the classical model, to equilibrating tendencies that came to rest at full employment. It was not the insufficiency of savings that was responsible for low investment and unemployment, but rather because investment was insufficient to generate higher incomes and hence savings and employment. He advocated restoring stability and full employment to the real economy. Participating governments were to be subjected to a regime of known rules. They would minimise uncertainty, generate confidence, and facilitate their power over domestic and international financial flows.

The United States emerged from the Second World War as the world's hegemon. By contrast with its policy of withdrawal from foreign responsibilities during the inter-war years, it now shouldered responsibilities for Free World leadership in defence, monetary stability and freedom of trade. The United States assumed leadership in creating the United Nations, the International Monetary Fund, of which Keynes was an influential architect, and the World Bank. Instead of sustaining one of the highest tariffs in history (the 1930 *Smoot-Hawley Tariff*), the United States pursued multi-tariff reductions under the General Agreement on Tariffs and Trade (GATT).[23]

International transport and telecommunications, however, were contained within regulations enforced by governments that pursued neo-mercantilist objectives. The *Merchant Marine Act* of 1936 stipulated that the United States should have a merchant marine sufficient to carry all of the nation's domestic waterborne commerce. It was also to have a substantial share of its exports and imports and be capable of serving as a military auxiliary in time of war.

The modern administrative state of the United States rose up out of the despondency of the depressed thirties. It was founded upon disillusionment over the market order and faith in the efficacy of government to re-order market outcomes.[24] The Roosevelt Administration set about limiting the market power of those who were alleged to have precipitated the stock market crash of 1929 and the ensuing banking crisis. *The Securities Act* of 1933 was aimed at curbing the excesses found in the new issues market. To eradicate manipulative activities, the *Securities and Exchange Act* of 1934 was introduced to regulate the trading of issued securities. The *Glass-Steagall Act*, or as it was formally known, the *Banking Act* of 1933, attempted to restore confidence in the American banking sector. Banks were to be confined to the loans business and were no longer to be allowed to hold sway in the brokerage business. Under the Act, commercial banks could receive no more than 10 per cent of their income from the securities market. To provide a safe haven for the savings of individuals, the Act established the Federal Deposit Insurance Corporation. The *Bank Holding Company Act* of 1956 restricted the activities of banks in the insurance market. Banks, stock brokerages and insurance companies were separated to ensure that a catastrophic failure in one pillar of the financial industry would not bring down the other two.

Regulations, protective of the transport modes, were enhanced and introduced during the 1930s in the United States as they were in all the major trading countries. International air transport [25] was subjected to a regulatory framework established at the close of the war. Entry was decided in terms of bilateral agreements among governments. Rates were set by an international conference, subject to the approval of each member government. Pooling agreements and capacity restrictions prevailed in many markets.[26]

The political system of the United States had a bias towards regulation rather than towards federal government ownership. As a result, some singular and far-reaching structures emerged. The ensuing regulation of the railroads, established, not only a precedent for the pursuit and correction of the distortion of monopoly power, but also the centrality of 'the regulator' in the concerns of the administration. The regulatory model was to be deployed to correct perceived distortions in other markets. In air transport, the failure to introduce an efficient mail subsidy contract system in the 1930s was to have a half-century of consequences for the US civil aviation industry. The failure of such a contracting system (and the ensuing fraud) engendered the view in government circles that the civil aviation carriers were prone to engage in destructive competition and could be saved from such a fate only by the imposition of protective economic regulation. The 1938 *Civil Aviation Act*, premised, in part, on the notion that carriers would, without protection, engage in destructive competition, was to endure for fifty years. During this time, the industry grew to be the major inter-city passenger public mode and aircraft technology from the propellered DC-3 to the wide-bodied jumbos.

In the telecommunications sector, the United States system was also atypical. In most countries, a single monopoly was granted with the assumption of control over communications. The telephone company was generally merged with the postal service. Both were placed within a government ministry. But the postal and telecommunication services were not merged in the United States. Each was subjected to a different regulatory agency.

In 1885 American Telephone & Telegraph (AT&T) became a wholly owned subsidiary of American Bell. AT&T then began to establish the first long-distance network. By 1902, Bell was competing with over 1,500 independent telephone companies. By denying them connections to its long-distance network and refusing to sell its patented telephone equipment to rival companies, Bell was able to pick off its would-be competitors. Bell claimed that its market consolidations constituted, in effect, a natural monopoly. In exchange for providing uniform, efficient and reliable service, Bell requested protection and regulation. In 1913 the Department of Justice granted AT&T protection from competition.

The *Communications Act* of 1934 established the Federal Communications Commission (FCC). The Act authorised monopolies in communications but subjected their prices and services to FCC regulations. As an independent agency charged with regulating interstate and international communications, the FCC came to regulate what later became known as the 'five lanes' of the information highway: broadcast, wire, wireless, cable and satellite. These lanes were legally separated and for the most part, they were not permitted to merge or engage in inter-lane competition.

The dominant telephone company was allowed to own its own equipment supplier. The US system and all the other major systems, however, operated under the rationale that the most efficacious and equitable means of providing public service, both domestically and internationally, was by means of monopoly supply of service and equipment. Regulated rate structures were usually uniform rates pitched at average costs. The standard arrangement was for the telephone services to subsidise the national monopolies that supplied the equipment; for telephone operations to subsidise postal services and for long-distance telephone services to subsidise local telephone services. Such domestic regimes were reinforced by international organisations that enforced bilateral monopolistic exchanges.

International standardisation and co-ordination measures were put into place: the International Telegraph Union of 1865; the Universal Postal Union 1875; the International Meteorological Organisation 1878; and the International Signals Code of 1871.

The 1906 Berlin Radio Conference established governmental control of the electromagnetic spectrum. The spectrum was carved into blocs, the applicant having to compete for channels in the relevant bloc, and to use them only for the purpose prescribed by government. The eventual establishment of standards facilitating interconnection or radio systems were agreed at an international conference in 1912, a move that reinforced government control of the electromagnetic spectrum. Marconi, in the 1920s, orchestrated an international cartel agreement for radiotelegraphy patents rights.[27] In 1932, the signatories of the 1906 International Radio Telegraph convention and the members of the

International Telegraph Union formed the ITU, from which emerged three bodies: the International Consultation Committee for Radio (CCIR), the International Consultation Committee for Telephones and Telegraph (CCITT) and the International Frequency Registration Board. The ITU operated on a one-nation, one-vote basis. Thus, the ITU delegated power to a specialised government bureau, which, in turn, patronised a monopoly supplier and, in this way, raised obstacles to entry. The CCITT, it is charged, in effect acted as a cartel for the respective domestic telephone and postal monopolies.

They (the CCITT and CCIR) were the anchors of a regime that facilitated bilateral monopolistic bargains, reinforced national monopolies and limited the rights of private firms in the global market.[28]

In 1962 the US Congress created the Communication Satellite Corporation (COMSAT). Although privately owned, COMSAT had three government appointees among its fifteen directors. COMSAT acted as the sole link between US carriers and international traffic. The FCC forbade it from providing direct domestic services.

Until 1979, COMSAT managed the International Telecommunication Satellite Corporation. Intelsat was established by an agreement entered into by eleven member governments in 1964. The enterprise is owned and funded by its members in proportion to their share of total Intelsat traffic, overwhelmingly transatlantic telephone traffic.

Article XIV (b) of the Intelstat agreement permits member countries to operate other satellites for 'international public telecommunications services,' only if the satellites are technically compatible with Intelsat and so do it no 'significant economic harm.' Over time, five regional satellite systems outside of Intelsat have been launched: Eutelsat in Europe, Arabsat in the Arab countries, Papala-B in Indonesia and the Soviet Intersputnik (in co-operation with Algeria).

Although radio frequency spectrums are technically equal, tangible and interchangeable, signatory bodies in all countries adhered to the allocation methods established in 1906, at which time spectrum blocs were divided, allocated to the broadcasters and often accompanied by geographic sale and programme restrictions. In the United States, the FCC allocated two (adjacent) parts of the spectrum to VHF services and divided the relevant spectrum bloc into twelve channels of 6 MHz each. By limiting the spectrum to television, specifying the channel band-width, and establishing mileage separation, the FCC guaranteed that there would be no more than three (over-the-air) networks (ABC, NBC and CBS).[29] In the 1979-1980 broadcast season, these networks captured almost 90 per cent of the prime time viewing audiences.[30]

The war-damaged economies operated for a while behind protective tariffs and international transport moved within government-enforced cartel agreements. The United States, along with its minor partner in the United

Kingdom, acted as the world banker to the International monetary system then known as the Gold Exchange Standard.

Exchange rates were fixed against the dollar price for gold. Governments maintained currency parity by responding, on the one hand to inflation and the resulting balance of payments deficits by tightening the money supply, and, on the other, to deflation and unemployment, by cutting taxes, increasing government spending and easing terms of credit. For approximately two decades, the resulting monetary action implicit in demand management appeared to be compatible with the maintenance of exchange rate parity and full employment. Conflict occurred, and the international system broke down when the supply of money concomitant with demand management led to steeper inflation and unsustainable exchange rates. In 1971, when President Nixon formally suspended the dollar's convertibility, the system finally broke down.

This is an appropriate date at which to take stock of the development of the mass industrial order.

The century had seen the representative democracies depart from Gladstonean fiscal policy. Expenditure was limited to the minimum required for essential services. Budgets were balanced and taxes raised revenue rather than redistributed income.

By the middle of the 1970s, the situation was dramatically different. The revenues of public authorities accounted for the equivalent of one-third to a half of such nations' economic product.[31] Keynesian notions of demand deficient unemployment appeared to have arisen, not from insufficiency of investment, but from labour-substituting technology that stimulated growth but not necessarily employment. The dead-weight losses resulting from zero-sum redistribution were seen to rise to intolerable levels, and, it was argued by some, contributed to the slow growth and rise in unemployment and inflation. Radical measures were proposed.

The unwelcome appearance of higher energy prices, higher inflation and higher unemployment in the early 1970s and its persistency in the face of higher government spending, added credibility to the monetarists position, which was that the long-run effects of total spending are on the price level. The stimulating effects on output and employment are transitory. As well as reinstating the revised aspects of the classical quantity theory of money, consideration was given to the rate of unemployment at which inflation neither falls nor rises. (The natural rate or non-accelerating inflation rate of unemployment.)

If this underlying rate of unemployment is regarded as being too high, the way to reduce, permanently, its level is to influence the market process. Prices should become flexible and responsive. Such measures might include the removal of the protective regulations of neo-mercantilist labour, capital, product and service markets in such a way that rigidities are removed and fuller uses of the resources of the economy are facilitated.

Growth rates slowed under the weight of the welfare state and demand management failed to contain inflation. Inflation duly prompted the application of measures that chipped away at the pillars of the welfare state.

Over time it was observed by some that political liberty, expressed through representative democracies, by substituting regulatory and government planning for unrestricted market exchange, led to a diminution in economic liberty. Moreover, equality was not enhanced. The reason was that the means employed were designed to retard levels of opulence, and the emerging redistributions were considered incongruous with notions of equality. The unwelcome combination of slowing growth, rising unemployment and inflation forced the attention of the political marketplace into considering whether security had been acquired at the cost of economic liberty, and redistribution at the cost of growth. At the same time that the main industrial order was stagnating and declining, there were changes in computation, transport and communications technology that were to shape the formation of a post-industrial order.

THE ASSAULT ON NEO-MERCANTILISM

The introduction of Ford's Model-T in 1908 was a defining moment in Western culture. The mass manufacturing and marketing of the motor car had begun. Nine decades later, it is still the dominant mode of transport. Although Daimler and Benz had adopted the petrol engine in 1885, it was Ford who demonstrated that the complete process car manufacture could be by assembly-belt. By 1927, he had built fifteen million 'Tin Lizzies.' The car came quickly to influence how people lived, worked and played. The possibilities of travelling ever further for leisure and work had begun. These possibilities were further extended by the arrival, after the Second World War, of large four-engined planes derived from wartime bombers. The adoption of the gas turbine – the jet engine – in place of the conventional reciprocating engine, increased the ratio of power to size. The jet age arrived in the late 1960s with the launching of large, wide-bodied jumbo jets capable of carrying hundreds of passengers on long haul routes.[32]

Wartime competition and Cold War rivalry was also to give a spur to a whole range of applications that were to lead to what became known as information technology. In 1833, Charles Babbage showed with his 'difference engine' and 'analytical engine' that a computer was an arithmetical machine that could do sums. A century later, Alan Turing solved many of the problems of computing with his design of the hypothetical Turing machine. George Boole, a nineteenth century British mathematician, expressed logical statements as a sequence of binary numbers. Claude Shannon of the Bell Telephone Laboratories adopted this in

1938. By using an electric component of the 'on' and 'off' to represent two values a viable basis for computer logic was built.

During the ensuing war, Turing contributed to the development of a machine that deciphered secret German codes. In the United States, the automatic digital computer – the Colossus – was developed in 1943 using 1,500 thermonic valves.[33] In 1944, IBM completed the automatic sequence controlled calculator and designated it as the Mark I computer. Until 1948, all these machines incorporating electronically-stored programmes used thermonic valves. Then Bell Labs identified point-contact transistors. This led to the development of large-scale systems of information processing. The so-called 'third generation' computers arrived in 1959 with the patenting of the integrated circuit. This facilitated the performance of the computer by the use of a small semi-conductor or chip with transistors printed on it

In 1965, Donald W. Davies, a British engineer, put forward a suggestion to make it possible for conventional telephones to carry huge amounts of computer-generated data in short bursts. He suggested the development of a network that would allow data to follow a variety of pathways. The data would be broken into small packets, each carrying a code indicating where it came from and where it was to end up so that a complete document could be compiled at the receiving computer. Packets would move along the fastest available route. Davies termed the concept 'packet switching.'

Davies built a demonstration packet-switching network within the National Physical Laboratory in 1969. Paul Baran of the RAND Corporation formulated a similar concept for the government of the United States. The intention was to make the government less vulnerable to a nuclear attack. Lawrence Roberts, program director for the Advanced Research Projects Agency, aimed to improve communications among the many laboratories and universities working on research financed by the agency. When informed of Davies' concept, Roberts, and others, set about melding this concept with that of Baran's. Concurrently, officials involved in the air defence systems encouraged the development of computers that could assimilate and analyse vast amounts of information involving complex military operations. The outcome was the creation of ARPONET – the Pentagon's Advanced Research Project Agency – which connected networks of computers across the country. This became the forerunner of the Internet.

In 1969, a team from the firm Bolt, Beranek and Newman (BBN) installed a prototype packet switch at the University of California-Los Angeles. By the end of that year, three more packet switches were in place and tests were made as to the ability of the network to carry data between the computers. Most significantly, the early pioneers who developed the common communications protocol known as the Internet protocol (IP) shared it with all users. As a result Internet transmissions could use any or all inter-linked networks - hence the 'inter' and 'net' of the neologism.

The seminal technical development was the invention of the microprocessor by Intel Corp. engineers in 1971. This 'brain' led to the building of personal computer (PC) prototypes. In 1975, MITS Altar 8800 became the first PC to gain widespread usage. Bill Gates and Paul Allen developed the first successful software programme for the computer, and, in so doing, established Microsoft Corporation. Two years later, in 1977, Steve Jobs and Steve Wozniak marketed their Apple II computer to a mass market and formed Apple Computer Inc. The spread of the PC was held back by its complexity. In 1981, IBM developed a personal computer with a technical specification that other manufacturers could copy. IBM licensed its micro-processor circuitry from Intel and its operating system from Microsoft. Both were free to licence the same technology to other entities. In 1983, the industry shipped 11·1 million computers worldwide. This figure increased, in 1989, to 21.3 million.

In the following year, a system of protocols aimed at transforming, linking and addressing documents to transmit over the Internet became operational. It was known as the World Wide Web,[34] and it opened up the possibility of economies of scale and network externalities. With the protocols in place, engineers began making navigation of the web easier by inventing point-to-point and click browsers. Here was an interface with the growing number of computers on the World Wide Web. In September 1994, Netscape shipped its first Internet browser. Earlier, in 1991, Microsoft had launched its Windows 3.1, which supplied an interface to the desktop computer. Then, in August 1995, Microsoft introduced Windows 95 and in November, its own web browser, Internet Explorer 2.0.

In 1994, PC shipments worldwide rose to fifty million. Four years later, they were approaching a hundred million. Between 1995 and 1998, users of the Internet doubled to around seventy million in at least 252 countries. In terms of the cost per million instructions a second, the price of a PC fell, in 1998, to one thousandth of the level of 1988.[35] By this time, a third of all households in the United States had a PC and half of those had modems.

In November 1999, Judge Thomas Penfield Jackson concluded in his 'findings of fact' that Microsoft had a monopoly in one market operating systems for Intel-based personal computers and that it had aggressively extended into the adjacent, but distinct, market of browsers. In April 2000, in his 'conclusions of law', he ruled that Microsoft maintained its monopoly power by anti-competitive means and had attempted to monopolise the Web-browser market. Both actions were in violation of Section 2 of the *Sherman Act*. The Justice Department immediately filed with Judge Thomas Penfield Jackson a plan that would create two companies, one an operating system consisting of Windows platforms, the other a range of software applications and development tools, including Internet and consumer services.

In a unanimous decision announced in June 2001, the District of Columbia Circuit Court of Appeals rejected the lower court's order breaking up Microsoft into two corporations. The court ruled for Microsoft on the claim that it had attempted to monopolise the browser market but affirmed the lower court's ruling that Microsoft had illegally maintained its monopoly in the market for computer operating systems. In the absence of a settlement, there will be a new trial to decide whether Microsoft tied its browser to the Windows operating system.

In the meantime, the Internet had emerged as a universal, common carrier network. Owned by no one and open to all users, the Internet was, in effect, a loose confederation of interconnected networks. In 1993, it moved from being a means of sending e-mail to a new medium occupying 'cyberspace' based on broadcasting, publishing and 'interactivity.' Such interactivity made the Internet both a community and a marketplace. In effect, an evolving highway upon which the five 'lanes' of the information highway - broadcast, cable, wire, wireless, and satellite - were wrestling with convergence.

While Microsoft products dominated operating systems, software applications and browsers, America On Line (AOL) was the dominant Internet server, Yahoo the major search engine and numerous companies, including Amazon, competed in the e-commerce, content and applications markets. Most of the Web's mainframes and servers do not use Microsoft software. Indeed, the centre of attention has shifted away from telephone lines and PCs towards the potential of broadband wires and cables to deliver all types of digital data-text, video, audio, film - anywhere, any time, on computers, television screens and telephones.

The potential of broadband has been widely touted. It is likened to the railways in its potential for global transformation. But rather than opening vast territories to settlement and commerce, as the railways did, the broadband is seen as going further and eliminating distribution limits to create what is in effect a 'borderless universe.' The ways of producing, distributing and retailing were under threat from the Internet, which facilitated interaction between producers, on the one hand, and between consumers and distributors, on the other. The 'infotainment' and communications industries competed for the Internet market by pursuing mergers and strategic alliances.

Alfred Marshall identified knowledge as the most powerful engine of production. Later commentators identified the contemporary transformation, from the mass industrial order to the age of information, as being characterised by additions to the stock of knowledge disseminated through information and communication networks. The age is described by its essence, knowledge, and its process of dissemination is identified as information.

This knowledge is, in part, dependent upon the converging communication and computational technologies. The application of cellular systems and the silicon chip have facilitated the merging of communication functions with those of information processing. As a result, the boundaries between distinct modes and activities have become blurred. These technical developments led to displacements and convergence, which, in turn, undermined the rationales of public utility regulation and the policing of natural monopolies. But the crucial factors in this seemingly irresistible momentum towards convergence were the choices made by the regulatory agencies. The FCC's imposition of cross-subsidisation facilitated the widespread adoption - the 'universality' - of the telephone. and, in a crucial decision, the FCC determined that computer-based data services, offered over the telecommunications facilities, should not be subject to common carrier regulation. In so doing, the FCC established the pricing structure and unregulated market in which the Internet was to grow and envelop the telecommunication infrastructure of the United States. In 1997, the Clinton Administration championed the spread of the Internet around the globe. In announcing the release of 'The Framework for Global Electronic Commerce,' President Clinton stated that the Internet 'should be a global free trade zone with minimal regulations and no new discriminatory taxes.'[36]

TRANSPORT

Rocked by steep fuel price increases, on the one hand, and declines in load factors on the other, air carriers operating the North Atlantic plunged into conflict in competition for traffic. In 1977, the United States and Britain re-negotiated their bilateral air agreement which came to be known as Bermuda II. The Carter Administration adopted a liberal approach to bilateral agreements. The policy, characterised by 'multiple permissive awards', allowed numerous carriers freely to enter and exit routes and unilaterally to establish low-fares and charter rates. The US, in a strong bargaining position, offered new continental gateways into the country in return for new routes elsewhere. In 1978, the Civil Aeronautic Board (CAB) directed the International Air Transport Association (IATA) and other interested parties, to 'show cause' as to why anti-trust immunity should not be withdrawn. Two years later, the CAB brought down a decision barring the participation of US carriers in IATA conferences that co-ordinated rates for traffic between Europe and the United States. Beginning in 1979, member carriers were no longer required to participate in tariff arrangements, nor to adopt tariffs agreed upon by IATA conferences.[37]

The CAB initiated domestic scheduled air carrier deregulation. The 1977 *Airfreight Deregulation Act* created a special certificate for all cargo services on domestic routes, one that did not require the condition of public convenience and necessity. In the following year, the *Airline Deregulation Act* phased in entry and fare deregulation of scheduled passenger air transport, and phased out the CAB. The process was completed in 1985. The deregulation of the US domestic transport system moved at a pace in the early 1980s. The *Staggers Rail Act* of 1980, accorded rate-making capabilities to the railroads and facilitated easier entry into and exit from the industry. The *Motor Carrier Act* of 1980, eased entry, rate-flexibility and a diminution in the scope of anti-trust immunity.

In Canada, the 1988 *National Transport Act* comprehensively deregulated the air, rail, bus and truck carrier market. Air Canada and the airframe manufacturers, de Havilland and Canadair, were privatised.

The British Conservative government was one of the first to deregulate its domestic transport carriers. In 1987, British Airways (BA) was privatised and parts of British Rail passenger operations followed in 1992. The government of Japan sold its share in the national airline (JAL) in 1987, as did the Austrian government in Austrian Airlines. In the spring of 1993, the newly-elected government of France stated its intention to privatise Air France.[38] In 1994, the German government reduced its stock holding in Lufthansa from 51.4 to 35.7 per cent. The Israeli government announced its intention of selling 49 per cent of El Al airline in 1999.

In the United States, air carriers built up their networks around hub and spoke systems. Armed with control of computerised reservation systems and deploying frequent-flyer programmes, a number of large carriers emerged. These carriers have presented a challenge to Japanese and European-based airlines for the global market.[39]

On 15 December, 1992, Alitalia, still government-owned, bought a 35 per cent stake in Malev of Hungary. Two days later, BA acquired a stake in Australia's Quantas. During the year, KLM moved into the United States market by acquiring a share of North Western, while the Dutch and US governments, in September 1992, agreed to allow their respective carriers entry into each other's markets. American, United and Delta Air Lines successfully opposed BA's attempt to link with US Air. They argued that such an arrangement would grant BA access to the whole of the market of the United States, while they would be denied reciprocal access to all the routes that BA serves from Heathrow Airport.[40] Later, however, US Air was linked with BA. In 1993, KLM, Swissair and SAS failed to agree on a proposed merger plan. In 1995, the European Union Commission approved the link between Swissair and Belgian's Sabena. In 1994, Lufthansa arranged a partnership with the UAL Corp., the parent company of United Airlines.

The liberation of air transport within the European Union occurred as a result of three packages of legislation over the period 1987 to 1992. They coincided with the *Single European Act's* overall aim of achieving a Europe without frontiers. However, the 'Third Package' left significant discretion in the hands of member states .[41] Since 1997, any EU citizen may own and operate an airline in any EU country, while non-citizens are limited to 49 per cent ownership of an EU carrier. Such limitations have placed a break on international mergers and encouraged substitute-marketing alliances.

In 1998, BA attempted to enter an alliance with American Airlines. Britain's Office of Fair Trading urged that the two airlines should be allowed to sell off 267 weekly landing and take-off slots in return for approval of their proposed alliance. The European Commission, however, maintained that such sales would be unlawful. BA went ahead and formed an alliance known as 'Oneworld.' This alliance includes American Airlines, Canadian Airlines, Quantas Airways and Cathay Pacific Airlines. The five carriers serve a total of 632 destinations in 138 countries. The alliance is a marketing agreement that links the frequent-flyer programmes of the five carriers and enables them to reduce costs through shared baggage handling. This agreement will rival the association known as the Star Alliance which ties together Deutsche Lufthansa, UAL, Thai Airways, Varig, Air Canada, South African Airlines (SAA) and, possibly, Air New Zealand. The constituent carriers, unlike those in Oneworld, engage in code sharing. This enables one airline to sell seats on an allied airline's flights, so partners draw revenue from one another.[42]

The proposed alliance between BA and American Airlines has influenced negotiations between European countries and the United States. The policy makers of the European Union have opposed agreements between Washington and individual European governments. In November 1998, however, Italy signed a bilateral agreement that stipulated there would be no government control over fares or frequency of service. This leaves Britain as the only major European nation without a liberalised bilateral agreement. Talks between the two broke down after US carriers claimed they were afforded too little access to Heathrow airport.

In May 2000, the UAL Corporation agreed to buy US Airways Group Inc. This move stated a series of proposed mergers in the US and Europe. AMR Corporation opened talks with Northwest Airlines and Delta Air Lines. In April 2000, Swiss Air's parent SAir Group raised its stake in SABENA to 85 per cent. KLM Royal Dutch Airlines, having failed to secure regulatory approval for its joint venture with Alitalia in 1999, opened talks with BA in June 2000 concerning a merger of the two carriers.

In Europe, the U.K. government negotiated pro-competitive bilateral air transport agreements with Luxembourg, the Netherlands, Belgium and the Federal Republic of Germany. Although the member states were legally bound to full liberalisation of all carrier modes by 1 January 1993, air travel has been subjected, since September 1989, to the so-called Second Phase. This allows for more flexible fares without the requirement of government approval, double disapproval of bilateral agreements and the ending of capacity sharing arrangements.[43]

In road transport, as from 1 January 1993, all bilateral quotas were abolished and admission to the occupation of road haulage operators in international trips is issued solely on the basis of agreed qualitative criteria. An expansion in the number of authorisations of road hauliers to operate on *cabotage* routes had been in effect since 1990.[44]

At the end of the 1990s, the railways' share of Europe's goods transport is less than half of what it was thirty years ago. Although high-speed passenger trains have been widely put into service, rail freight transport is mired in incompatible equipment and standards as well as protectionism. The European Commission called upon all members to split their national railway networks into two operations, the railways and the rail-service operators. According to a 1996 proposal, networks were to be dedicated to a 'freight freeway' and a single marketing service. Outside operators were to be encouraged. In Britain, a company, known as Railtrack, owns and manages Britain's rail-network. Private sector operators have been formed to move freight traffic. Dutch and German national railway companies have agreed to merge their freight operations. Denmark's Danske Stats Baner (DSB) and Germany's Deutsche Bahn Gruppe (DBG) have abolished protected civil-service status for newly recruited railway workers. But the proposed entry of outside operators has been met with strong resistance.

The market liberation of international shipping was slow in starting. International shipping was heavily cartelised, the cartelised liner sector, accounting for approximately 80 per cent by value of world sea borne traffic[45] had been supported by UNCTD.[46] The code of conduct, which called for the division of trade between exporting and importing country fleets, leaving 20 per cent to third parties, and its support of deferred rebates, was passed by the UN.[47] In 1983, the EEC acceded to the code with reservations The US government summarily rejected the code,[48] but, on 1 May 1999, it became legal for US customers to enter into confidential contracts with individual carriers. However, the passage of the 1998 *Ocean Shipping Reform Act* [49] shifted the industry from one of common carriage to one of contract carriage. Although shipping conferences retained anti-trust immunity they quickly came under pressure as carriers broke away and signed confidential contracts with key shippers. The once dominant shipping conference, governing the $140 billion a year cargo trade over the North Atlantic had met with opposition from the European Commission (EC). The Trans Atlantic Conference Agreement, according to the EC, had violated price-fixing agreements and was fined $318 million. Members have defected, many joining the North Atlantic Agreement, under which participants are allowed to exchange information on vessel capacity and utilisation. A similar organisation, known as the Transpacific Stabilisation Agreement, has replaced the largest shipping conference in the Trans-Pacific trade. The Asia North America Eastbound Rate Agreement (Anera) represented more than 50 per cent of ship space on trade valued at more than $200 billion a year.[50]

FINANCIAL

Less than 10 months after President Nixon closed tight the gold window in 1971, the International Monetary Market (IMM) was established. This was a public market in foreign currency futures and it was created, in large part, through the efforts of a financial entrepreneur, Leo Melamed and his associates on the Chicago Mercantile Exchange. In 1981, by substituting cash settlements for physical delivery, the IMM made it feasible to trade futures in Eurodollars. Trading in a widening range of financial futures then followed, including interest rates and stock price indexes.

The *Securities Act Amendment* of 1975 abolished fixed commission rates and minimum commissions agreed to by members of the New York Stock Exchange. Competition among brokers increased. The trading of securities not listed on an exchange, known as the over-the-counter-market, is regulated by the National Association of Security Dealers. Until mid-1979, the New York Stock Exchange (NYSE) had a rule that if a member firm had an order to buy or sell exchange-listed stock during the hours the exchange was open, the trade had to be performed on the exchange floor. This was deemed as anti-competitive. Accordingly, the Exchange agreed that any companies listed after mid-1979 on the NYSE could be traded anywhere. A twenty-four-hour market emerged of NYSE member firms making trades in NYSE listed issues. By 1995, however, the volume of trades in the over-the-counter-market exceeded those of the exchanges. Some five thousand companies are quoted on the NASDAQ (NASD Automated Quotations) system. In 1989, Reuters bought Instinet (Institutional Network), an electronic bulletin board used as an institutional intermediary for both NASDAQ and NYSE stocks. This was the first of the electronic communications networks (ECNs) that match customer buying and selling orders twenty-four hours a day.

In December 1999, the NYSE sought the approval of the Security Exchange Commission (SEC) to rescind Rule 390. This rule restricted member firms from trading 'Big Board' stocks in competing stocks. The SEC agreed in May 2000 to scrap this regulation, and so one of the last barriers facing market participants wanting to compete with the NYSE had fallen. In the same week, the stock exchanges in London and Frankfurt announced that they intended to merge (as had, earlier, the stock exchanges of Paris, Amsterdam, and Brussels). However, the merger agreement was called off in September. Nevertheless, the 200-year-old London Stock Exchange is no longer dominant in Europe and remains vulnerable as is demonstrated by the failed hostile take over from the Swedish trading and technology group, OM Gruppen AB in late 2000.[51] The NASDAQ Stock Market combined with the American Stock Market and went public, stating its intention to form partnerships in Canada, Europe and Asia.

Two of the most significant financial innovations since the railroads introduced financial instruments in the middle of the nineteenth century, emerged, not from deregulation, but from entrepreneurial opportunism. The credit card was second only to money itself, as the greatest economic invention, while 'junk' bonds opened the capital market to a wider range of companies, including the purveyors of the new communications technology.

It is believed that coins were first used in Asia Minor some 2650 years ago. They acted as store of value, a medium of exchange and as a unit of account - in other words, as money. The early bankers made money by extending credit, but only to those who could show collateral. Much later, banks made loans to individuals for major purchases in which the goods purchased were the collateral. Then in 1951, William Boyle (1912-2000), a manager in the Franklin National Bank of Long Island, developed the Franklin Charge Card. This combined two old banking ideas: one, the charge account that merchants had offered affluent customers, and two, the line-of-credit that banks had offered their most reliable commercial customers. Merchants no longer had to check the credit-worthiness of customers while the customer could finance purchases without applying to a bank for each transaction. Franklin National charged the merchant a percentage of the total amount and charged customers a high rate of interest on unpaid balances. During the 1970s, Visa and MasterCard were founded. They transformed local operations into national and then global networks. The average consumer could now purchase a product in almost any place on the globe and charge it to the card. William Boyle had made a major contribution to the democratisation of capitalism.

As a result of habit, custom and organisation, those who are risk-averse invest money owned by others. Regarding investment as a loser's game, investment managers thought it better to make a little money rather than to run the risk of losing a great deal. Consequently, bonds were the preferred investment of risk-averse fiduciaries and one result was a 'disequilibrium', exceptions from which above-average risk adjusted gains could be earned. One investment banking firm in particular, Drixel Burnham Lambert, observed that the past evidence of default did not support the traditional aversion to low-rated debt. New issues of such securities - high yield or junk bonds were deemed to be saleable. In 1975, low-rated debt was merely 4.1 per cent of the public straight debt outstanding. Companies that failed to qualify for high ratings were unable to issue debt to the public and had to resort to bank debt or to severely restricted loans. By 1984, 11.2 per cent of public debt outstanding was in low-rated debt. The rate of growth of such bonds had been three times that of higher-rated bonds. [52] Second tier corporations, rather than just the blue chips, now financed their activities in the bond market. More controversially, these junk bonds were deployed in battles between rivals, some resulting in the unbundling of conglomerates and the formation of flexible organisational structures.

The destabilising inflation, high nominal interest rates (at record levels) of the late 1970s and the offshore currency market, which grew in its power to influence exchange rates, activated changes in financial regulation. The IMF's Article VIII of Agreement required currency convertibility for all current account transactions. This meant that residents and non-residents of a country could exchange its currency for foreign currency when buying or selling assets. Western European countries came only to accept currency convertibility under Article VIII in 1961. [53] A major reason why capital controls were retained was that, under a fixed exchange rate system, allowing free movement of capital limited the capacity of the national monetary authorities to engage in counter-cyclical monetary policy. Countries that did not have capital controls included the US, Canada, Switzerland and Germany (after the 1960s). The controls on capital outflows imposed by President Johnson in 1967 were lifted in 1974. Faced with a changing foreign exchange market, the newly-elected British Conservative Government responded by abolishing exchange controls in October 1979. [54] France and Italy were committed to removing their remaining capital controls by 1990, while Portugal, Spain and Greece were granted a couple of years longer.

In the United States, inflation pushed market interest rates above the ceilings on rates that could be paid on deposits with the result that depositors were in the position of paying the depository institutions to take their money. The competing instruments, particularly money market funds, sucked the funds away, prompting deregulatory legislation. [55] The 1980 *Depository Institutions Deregulation Act* phased out interest rate ceilings over a six-year period, title IV allowing the Savings and Loans institutions to move out of their exclusive dependency on mortgage loans and to invest in commercial loans, commercial paper and corporate debt securities. The 1982 *Gare St. Germain Act* accelerated this phase out of interest rate controls and permitted Savings and Loans and the newly-created 'federal savings banks' to engage in commercial lending. In 1983, commercial banks were allowed to engage in securities brokerage, and some proceeded to move in on the underwriting market of corporate securities.

The balkanised, fragmented American banking system, which in 1980 had 14,400 banks, began to change as the cartel created by the 1933 *Banking Act* disintegrated. [56] From the fragmented cartel emerged transnational, multi-service financial institutions with networks of hundreds of thousands of points of sales.

These reflected the economies afforded by the electronic funds transfer technology (EFT).

According to Barry Eichengreen,

> the establishment of deposit insurance, securities regulation and sound monetary policy led to fewer restrictions on domestic financial markets. Partly because of the changing ideology, and partly because fewer domestic markets opened opportunities for international arbitrage among markets, the restrictions on international flows were eased.[57]

Under regulation, limits were placed on how much banks could charge and how much they could pay depositors. Lending was proportionate to assets, and lending determined earnings. Banks traded on their money and information. Deregulation and electronic communications removed the banks' comparative advantages. Large industrial conglomerates traded currencies and floated their own bonds. To survive, banks have had to discover their economies of scale and scope. Their clout in the market is determined, not by their assets, but by their market capitalisation. As with other private corporations, growth in earnings matters. One means of achieving these reinforcing objectives has been to merge.

The Bank of America and Nations Bank merged. Citicorp merged with Travellers Group to form Citigroup. Travellers Group had been a conglomerate that included fund management and insurance. As this mega-merger indicated, over time the rulings of the courts had eroded the three-way division of the financial industry established under the *Banking Act*. In November 1999, the *Banking Act* of 1933 was repealed and the *Bank Holding Company Act* of 1956 was substantially changed. In essence, banks were to be allowed to move into new lines of business as long as they had satisfactory lending records.

In August, the Credit Suisse First Boston unit of Credit Suisse Group purchased securities firm, Donaldson, Lufkin & Jenrette Inc. for $11.5 billion. In September 2000, the Chase Manhattan Corporation, the third-biggest banking company in the United States, acquired J.P.Morgan & Company for $30.9 in stock. Chase has been striving to become a global banking enterprise, while J.P.Morgan had specialised in investment banking. Under the triple forces of convergence, globalisation and technology, two institutions appear to be emerging.[58] The first group has evolved out of the commercial banks and is essentially made up of financial conglomerates. The second group are investment banks that manage the raising of capital, brokering of mergers and trading in a growing range of activities. Included in this group are Goldman Sachs, and Merrill Lynch.

There is, however, a doubt that overshadows these mergers and 'cross-sells.' It originates from those who are exploring the potential of the Internet. Entrepreneurs have been adept at replacing intermediaries in the distribution of information, such as bookstores, travel agents, stockbrokers and analysts. A tempting new target for Internet entrepreneurs is the transactions between borrowers and lenders. Raising money for a company over the Internet could be the start of the substitution of on-line services for expensive investment bankers - a development that could show bank mergers as being ill-conceived and far too expensive.

Realising the potential of the Internet also threatens to transform what is traded and the means of trading. Lower communication costs mean that all manner of cash flows, from used-car loans to sheet-music royalties, can be securitised, packaged and offered to the smaller investor. Most events can be hedged. Catastrophe bonds can be expected to become commonplace and traded by the smaller investor. The ECNs also threaten trading over the stock market. The ECNs are networks that facilitate speedy and convenient electronic execution. Not only is trading by this means more efficient and flexible than the floor trading of the exchanges, it is more transparent. As markets move online physical location becomes irrelevant. The regulatory apparatus of the SEC is side-stepped. But risks remain and transaction fraud has taken on new forms.

During the 1990s, the US market was characterised by the increasing size of the securities markets and, in particular, by the rise in assets of the mutual fund sector. A particular feature of this market was the presence of privately-owned, largely unregulated funds, which were often steered from offshore sanctuaries. Generically known as hedge-funds, some of these private partnerships were able to leverage huge loans and, as a result, were to become the dominant trading entities in emerging markets, high yielding debt and mortgage derivatives. Deregulation and information technology made buying and selling much easier. But these more liquid financial markets grew to be interdependent and dependent on highly-leveraged investors to allocate capital.

In 1996, the Government of Japan announced its 'Big Bang' banking policy. The state was to reduce its involvement in the banking sector and to encourage the growth of private capital markets. Instead, the financial crises of the ensuing year left the government not only as the regulator, but also as the most important intermediary in the financial system.

In the 1970s the commercial banks in Britain[59] had started to move into the mortgage lending business and into merchant banking. By 1983, the building societies' cartel had collapsed. For the last decade these building societies or saving-and-loan institutions, had been turning themselves into banks by providing, not just mortgages, but also over-the-counter retail services. In 1984, the government concluded an agreement with the London Stock Exchange under which the Exchange abandoned fixed minimum commissions paid by brokers in securities dealings. This measure came into effect in 1986 and with it the so-called 'Big Bang.' Mergers between banks, securities, dealers, jobbers, insurers and investment managers followed the facilitation of freely-negotiated commissions. More recently, upstarts from supermarkets and Richard Branson's Virgin Group have been offering financial services. In early 2000, the Royal Bank of Scotland acquired the National Westminster Bank (NatWest) for $31.5 billion. In May 2001, the Bank of Scotland PLC merged with Halifax PLC and so created Britain's fifth-largest bank.

France, Australia and Canada have been notable in their restructuring. Since 1984, the French government has removed ceilings on lending by domestic banks, privatised the Societé General and the Paribas banks, and liberalised the issuing of a number of financial instruments. In early 1999, Societé Generale and Paribas announced plans to merge in a $17 billion stock deal. Then *Banque Nationale de Paris* (BNP) bid to join the proposed two-way merger. Beginning at the end of 1992, banking in the EC has been subjected to 'a partially consistent regime.' Chartered banks are free to engage in any activity permitted either by their respective chartering authority or authorities in 'host' jurisdictions.[60] At the start of 1999, Europe had about 7,500 banks, of which 40 were considered large.

However, the French government continues to block foreign banks from taking over French institutions. In Germany, where 80 per cent of the banking industry is controlled by either non-profit co-operatives or state owned institutions, private banks are essentially prohibited from buying these institutions. Despite these constraints, financial institutions have been re-organising. They are marketing bank and insurance services through the same channels. It is known as 'bank assurance.' To meet the challenges of the single European currency, they are forming alliances among themselves and with those American investment banks that are playing a major role in orchestrating Europe's biggest industrial mergers.

UBS AG merged with Swiss Bank Corporation. In July 2000, UBS bought Paine Webber, the fourth largest brokerage firm in the United States. *Creditor Italian* acquired *Unaccredited* and then bid for *Blanca Commercial Italian*. San Paulo - IMT acquired *Blanca di Roma*. *Bearish Vereinsbank* and *Bayerische Hypobank* merged. ABN Amro of the Netherlands bought smaller finance businesses across Europe to rival German private banks in size. *Deutsche Bank's* acquisition of Bankers Trust signified the bank's desire to enter the investment banking business. *Axa*, originally an insurance company in France, with significant stakes in BNP and Parisbas, has a majority stake in the US-based Equitable. It is now the world's third largest money manager, after Fidelity Investments and UBS. In April 2001, *Alliance AG*, the insurance conglomerate, bought *Dresdner Bank*, Germany's third largest bank.

In the first three months of 1999, five acquisitions and mergers were announced in three different countries, Spain, Italy, and France, with a combined value of more than $90 billions. A year later, the proposed mergers in Italy and France had yet to win the approval of central banks and finance ministries. They expressed concern at the hostility of the proposed take-overs and stressed the national interest.

In Canada, reforms started in 1980, when the *Bank Act* was amended. By September 1992, fifty-eight closely held or wholly-owned Schedule II subsidiaries of foreign financial institutions were licensed and operating alongside the eight domestically owned Schedule I banks.[61] Reforms have permitted the common ownership of banks, trust companies, insurance companies and security dealers. Business lending is no longer the preserve of the chartered banks; mortgage loans and the fiefdom of trust and loan and life insurance companies and market making in securities no longer the monopoly of an independent set of investment entities. However, 'despite market and international pressures towards increased regulatory harmonisation within nation states, financial services regulation in Canada emerged less harmonised than any time in the post war period regulatory reform was drawn into the vortex of federal-provincial conflict.'[62]

In 1998, a federal Canadian task force recommended that the Canadian government drop its bar against mergers among major banks. The proposed mergers would unite the Royal Bank of Canada with the Bank of Montreal, and the Canadian Imperial Bank of Commerce with the Toronto Domestic Bank. The report also recommended that Canada remove protectionist barriers against foreign banks, and that Canadian banks be allowed to sell insurance through their branches and compete in the auto-leasing business. These recommendations did not meet with the approval of the Minister of Finance. In response, Canada's big five banks have formed online links with Internet banks in the United States. There is the promise of legislation that will allow individual entities to own stakes of 20 per cent, up from the present 10 per cent, in banks with over five billion dollars. By contrast with the Royal Bank of Canada, which owns a diverse collection of little-known US banks, the Toronto-Dominion purchased discount broker T.D. Waterhouse Group Inc. This brokerage operation, in turn, sells services of a subsidiary electronic bank. The Canadian Imperial Bank of Commerce provides store-label banking for supermarket companies Safeway Inc. and Winn-Dixie Stores Inc. The Bank of Montreal owns Chicago-based Harris Bank.[63]

American banks have been more aggressive in the Mexican market. In May 2001, Citigroup's vice chairman, Robert E. Rubin (former US Treasury secretary) engineered Citigroup's purchase of Grupo Financiero Banamex-Accival, Mexico's second largest bank, for $12.5 billion. This is the largest direct investment by a foreign company in Mexico. As a result, Citi will be the dominant bank in Mexico.[64]

TELECOMMUNICATIONS AND ELECTRICITY

Since the enactment of the *Communications Act* of 1934, the constituent agencies as well as federal and state regulators have pursued the goal of universal service. Regulation was designed to ensure the availability of an affordable basic telephone service to all Americans. Local telephone companies priced services to inter-change carriers and to some intrastate services above costs. These surpluses facilitated the supply of high-cost phone services to rural communities. As a result of this cross-subsidisation there was a very high level of telephone subscriber rates in America.

These were primarily circuit-switched analogue communication systems. Meanwhile, microchip technology made it possible to shift from electrical to digital and optical fibre technologies, so blurring the distinction between data processing and communication. It was now possible to use packet-switches[65] to deliver data at a much lower cost than on circuit-switched analogue systems.

In 1969, the FCC permitted MCI WorldCom, a pioneer in microwave technology, to enter the intercity private line market. The public, and more particularly, the data service providers, were presented with an alternative to the monopoly provider, AT&T. During the 1970s, the number of computer-based data services offered over the telecommunications facilities started to increase. The FCC was sensitive to the importance of the data-processing industry and its reliance upon and use of communication facilities and services. The Commission made five decisions. They served to differentiate between communication services, which were regulated, and data services which were not.

- One, in a 1971 decision, the data industry was exempted from the common carrier requirements of Title II of the *Communications Act.*
- Two, common carriers were permitted to enter and compete in the data market. However, safeguards were to be introduced to ensure that data-providers were not discriminated against by being denied access to the underlying communications component.
- Three, Part 68 of the FCC's rules concerning the connection of terminal equipment to the public telephone network was adopted in 1973. Consumers were permitted to connect equipment from any source to the public network so long as the equipment fitted within the technical parameters as stipulated in Part 68.
- Four, in 1980, the FCC reiterated its commitment to regulating only the common carrier 'basic' services. Enhanced services, such as a telephone service with an enhancement such as computer-processing, were exempt from common carrier regulation.

Common carriers that offered enhanced services were to provide them through separate affiliates.
- Five, in 1983, the FCC determined that enhanced service providers (ESPs) would be exempt from access charges. The Commission reasoned that because the ESPs were not subject to common carrier regulation, they should be treated as end users of the network rather than as carriers.

In the same year, the telecommunications industry was to undergo major structural and deregulatory changes. In 1984, after eight years of litigation, a joint Justice Department-AT&T break-up plan mandated the division of the American Telephone and Telegraph Company (AT&T), with its $150 billion in assets and one million employees, into seven regional phone companies. Each was to provide local service while AT&T retained its long-distance subsidiary (AT&T Communications) and its unregulated research and phone equipment manufacturing communications business. Local telephone companies were instructed by the regulatory bodies to make, by 1987, equal quality services available to every long-distance carrier. Companies such as Western Electric and Bell Labs were free to expand into data-processing and enhanced communication services.

The break-up of AT&T served as a template against which the electricity power industry was re-ordered. (It is worth noting that the US's electricity market, at $220 billion, is larger than those for cellular and long-distance telephony combined.) The vertically integrated electricity industry was subject to state regulators. Planning for new plants was overseen by state public utility commissioners who tended to stress the need for excess generation capacity and guided the utilities to buy or to generate power from varied fuels, including coal, natural gas, nuclear and hydro. Rates were set high enough for private companies to cover their costs and earn a guaranteed rate of return on their investment.

The 1978 *Public Utility Regulatory Policies* forced the utilities to diversify the types of fuel used for power plants, including renewable energy sources such as solar and wind power. They were compelled to enter contracts with independent power producers. Twelve years later, the *Energy Policy Act* opened the door to competition by ordering utilities to allow others to move power down their lines. A 1996 order of the Federal Energy Regulation Commission required utilities to provide, to all power markets, open access to their transmission lines at the same time. The goal was to allow customers to buy electricity from the power company of their choice. Competition, it was argued, would reduce rates and encourage the development of clean and efficient power plants.

By mid-2000, some twenty states had enacted legislation to re-organise and to move away from the model of monopoly utilities with regulated rates and guaranteed rates of return. The production of electricity across the country has been deregulated, as has the trade in power and billing and metering. Generators are free to build whatever type of plant they desire and more than 90 per cent of the plants under construction or planned, will run on natural gas. Independent companies, in 2000, accounted for more than 20 per cent of domestic electricity generation. In the wholesale power market, close to 3 billion megawatt-hours of electricity changed hands in 2000. The transmission and distribution of electricity remain regulated. Some states have established independent system operators (ISOs) to control their transmission grids. Typically ISOs receive offers to produce electricity from generators. They then select the lowest bid first, then the next lowest, and so on. To avoid costly duplication, transmission infrastructures, which are owned by the utilities, are subject to rate review by federal regulators. Local lines are regulated by the states. [66]

States have differed in the ways they have encouraged electricity supply and in which they have approached retail deregulation. Pennsylvania set rates charged by existing utilities high enough to make it attractive for new power suppliers to enter the market. This rate appears on customers' bills, so, if they switch to other utilities with lower rates, they would know the extent of their savings. Texas has attempted to increase supply ahead of full retail deregulation. Wisconsin has updated and expanded its grid to make sure all power supplied in nearby states ready access to their market.

On 1 April 1998, California opened up a market for wholesale electricity. Power was to be sold to utility companies by unregulated suppliers at wholesale prices subject to the state's ISO. The state's major utilities had been subject to strict environmental and other regulatory standards and many of their plants were costly. Over the last eight years, supply has increased by only 6 per cent, while demand has grown by some 25 per cent, in part, because retail prices were fixed at low levels. Wholesale prices were deregulated but retail prices were not. Customers had no incentive to consume or to seek better deals. Unable to compete, the utility companies sold their plants to out-of-state companies and were required to buy in the spot market. In mid-2000, a rapid rise in gas prices, a rise in demand and a contraction of supplies sent the spot rates shooting upwards. With their retail rates fixed well below these rising rates by the fall, these utilities faced bankruptcy.

The well-publicised crisis of blackouts in this state that accounts for 12 per cent of the nation's GDP is not the result of deregulation. It is the result of a combination of rigid regulation of retail prices along with rising energy prices and demand that drive the wholesale prices upwards. The California

Legislature's initial response has been to subsidise retail prices, to cap in-state wholesale prices and to order the state to consider building and operating new power plants. Daniel McFadden's comment was:

> The lessons of history suggest that in making the Hobson's choice between a dysfunctional, partially regulated one that promises to be even more dysfunctional, California is picking the greater of two evils. If it fails to move to sensible electricity pricing in which both consumers and suppliers see the real economic price at the margin, it will face another even more serious crisis in the not too distant future.[67]

The trend towards decentralised generation and use and away from central-station electric systems is, in part, due to the break-up of the monopolies. These were viewed as being based on the economies of scale of water and steam turbines. In Britain, however, the Conservative Government not only privatised the electric industry, it decided that electricity supply should no longer be a monopoly.

Chile had privatised its industry, and established a competitive market for generation by 1986. In 1991, the Conservative government sold the Crown's non-nuclear generation capacity to private companies. Other countries followed suit. This gave an impetus to gas-turbine power stations and new technologies. These include mini- and micro-turbines, fuel cells and renewable sources such as wind power, biomass power and solar photovoltaics. These have provided options for local generators and users. The gas-turbine systems, in particular, have been shown to be economical at much smaller sizes, and can be located nearer users and sometimes on site.

In 1993, the incoming Clinton Administration charged Vice-President Al Gore with the responsibility of handling the nation's communications policy. The Vice-President set about re-defining the meaning of universality. The concept was to become more inclusive. Schools, libraries, and health care providers, as well as residential and rural customers, were to be the primary universal service beneficiaries. They were plugged into the emerging interactive information superhighway.

The policy of regulating communications services and deregulating the data services market had, by 1993, provided a universally accessible telephone service that was the open gateway to the Internet. Telephone customers could access any Internet service provider of their choosing. They could attach their own equipment to the phone lines, through which they could link into the information superhighway. Soon, hundreds of Internet service providers (ISPs) - which can both send and retrieve and store and transform data to different protocols that allow the end user to interact with other computer networks - were offering unlimited dial-up Internet access over the inexpensive phone lines. These enhanced services were not regulated, though the telecommunications service remained regulated. Similarly, Internet backbone providers (including MCI WorldCom, Sprint, and PSINet) started to propel traffic through fibre optic cables, and exchanged traffic with one another both at public network access points (NAPs), and at private points of interaction. Because the FCC determined that such data should not be regulated, the Internet backbone was an unregulated information service.

Reed E. Hundt was appointed Chairman of the FCC in 1993. He re-ordered the priorities of the Commission. Instead of protecting consumers from monopoly prices, the Commission was to promote competition and to stimulate investment and innovation. Its task was facilitated by two pieces of legislation: the 1993 *Omnibus Budget Reconciliation Act* and the 1996 *Telecommunications Act.*

The former Act permitted the FCC to auction the rights to use the public's airwaves for mobile telephone services. The auction, held in 1995, raised $7.7 billion. The duopolies in 500 markets were no more. The wireless industry was deregulated. The FCC then proceeded to promote a national over-the-air Internet access network.

In interpreting and implementing the *Telecommunications Act*, Chairman Hundt claimed that 'our fundamental goal was to encourage any business to attack monopoly incumbents.'[68] The central concept of the Act was a reliance on private contracts to shape the relationships between entities rather than government dictates. The hope was to unleash inter modal competition with Baby Bells, long-distance carriers and cable operators competing in each others' markets. Section 271 of the Act was designed to allow the Baby Bells to enter the long-distance market. This reversed the provisions of the 1984 break-up. However, before they could enter long-distance markets, the Bells had to persuade the FCC that they had opened their local markets to competition. The FCC intended to release competitive pressures that would force the Bells to contribute to technologically innovative systems. The Commission's primary instruments were the interconnect rules. Local companies were required to provide unbundled network prices to new entrants, and, therefore, to rivals, in a single, integrated package. The lease prices were to be set at levels that reflected, not historical costs, but current, most efficient technologies. In January 1999, the Supreme Court upheld the FCC's authority to prescribe the interconnect rules.

Section 254 of the Act dealt with 'universal service.' This requires that the FCC and the states base the revision of the universal service system on seven principles, including the principle that elementary and secondary schools, libraries, and healthcare providers should have access to advanced telecommunications services. According to the *Snowe-Rockefeller-Exon-Kerrey Amendment*, individual telecommunications carriers must provide services to schools and libraries at 'affordable' rates. Known as the E-Rate, funds provide discounts of 20-90 per cent on telecommunications services, Internet access and internal connections to schools and libraries. The funds were initially to come from about 1 per cent of the revenues of all communications companies. However, local telephone companies were allowed to reimburse themselves by charging long-distance companies higher access charges in an amount equal to the contribution. At the same time, the FCC ordered a reduction in those charges. The argument was that technological applications were facilitating lower operating costs.[69]

Cable began as a means of delivering network programming to areas where the broadcast signal was weak. Cable television, however, could be financed by direct 'per channel' or 'per programme' viewer charges. Programmes were sold to viewers instead of viewers to advertisers, hence facilitating the provision of a diverse range of tastes. In 1980, the remaining distant signal carriage rules for cable television were deleted, so that, by the mid-1980s, entry into the television market of direct broadcast satellites was possible. But the 1984 *Cable Act* mandated that cable systems have municipal franchises. This usually worked out as one franchise per town. Telephone companies were blocked from competing in video. Cable operators re-broadcast TV-signals and then re-sold them to customers for a monthly fee.

The 1992 *Cable Act* reversed the relationship between the cable companies and the broadcasters. Either the cable company 'must carry' the broadcaster signal for free, or negotiate for transmissions, selling the signal for whatever the market would bear. These rates, however, were then subject to regulation, and then deregulation. As a result of the implementation of the *Telecommunications Act*, the majority of US cable subscribers have faced unregulated pricing since April 1999. As for direct broadcast satellite (DBS), the FCC allowed, in November 1999, dish owners to receive local signals. The 'must carry' policy was waived, but only until 2002. DBS systems that carry signals will then be forced to carry all local signals.

The FCC's policy of favouring data-transmissions, packet-switched technology, and the exclusion of Internet traffic from charges normally imposed on long-distance voice communications, stimulated the growth of service providers and of data networks. In 1993, the first year of the commercial browser, 1.3 million computers were linked to the Internet. In 1999, eighty million Americans were online. Over 6,000 Internet service providers (ISPs) offered dial-up service to the Internet. America Online, with eighteen million worldwide members in 1999, dominates this market. Exempt from access charges, tens of millions of American enjoy unlimited use of the Internet. This is by contrast with to Britain and Europe. ISPs may offer a flat rate for monthly service, but end users are subject to per -minute charges for local dial-up connections to their ISP. In 1998, the ISP market generated over $15 billion in income while the whole of Europe generated $4billion.[70]

The growing millions of users of the Internet used slow narrowband services via copper wires belonging to the telephone companies. Businesses were already enjoying faster and more reliable access for their data-transmissions by using bandwidth or fibre-optic networks. These cables were not the analogue lines that piped television. They could carry two-way data in voice, pictures and print. These converging media had the potential to transform the static Internet, with its pictures and text into an area of interactive communications, television-quality video and high quality sound accessed from many devices other than just the PC. The possibility existed that the Internet would become an interactive, mass marketing, entertainment medium.

The fixed costs of delivering the Internet are substantial. Average costs per subscriber decline as the number of subscribers grows. A world-wide network also allows the subscriber to by-pass international toll calls. There are also three distinct sub-markets: long-haul bandwidth, local access and interactive content.   The Baby Bells, long-distance carriers, and cable companies are competing to deliver bandwidth. It is as yet uncertain which broadband standard CableLabs, the industry's specification-setting body, will adopt.   The Baby Bells, cable companies and long-distance carriers are competing for the so-called 'last mile' into the 100 million homes of America by establishing cable modems, wireless and fibre optics and digital subscriber lines.   The interactive market consists of those who bundle content with bandwidth and consumer access.

The seven Baby Bells acquired one another until only five remained of which Bell Atlantic alone has been permitted to provide long-distance service to customers in New York State. AT&T purchased major cable companies Tele-Communications Inc. and MediaOne Group Inc. WorldCom Inc. purchased MCI to become the second-largest long-distance carrier in the US. Then MCI WorldCom acquired Sprint, the number three long-distance carrier, in an all-stock deal worth $115 billion This merger was cancelled, in July 2000, following objections from the US Justice Department and the European Competition Commission.   Time Warner Inc. bought Turner Broadcasting.   Viacom, the cable operator that also owned Paramount Pictures, Blockbuster and publishers Simon & Schuster, acquired CBS for $37 billion.   America Online (AOL), the major Internet server, bought Netscape, a major browser and on 10 January 2000, acquired Time Warner for $156 billion in stock.

In June 2000, Rupert Murdoch announced that News Corp was to spin-off its satellite division, which reaches 65 per cent of the world's viewing population, and create an Internet service provider. Then Murdoch sold John Malone a stake in News Corp. in return for Mr. Malone's shares in Gemstar-TV Guide International, a leading producer of on-screen guides. Murdoch is also negotiating to acquire satellite broadcaster, DirecTV, now owned by General Motors (GM). The proposed $70 billion deal would place Sky Global Networks, that includes British Sky Broadcasting and Star TV, in Hughes, the GM's satellite and electronics business with its 11 billion customers in the Americas. Microsoft has also shown interest in the alliance. The software group is expected to invest between $4 billion and $5 billion in the belief that the set-top box is the digital gateway into to the home.

The AOL-Time Warner merged entity appears to be aiming to sell information and entertainment services to subscribers who use, not only PCs, but also digital cell phones and television set-top boxes. Not only was AT&T the largest telephone company, it became the largest cable television provider. Its strategy appeared to be to offer TV, local telephone service and high-speed Internet links using the same up-graded systems. While AOL-Time Warner are seeking to move 'old' content into new media, AT&T appeared to be shifting from controlling the wires, on which the phones travelled, to controlling the cables that provide access to digital services. Local cables are effectively monopolies, but unlike the local telephone monopolies, they have not yet been forced to provide equal access. Satellites are a fast means for downloading information on the Web and Murdoch would appear to be assuming that consumers will gravitate to using more media-rich content.[71]

The Chairman of AT&T, C. Michael Armstrong, acknowledged, in October 2000, that the corporation's core activity, voice services to business and residential customers, was in 'systemic decline.' He launched what was termed 'Project Grand Slam.' AT&T's three-year project, to become a one-stop seller of long-distance, wireless, cable television and Internet services was ditched. Instead, three independent companies with four separate stocks are to be formed. Cable television operations and the wireless operations will become separate companies over the next two years. The global communications network and the business customer unit will remain within AT&T, which will also control AT&T's consumer unit. Similarly, WorldCom, second in long-distance, has scrapped its strategy of becoming a communications conglomerate. By planning to issue a new, separate stock for its MCI consumer unit, while focusing on business customers. Sprint Corporation, the number three long-distance carrier, deliverer of local phones to almost eight million homes, controller of the fourth wireless company and the second largest Internet transport, is the odd man out. After the WorldCom-Sprint merger was rejected, Ronald T. LeMay, president and chief operating officer of the Sprint Corporation, said that his company would pursue a one-stop communications strategy.[72]

The Clinton administration launched a pro-competition international policy that was to be activated, not through bilateral, but through multilateral agreements. The aims were to encourage foreign investment in the communications industry; to establish regulatory agencies with powers exercised by the FCC in order to create the rule of law for competitive entry into protected markets; and to promote interconnection rules that were similar to those in the US industry.[73]

As Pekka Tarjanne, Secretary General of the International Telecommunications Union (ITU) has noted, the market for telecommunications technology is in developing countries.[74] The World Trade Organisation (WTO) Agreement on Basic Telecommunications Services became effective in January 1998.

In general, deregulation and privatisation of parts of the telecommunications industry outside the US have been undertaken in series of small rather than big, bangs. The separation of postal and telephone services from government departments and the establishment of regulatory authorities for both have generally been undertaken. However, many postal systems have retained their monopolistic powers. In 2001, the European Parliament contained commercial competition to just 6 per cent of the $70 billion-a-year business. The privatisation, in 1994, of British Telecom, for US $6 billion, was the largest share issue in British history.[75] Other major privatisations were Nippon Telegraph and Telephone, in 1987, Deutsche Telekom, in 1996, Telecom Italia and Telsa (Australia), in 1997, and Brazil's Telebras, in 1998. Over the period 1988-98, some 30 per cent of the approximately one trillion dollars raised by privatisation was accounted for by the telecommunications sector.[76]

Although Japan has not deregulated to the extent that have the UK and the US, regulators appear to be moving towards the encouragement of alternatives. Competition has been stimulated in the provision of basic network services, shared use and freedom of routing in all international communications. The resale of basic services has been allowed. More than one international carrier has been encouraged in the UK and Japan. They have promoted both different and new forms of supply of international transmission facilities, including satellites and transoceanic cable systems.[77]

Following deregulation in Canada, Bell Canada, a unit of BCE Inc., operating mainly in Ontario and Quebec, announced, in 1999, an alliance with MCI World Com. Inc. to sell the US company's services in Canada. This is part of a strategy aimed at building a national fibre-optic network. In March 1999, AT&T announced a pact that allows it to merge partially with, and eventually to buy, Canada's largest provider of local phone hook-ups to business, MetroNet Communications. The pact will merge AT&T Canada's national long-distance network with MetroNet's local connections in major Canadian cities and MetroNet's Internet interests.

In Japan, NNT invested in Integrated Switched Digital Network (ISDN), facilitating, through simple copper telephone lines, a range of services. Growth has been limited by the relative slow growth of PC sales. Controversy raged over the break-up of NNT and the deregulation of the system.

Cable and telephone companies do compete in Britain, but BT claims that it is inhibited in laying cable because of legislation which excludes it from providing entertainment on its wires until the year 2002. In the meanwhile, some eighty-three cable-TV franchises are busily laying down fibre optic cable. In Australia, the government privatised and deregulated the telecommunications industry in 1992, so ending a ninety-year-old monopoly. The renamed Telstra is now facing competition from entities that are laying down broadband networks and establishing a pay-TV service.

In France, the monopoly France Telecom pioneered their wired Minitel, a video terminal. Although, initially, a rapid penetration rate was secured, growth presently slowed down. Consumers showed resistance to the programme quality provided by the private companies. France Telecom's monopoly of telephone services ended, as in most European countries, in January 1998. Beyond simply allowing other companies to offer telephone service for the first time, the European Union's rules require the traditional monopolies to give rivals access to their networks at reasonable rates. In Germany, regulators forced Deutsche Telekom (DT) to give access at low prices. Some, such as Arcor, are substantial ventures, backed by large corporations while others are small entities. Whatever their size, within the first nine months DT had lost 25 per cent of its business to new entrants into long-distance markets.[78]

Telecom Italia was privatised in January 1998, incurring poor financial results. In early 1999, Olivetti, a typewriter manufacturer, computer and communication provider, launched a hostile take-over bid for Telecom Italia. A little later, Deutsche Telekom and Telecom Italia announced that they were negotiating a $76 billion merger. Olivetti, however, became the controlling shareholder with 55 per cent. In 2001 Pirelli and Benetton gained managerial control by purchasing a 23 per cent stake in Olivetti Spa.

In July 2000, DT announced its plans to acquire, for $50.7 billion, VoiceStream Wireless Corp., the eighth largest wireless carrier in the United States. VoiceStream, unlike most US carriers, uses the most popular of digital cellular standards, GSM. The deal, if completed, will be the first purchase in the United States by an entity in which a (foreign) government holds a controlling interest.

The spate of privatisations spurred international mergers and joint ventures. There was the merger of Sweden's Telia AB and Norway's Telenor AS. British Telecom and AT&T formed a joint venture to sell voice and data services to multinational companies. This venture subsequently bought a stake in Japan Telecom Company. Spain's Telefonica made extensive acquisitions and joint ventures with telecommunication companies in Latin America. In May 2000, Telefonica's Internet service provider, Terra Networks, acquired Lycos, the number three portal in the United States. Bertelsmann AG, one of the world's largest media companies and Lyco's partner in Europe made a commitment to purchase the services of the merged company.

Not all mergers have gone unopposed. The European Competition Commission forced MCI to sell its Internet business to Cable & Wireless PLC when MCI sought regulatory approval of its merger with WorldCom in 1998.

Unlike the United States, which is fractured into multiple standards, much of Europe, South Africa and parts of Asia have adopted a global system for mobile communications, known as GSM. Vodafone Ltd. formed a joint venture with Bell Atlantic and GTE and so created the largest wireless network in the United States with more than twenty million subscribers. Then in 2000, Vodafone Air Touch PLC acquired Mannesmann for $179 billion. This union offers the possibility of exploiting the seamless network of Europe and beyond. Later in the year, the UK government auctioned the so-called 'third generation' (3G) wireless spectrum for $35.45 billion. With the rights to offer Universal Mobile Telecommunications Systems (UMTS), the competing companies are expected to include high-speed wireless access to the Internet and to offer services such as banking and e-mail. In August 2000, the German auction of 3G licences raised DM 1000 billion. In January 2001, the French government failed to net the $19 billion it had expected to raise from its corresponding auction.

In November 2000, BT followed AT&T in announcing a restructuring. This has been put forward for regulatory approval. The corporation's regulated wholesale operations are to be placed in a new corporation, NetCo, a quarter of which will be sold off. BT Wireless, Yell, its electronic directory and Ignite, which sells broadband to businesses, will be linked to NetCo through a holding company.

TRADE AND INTERNATIONAL CURRENCY REGIMES

The increasingly liberal regimes of international trade and investment have contributed, not only to growth and development by extending markets and consolidating integration, but they have also played their part in deregulation and privatisation processes. The seven rounds of GATT reduced the tariffs on manufactured products of the major industrial markets from about 40 per cent to an average of 4.7 per cent.[79] Such reductions in protection placed pressure on the trading countries' non-traded services to become more efficient.

Accordingly, their promoters depicted liberalised trading regimes as the lynchpin of the new, beneficent order of globalisation. Liberating trade, it was argued, would promote economic development and interdependence and, thus, erode authoritarian rule and help in establishing both economic and political freedom. The difficulties encountered in navigating the Uruguay Round of GATT in 1994, however, generated uncertainty as to whether a truly global market would be achieved by unilaterally extending increasingly unrestricted trade. By this time, the set of assertions concerning trade liberalisation were challenged by an array of interests, ranging from organised labour to environmental protectionists, violent anarchists and to old- fashioned Marxist opponents of capitalist domination. To these groups, globalisation was neither inevitable nor beneficent. They took aim at the rationale, transparency and resulting forms of regulations of the World Trade Organisation (WTO).

GATT was laid to rest in December 1995, but the WTO entrenches and strengthens the rule-based regime for which GATT stood. Over the next four-and-a-half years, however, trade multilateralists were to suffer three major reverses. In 1997, the Clinton administration shelved the proposed fast-track trade authority. If passed, Congress would have allowed the US President to negotiate trade agreements that would have been put to the vote without amendments. In 1998, the talks in Paris at the twenty-nine-nation member Organisation for Economic Co-operation and Development (OECD) over the Multilateral Agreement on Investment (MAI) (described by the then head of the WTO, Renato Ruggiero, as 'the constitution of the global economy') were suspended after a concentrated attack from protestors. The agreement would have admitted international investment with limited exceptions and would have given such investments a legal status equal to that afforded domestic investments. The Washington-based Public Citizen's Global Trade Watch heisted the almost completed agreement and placed it on its web site. Government support for the measures started to erode. The OECD countries failed to reach an accord. Then, in late November 1999, a mob of protesting Greens, consumer, labour and anarchist groups stormed the meeting of the WTO in Seattle. Martial law was declared and the so-called New Millennium Round of trade negotiations, that included agriculture and trade in services, was suspended.

In a widely displayed advertisement prior to the Seattle meeting, a coalition of interest groups claimed that economic globalisation and institutions such as the World Bank and the WTO were promoting 'a specific kind of homogenising development. This development, it was claimed, frees the largest corporations in the world to invest and operate in every market, everywhere.' [80] The Public Citizen's Global Trade Watch asserted that all governments are fronts for their corporate interests and that the resulting rules of the World Bank do not constitute free trade but 'corporate managed trade.' The said rules were allegedly formulated by a secretive and non-accountable intergovernmental bureaucracy, which, in turn was manipulated by business corporations. In terms of these rules, the corporations enjoyed transport subsidies while educational subsidies were denied to the poor. Upholding the intellectual property rights of the corporations, it was argued, resulted in attenuated trade, which caused poor countries to incur enormous burdens. The rules of the World Bank, in effect, set corporate profits above aspects of human rights, public health, safety and the environment.[81]

These groups were also critical of integrating less developed countries (LDCs) into the global economy. The nationalistic, anti-colonial objectives - complemented by government ownership and trade protection - of many of the LDCs had, in some cases, been reformulated by means of privatisation, deregulation and the acceptance of GATT agreements. Such acceptance, it was argued, had not been prompted by reduced fear of dependency on the multinationals. Rather, the LDCs had been forced to accept the terms imposed by the international banking institutions as a condition for the granting of loans.[82]

The major criticism of the *African Growth and Opportunity 2000 Act* was not that the United States had unilaterally lowered tariffs and eliminated import quotas for African textiles made with native or American material, but that, over time, African countries would receive favourable access to the United States only if they satisfied a set of conditions. These conditions were similar to the 'unfair and exploitive' investment and intellectual property rules established under NAFTA.

In the United States, organised labour complained that NAFTA facilitated the export of old economy, and largely unionised, jobs to Mexico. Trade was shifting the industrial mix of the United States and resulting in factor (labour) price (wage) equalisation. The unions also pointed out that jobs were being lost to China. Advocates of human rights argued that extending trade with China and granting that country membership of the WTO would do little to reform what were, effectively, slave labour factories, neither would the abuses of this Communist one-party state be lessened. Entry into the WTO was in fact to be determined by the members themselves. During 1999, both the European Union and the United States conducted negotiations with China over the terms of its membership.[83]

In late May 2000, Congress granted Permanent Normal Trade Relations (PNTR) to China. For the last twenty years, the government of the United States had been renewing normal trade relations with China annually, but, while China's exporters have enjoyed the same access to the US market as did those of Japan and Europe, US exporters have faced stiff tariffs and restrictive regulations in China. In November 1999, American and Chinese trade negotiators agreed to an accord. By 2005, tariffs on most US exports will be reduced from 24.6 per cent to 9.4 per cent. Tariffs on US agricultural exports will fall from 31.5 to 14.5 per cent. Up to 49 per cent of China's telecommunication industries may, in terms of the agreement, be foreign-owned. In the second year of the agreement, this rises to 50 per cent.

Earlier, in May 2000, the EU had concluded negotiations over China's entry into the WTO. The resulting trade agreement brought the timetable forward by two years for investment in mobile phones. License rules on foreign insurance were eased. The limit on foreign ownership of large retail stores was ended and some of the restrictions imposed on joint ventures in the motor car industry were lifted.

China's accession to the WTO means that this economy of 1.3 billion people will be subject to obligations and commercial law that will be imposed by the multilateral weight of 135 members rather than by the US alone. Despite this victory, there are doubts as to how far trade liberalisation will be extended through WTO-brokered multilateral agreements. In Seattle, a beleaguered President Clinton asserted that national labour and environmental policies must meet 'acceptable' standards and that these should form part of the trading rules. The President also suggested that he would seek to impose sanctions on developing countries that violate environmental or labour standards. President Ernesto Zedillo spoke for many leaders in the developing world when he stated that labour and environmental standards are code words for rich-country protectionism, which will 'save developing countries from the effects of development.'[84]

On 24 October 2000, the Clinton administration announced that it had concluded a free trade deal with Jordan. This was the first trade deal to include language in the principal text committing the signatories to meet their own labour and environmental standards. (NAFTA covered these areas in side accords.) On 29 November 2000, President Clinton announced that the United States had opened negotiations over trade with Chile. The most notable feature of the agreement was that it was based on the Jordan pact. This was also the next step in getting the Free Trade Agreement of the Americas off the ground. The aim is to include the thirty-four democracies of the Western Hemisphere in a free trade zone.

The new trade representative in the Bush administration, Robert Zoellick, indicated at his confirmation hearing that the President would push quickly to recover for the Presidency the large measure of trade-negotiating authority that the Clinton administration had lost to Congress. While campaigning, President Bush said he favoured free trade deals and, in particular, the Americas deal, but that he was against including labour and environmental standards that could interfere with trade. It is unlikely that the Bush administration will be able to avoid 'triangulating' with organised labour and environmental protectionist interest groups. The incentives have been re-ordered. They would appear to encourage, not multilateral, but bilateral deals, in which the costly and probably ineffective labour and environmental regulations are avoided and exchanged for complex, indirect trade deals that have the potential to be trade-diverting rather than trade-enhancing.

Between 1990 and 1994, some thirty-three trading blocs were formed. MERCOSUR, an economic union between Uruguay, Paraguay, Argentina and Brazil was formed in 1991. Now it is the third largest bloc behind NAFTA and the EU. Some are more liberal than the WTO deals - those between Australia and New Zealand and the United States and Israel are examples - others are more restrictive, and especially so with respect to trade outside their blocs.[85] NAFTA stops far short of a common market, let alone a political union of the United States, Canada and Mexico. While the establishment of a common market was the stated aim of the victor in the Mexican election in 2000, allowing the free movement of labour between the three countries appears to have little support in the United States.[86]

However, the Bush administration has moved to legalise three million illegal Mexican immigrants and to forge a temporary-worker programme for Mexican immigrants. The unions have also been encouraged to recruit immigrant labour. The administration has also pursued the goal of integrating Central American economies into NAFTA, even though there appears to be little enthusiasm from the public at large in both the United States and Canada, for this proposal.

The proposed enlargement of the common market of the EU from 15 to 23 members is placing strain on the welfare programmes and decision making mechanisms of the constituent bodies. The proposals, which include the down-scaling of welfare programmes and the establishment of a European federation with a directly elected president and a parliament sharing executive and legislative powers, are unlikely to win widespread approval.[87] It remains to be seen whether Western Europeans will compromise what, in effect, are their nation states, in order to accommodate Turkey and Europe's transitional countries (the former communist countries).

The major trading blocs have tended to protect their interests. The EU has been loathe to reduce farming subsidies; Japan to increase trading access. The Uruguay Round left out banking and insurance services which have become the subjects of American strategy. In essence, if restrictions are not removed, the US has threatened to erect its own restrictions. In June 1999, the EU and MERCOSUR were unable to agree on a timetable or on an agenda for negotiations for a free trade agreement. The EU was, however, more successful with South Africa and Mexico. Starting in July 2000, tariffs on trade between the EU and Mexico will be gradually reduced through to 2007. At the end of 2000, there was renewed interest in the EU about eliminating tariffs and most trade barriers with MERCOSUR. Canada and Mexico, unlike the United States, already have free trade agreements with Chile. Japan has launched bilateral free trade talks with South Korea, Singapore and Mexico.

Although the United States rightfully claims to have led the move towards open trading regimes, there are indications that the Clinton Administration's 'fair trading policy' has closed up corners of this regime. In 1994, Japan turned down the Administration's managed-trade demands for import targets. In his January 1999 'State of the Union' address, President Clinton vowed to fight for a freer and fairer trading system for 21st century America. Section 301 of the US trade law authorises retaliatory tariffs against countries whose trade policies the United States deems unreasonable. Unilateral action in the name of fair trading is contrary to the expressed goal of liberalised trade and, as such, serves to undermine the integrity of the leaders of liberalisation. When implemented, these measures have served to attenuate trade and to heighten, in particular, the tension between the EU and the United States.

In the summer of 1999, the Clinton administration responded to a report from the US International Trade Commission (ITC). This body deemed imports of lamb from New Zealand and Australia to be 'a substantial cause of a threat of serious injury' to the domestic sheep producers. The administration, although a supposed supporter of reduced agricultural protection at the Seattle meeting of the WTO, opted for far tougher trade restrictions than the ITC had proposed. The President imposed a 9 per cent tariff on all imports in the first year and a 40 per cent tariff on imports above 1998 levels.

In March 1999, the House voted to impose, for three years, a quota on imported steel. The aim of the quota would appear to be to save the markets of the large, integrated but uncompetitive steel companies. However, setting unilateral import limits violates the treaty that established the WTO. The Bush administration requested the US International Trade Commission to launch a 'Section 201' inquiry to determine whether import restrictions are needed. In a related move, the administration initiated a multinational steel agreement under which governments, not the individual steel makers, would be 'volunteering' to limit production.

Earlier, the WTO was faced with adjudicating a dispute between the EU and the US over bananas. The administration fought Europe's banana import regime by placing prohibitive tariffs on a range of European goods. The European farmers claimed that hormone-treated American beef was unsafe. The administration countered by raising $202 million in tariffs on a new range of European goods.

Then three other contentious issues appeared. The Americans objected to the subsidisation, by European governments, of a double-decker passenger jet built by Airbus Industrie. The Europeans countered by objecting to a tax break the United States grants to major corporations that set up operations in offshore tax havens. The Americans, in turn, objected to a European imposed regulation aimed at reducing aircraft noise.

There have also been growing tensions between the United States and its partners in NAFTA. The social clause in the World Trade Organisation Agreement was opposed by the administration. The Clinton administration also responded to the pleas for protection from the US trucking industry. According to NAFTA, the borders were to be opened to each other members' trucks on 17 December 1995. The Clinton administration argued that the provision would not be implemented because of safety concerns over Mexican trucks. As a consequence, cross-border traffic has been subject to time-consuming and expensive transfers. Mexico brought a formal complaint before the dispute resolution panel that succeeded. The US is obliged to open its border to Mexican trucks or face a penalty that could amount to as much as \$2 billion a year.[88] (President Bush opened the border in June 2001. This move met with opposition in Congress.)

In turn, the Clinton administration pointed out the failure of the Mexican regulatory authorities to implement their commitment to the WTO's agreement to an open telecommunications market. Major investors in companies in competition with the former monopolist, Telmex, such as AT&T and MCI Worldcom, have complained that the regulatory agency has allowed Telmex to charge predatory prices that are thwarting their entry into the Mexican market. Network access rates are pitched at levels that have put a break on the expansion of the Internet.[89] The Clinton administration rejected the measures proposed by the Canadian government to safeguard the Canadian content of part of the media.

Paralleling these shifts into trading blocs is a move of nation states away from their independent currency and central banks and into linking with one or other of the world's major currencies. If trends continue, the globe could eventually divide into two or three currency zones, one ruled by the euro, one by the dollar and a third that uses either the Japanese yen or the Chinese yuan. Whatever the composition of the currency blocs, there are forces pushing away from the present system and others are pulling towards stable currencies. The managed regime of fiat currencies that float against each other is seen, by many observers in emerging markets, as having led to instability, while stable currencies facilitate trade, investment and growth.

According to Joseph Stiglitz, chief economist at the World Bank (1996-9), the reason for the liberation of the capital and financial markets in East Asia was not that they needed to attract more funds, but 'because of international pressures, including some from the US Treasury Department.'[90] Elsewhere, financial and capital markets have been liberated, in part or in whole, by conditions stipulated in bilateral agreements and by the conditions attached to the International Monetary Fund's (IMF) Structural Adjustment Programmes.

Under NAFTA, the respective nations have to treat foreign investors and their investments 'no less favorably' than domestic investors. As a condition of the 1994 bailout, the Mexican government had to ease restrictions on the ownership of financial institutions.

As the central agency of the Bretton Woods Agreement, the IMF's primary function was to control international capital flows among Western economies so as to reconcile the goals of stable, convertible exchange rates with high employment and welfare capitalism. Since 1971, successive administrations have deployed the IMF as an enforcer of foreign debts and a promoter of the integration of developing economies into the Western (Group of Seven) financial markets. From about 1980 onwards, supplicant economies have been encouraged to ease capital controls, raise interest rates and so attract capital. Structural Adjustment Programmes (SAPs), whose aim is to restore growth by attracting foreign capital, typically stipulate the privatisation of state assets, reductions in government expenditures and the removal of regulations that protect domestic over foreign corporations.

By the mid-1990s, the US Treasury Department, in tandem with the IMF, had pressured South Korea, Thailand, the Philippines, Mexico, Brazil and Russia to open their financial markets. In April 1997, the Interim Committee of the IMF proposed amending the Fund's Articles of Agreement to make currency convertibility for capital transactions a fundamental objective. Integrated financial markets were expected to bring forth a convergence of real interest rates, an efficient allocation of investment funds and a subsequent increase in productivity and output across the globe. They were not expected to contribute to the financial instability that marred the end of the decade.

The recent past has shown that the most unstable regime was a pegged exchange rate with a monetary policy that had involved deficit financing. Not only have such policies stoked inflation and a depreciation of the currency; they have also undermined attempts to peg the exchange rates.[91] There have also been objections to the remedial policies favoured by the IMF-US Treasury. Fashioned in order to regain investor confidence, they have usually comprised a sharp increase in interest rates and the offer of a dollar loan in return for cutbacks in public spending and the promise to pay back foreign bankers. The reasoning appears to have been, that if inflation and depreciation of the currency can be limited by such means, investor confidence will return, and with it renewed investment and growth. The main objection to these policies is that they generate destructive recessions. To avoid such devastation, others recommend exactly the reverse course of action. Interest rates should be lowered to encourage investment, while the exchange rate (and inflation) should find their own levels.

Many have doubted that the policies of the IMF-US Treasury have achieved their objectives. While interest rates have risen and precipitated recessions, the dollar loans have been dissipated in vain attempts to stabilise the exchange rates. At best, the IMF-US Treasury has been seen to act as lender of last resort to Western bankers and corporations, not to the central banks of the respective countries. Leaders among the so-called Asian tigers point to their high savings rates and ask why their financial markets should have been exposed to such a devastating instability. An increasing number of states are rejecting the destabilising regime of liberalised financial and capital markets and are seeking to align with stable currencies that offer a meaningful unit of account and a reliable store of value. With a stable currency, it is thought, investor confidence will return, followed by investment and reinforced growth.

Three countries, Argentina, Hong Kong, and Bulgaria, have operated currency boards with notable success. According to this system, the country issues a currency and the central bank, by law, agrees to exchange the currency for a 'hard' foreign currency. The money supply is determined by the central bank's reserves of hard foreign currency. Hence, the quantity of local currency fluctuates, depending on how much foreign currency the country acquires through trade and investment. Interest rates adjust automatically to defend the currency. Argentina and Hong Kong, which are linked to the US dollar, and Bulgaria, which is linked to the German mark, have retained the confidence of investors, although the devaluation of the real by the Brazilian authorities, in 1999, placed severe pressure on the Argentine currency as factories moved from Argentina to the lower cost Brazilian market. These pressures intensified in 2001 and the Argentine authorities introduced modifications to the peg in order to assist exports and to discourage imports. Estonia, Lithuania, Bulgaria and Bosnia also introduced currency boards, while Kosovo, East Timor and Montenegro granted foreign currencies legal tender status. In 2000, Ecuador replaced the sucre with the dollar. Other countries that have considered currency boards are Brazil, Mexico, Russia and Indonesia. Meantime , in January 1995, eleven of the member countries of the European Union (EU) agreed to replace their currencies with a single currency, the euro, and a single central bank. In January 1999, the members had fixed exchange rates among themselves, while the euro floated against the dollar and other currencies.

Notes

1.   Marx, Karl and Friedrich Engels (1872), *The Communist Manifesto*, translated by Samuel Moore (1888), reprinted, with an introduction and notes by A.J.P. Taylor (1985), London: Penguin Classics, p.85.
2.   Hadley, Arthur T. (1888), *Railroad Transportation. Its History and its Laws*, New York and London: Putnam, p.18.
3.   Keynes, John M. (1936), *The General Theory of Employment, Interest and Money*, reprinted (1961), London: Macmillan, p.150.

4. President Clinton, W. J. (1993), Speech, 'Prosperity Aids Freedom,' *The New York Times*, 27 February.
5. Keohane, Robert O. and Joseph S. Nye, Jr. (2000), 'Globalization: What's New? What's Not? (And So What?)', *Foreign Policy*, **118**.
6. Marx, Karl and Friedrich Engels, op.cit., p.83.
7. Williamson, John (1990), 'What Washington Means by Policy Reform,' in John Williamson (ed), *Latin American Adjustment: How Much Has Happened?* Washington Institute for International Economics.
8. Gellner, Ernest (1991), *Plough, Sword and Book. The Structure of Human History*, London: Paladin. Grafton Books, p.17.
9. It is recognised that the terms Medieval, modernity and Renaissance are generalisations covering periods which were undergoing continuous change and in which there are doubts as to the meaning of the descriptions. However, this section is an attempt to give a concise account of a complex period. It is, therefore, considered permissible to deploy reductions and generalisations.
10. Harvey, David (1989), *The Condition of Post-Modernity*, Oxford: Blackwell.
11. Wassenbergh, H. A. (1984), 'Parallels and Differences in the Development of Air, Sea and Space Law in the Light of Grotius' Heritage,' *Annuals of Air and Space Law*, **9**, pp.163-175.
12. Mahan, Alfred Thayer (1890), *The Influence of Sea Power upon History, 1660-1783*, reprinted with an introduction by Louis M. Hacker (1961), New York: Hill and Wang.
13. Oliver Wendell Holmes had argued that the protective system was a sign that the law 'was administered in the interests of the upper classes.' Basedow goes on to state: 'In a sector of the economy where both monopoly and competition co-existed, the dependency of the upper classes on public transportation is the better explanation for the particular burden which the common law imposed indiscriminately on all common carriers.' Basedow, Jürgen (1983), 'Common Carriers: Continuity and Disintegration in US Transportation Law', *Transportation Law Journal*, **12**(1:1), p.8.
14. Hayek, F. A. (1955), *The Counter Revolution of Science. Studies on the Abuse of Reason*, London: Collier-Macmillan, p.105.
15. Nelson, James R. (1965), 'Pricing Transport Services' in Fromm, Gary (ed), *Transport Investment and Economic Development*, Washington DC: The Brookings Institution, Transportation Research Program, p.211.
16. Ekelund, Robert B. Jr. and Hebert, Robert F. (1990), *A History of Economic Theory and Method*, London: McGraw-Hill International, pp.64-65.
17. The capital requirements of the railways and the magnitude of the failure of the financial markets prompted the consideration of a range of new legal entities, including limited liability: 'The technology enabled exciting visions of railroad and development, and these visions were expressed in the law, especially in the legislation about financing and the structure and powers of the individual corporation. The apparent benefits of encouraging the development may have affected the allocation of liability for use of land and accidents, but attitudes towards individual fault and responsibility were probably much larger in influence.' Risk, B. (1973), 'The Nineteenth-Century Foundations and the Business Corporation in Ontario', *University of Toronto Law Journal*, **23**(270), p.238.
18. Chandler, Alfred. D. (1973), 'Decision Making and Modern Institutional Change', *Journal of Economic History*, **33**(1), pp.1-75.
19. Buchanan, R. A. (1994), *The Power of the Machine*, London: Penguin, pp 72-77.
20. Spengler, Joseph J. (1969), 'Evolution of Public-Utility Industry Regulation: Economic and Other Determinants.' *South African Journal of Economics*, **37**(3), p.9.
21. 'The obvious conflict between the traditional ideology and the public utility concept was resolved by resort to rationalisation. It was said that enterprises supplying gas, electricity, street transportation, water and telephonic communication were 'inherently' or 'naturally' monopolistic. Thus the fiction of 'natural monopoly' was invented to explain the centripetal tendencies then observable...,' Gray, Horace M. (1940), 'The Passing of the Public Utility Concept,' *Journal of Land and Public Utility Economics*, **8**, p.9.

22. The 'neo' refers to an institutional change, from monarchies to representative governments which supplied the regulatory protection and subventions desired by rent-seeking agents who used political means to secure differential gains at the expense of the general polity.

23. 'In the early thirties, change set in with abruptness. Its landmarks were the abandonment of the gold standard by Great Britain; the Five-Year Plan in Russia; the launching of the New Deal; the National Socialist Revolution in Germany; the collapse of the League in favour of anarchist empires. While at the end of the Great War, nineteenth century ideals were paramount and their influence dominated the following decade, by 1940 every vestige of the international system had disappeared.' Polanyi, Karl (1944), *The Great Transformation*, Boston: Beacon Press, reprinted in paperback edition with a forward by Robert M. MacIver (1975), p.25.

24. The father of GATT was Cordell Hull, US Secretary of State. Under his leadership, the US undertook steep tariff reductions that were spread by means of multilateral concessions among member states.

25. In explaining the 'drastic increase over the past fifty years in the role of government', Milton and Rose Friedman stated that 'the major reason these changes took place when they did was the basic shift that occurred in public opinion.' Friedman, Milton and Rose Friedman (1984), *The Tyranny of the Status quo*, Harmondsworth, Middlesex: Penguin Books, pp.40-41. The Friedmans interpret the election in 1931 of F. D. Roosevelt to the Presidency of the United States as a watershed, as 'it marked a major change in both the public's perception of the role of government and the actual role assigned to government.' They identify the epistemic community and its role in the shift in ideology: 'The members of FDR's brain trust were drawn mainly from the universities – in particular, Columbia University. They reflected the change that had occurred earlier in the intellectual atmosphere on the campuses – from belief in responsibility, *laissez-faire*, and a decentralised and limited government. It was the function of government, they believed, to protect individuals from the vicissitudes of fortune and to control the operation of the economy in the 'general interest', even if that involved government ownership and operation of the means of production. Friedman, Milton and Rose Friedman (1981), *Free to Choose. A Personal Statement*, New York: Avon Books, p.83.

26. 'Freedom of the air', however, has so far not existed in international law. The sovereignty of the state over the air column above its territory replaced the doctrine of national '*res communis*', the height of the sovereign air column in practice being determined by the definition of 'aircraft.' The sovereignty over the 'national' air column became used for the protection for the national air traffic market. Ching, Bin (1962), *The Law of International Air Transport,* London: Stevens & Sons, p.120.

27. The Chicago Convention, negotiated by 52 nations in 1944, formalised the principle that in effect every nation has exclusive sovereignty over the airspace above its territory. The failure was to achieve a multilateral agreement linked to a system of bilateral agreements, the prototype of which was Bermuda I, contracted between the British and US governments in 1946. The bilateral regulated market access, the number and scope of air transport rights, tariffs and capacity. Tariffs were negotiated within the International Air Transport Association (IATA), established in Havana in 1945. Rate-making was based on a unanimity rule, subject to government approval and the residual government powers provided for in the Bermuda agreements.

28. Cowhey, Peter F. (1990), 'The International Telecommunications Regime, the Political Roots of Regimes for High Technology', *International Organisation,* **44**(2), p.186.

29. Ibid., p.176.

30. 'Japan is a country of about 145,000 square miles, one twentieth the land mass of the United States. In 1978, it used only about 264 MHz of spectrum, divided into twelve VHF and thirty-two UHF channels, to distribute television programming through a total of some 7,300-broadcast TV stations. Of that number, 212 were the full service variety prevalent in the United States, and the balance was relay outlets. By comparison, in the United States that year, the FCC allocated 408 MHz of spectrum, divided into twelve VHF channels and fifty-six UHF, to provide broadcast TV through some 1,000 full service stations (600 VHF and 400 UHF) and 3,000 relay or translator outlets. and in California, which is 10 per cent

larger than Japan, FCC regulations allowed just 66 full-service and 349 translator stations.' Robinson, Kenneth (1983), 'Some Thoughts on Broadcasting Reform', *Regulation*, May/June, p.20.

31. Besen, Stanley M. and Thomas G. Krattenmaker (1991), 'Regulating Network Television', *Regulation*, May/June, p.27-28. 'Historically, the FCC had been concerned solely with preventing network practice that restricted competition within the existing system.'

32. Cameron, D. R. (1978), 'The Expansion of the Public Economy: A Comparative Analysis', *American Political Science Review*, **4**(72), pp.1243-1261. Mueller also estimated that total government expenditure in the US as a percentage of GNP was 1.4 per cent in 1799, 10 per cent in 1960 and 47.8 per cent in 1984. Mueller, Dennis C. (1989), *Public Choice II*, Cambridge: Cambridge University Press, pp.320-322.

33. Buchanan, R.A.,op.cit., pp 38-40, uses, not an evolutionary, but a mechanical concept, the ratchet. He uses the example of the development of the internal combustion engine making available a sufficiently light power pack to be applicable to the first flying machines.

34. McCartney makes a case that two men at the University of Pennsylvania, John Mauchly and Prester Eckert created the ENIAC, the first digital, general-purpose, electronic computer. McCartney, Scott (1999), *The Triumphs and Tragedies of the World's First Computer,* New York: Walker &Walker Company.

35. Berners-Lee, Tim (1999), *The Original Design and Ultimate Destiny of the World Wide Web by Its Inventor,* San Francisco: HarperSanFrancisco.

36. Carton, Jim (1988), 'It Seems Like Yesterday,' *The Wall Street Journal*, Technology Supplement, 16 November.

37. 'Remarks by the President in Announcement of Electronic Commerce Initiative,' Washington: The White House, Office of the Press Secretary, July 1, 1997.

38. Jonsson, Christer (1981), 'Sphere of Flying: The Politics of International Aviation', *International Organisation*, **35**(2), pp.273-350.

39. 'Europe for Sale. A Privatisation Drive Could Raise $150 Billion,' *International Business Week*, 19 July 1993.

40. 'Global Dogfight: World's major airlines scramble to get ready for a world wide competitive battle,' *The Wall Street Journal*, 14 January 1992.

41. 'Airlines Going Global,' *The Economist*, 19 December 1992.

42. Duchene, Dennis A. (1995), 'The Third Package of Liberalization in the European Air Transport Sector: Shying Away from Full Liberation,' *Transportation Law Review*, **23**.

43. Cowell, Alan (1988) 'Five Airlines in Marketing Pact to Rival Star Alliance,' *The New York Times,* 22 September.

44. Ebke, Werner F. and George W. Wenglorz (1991), 'Liberalising Scheduled Air Transport Within the European Community: From the First Phase to the Second and Beyond', *Transportation Law Journal*, **14** (2), pp.417-452.

45. Papaioannou R. and D. Stasinopoulos (1991), 'The Road Transport Policy of the European Community', *Journal of Transport and Economic Policy*, **25**(2), pp. 203-205.

46. Cafruny,Alun W. (1985), The Political Economy of International Shipping: Europe versus America', *International Organisation*, **37**(1), p. 94.

47. The UN Conference of Trade and Development (UNCTAD) was founded in 1964 primarily as a trade and development watchdog on behalf of the developing world. At its eighth conference in Cartagena, Columbia, in 1992, UNCTAD restructured itself so it could play a larger part in influencing world trade and development.

48. 'The world markets in which the merchant marine operates, however, do not strictly observe competitive rules. On the contrary, attempts at the extra-territorial extension of US anti-trust laws into international markets have produced strained relations abroad and serious embarrassment at home. Conferences of lines (shipping cartels) set rates and control services on trade routes outside the national jurisdiction, they are generally exempt from US Anti-trust laws as long as they do not subscribe to certain outlawed practices like deferred rebates and fighting ships. Also, an increasing number of ship lines within and outside the conferences are owned by the state and subscribe to cargo-sharing rather than to competitive rules. Any attempt to reform or deregulate US economic regulation must come

to grips with these unique conditions.' Hazard, John (1980), 'A Competitive US Marine Policy', *Transportation Journal*, **19**(2), pp.43-44, 49.

49. Ibid., p.40 'The US merchant marine, however, does not operate in a completely open and competitive market. Instead, it receives protection from foreign competition in domestic markets. *Cabotage* legislation simply prevents all domestic waterborne commerce for US flagships. In foreign commerce, US flag ships are accorded preference on government cargoes (50 to 100 per cent allocations), differential subsidies calculated to equalise US and foreign costs, and certain other types of assistance. US flag ships are also accorded preferences in the defence market, if they are willing to place half of their ships on a ready call-up reserve list.'

50. Stapleton, Drew H.M. and Soumen N. Ghosh (1999), 'The Ocean Shipping Reform Act: Practical Implications for Both Buyers and Sellers,' *Journal of Transportation Law, Logistics and Policy*, **67**(1), pp.53-68

51. Machalaba, Daniel (1999), 'North Atlantic Shipping Firms Propose Pact to Allow Exchange of Market Data,' *The Wall Street Journal*, 16 February. Machalaba, Daniel and Anna Wilde (1999), 'Big Pacific Shipping Cartel Fades Away, But Looser Group Appears to Succeed It,' *The Wall Street Journal*, 19 March.

52. Portanger, Erik and Vanessa Fuhrmans (2000), 'How it Became a Foggy Day on the London Exchange,' *The Wall Street Journal*, 2 November.

53. Marks, Howard S. Fabozzi, Frank and Irving M. Pollack (eds) (1987), 'High Yield Bond Portfolios,' *The Handbook of Fixed Income Securities*, Homewood, Illinois: Dow Jones–Irwin, pp.751-764.

54. Cooper, Richard N. (1999), 'Should Capital Controls Be Banished?' *Brookings Papers on Economic Activity*, **1**, pp.89-142.

55. Lawson, Nigel (1992), 'Side Effects of Deregulation,' *Financial Times*, 27 January. Gilmour presents a different interpretation as to why exchange controls went in 1979: 'the decision owed less to concern at the pounds rise than to Thatcherite ideological belief in the invariable beneficence of market forces. Yet the ideological objective, for the dismantling of exchange controls, made the governments primary objectives – control of the money supply – virtually unattainable.' Gilmour, Ian (1992), *Dancing with Dogma. Britain under Thatcherism*, London: Simon and Schuster, p.25

56. Scott, Kenneth E. (1980), 'The Uncertain Course of Bank Deregulation', *Regulation*, May/June, pp.41-45.

57. The Banking Act of 1933 sought to deal with the problems of the depression by creating an industry cartel to fix rates and divide markets. Competition would be constrained and so the main course of the depression would be contained. A buyers banking cartel was created which limited the demand for deposits. Maximum rates of interest were to be established by the regulatory agencies, the Federal Reserve Board and the Federal Deposit Insurance Corporation (FDCC). The maximum rate to be paid on checking accounts was fixed, by law, at zero. In the wake of the Great Crash, the *Glass-Steagall Act* of 1933 precluded banks from acting as dealers in commercial paper. In consequence, a number of new entities arose, such as Morgan Stanley, which, unlike Morgan's could deal with securities.

58. Wescil, David and Bob Davis (1998), 'Currency Controls Gain a Hearing in Asia,' *The Wall Street Journal*, 4 September.

59. Norris, Floyd (2000),'Consolidation Changes Industry's Face,' *The New York Times*, September 13.

60. In Britain there had grown a tradition of specialisation and separation of financial activities, which was generally reinforced by the informal policies of the Bank of England.

61. European Commission, Brussels (1990), *A Common Market in Services*, DGXV-Internal Market and Financial Services.

62. Kintner, Evelyn (1993), 'Politics and Deregulation in the Canadian Banking Industry,' *The American Review of Canadian Studies*, **23**(2), p. 232.

63. Coleman, William D. (1992), 'Financial Services Reform in Canada: The Evolution of Policy Dissension', *Canadian Public Policy*, **18**(2), p. 139.

64. Zweig, Phillip L (2001), 'Mexico will reap Dividends from Citibank, *The Wall Street Journal, 22 May.*

65. Cherney, Elena (2001), 'Canada's Banks Head to US, but they take different Routes,' *The Wall Street Journal, 22 May.*

66. Packet switches take information that is partitioned into small packets and route them to their destinations. They are routed on the best available pathway. Circuit-switches establish a single dedicated transmission for the delivery of information.

67. During the summer of 2000 there were numerous well-publicised blackouts and rate increases. See Banerjee, Neela, (2000), 'A Dwindling Faith In Deregulation,' *The New York Times,* 15 September.

68. McFadden, Daniel (2001) 'California Needs Deregulation Done Right,' *The Wall Street Journal,* 13 February.

69. Hundt, Reed E. (2000), *You Say You Want a Revolution,* New Haven & London: Yale University Press, p.155.

70. Ibid., pp.214-215.

71. Oxman, Jason (1999), 'The FCC and the Unregulation of the Internet', OPP Working Paper No.31, Federal Communications Commission, Washington D.C.

72. Perkins, Anthony B. (2000), 'Interactive TV Is Coming Soon. Really,' *The Wall Street Journal,* 2 October.

73. Schiesel, Seth, (2001) 'Sprint Still Aspires to Offer One-Stop Communications,' *The New York Times,* 15 January.

74. Hundt, Reed E., op.cit., p.203.

75. Tarjanne, Pekka (1997), 'Telecommunications and World Development: Forecasts, technologies and services.' Moscow: ITU.

76. Laux, J. K. and M. A. Molot (1988), *State Capitalism: Public Enterprise in Canada*, Ithica: Cornell University Press, p.184. In 1968 the Labour government amalgamated the Post Office and Telecommunications into a huge, monopoly public corporation. In 1980, British Telecom (BT) was separated from the Post Office. Gilmour asserts that this decision to privatise was prompted by BT's lack of financial resources, causing the corporation to go to the market: 'Ideological commitment was happily joined with party advantage and government necessity. In consequence, during the Thatcher years, about half of the previously state-owned industries were sold to the private sector.' Gilmour, Ian, op.cit., p.118.

77. Megginson, William (2000), 'Privatization', *Foreign Policy,* 118(Spring).

78. Gilmour, Ian, op.cit., pp.191-195.

79. Andrews, Edmund L. (1999), 'Deutsche Telekom, Phone Home,' *The New York Times,* 26 February.

80. Wolf, Martin (1992), 'The GATT makes its Last Stand,' *Financial Times*, 20 January.

81. Advertisement (1999), 'Global Monoculture', *The New York Times*, 15 November.

82. Wallach, Lorri (2000), 'Lori's War. The FP Interview', *Foreign Policy,* 118(Spring).

83. Three quarters of all actions to restrict imports under GATT safeguard essentially three groups: steel, textiles and clothing. See Lipson, Charles (1982), 'The Transformation of Trade; the sources and effects of regimes change,' *International Organisations* 36(2), p.428.

84. Winestock, Geoff (2000), 'Trade Chief Tries New Fighting Style,' *The Wall Street Journal,* 6 June.

85. Phillips, Michael. M. and Christopher Rhoads (2000), 'In a Repeat of Seattle, Economic Forum Draws Protests', *The Wall Street Journal*, 31 January.

86. Three quarters of European countries' trade is with one another. However, 40 per cent of all world trade is inter-regional, such that regional blocs would not appear to provide a long run alternative to multi-lateral liberation. Of the total value of world exports in 1990 of $4300 billion, total services (travel, transport, and other private services) accounted for almost 19 per cent; manufacturers (almost) 60 per cent; and the rest 11.5 per cent and agriculture 10.1 per cent. Wolf, Martin, op.cit.

87. Borjas, George J. (2000), 'Mexico's One-Way Remedy,' *The New York Times*, 18 July.

88. Cohen, Roger (2000), 'Germany's Foreign Minister Urges European Federation,' *The New York Times,* 15 May.
89. Cooper, Helen and Kathy Chen (2001), 'US Is Told to Let Mexican Trucks Enter,' *The Wall Street Journal,* 7 February.
90. Peters, Philip (2000), 'A Final Test of Courage for Clinton and Zedillo,' *The Wall Street Journal,* 9 June.
91. Stiglitz, Joseph (2000), 'The Insider. What I learned at the world economic crisis,' *The New Republic*, 12 & 24 April.
92. Mundell, Robert (2000), 'Threat to Prosperity,' *The Wall Street Journal*, 30 March.

3. Future Imperfect

Computerised and electronic communications systems have, during the past decade, formed a set of interlocking markets that have enabled almost instantaneous movement of information around the globe. The resulting compression of time has accelerated the geographic mobility of data and funds, resulting in a swifter response to changes in relative costs and an almost instantaneous response to movements in exchange rates within a global stock market through which currencies, debt and futures are continuously traded.

Running parallel with these revolutionary developments, there has been a thoroughgoing transformation of the regulations governing trade, transportation, communications and every element of exchange. The reform and removal of protective economic regulation has increased competition, thereby reducing costs. Prices have moved in line with costs, and demand has risen for transport and communications services. Shifts in production and trade have occurred and transnational manufacturing has been facilitated.

Estimates published by Crandall and Ellig show that the five US 'network' industries - natural gas, telecommunications, airlines, trucking and railroads - all registered price falls of between 4 per cent and 15 per cent during the first two years of their respective deregulations. Prices have been lowered by at least 25 per cent within the last ten years. Competitive forces have aligned service quality with customers' desires and stimulated innovation and consumer choice.[1]

According to the Bureau of Labour Statistics, the Consumer Price Index (CPI) rose at an average annual rate of 3.2 per cent over the period 1989-1999. The average rates of increase for telephone services were 0.9 per cent, transportation 2.8 per cent and electricity 1.2 per cent.

Steven Morrison testified before the Senate Judiciary Committee that airfares in 1997, adjusted for inflation, were 40 per cent lower than they had been before deregulation.[2] While in 1978, 275 million people flew on domestic carriers,[3] by 1997, the number had risen to 600 million. Statistics from the International Air Transport Association (IATA) show that the average consumer of scheduled airline flights is today paying 70 per cent less in real terms than he paid twenty years ago. In 1999, 1.6 billion journeys were undertaken. Travel and tourism account for 12 per cent of the global economy.[4]

According to a study by the Center for Research in Electronic Commerce of the University of Texas, the Internet economy, in 1999, accounted for nearly $524 billion in revenue, an increase of 68 per cent over 1998.

Between 1995 and 1999, the US Internet Economy grew at an estimated annual average of 174.5 per cent, compared with an average annual GDP growth of 2.8 per cent in the United States. A substantial part of this growth can be assumed to be transactions that have moved from the 'physical world' to the Internet.[5] Such substitutions are accelerating, in part, because every Internet purchase is tax free up to the end of the year 2001. Currently some 7,600 state and local governments rely for revenue on sales taxes. Since 1992 companies have been obliged to collect sales taxes only from consumers in states where the company has a physical presence. Some states have voiced their concerns to the Advisory Commission on Electronic Commerce that the shift to on-line retailing is eviscerating their sales tax revenues.

In 1998, for the world as a whole, the total reported output of telecommunication traffic aggregated to 93 billion minutes. International telephone calls totalled 4 billion minutes in 1974, 33 million in 1990 and 68 billion in 1996.[6] International calls have been growing at an annual average of 15 per cent a year, while the overall world-wide average annual economic growth rate in the same period (1995-1998) has been 3.8 per cent. However, the growth in traffic is known to be an underestimate because increasing volumes of voice and fax traffic passes over private rather than public switched telephone networks.[7]

The arrival of affordable desktop personal computers and the Internet have drastically reduced consumers' search costs. The resulting instant re-orientation in fashion and public tastes and changes in patterns of consumption have necessitated a flexible response from manufacturers. This has impacted on labour, which has also had to become more flexible. Work rules have been eased. Part time employment, outsourcing and sub-contracting are now characteristics of many labour markets. Transnational companies have moved production between countries, often removing the mass production functions from the organised to the less organised labour markets.

In the half-century since the founding of GATT in 1948, the world economy has expanded six-fold while trade has expanded sixteen-fold.[8] Between 1973 and 1993, merchandise exports (in US dollars) grew by a factor of seven, twice as fast as gross world product in real terms.[9]

Since technology has displaced the physical weight of output with weightless concepts, shipping costs have been steadily declining as a proportion of the value of commodities. Manufactured goods have come, increasingly, to resemble 'congealed' brainpower. [10] Today, 40 per cent of the world's manufactured exports, by value, are transported by air.[11] But this evolution in trade is not occurring in all countries. The globe's least developed countries accounted for 13 per cent of the world's population in 1997 but generated only a 0.4 per cent share of the globe's exports and absorbed only a 0.6 per cent share of imports.[12]

In advanced economies, computer technology influences every aspect of existence, from the provision of utilities to the operation of cars. The emergence of the Y2K problem – the widespread belief that computers that had not been re-programmed would confuse the year 2000 with the year 1900 – was illustrative of how extensive computer technology had become. Estimates were that the cost of litigation in the Unites States, following the Y2K fiasco, would run as high as $1 trillion.[13]

These figures contrast starkly with those emanating from the developing world. According to the International Telecommunications Union (ITU), the 'teledensity' – the number of main lines per thousand inhabitants – in eight African countries fell between 1990 and 1996.[14] In 1996, fully one-quarter of ITU member states still had a teledensity of less than one. There is hope that global mobile personal communications by satellite (GMPCS) will enable users to make and receive calls via mobile handsets from almost anywhere in the world. Low-earth orbit (LEO) systems operators plan to provide global voice service coverage that will link public telephones to the system. The ITU suggests that the goal of ten telephone lines per hundred inhabitants, with more than 50 per cent of the households served in developing countries, 'seems reasonable as a target for 2010.'[15]

The multi-dimensional market, which, thanks to technology, shrinks space and compresses time, is potentially a more efficient co-ordinator and distributor of resources than its predecessor. Connectivity with computer power, and therefore with the market, has enabled knowledge, education and power to migrate to those who are more technically proficient. Improvements in the immediacy and accuracy of information has enhanced the control of branch operations, facilitated the outsourcing to emerging markets and encouraged the flow of capital across the globe. This flow, in turn, has been influenced by the liberalisation of capital and financial markets.

Banks mobilise the savings of households and assess the risk profiles of the companies to which they lend their capital. Opening up the banking sector to world competition could result in the augmentation of domestic savings and diversification of risks. This was among the arguments put forward by the United States treasury and the IMF when they encouraged economies to open up their financial transactions to competition. As a consequence, there has been a notable rise in cross-border private banking and increases in direct investment in the financial services sectors of emerging markets.[16] The resulting competition has increased the availability of loans to governments and private corporations.

Between 1990 and 1994, long-term financial flows to the developing world have more than doubled to US $275 billion. (But between 1985 and 19995, the net outflows of foreign direct investment from industrial to developing countries were only about 2 per cent of the total capital formation in the developing countries.[17]) In 1998, direct foreign investment accounted for 56 per cent of net long-term resource flows. Bonds, private loans and portfolio equity flows aggregated to 26 per cent of the total in 1998, having been 40 per cent of the total in 1994.[18] Between 1990 and 1997, short-term borrowing by emerging market economies nearly tripled. In 1977, global foreign exchange turnover was $4.6 trillion. By 1995, this turnover exceeded $300 trillion. Most transactions involved round trips of a week or less. In the 1970s, 30 per cent of the foreign exchange turnover was used to finance trade in commodities and non-financial services. By 1995, the percentage had fallen to around 5 per cent, while global foreign exchange reserves totalled less than one day of foreign exchange turnover.[19]

Short-term lending has proved to be pro-cyclical, magnifying booms and busts.[20] There have also been the not altogether welcome effects of innovative financial instruments, market deregulation and new information technology. Not only have global markets become more liquid because of the reduced cost of borrowing and lending across borders, but the new technology and deregulated markets have also facilitated the transmission of financial oscillations.

Unlike the preceding Bretton Woods era, when capital controls and financial sector regulation limited capital flows to emerging markets, the surge in private capital flows has been punctuated by frequent crises in banking and exchange rates. Between 1994 and 1999, ten middle-income emerging markets suffered major financial crises. The financial crisis in 1997 and the emergence of over-production, deflation and recession in Japan as well as in neighbouring South East Asia, were signal events in the history of global markets. These economies had expanded in such a way that, for the first time in 350 years, their vicissitudes adversely affected the economies in the Northern Hemisphere. After being hailed by the World Bank for their high savings rates, in their 1993 study, 'The East Asian Miracle,' the tigers found themselves floundering as capital departed and their exchange rates plunged.

The resulting dislocations have been severe. In 1997, per capita income fell in twenty-one countries, accounting for 10 per cent of the developing world's GDP and 7 per cent of its population. In 1998, Brazil, Indonesia, Russia, and 33 other developing economies, accounting for 42 per cent of the total GDP for the developing world, experienced negative per capita growth.[21] Those who were unable to hedge against massive drops in the value of local money suffered greatly. Mexican taxpayers face a bill of $71 billion to pay for the government's bailout of the banking sector following the crisis in 1995.[22] In Brazil, at least half the workforce earns the minimum wage of $77 a month.[23] Under the IMF's programme for Indonesia, three-fourths of the population are expected to live on $1 per day.[24] In 1997, the overall capital investment in the productive sector of

Russia was just 17 per cent of the 1990 level, while GDP, if measured at market exchange rates, was no more than 6 per cent of the GDP of the United States.[25]

ENVIRONMENTAL CATASTROPHE

In spite of the huge benefits that the changes outlined above have brought, especially to the West, entailing among other things, the increased mobility of labour and rapid shifts in consumption, this 'phase of capitalism,' as it is called by the Marxists and democratic socialists, has not been universally acclaimed. Some have retained Marx's apocalyptic plot but have written the working class out of the script. According to these Green Marxists, the coming conflagration in capitalism will be a combination of ecological crisis and social polarisation.[26]

Democratic socialists point to Polanyi's thesis that the disembodied, self-regulating global market has subjected growing numbers to its blind forces.[27] Others go further and assert that free market capitalism is unleashing chaos, conflict and antagonistic rivalries within and between nations.[28] Those along this spectrum of opinion express concern as to what is seen as the autonomy of the global financial system.

But global capitalism or the limits of growth do not, according to media commentators, cause declines in bio-diversity, pollution, famines global warming and ozone depletion. So the predictions and analyses of Marx and Malthus are insufficiently dramatic to grab the attention of the broad public. In fact, they are now way down on the billing. It is the alleged environmental trends and occurrences that are sensationalised and depicted as apocalyptic. The end of nature is widely heralded. Oceans are said to be dying. Bio-diversity is in a terminal decline. Global warming, it is warned, will cause a catastrophic flood.

The culprit is not the mode of organising production and consumption, but the nature of humans. The human species craves for mastery over nature. Yet nature is sacred and should be left alone. In mastering nature with their technology, humans destroy nature. Redemption from their evil ways and the salvation of nature can only be attained by the conversion of the human species to a new set of values. Conversion starts by confronting humans with the catastrophic consequences of their actions.

There is an analogy here with radical economics whose practitioners attack the notion that self-interest is a non-expungible aspect of human nature. In their rationalistic utopia, human beings are supposed to subordinate their particular selfish wants to the profound needs whose satisfaction produces a community of autonomous but selfless individuals. Such utopian socialistic projects have not been successful. Similarly, the conversion of humans away from their seeming innate drive for mastery of their environment has proven, so far, to have been attended by only limited success. No more than an admired, but pitied few individuals, like Mother Theresa, have really practised self-denial.

Third world economies have been encouraged and in some cases cajoled, with pecuniary enticements, into reducing their population growth rates, containing their consumption of energy and adopting environmentally friendly, if not notably efficient, technology. Environmental groups have succeeded in attracting corporate support. Some of California's major corporations, for instance, have teamed with the Sierra Club and the Environmental Defence Fund to form the California Environmental Dialogue, whose aim is to make 'safe' from development some 5.4 million acres of private land. Electors have been encouraged to adopt conservation measures. In March 2000, the voters in California approved Proposition 12, committing taxpayers to a $2.1 billion bond issue to acquire and set aside more parkland. In 2000, the Federal government joined the state of Florida in funding the $7.8 billion project to restore the Everglades.

All over the developed world, groups have succeeded in closing down atomic energy programmes. They have been less successful, however, in controlling emissions of greenhouse gases. Reports by the Intergovernmental Panel on Climate Change, a body that operates under the auspices of the United Nations, purport to show strong links between recent global warming and rising emissions of greenhouse gases. Emissions of carbon dioxide - the greenhouse gasses - collect in the Earth's upper atmosphere, where they slow the natural loss of the sun's heat into space, just as a greenhouse does.

Yet, although a hundred countries have signed the Kyoto Protocol of 1997, and major concessions were made in Bonn in July 2001 to entice governments to ratify, the main industrialised countries, including the United States, have still not ratified it. Its adoption would require signatory states to cut their combined emissions of greenhouse gases by the year 2012 to 5 per cent below 1990 levels. The United States, which produces a fourth of the world's emissions and a fourth of its economic production with 5 per cent of the world's population, stands to be affected most by any such agreement. Perhaps because of this vulnerability, there are those in the United States who question the objectivity of the scientific enquiries into global warming and the motives of the European governments.[29]

The dispute over global warming involves complex scientific enquiries that remain highly speculative. This has not dissuaded the contestants and, in particular, some of the environmental interest groups, from asserting their allegedly unassailable values. They are, in effect, expressing their revulsion against contemporary capitalism and propounding their brand of utopian socialism. Common resources are not to be contaminated by market processes. The possibility of trade-offs is unthinkable, for this would constitute a sell-out to sordid commercial interests. But free commercial transactions direct self-interested impulses toward the common good of improved material conditions. Trade-offs are at the heart of the capitalist process and underpin the economic well-being of society. To attenuate such transactions is a sure way to court real economic disaster, as the desperate Californians realised.[30]

FINANCIAL CATASTROPHE

Contrary to their usual analysis based on the deterministic mode of production, the Marxists allege that the financial system is driving 'geographic and temporal flexibility.' They describe the characteristic forms as capitalism's phase of 'flexible accumulation.' Detached from real production, the financial system, according to David Harvey, will carry 'capitalism into an era of equally unprecedented financial dangers.'[31]

Democratic socialists also perceive the world's autonomous financial systems as 'spinning out of control.'[32] There are frequent characterisations of the market process in negative, anthropomorphic terms.[33] The balances of forces, it is argued, have shifted in favour of the financial system as against corporate, personal and state finance. Speculation and short-term horizons are driving the real economy on to the rocks as investment declines and inflation is contained, only after attaining higher and higher levels of unemployment.

Two inter-linked and reinforcing factors are allegedly the source of the instability. One is that the participating agents in the financial markets act in a manner that is neither stabilising nor co-ordinating. The second is that, when the United States, in 1971, refused to continue its commitment to buy and sell gold at $35 an ounce (and once the deregulation of the financial market was launched), there was little agreement on how the instruments of control were to manage the international supply of money.

It is claimed that the markets in short-term capital flows are inherently unstable. The participants exhibit a herd instinct, producing a cycle of panics, manias, booms and busts. Because of the type of financial instrument employed and the volume of transactions, such flows, it is claimed, not only destabilise the smaller 'emerging markets,' they also threaten to destabilise the established financial markets.

Thanks to deregulation and advances in communication and information technology, the financial markets have become massive, complex and diverse industries of investment management. The innovative instruments known as derivatives, which include futures and options, derive their value from the underlying asset of the stock, bond or currency. Derivatives make it possible to diversify risks more effectively and thus have enhanced the efficiency of capital allocation. Hedge funds have become major players in the derivatives market. As private partnerships, which trade for themselves, they are exempt from the regulation of disclosure fees and borrowing that are applied to mutual funds. At the end of 1998, hedge funds had expanded to about 4,500 domestic and offshore funds in the United States with almost $300 billion in assets. A few have been able to obtain enormous leverage. Their assets include all investment made with partners' capital plus investment made using leveraged arranged by financial counterparts and, in particular, by major investment banks. While commercial banks are leveraged 20 to 1, some of the largest funds, such as the Long Term Capital Management (LTCM) have been leveraged by 300 to 1.[34]

A 1992 report of the Security and Exchange Commission, the Federal Reserve Board and Treasury made the observation that '…the potential of these funds, due to their size, active market presence and use of leverage, is to cause market disruption.'[35]

The celebrated hedge fund entrepreneur, George Soros, warned of the exposure of banks in the derivatives market: 'The transactions form a daisy chain in which each intermediary has an obligation to his counterparts without knowing who else is involved.'[36]

Barings, the UK investment bank, went bankrupt in 1995. This failure revealed the vulnerability of investment banks to unauthorised trading. The losses incurred by LTCM in September 1998, threatened a sudden liquidation of its portfolio, which would, it is alleged, have created an unacceptable systemic risk to the entire financial system in that tens of billions of illiquid securities would have been dumped on to an already panicking market. Faced with the potential collapse of LTCM, together with its highly leveraged investment portfolio of nearly $80 billion, the Federal Reserve Bank of New York orchestrated a private rescue.[37]

The immediate cause of LTCM's demise was the decision of the Russian government to default on its loans. Hedge funds were forced to shore up their finances, as their lenders demanded more collateral. Under the pressure of selling, the urge to flee became 'contagious.' There was a headlong flight out of emerging markets into safe US treasury securities and German bonds. The losses made by LTCM, estimated at $1.8 billion, questioned the shortcomings of computer forecasting, the quality of unregulated, privately negotiated contracts and the extent of unregulated leverage. As lenders, the banks had failed to regulate the hedge funds. The 'private bailout' encouraged by a major banking regulator, implied that government protection could be extended to non-banks as well as banks. In the absence of diligence from lenders, government regulation, not market discipline, was used.

The Federal Reserve Bank's orchestrated bailout revealed a world of interlocked partners and lenders that attracted the charge of 'crony capitalism.'[38] Whatever the degree of collusion and collaboration, some in emerging and established markets were concerned at the power that a few hedge funds could exercise over their markets. Malaysia's Prime Minister blamed the machinations of speculators for his nation's financial crisis in

1997. Sir Donald Tsang, the Finance Secretary of Hong Kong, claimed that there was a co-ordinated conspiracy against the economy. His allegation was that a cabal of speculators was attempting to sell his country short and then spread rumours about its future plans. Hong Kong officials purchased shares in August 1998, because there were no international rules that protected markets from such short-selling strategies,[39] and because of the fear that the speculation would be self-fulfilling. That is, when stocks plunged those not in on the speculation might not rush in to buy the falling stocks because of the expectation that the ploy would succeed.[40]

Another explanation for the destabilising effects of short-term capital movements asserts that speculation is self-justifying. Instead of the speculators who bet against the fundamentals being 'wiped out,' the fundamentals may change to reflect the speculation. This, it is alleged, is what happened to the Asian tiger economies.[41] Out of panic, investors pulled out their capital when they perceived these economies to be weak. In so doing, they further weakened economies that, while subject to inefficient but deregulated capital markets and corrupt governments, were fundamentally strong.

Those who have identified capital movements as the source of the instability have advocated a range of policies, from the taxing of short-term capital flows[42] to the outright abandonment of free capital movement. Others have identified the inability of the financial institutions to regulate their own entities. Some advocate the imposition of banking regulations on to 'near banks' and the eradication of 'safe haven' jurisdictions.

There are those who say that this approach confuses cause with effect. The implication is that, because of the deficiencies of the participating agents, the market process does not stabilise and co-ordinate activity. On the contrary, it is the cause of the instability. Markets, by transforming information into opportunities by co-ordinating the plans of participants, harness the underlying flux of economic and political activity. Markets are possible when prices are allowed to respond freely to changes brought about by forces of demand and supply. The term 'speculator' is not pejorative. Rather, it is a term denoting the crucial function of constantly providing bids and offers in markets. This facilitates liquidity, without which the commercial participant could not effectively use the market.

The instability that became a full-blown crisis was not caused by market failure. It was the result of government intervention in domestic markets and the attempt of international agencies, such as the IMF and the World Bank, to supersede the international markets. Taxpayer's money was spent or lent, and so replaced private spending and loans. This constitutes the core of the counter argument.

The first major controversy involving hedge funds occurred in September 1992. Members of the European Union had devised a system of fixed exchange rates known as the European Exchange Rate Mechanism (ERM). The United Kingdom joined the ERM in 1990. This meant, essentially, attempting to maintain the value of the pound against the German mark, which was at a high value, in part because of high interest rates.

But the UK had entered at too a high a rate. Hedge fund operator, George Soros, spotted the opportunity. He forced the pound to its 'right' level. After three days, during which interest rates were raised, the UK dropped out of the ERM and started to float. The pound stabilised at around 15 per cent below its ERM level, while Soros was reputed to have made a return of a billion dollars.[43] Speculators then attacked the French franc, the currency of the fourth largest economy in the world.[44] Although the fundamentals of the French economy were considered to be sound, the French government had to raise interest rates and introduce austerity measures in order to re-enter the ERS. Interest rate increases dampened growth. Higher rates also attracted capital in-flows. The UK government lowered interest rates and enjoyed a higher growth rate. Five years later, the emerging markets discovered that when their currencies lunged in values and they raised interest rates, capital did not flow in. Investors panicked and capital flowed out.

The crisis in 1997/98 can be traced to the response of the IMF and the United States Treasury to the Mexican crisis in 1994/95. The IMF and the US Treasury bailed out the banks and financial institutions that had made dollar loans to Mexican institutions (that the latter, in turn, could not repay). The Mexican people were left with lower incomes and faced sharply rising prices for basic commodities. The financial bailout encouraged the belief among investors elsewhere that they would be likewise bailed out if currencies came crashing down. That elsewhere was East Asia, where investors poured in money after the Mexican crisis.[45]

These tiger economies were encouraged by the IMF-US Treasury to pursue three objectives: free capital movement, fixed exchange rates and a domestic monetary policy that favoured growth. However, when they faced deficits in the current account of the balance of payments they failed to reduce foreign payments and to increase foreign receipts. Instead, these countries drew on their dollar reserves or borrowed dollars from abroad to finance their deficits. But the deficiencies in the fundamentals of these economies could not be obscured. Without the application of economic discipline, their fundamentals grew more incongruent with their pegged exchange rates. The drastic subsequent devaluations indicated the extent of the distortions. They were inevitable, for it was not possible to achieve all three objectives simultaneously.[46]

This analysis stresses the point that the economies of South East Asia, South Korea, Russia and Brazil failed to adhere to a free-floating currency regime. They were all striving to attain a pegged exchange rate while allowing their central banks to manipulate their money supplies. All had, in varying degrees, defective fiscal and financial regulatory policies. These internal policies unleashed pressures that worked downward against their pegged exchange rates. The drastic devaluations and economic dislocations were primarily the result of these domestic policies.

The crisis also exposed the weakness of the IMF-US Treasury's so-called shock-therapy strategy for Russia's transformation to a market economy. There were many weaknesses in this strategy: the omission of a legal structure to facilitate the voluntary exchange of property and assets through market transactions; a weak corporate governance; lack of effective bankruptcy laws; and general absence of transparencies, were most damaging. The criminal oligarchy of the Soviet system was consolidated.[47] The privatisation of the huge petroleum, natural gas and telecommunications industries, and the notorious 'loans for shares' scheme, under which the well-connected obtained controlling shares in the country's most valuable assets for a fraction of their worth, went ahead. The IMF-US Treasury had not activated the transformation to a market economy but had facilitated the transfer of most of this mobile wealth out of the country.[48] Fitch IBCA, the international credit rating agency, estimated that $136 billion of capital moved out of Russia between 1993 and 1998. This estimate was far in excess of the capital flowing in from foreign investors and international financial institutions.[49] According to the US General Accounting Office (GAO) Russia had received only $66 billion in aid from the US, Europe and the leading international lending institutions.[50]

In response to a request from the IMF for further funding for a bailout of Russia, Congress created the International Financial Institution Advisory Commission (IFIAC). Since the currencies supplied by 80 per cent of the member countries are not usable in international transactions, the wealthy countries, and the United States in particular, bear the burden of lending. In 1988, the IMF lent Russia $3.7 billion, in 1993, $40 billion and in 1999, $94 billion.[51] There were questions as to the efficacy of the IMF-US Treasury policies and the functions of the World Bank. At the same time, the leaders of the G-7 countries contemplated making changes to the international financial 'architecture.'

While these deliberations were underway, a range of issues, revelations and accusations surfaced in the media. The World Bank admitted that its officers had failed to inform the market of the extent of incompetence and corruption in some South East Asian countries. The IMF–US Treasury repeatedly miscalculated the market's response to the imbalances and effectively dissipated billions of US taxpayers' money in futile attempts to sustain the exchange rates. Their subventions and advice were marshalled in failed attempts to stymie the operation of freely-floating currency regimes. Some raised the question as to whether their support of international investors had contributed at all to the stability and integrity of the 'freely floating' international currency regime.

The IFIAC report was issued in March 2000.[52] A central theme of the report was that the institutions should specialise according to their respective comparative advantages. The majority report stated that the World Bank had failed in its primary goal of combating global poverty. Its banking function had been supplanted by private capital flows. The IFIAC recommended that the Bank phase out its lending operations to the richer developing countries and those with access to private capital. It should become a development agency primarily for the poorest countries. The Poverty Reduction and Growth Fund (PRDGF) should be taken from the IMF and placed within the World Bank. The IMF should return to short-term, emergency lending and move away from long-term development finance. The IMF's loans to the poorest countries should be cancelled, and the micro-managing of developing economies should cease. The IFIAC and four other reports that addressed the changing roles of these institutions saw the IMF playing a central part in preventing, and then managing, financial crises.[53]

The Clinton administration was not enthusiastic about the IFIAC report. The Secretary to the Treasury, Lawrence Summers, gave a speech in London in December 1999, in which he argued that the IMF should focus its financing on emergency situations, acting not as a first, but as a last resort.[54] Summers suggested that the Fund should collect and disseminate information to investors and markets. He did not endorse the shift of the PRGF from the IMF to the World Bank. The IMF's expertise should be deployed in promoting sound macroeconomic policies and structural reforms in tax policy and fiscal management.

Stanley Fisher, then the acting managing director of the IMF, said that there was no support among the developing countries for the move towards short-term crisis management.[55] The G-7's communiqué of 15 April 1999, stated that crisis prevention and response should be at the core of the IMF's work. The IMF launched an Independent Evaluation Office, rationalised and re-designed its lending facilities, and promoted greater transparency in both the operation of the Fund and in relation to its members. The IMF Executive Board, meeting in Washington in April 1999, approved a programme for contingency credit. The World Bank and the IMF, jointly, launched a programme to provide 'faster, deeper, and broader debt relief for the poorest countries that demonstrate a commitment to reform and poverty alleviation.'[56] In its annual report for 1999, the World Bank stated its re-ordered priorities. Clean government and respect for human rights were to be the foundation of its development lending.

On the eve of the joint meetings of the IMF-World Bank in April 1999, Chancellor of the Exchequer, Gordon Brown and Secretary of the Treasury, Robert Rubin, outlined their proposals for the international financial architecture. Chancellor Brown stated that 'global stability consistent with national sovereignty' could be attained if governments and private businesses were to adhere to international codes of conduct. The new rules for the IMF were designed to 'promote orderly and co-operative management of crises and to address the moral-hazard concerns associated with public sector rescue packages.'[57] Secretary Rubin discouraged most countries from deploying fixed exchange rates. Lenders should pay a greater share of the cost of bailing out economies. He encouraged countries to rely more on long-term borrowing and less on short-term loans and said that they should disclose more information about outstanding debt. During crises, provision should be made for the protection of the poor and the middle classes.[58]

These proposals affirmed the *status quo*. Radical measures had not been necessary, for within six months the crisis had blown itself out. There was to be no retraction, even though policy-induced distortions - such as the rapid liberalisation of domestic banking systems and the opening of capital accounts - were deemed to have contributed to the destabilising boom in short-term borrowing. Safeguarding measures, including restrictions on capital inflows and outflows, were regarded as costly and difficult to implement. Such measures were no substitute for 'better macroeconomic fundamentals.' International agencies were to assist governments in implementing structural reforms and funding domestic safety nets for the poor.[59] The more transparent of the public sectors, reformed banking sectors and deregulated capital markets, would lubricate the workings of the market. A more efficient market would effectively handle imbalances.

The stock markets in the tiger economies rebounded, while the US markets went roaring ahead. (However, if measured in dollar values, the South East Asian markets were way below their mid-1997 levels). The sense of relief was demonstrated in the report of President Clinton's Working Group on Financial Markets. Issued in April 1999, the report recommended heightened disclosure and possibly more detailed reviews of the trading practices and capital requirements for brokerage firms and banks that deal in derivatives and make loans to hedge funds. However, an unnamed hedge fund spokesperson observed that if the Working Group had recommended the direct regulation of hedge funds, then 'every hedge fund would leave the United States.'[60]

The Group of Eight (G-8) appeared to be more determined to close international tax havens.[61] Drug cartels and corrupt officials were responsible, the Financial Action Task Force opined, for at least $600 billion a year of the money that was flowing into these havens.[62] This was a body created by the G-8, in 1998, to counter money-laundering, which was allegedly distorting capital flows. The Task Force released a list of sixteen 'non-co-operative' nations. These included the Bahamas, Russia, Israel, the Cayman Islands and Liechtenstein. At the G-8 meeting at Fukuoka, Japan, in July 2000, ministers approved a paper that called upon regulators to send official advisory notes to private sector banks, warning them of the risks of dealing with countries that do not take sufficient measures against money-laundering and other financial crimes. By the end of 2000, seven of the listed countries, including Israel, had enacted laws to criminalise money-laundering and to allow closer scrutiny of suspect bank accounts.[63]

A report released by the National Security Council claimed that well-connected networks of international criminals from Russia, China, Nigeria, Italy and the Middle East had embraced globalisation and technology in order to expand their activities. These included terrorism, illegal drug trafficking, smuggling of aliens, trafficking in women and children, copyright violations and motor car theft. (Some have also claimed that the spread of HIV-AIDS is primarily a by-product of the international organised crimes of drug trafficking and prostitution.) The US, along with other countries, promised to sign the United Nations Convention Against Transnational Organised Crime. The document committed the signatories to treat money-laundering, corruption, obstruction of justice and participation in organised criminal gangs, as crimes.[64]

The intentions of such police activities are, however, not always honourable. In January 2001, the Organisation for Economic Co-operation and Development (OECD) held a conference in the Caribbean, at which they hoped to persuade some sixteen 'harmful tax regimes' or 'tax havens' in the region to re-write their tax and privacy laws in accordance with the OECD's Collective Memorandum of Understanding. This would oblige low-tax countries to eliminate tax and privacy laws that attract investment. Tax collectors from OECD nations would then have access to financial accounts, so enabling them to impose taxes on income earned in other countries. Not a single country was persuaded to sign the Memorandum. Indeed, there is overwhelming evidence that money-launderers do not use tax havens and instead access so-called 'correspondent banking relationships' that mainline US banks have with offshore banks.[65] According to Daniel J. Mitchell, many leaders from the Caribbean region view the OECD as a 'rich nation's club arrogantly re-writing the rules of international competition to protect the interests of politicians from high-tax nations.'[66] Mitchell goes on to echo the warning of the leaders of this region, namely that an attack on the financial sector of the region will devastate their economies and lead to economic and political instability. The international financial architecture started to undergo change in 2001. The Bush administration's Treasury Secretary, Paul O'Neill withdrew US support for the OECD's Memorandum. This was because the intention of OECD, according to the Treasury Secretary, was to 'harmonise' the tax regimes around the globe. Instead, the Bush administration favoured negotiating separate treaties with foreign jurisdictions that would call for sharing information on suspect tax cheats. In late 2000, Horst Koehler assumed the post of managing director of the IMF, while six months later, Stanley Fisher announced that he would step down at the end of 2001. In April Koehler pledged the IMF to develop an improved 'early warning system' in order to identify and expose weaknesses in member nations before they became emergencies. At the same time the IMF extended a loan of $19 billion to Turkey. The early warning is regarded by some as an inadequate measure.[67] Furthermore, senior figures in the Republican party have voiced concern at the intermediate position of the IMF. Lying between Western governments and borrower countries, the IMF has allegedly multiplied the so-called 'global moral hazard'. The best move, according to these critics, would be to shut the IMF down.[68]

The launch of the euro, in 1999, meant that the global economy had not one currency managed by a world central bank, but a tripolar system based on the dollar, the euro and the yen. The question is whether there will be a commitment among the Europeans, Japanese, the Americans and the IMF, to guarantee the value of money by establishing stable currencies. Such commitments will be conditional upon: central bankers having the will and the means to defend their fixed exchange rates against speculators; regulation of financial institutions in both tripolar economies and emerging markets; and a convergence of inflation rates between the three blocs. It remains to be seen whether the international regime exhibits the instabilities associated with oligopolies. Whatever form the international financial regime takes, it will be effective only if conditions are conducive to sustaining international co-operation.

GLOBAL OLIGOPOLIES

Other deregulated or reformed regulatory regimes also appear to have become re-ordered into oligopolies. According to Thomson Financial Securities Data, there were 44,518 mergers with a combined value of $2.17 trillion during the twelve years of the Reagan-Bush administrations, and 71,811 corporate deals valued at $6.6 trillion in the seven-and-a-half years of the Clinton administration.[69] In the two decades of deregulation, a handful of carriers, including a new entrant, Southwest Airlines, have come to dominate the domestic and international routes of the United States. If United Airlines' bid to buy USAirway Group Inc., and American Airline's proposed take-over of Trans World Airlines had gone through they would have occupied approximately half of the US domestic air travel market. Air Canada has emerged, effectively, as a monopoly carrier in Canada. Other examples of the consequence of mergers help to illustrate the new phenomenon:

- In 1980, there were forty large railroad companies in the United States. Twenty years later there were just seven, with no more than two serving almost any market.
- The seven Baby Bells have shrunk to four.
- AT&T's acquisition of Media One, means that the company will occupy around a third of the cable television market. Vivendi SA's acquisition of Seagram, with its Universal entertainment interests, further concentrates the entertainment-internet market.
- The Seven Sisters oil companies have shrunk to four.
- Bank mergers in Japan, France, Italy, Spain and the United States are creating oligopolistic structures.
- London, New York and Tokyo combined, hold a third of the world's institutionally managed equities and account for 58 per cent of the global foreign exchange market.[70]
- The Vodafone Group's purchase of the US's Air Touch Communications and Germany's Mannesmann, creates the world's largest wireless carrier.
- Daimler's merger with Chrysler, Renault with Nissan and Ford with Volvo, has created a global oligopoly in autos.
- In commercial aviation, there is a global duopoly of Boeing and Airbus Industries.
- General Electric's purchase of Honeywell, in 2000, further concentrated the aircraft components industry. (Although approved by US anti-trust authorities, twenty European commissioners, in 2001, unanimously rejected the merger.)
- There are four global mining and metals producers and six companies that dominate global advertising.
- Smurfit-Stone, Weyerhaeuser and International Paper, now account for more than 35 per cent of the US domestic linerboard and corrugated box production.
- In accounting, there are five big companies; in soft drinks three: Coca-Cola, Pepsi-Cola and Cadbury- Schweppes.

A century ago, giant corporations were formed to meet the demands of the rapidly growing national marketplace of the United States. Today, a small number of corporations are forming in response to the global economy with its almost instant communications and computer technologies. Opponents of these recent developments echo the charges made by the progressives of a century ago. They lament the loss of competitive markets and their replacement with corporate oligopolies. Competition is a myth, so their argument goes. Competition and a modicum of economic democracy necessitate either the strict application of anti-trust measures or economic planning. The counter-argument is that, to survive and prosper in the global marketplace, corporations have to be allowed to exploit economies of scale and scope. Similarly, corporations in smaller economies, such as Australia and Canada, must grow even to the point of dominating their domestic industry before they can consider competing in the global marketplace.[71]

The consequences of market concentration, global oligopolies and growing transnational entities are ambiguous. Market structures, characterised by a few sellers, are frequently highly competitive, if not always stable. Nor are they necessarily long lasting. Innovation is encouraged and the resulting competition is often the reason why markets fragment. Indeed, it is arguable that concerns over corporate stability have superseded fears of their domination of particular markets. The convergence of deregulation, technical change and freer trade has presented corporations with unprecedented opportunities and enormous risks. The rapid turnover in chief executives testifies to the speed with which the financial markets punish mistakes.

Deregulation has stimulated innovation, but at a cost. There are casualties, for only successful innovators earn profits. The process of creative destruction is underway. When competing companies make the same quality of products in the same way, they tend to cut prices to gain market share. This results in prices dropping to the level of costs. An innovative producer with a new process or product has room to cut prices and gain market share until the innovation is copied or surpassed by rivals. The telecommunications, electricity and financial markets were, until recently, regulated. Markets were protected from competition and earnings were regulated. The incentives to innovate were weak. But this is no longer the case. Investment houses compete with banks. Phone monopolies compete with wireless companies. Electrical utilities compete with independent electricity generators.

When the corporate decision involves technological innovation, the costs and risks can be enormous. The former monopoly telecommunication operators in Europe and North America are struggling in the deregulated, competitive and high-risk markets. AT&T spent $100 billion on buying high-speed Internet access companies, but found itself in a price-squeeze on its long-distance telephone market, as Sprint and WorldCom, in competition, forced prices downwards. AT&T just did not make the right innovations with which to restore its profit margins and had to re-organise.

The electrical utilities in California were hampered by expensive plants, and simply could not survive by buying at high prices and supplying to consumers at lower, regulated rates. Only a very short time ago, these two industries - telecommunications and the utilities - were considered by the financial markets to be almost risk-free blue chips. Their vulnerability and debts could herald a change in attitude.

The size of the telecommunications and utility companies no longer poses the threat of market domination, but defaulting on their debts could overwhelm the financial markets and greatly damage the banks that have lent them money. As their deregulated, competitive markets are now subjected to creative destruction, politicians will be tempted to regard them, and possibly the large financial institutions, as 'too big to be allowed to fail.'

Figures purporting to describe market structure can also be misleading. Fragmented markets yield producers whose products are often more costly to consumers, while the losers are sometimes successful in acquiring government protection. One of the threats to the open trading regimes is the uneconomical 'big steel' producers of the United States, who have been attempting to persuade Congress to impose a selective steel quota. In some cases, transnational entities offer opportunities to courageous entrepreneurs that are denied them in their own communities. Alternatively, while transnational entities may be able to reduce trading barriers, they may be tempted to introduce price-fixing and market share agreements. In approving and harnessing the talents of people, irrespective of their backgrounds, transnational enterprises threaten the loyalties of the subjects and citizens of their nation states. One of the emerging issues will be the number and form of transnational entities that successfully transcend the ethnic, cultural and religious division to form truly global enterprises.

CULTURE, FREEDOM AND GLOBALISATION

Globalising broadcasting systems are seen by some to threaten cultural and ethnic identities. Telecommunications and the communications media can serve to enhance the citizens' autonomy, holding governments and entities of authority to account, or, alternatively, they can be used to attenuate autonomy, shackling their citizens to systems of authority, facilitating totalitarianism rather than liberty. Although satellite broadcasting and the spread of cables has made the control of communications much more difficult, the entry of private carriers and broadcasters has balkanised many national telecommunications and broadcasting industries, undermining the government owned-system of cross-subsidisation that underpinned the provision of the public good.

These global communication regimes have not passed unnoticed among democratic socialists. Their counter-attack is grounded on the distinction between the consumer and the citizen. In a democracy, citizens should have similar rights, expressed through the market. They reject the privatisation and deregulation of communication systems because they merely open the door to American and European domination. Instead, they advocate a policy of re-regulation. It should be one of maximum possible de-commodification and should re-embed the communications media in the social life of civil society - for this, they argue, is a vital condition of freedom from state and market ownership.[72]

In the United States, questions have been raised at the assertion that corporate consolidations would enhance competition and diversity and thereby serve the public interest. Indeed, an argument has been put forward asserting that competition alone cannot produce a quality product. Critics of the proposed AOL-Time Warner merger have argued that news and entertainment would be retained in an ever-diminishing number of hands. Time Warner is a very large entertainment company with both a major motion picture studio and a major record label in its portfolio. Furthermore, Time Warner controls the country's second-largest cable television company, while AOL is the largest Internet company. One argument was that the merged behemoth would be able to encase customers in a 'walled garden' of its own programme content and so prevent them from obtaining news and entertainment from competitors.

In the spring of 2000, Time Warner found itself in a tussle over contracts with the Walt Disney Company. Time Warner briefly blacked-out Disney over its cable systems. This display of power evidently caused the Federal Trade Commission (FTC) to consider forcing Time Warner to open their cable systems to multiple competing Internet access services in each market.[73] In December 2000, the FTC approved the merger after the two companies had agreed to such restrictions on their conduct.[74] The argument was that, without this agreement, broadband could have stayed captive to cable operator-owned Internet services such as Road Runner, which is owned, jointly, by Time Warner and At Home.

On 12 January 2001, a year and a day after America Online and Time Warner had announced their intention to merge, the FCC granted permission for the merger. There were conditions attached. Fearing that the merged company would exploit its dominance over instant messaging by monopolising related Internet services that might be developed for high-speed cable connections, the FCC stipulated that AOL's instant-messaging be made compatible with the systems of Internet rivals. AOL's instant messaging allows 140 million computer users to communicate in real time. Competing services are offered by a number of companies, including Microsoft and Yahoo. Under the ruling, should AOL upgrade its Instant Messenger and ICQ services, for instance, by allowing the exchange of live video, it will have to make them compatible in under six months, with the software of at least two rivals. William E. Kennard, the retiring chairman of the FCC, claimed that by making interconnect possible, the FCC hoped to avoid a repeat of AT&T's growth into a monopoly 'that effectively shut out any competitors by making its telephone system incompatible with those of rivals.'[75]

There were dissenters to these rulings. Incoming chairman of the FCC, Michael K. Powell, wrote that this 'order makes clear that the FCC has jurisdiction to regulate virtually every Internet product.' The two commissions were not only using the merger to impose regulatory controls, but they clearly intended to set the rules within which the Internet will evolve. Some see these rules as stripping companies of their property rights. This is a development that would deter investment in innovation.[76]

The flow of information over the Internet is no longer uninterrupted. The real-space location of Web users is beginning to determine the virtual places they can visit. The governments of France and Germany want to block Nazi sites; the United States tries to prosecute offshore gambling sites; China, Saudi Arabia, Singapore and others try to censor sites for political or religious reasons.[77] According to data collected in 2000, the Internet harbours more than two thousand groups promoting anti-Semitism or white supremacy. Organisations such as the Wiesenthal Centre have exerted pressure on online services and shopping sites to stop the proliferation of these sites in the belief that such actions will eradicate these hatreds. Yahoo's response, for instance, was that it wished to avoid becoming a safe haven for hate, but at the same time it wanted to provide a neutral area for users.[78] The company was ordered, in November 2000, to use filtering technology to block hate-promoting material from appearing on computers in France or face fines equivalent to $13,000 a day.

OPPOSING GLOBALISATION

Others have challenged the Washington Consensus of market capitalism. To some critics, open markets, free trade in goods, information and capital do not constitute a universal civilisation. Huntington has argued that imperialism is the necessary, but unwanted, consequence of universalising market capitalism.[79] Others argue that 'corporate-led economic global-isation, as expressed and encouraged by the rules of global trade and investment,' is leading to destructive volatility in global financial markets. This deliberately designed economic globalisation is leading to dislocation in all regions. Furthermore, all peoples of the world 'have been made tragically dependent upon the arbitrary, self-interested acts of giant corporations, bankers and speculators.' Rules of the deregulated global market 'suppress the abilities of local economies and nations that protect resources, public health and human rights.' The success of this 'never ending expansion of markets, resources and consumers' is failing to achieve social equality and a meaningful livelihood for all. As a result, 'social unrest, economic and ecological breakdown are the inevitabilities of such a system.'[80]

George Soros, the famous hedge fund billionaire and philanthropist, does not adhere to this conspiratorial thesis of monopoly capitalism but argues that the globalisation of the capitalist system is subject to weaknesses.[81] Indeed, he claims that the threat to his notion of the open society does not emanate from either communism or fascism, but from the capitalist system. Soros argues that capital is more mobile than labour and portfolio investors enjoy greater freedom than do investors of fixed investment. Capital is attracted to financial centres, which are increasing in size and importance. Capital's mobility favours capital over labour and the financial centres over the extractive and industrial peripheries. But financial markets are inherently unstable. Investors exhibit a herd instinct, producing a cycle of boom and bust. Such oscillations, in turn, can cause serious economic and social dislocations.

Despite these statements, economist Paul Krugman alleged that Mr. Soros had taken advantage of his privileged position and engaged in insider trading of the 'real,' the currency of Brazil. This currency fell sharply in early 1999. Later, Professor Krugman withdrew his allegation.[82] Bhagwati is one who has also suggested the operation of an information network. 'Few would deny,' he says, 'the role of Wall Street lobbyists - with the acquiescence of Treasury officials - who pushed for breaking down capital account restrictions worldwide and helped precipitate, among other things, the Asian financial crisis.'[83]

Underpinning the approach of some critics is an opposition to the 'totalising' notions of modernisers with their grandiose notions of the Enlightenment. They reject the so-called revelation of eternal and immutable qualities of humanity that emerged from the reinforcing growth of science, rationality and universal freedom. In particular, these critics oppose the consequences of economic rationality, in which work is solely for the purpose of commodity exchange. Regulated by money or the state, the costs of this order emerge in the form of 'pathologies' or dislocations of the real-life world. The untrammelled market is destroying the complimentary institutions and networks that facilitate a functioning market. Instability is engendered, while the autonomy of the individual is undermined. The central problem is seen to be 'the limits inside which economic rationality is to operate.'[84]

These critics purpose to constrain economic rationality and to convert global markets and transnational corporations. Their true function is to promote the cohesion of societies and the integrity of citizens and the states in

which they live.   Sociologist Anthony Giddens has stated that 'we have to
produce a politics which allows us to create an inclusive society locally,
nationally, and globally, and to harness these processes for the betterment of
human beings.'[85] Presumably, these social needs of the citizen, such as
diversification, are to be articulated by the elite planner and substituted for
the consumers' wants as expressed through the market and the polity. Some
advocate a framework of global regulation of currencies, capital movements,
trade and environmental conservation. Others suggest limiting capital flows
by taxing short-term movements.   A second UN Security Council for
Economic Affairs, to include the smaller developing countries, has been
advocated.[86]

George Soros has called for an International Credit Insurance Corporation
to guarantee loans made to periphery countries.   The resources for this
venture would come from taxpayers in the G-7 countries. Henry Kaufman, a
Wall Street economist, would create what he calls a Board of Overseers of
Major International Institutions.   This body would establish uniform
accounting and lending standards, monitor performance, set minimum capital
requirements for all institutions and impose discipline on those who fail to
meet these standards by limiting their ability to lend, borrow, and sell.[87]

Despite such critiques, it would appear that collectivism, not capitalism, is
in crisis. Collectivists, it is argued, operate within an outdated conception.
Thanks to the opening of possibilities, due to bio-technology and information
technology, the issue is not the Malthusian concern with diminishing returns.
Nor is the issue whether global markets operate according to an order that is
linked with nature in the form of common patterns that could be
equilibrating.[88]   The issues emerge from the collision of the seemingly
chaotic market processes with defined states. There are now one hundred and
eighty-five nation states in the United Nations. There are a number of points
at which an increasingly competitive global economic system is in conflict
with the interests that the politicians and leaders of these nation states claim
to represent.

In the United States, some analysts are concerned that income distribution
is growing more inequitably.[89] Others feel that the demotion of fiscal policy
and the ascendancy of financial policy lessens the participation of elected
representatives and places increasing power among people who are not
elected and are, therefore, not accountable to the electorate.   Similarly,
international financial policy has effectively replaced foreign policy, with a
resulting reduction in accountability.[90]

Some analysts see the growing differences between the elite labour force
in the knowledge sector and the mass work force as the nub of a growing
crisis. This is allegedly heightened by globalisation, which lowers wages and
generates unemployment.   The dynamics of the competitive system are

implicitly assumed to result, not in some positive adjustment, but in a crisis. The consequent 'new' inequality - the increasing income, wealth, and opportunity gap - will, it is predicted, lead to social unrest, rising crime levels and violence.   This can, and should, be averted not by attenuating technological change and trade, but by changing the set of incentives. Jeremy Rifkin argued in his 1995 book, 'The End of Work,' that the new technologies should be used to generate more leisure rather than, as he alleged was happening, to offer less pay and to increase under-employment. His argument was used to support the legalisation of the 35-hour working week in France.

Professors Bruce Ackerman and Anne Alstott, in their 1999 book, 'Stakeholder Society,' address the issue of equality of opportunity.   They propose to increase equality of opportunity within the system by guaranteeing, as a matter of fundamental right, $80,0000 to every citizen at his or her twenty-first birthday.

The movement of corporations and labour across the globe presents challenges to all political systems.   To what extent can corporations engage foreign labour without threatening the national identity of the host countries? Can national corporations be downsized and can transnational entities be accommodated?   These are multifaceted issues that threaten the foundations upon which many nation states are anchored.   They also threaten the political system for they mean relinquishing influence over interest rates, monetary policy and immigration, while retaining responsibility for levels of employment, rates of growth and social cohesiveness.

The pessimism expressed over globalisation, the democratisation of technology and the threats to the governments' monopoly of coercive force, is reminiscent of that expressed at the turn of the twentieth century. Thanks to the railway, the mail and the telephone, time and space were shrinking. It took man two million years to invent the wheel, and then only 5,000 to propel them with a steam engine.   Those who had abiding confidence in technological progress and those who believed that human behaviour could be understood scientifically, and, therefore, could be predicted, more than matched the pessimists in number.   Forecasters noted a century ago, that trains travelled ten times faster than the mail coaches of a century before. According to their extrapolations, by the year 2000, trains would be travelling at six hundred miles an hour.   Air travel was imagined, but by dirigible and used primarily as an intra-urban mode.   H.G.Wells thought the wireless telegraph would make it possible to replace news dailies with 'hourly papers.' However, he thought this would be too much news for the reader and would be a commercial failure.   What he was implying was that machines may be predictable, but human behaviour was not.

In the last transforming decade, electronic mail, faxes and voice-mail, along with cellular phones, have come into common use. In the next decade, advances in high temperature superconductors, improved voice-activated computers, optical electronics and the arrival of new materials could see profound changes in the way we live. At hand are radically new developments. Included in these are the active use of super-efficient power lines, jetliners carrying up to eight hundred people, trains that fly on cushions of electromagnetic energy, wrist-sized cellular phones, light, as an information–processing medium, and voice-recognition technology becoming standard in most sorts of electronic information-processing devices. The Word Wide Web is likely to be transformed by the protocol known as Extendable Markup Language (EML). EML organises data so that computers can communicate directly without human intervention and so make possible the emergence of automated global markets.

These technical innovations will be the result of the continuous processes of trial and error engendered by relatively free and open societies. Their consequences are not predictable, for the universe is not deterministic. Similarly those who wish to impose a re-imaging of this universe cannot guarantee that the unintended consequences resulting from their impositions will necessarily be positive.

Notes

1. Crandall, Robert and Jerry Ellig (1997), Economic Deregulation and Customer Choice: Lessons for the Electrical Industry, Fairfax, Virginia, Center for Market Processes.
2. Robson, John E. (1988), 'Airline Deregulation,' *Regulation*, **21**(2), Spring.
3. Morrison, Steven A. and Clifford Winston (1995), *The Evolution of the Airline Industry*, Washington DC, Brookings Institution.
4. Junniot, Pierre J. (2000), 'State of the Industry,' Address to 56th IATA AGM, Sydney, Australia, 5 June.
5. 2000 Internet Economy Indicators, Cisco Systems, located at: http://www.internetindicators.com/features/html
6. International Telecommunication Union (1997), *World Telecommunication Development Report 1996/7. Trade in telecommunications*, Geneva, February.
7. Kelley, Tim and Mark Woodall (2000), 'Telecom Traffic Indicators,' ITU, March 2000.
8. Lukas, Aaron. (2000) 'Globalization and Developing Countries,' Center for Trade Policy Studies. Washington D.C. Cato Institute, 20 June.
9. Cooper, Richard N. (1999), 'Should Capital Controls be Banished?' *Brookings Papers on Economic Activity*, **1**, p.98.
10. Greenspan, Alan (1999), 'Trade and Technology,' speech before the Minnesota Meeting, Minnesota, 30 September, The Federal Reserve Board.
11. Junniot, Pierre J., op.cit.
12. UN Conference on Trade and Development (1998*), The Least Development Countries 1998 Report*. Overview :http://www.unctad.org/en/docs/lde98/ove/df
13. Jacobs, Margaret T. (1998), 'Some Big Companies Swear Off Y2K Suites,' *The Wall Street Journal*, 30 November.
14. Robyn, Charmers (1998), 'Continent must Tune in the Global Vision,' *Business Day*, 12 May; Simon, John (1998), 'White House to Unveil Plans to Expand Internet Projects in Developing Nations,' *The Wall Street Journal*, 30 November.

15. ITU (1998), World Telecommunication Development Report, Universal Access, Geneva, March, p.14.
16. Weller, Christian (1998), 'In Focus: Global Banking,' Foreign Policy in Focus, http:// www.foreignpolicy-infocus.org/briefs/vol3/v3n9gl.html
17. Golub, Stephen S.(1999), *Labor Costs and International Trade,* Washington D.C: American Enterprise Institute, p.15.
18. World Bank (1999), *Global Development Finance 1999*, Washington DC.
19. Felix, David (1998), 'In Focus: IMF Bailouts and Global Financial Flows,' *Foreign Policy in Focus*, 1998.
    http:// www.foreignpolicy-infocus.org/briefs/vol3/v3n5fimf.html
20. World Bank (2000), *Global Development Finance 2000*, Chapter 6, Washington D.C.
21. World Bank (1998), 'World Bank Predicts Lowest Growth Rates For Developing Countries Since Eighties' Debt Crisis,' News Release No. 99/2016/S Washington DC, 2 December.
22. Preston, Julia (1999), 'Runaway Banks Without Brakes: Mexico's $71 Billion Lesson,' *The New York Times*, 22 July.
23. Roher, Larry (2000), ' Brazil Collides with IMF over a Plan to Aid the Poor,' *The New York Times*, 21 February.
24. Malpas, David (1999), 'A Leadership Vacuum in International Economics,' *The Wall Street Journal,* 19 April.
25. Gaddy, Clifford.G. and Barry W. Ickes (1998), 'Russia's Virtual Economy,' *Foreign Affairs*, September/October. pp.54 and 62.
26. Anderson, Perry (1992), *A Zone of Engagement*, London: Verso.
27. Harvey, David (1989), *The Condition of Post-Modernity*, Oxford: Blackwell, p.55.
28. Gray, John (1998), *False Dawn: The Delusions of Global Capitalism*. London: Grante.
29. Glassman, James K. (2000), 'Forget Kyoto,' The *Wall Street Journal*,' 28 November.
30. Krauthammer, Charles (2001), 'Yet another "crisis,' *The Miami Herald*, 16 February.
31. Harvey, David , op.cit., p.55.
32. Hutton, Will (1995), *The State We're In,* London, Jonathan Cape, p.312.
33. Ibid., p.294. See also Keegan, William (1993), *The Spectre of Capitalism. The Future of the World's Economy After the Fall of Communism*, Reading, Berks.: Vintage, p.190.
34. Gerson, Mark and Lehrman, Thomas (1998), 'Most Hedge Funds Play it Safe,' *The Wall Street Journal,* 10 October. Abilson, Reed (1998), 'Survey Shows Big Growth in Hedge Fund Popularity,' *The New York Times*, 1 October.
35. Wayne, Leslie (1998), 'Congress to Debate Greater Oversight of Hedge Funds,' *The New York Times*, 1 October.
36. Soros, George (1998), 'The Crisis of Global Capitalism,' *The Wall Street Journal*, 15 September.
37. Schlesinger, Jacob M, 'Long-Term Capital Bailout Spotlights a Fed 'Radical' (1998), *The Wall Street Journal*, 2 November.
38. Plender, John (1998), 'Western Crony Capitalism,' *Financial Times*, Weekend, 3 October.
39. Cooper, Richard N., op.cit., p.123.
40. Krugman, Paul (1998), 'Dr. Mabuse Returns,' (1998), *The New York Times Magazine*, 8 November.
41. Bhagwati, Jagdish (1998), 'Yes to Free Trade, Maybe to Capital Controls,' *The Wall Street Journal*, 16 November.
42. In 1972 Professor James Tobin of Yale proposed a tax on unproductive currency speculation as a means of stabilizing the international monetary system. In France, a pressure group, the Association for the Taxation of Financial Transactions for the Aid of Citizens (Attac), has been formed to implement this proposal. Attac estimates currency speculators trade over $1.8 trillion dollars each day. Each trade would be taxed at 0.1 to 0.25 per cent of volume. If imposed, short-term currency trades would decline, leaving long-term productive investments. Governments would now be able to intervene in order to protect their own currency from devaluation and financial crises. The revenue generated ,estimated between $100-$300 billion a year, could go into earmarked trust funds to fund 'urgent international projects.'

43. Krugman, Paul (1999), *The Return of Depression Economics*. New York: W.W. Norton, pp.121-123.
44. Soros claims he 'refrained' from speculating against the franc. Soros, George (1994), *The Alchemy of Finance*, New York: John Wiley &Sons, Inc. pp.5-6.
45. Weinstein, Michael, (1998), 'Twisting Controls on Currency and Capital,' *The New York Times*, 10 September. Kristoff, Nicholas D. (1998), 'Experts Question Roving Flow of Global Capital,' *The New York Times*, 20 September. Wessels, David and Bob Davis (1998), 'Would-Be-Keynesians Vie Over How to Fight Global Financial Woes,' *The Wall Street Journal*, 25 September; Morgenthau, Robert M. (1998), 'On the Trail of Global Capital,' *The New York Times*, 9 November.
46. Friedman, Milton (1998), 'Markets to the Rescue,' *The Wall Street Journal*, 13 October.
47. Yavlinsky, Gregory (1998), 'Russia's Phony Capitalism,' *Foreign Affairs*, May/June, p.69.
48. Stiglitz, Joseph (2000), 'The Insider. What I learned at the world economic crisis,' *The New Republic*, 17 and 24 April.
49. Thornhill, John and Charles Clover (1999), 'The Robbery of Nations,' *Financial Times Weekend*, August 21/22.
50. GAO-01-8 'Foreign Assistance of Russia'.
51. Melloan, George (2000), 'A Short Primer on What the IMF is All About,' *The Wall Street Journal*, 7 March.
52. Sachs, Jeffrey. D. and Allan Meltzer (2000), 'A Blueprint for IMF Reform,' *The Wall Street Journal*, 8 March.
53. Williamson, John (2000), *A Guide to The Reports,* Washington DC: Institute for International Economics, May.
54. Summers, Lawrence (1999), 'The Right Kind of IMF for a Stable Global Financial System,' speech at the London Business School, December.
55. Editorial (1999), 'Lopsided Growth,' The *Wall Street Journal*, 19 April.
56. IMF (1999), 'Proposals to Strengthen the Initiative for the Heavily Indebted Poor Countries (HIPCs),' 23 September. See www.imf.org/external/np/hipc/proposal.htm.
57. Hanke, Steve H. (2001), 'IMF-Early Warning Should Start on the Web,' *The Wall Street Journal*, 1 May.
58. Editorial (2001), 'Fix the Fund' *The Wall Street Journal*, 25 May.
59. Brown, Gordon (1999), 'Toward a Strong World Financial System,' *The Wall Street Journal*, 30 April.
60. Sanger, David (1999), 'Rubin Proposes Modest Limits on Lending Risk,' *The New York Times*, 22 April.
61. World Bank, 'Global Development Finance 2000, Overview,' pp.4-5.
62. Oppel, Richard. A. Jr. (1999), 'Hedge -Fund Report Raises Few Wall Street Hackles,' *The Wall Street Journal,* 30 April.
63. 'Capital movements become allocationally efficient in a world of widespread potential for tax evasion only if marginal tax rates on capital are harmonized and if national tax authorities cooperate sufficiently closely to reduce evasion on capital income to negligible levels.' Cooper, Richard N., op.cit., p.106.
64. Kahn, Joseph, (2000), '15 Countries Named as Potential Money-laundering Havens,' *The New York Times*, 23 December.
65. Editorial (2001), 'Global Money Launderers,' *The New York Times*, 22 December.
66. Kahn, Joseph and Judith Miller (2000), 'Getting Tough On Gangsters, High Tech and Global,' *The New York Times*, 15 December.
67. Beckett, Paul (2001), 'Dirty-Money Flow in US Banks Is Huge, a Senate Report Finds,' *The Wall Street Journal*, 5 February.
68. Mitchell, Daniel, J. (2001) 'OECD Nations Want Caribbean Tax Havens To Tell All,' *The Wall Street Journal*, 19 January.
69. Labaton, Stephen (2000), 'Oligopoly,' *The New York Times*, 11 June.
70. Sassen, Saskia (1999), 'Global Financial Centres,' *Foreign Affairs*, January/February, p.77.
71. Gaylord, Becky (2001) 'Mergers in Australia Stir A Debate Over Competition,' *The New York Times*, 20 February.

72. '... exemplify and foreshadow the general principle: communications media should not be at the whim of 'market forces' but rather placed within a political and legal framework which specifies and enforces tough minimum safeguards in matters of ownership structures, regional scheduling, programme content and decision making procedures.' Keane, John (1992), 'Democracy and the Media – Without Foundation,' *Political Studies*, **XL**(116), Special Issue, p.117.

73. Labaton, Stephen (2000), 'Some Tangled Issues Kept FTC on Edge During Negotiations,' *The New York Times*, 15 December.

74. The companies agreed to open their cable lines to competing Internet services and to accept continued federal monitoring of their progress in this area. Angwin, Julia (2000), 'FTC Approves AOL-Time Warner Deal,' *The Wall Street Journal*, 15 December.

75. Labaton, Stephen (2001), 'F.C.C. Approves AOL-Time Warner Deal, With Conditions,' *The New York Times*, 12 January.

76. Glassman, James K. (2001), 'The FCC's Dangerous Internet Precedent,' *The Wall Street Journal*, 17 January.

77. Glater, Jonathan D. (2001), 'Hemming in the World Wide Web,' *The New York Times*, 7 January.

78. Guernsey, Lisa (2000), 'Mainstream Sites Serve as Portals to Hate,' *The New York Times*, 30 November.

79. Huntington, Samuel P.(1997), *The Clash of Civilisations and the Remaking of World Order*, London: Touchstone Books.

80. The Sienna Declaration. 'Should the People who Caused the Problems be the Ones to Create the Solutions?' *The New York Times*, 20 November 1998. Statement of the International Forum on Globalisation.

81. Soros, George (1998), 'Towards a World Wide Open Society,' *Johannesburg Star*, 5 January; Soros, George (1998), 'New Body is Needed to Regulate Markets,' *Business Day*,5 January.

82. O'Brien, Timothy L. (1999), 'Columnist Backs Off Soros Charges,' *The New York Times*, 18 February. 'In March 1999, the Brazilian central bank said that it was conducting an investigation into charges that nine banks used access to government officials in the days leading up to the January 13 policy shift to make trading decisions resulting in a combined project of roughly $ 1 billion.' Romero, Simon (1999), 'Brazilian Central Bank Plans A Currency Insider Inquiry,' *The New York Times*, 1 April.

83. Bhagwati, Jagdish (1999), 'It's a Small World After All,' *The Wall Street Journal*, 3 May.

84. Gorz, A. (1989), *Critique of Economic Reason*. London: Verso, p.127.

85. Giddens, Anthony ' The Second Globalization Debate,' *Edge*. See www.edge.org.

86. Cohen, Roger (1998), 'Redrawing the Free Market,' *The New York Times*, 14 November.

87. Haass, Richard N and Robert E. Latan (1998), 'Globalization and its Discontents,' *Foreign Affairs*, May/June 1988, p.4.

88. In pursuing the ideal of a unified science, proponents of what is called the 'science of complexity,' argue that soon shall be known the principles of order that link the worlds of chemical, biological, economic, social and cultural phenomena. All, it is claimed, are drawn to organise themselves into patterns. See Waldorf, Mitchell M. (1993), *The Emerging Science at the Edge of Order and Chao,* New York: Simon and Schuster.

89. Schlesinger, Jacob M. (2000), 'Working Full Time Is No Longer Enough,' *The Wall Street Journal*, 29 June.

90. Reich, Robert B. (1998), 'The Real Policy Makers,' *The New York Times*, 29 September.

4. Ideologues, Entrepreneurs and Explanations

INTRODUCTION

As was shown in Chapter 1, the regulation of the railroads constituted the divide between the era of *laissez-faire*, the era from which the railroads emerged, and the beginning of the era of mass industrial order driven by the state.

Under Britain's hegemony, and subject to the rules of the gold standard, labour and capital were free to flow where individuals considered them to be most productive. It was this freedom to move between markets, reflecting high transport costs and limited information, that established the key characteristic of this era, the separation of markets and the movement of capital and labour between them. The widespread use of the motor car, the aircraft, the telegraph and the telephone forged and cemented the links between these disparate markets.

However, at the turn of the new century, despite the rising prosperity of the participating states, in the emerging domestic market of the United States, opposition mounted to the intrusion of foreign competition and foreign immigration.

Then, in 1914, the open international system, by then fifty years old, gave way to a more restricted and regimented international regime as the erstwhile participants in that open system confronted one another in one of the bloodiest conflicts of all time. Moreover, after 1918, during the inter-war years, economies moved off the gold standard and operated behind protective tariffs. Open regimes were clearly not irreversible, as many had hoped; on the contrary, the global market of the mass industrial order became encased within a neo-mercantilist superstructure.

It was only in the 1970s that these regulatory structures started to crumble as the United States and Canada moved to dismantle the regulations that had encased, for most of the century, their transport, communication, energy and monetary markets.

After the Second World War, the Soviet Union devoted its energies, backed by a well-oiled propaganda machine, to an unrelenting global

126

campaign against the spread and establishment of democratic capitalism. This Herculean effort, however, came to a rather abrupt end when, in the early 1990s, a confluence of changes in the international arena occurred that offered an enormous opportunity to proponents of the free market to promote the market-orientated philosophy.

This was accomplished through what came to be known as the 'Washington Consensus.' Quite fortuitously, the Soviet empire had imploded at the very time that the 1990 US-Canada free trade agreement, establishing a customs union across the northern half of the continent, had successfully been launched. Suddenly, proponents of an inclusive, democratic and market order found themselves in the happy position of being able to contrast the patent success of the US-Canada market, comprising two democratic, capitalist and inclusive societies, with the degeneracy and ultimate failure of the Soviet's centrally-planned, totalitarian system.

Four years later, following the signing of the North American Free Trade Agreement (NAFTA), the North American market was extended into Mexico. Emboldened by the surging performance of the US economy, officials of the Clinton administration vigourously began to promote market-oriented policies through the forum of the World Trade Organisation (WTO), institutions of the World Bank and the International Monetary Fund (IMF). The Washington Consensus, according to Fred Bergsten of the Institute for International Economics, 'gained near-universal approval and provided a guiding ideology and underlying intellectual consensus for the world economy.'[1] The resulting policy of globalisation entailed, quite simply, the opening of markets around the world to foreign trade and investment on a scale never before possible. Globalisation was sold to the governing elites in what become known as the 'emerging markets' on the premise that it 'spurs economic growth, and growth raises living standards.'[2] The underlying assertion, supported by empirical evidence, was that there was a positive, causal link between economic freedom and economic growth.

During the second Clinton term, the policy of globalisation went through a metamorphosis, extending the concept of freedom beyond the economic sphere. The promoters of globalisation, no longer satisfied with the plain assertion that the necessary conditions for the successful launch of inclusive, decentralised, market-based orders consisted in the existence of constitutional guarantees of human and minority rights and a democratic polity, strove to separate free markets from universalised human and minority rights. The point is well illustrated by the following statement, made by Strobe Talbot, US Deputy Secretary of State in the Clinton administration, in the wake of the US led NATO attack on Serbia over that country's treatment of the inhabitants of Kosovo. He asserted that:

...the way a government treats its own people is not just an 'internal matter', it is the business of the international community, for there are issues of both universal values and regional peace at stake. This principle gives American diplomacy a template for supporting self-determination without necessarily encouraging secessionism.[3]

This new alliance between international liberals and unilateral neo-conservatives, the 'New Wilsonianism,'[4] has stirred a debate within the international community between those who support international intervention designed to preserve both lives and democratic institutions and those whose purpose is to assert the primacy of the interests of nation-states.[5] The subsequent actions of the Clinton administration, however, have prompted some to suggest that the administration was always more interested in opening markets than in improving human rights, in enhancing democracy or in serving the interests of nation-states. The sceptics have argued that the admittance of China to the WTO has shown that markets come before human rights.

Other commentators have detected a determinism in the process of globalisation. Noting the relentless advance of information technology, they have asserted that this shows that globalisation was inevitable and irreversible.[6] Their argument is that technical advances are dependent on the free flow of ideas and their message to dictatorships is that liberty is the price of sustainable economic prosperity. This deterministic thesis also has a corollary, namely that because the players, acting through the global market, now wield a stick, there is no need for the carrot. States that abuse human rights, persecute minorities, trample on democracy and oppose the market in information will witness the swift flight of capital and skilled labour and a resulting economic decline. Proponents of one-party systems of government and crony capitalists will soon get the message: change or lose out.

Nevertheless, as was argued in the closing section of Chapter 2, there remain those who are critical of the idea that a democratic, capitalistic order constitutes a universal civilisation worth striving for. Indeed, the assumption of global obligations and the propagation of American liberty are, to a Marxian, nothing but calculated deceptions.

In his view, the ruling class of the United States is propagating, ruthlessly executing and profiting greatly from a coercive neo-imperialist strategy under which 'the flag stays home, while the dollar goes everywhere - frequently assisted by the sword.'[7] The good news emanating from the capitalist press of an integrating global economy, in which living standards are converging, is, in Marxian eyes, mere propaganda. As ever, he argues, the world economy of capitalism is made up of interdependent and unequal zones. The Third World is subjected to an 'intensely exploitative form of dependent capitalism' into which investors go, not to uplift, but to enrich themselves.

China and India, he concedes, have been the exceptions, but only because they have prudently placed restrictions on the flows of international trade and private capital investment.

But elsewhere, he believes, it is a picture of unmitigated gloom. The transitional economies of the former Soviet block have been looted. The wealthy capitalist countries - the Group of Seven - trade and invest in one another's economies while the emerging markets - the Asian tigers and some Latin American countries - have been devastated by the fickle capital market. The resulting flows of capital, goods, technology and organisations are causing dangerous divergences that threaten to destabilise the global order. The failed states of sub-Saharan Africa, the Balkans and the former Soviet Empire are propelling millions of migrants to Europe's borders. The North American economies, likewise, face ever-growing migrations from the impoverished Caribbean, Central American and Andean economies.

Moreover, Marxian analysts are sceptical about the concatenation of forces that have shaped the global economy. What, they (and others) ask, were the constituent dimensions of Western civilisation that were decisive in establishing the region's precedence in technology and in the invention of the reinforcing culture of modernity? Did the market really emerge autonomously in the West? If so, what are the implications for Non-western societies? Can development models ever be effective?

Some have questioned the supposition that large-scale historical change can be explained as the product of a set of structural transformations alone. History clearly involves human intervention. Are there links between structure and human agency, and, if so, how do they aid explanation?

The Marxian interpretation, unlike most others, relies explicitly on the role of the ruling class or elite. The class that controls the means of production controls the bourgeois state. Although it may pretend otherwise, the ruling class exercises power exclusively in its own interest. Ironically, Milovan Djilas, who observed the power structure in the communist state, found the same phenomenon there. He defined the new ruling class as that which comes to power, not with the aim of implanting a new economic order, but to establish its power over society. Over time, the new class grows stronger than the party.

Pareto also distinguished between a governing elite, which dominates politics, and a non-governing elite. But Neo-Paretians argue that there are numerous competing elites, which rise by capturing the power structures.

In his writings, C. Wright Mills has also identified the group that wields power within the ruling institutions of the modern state, not as class but as an elite.[8]

On a somewhat different tack, Michael Young, in his 1958 study, 'The Rise of the Meritocracy, 1970-2033', discerned the emergence of what he called an 'aristocracy of talent' that was replacing an aristocracy of birth. Nurtured by the education system, an elite in the form of a meritocracy that takes charge of government.

Lasch has defined today's power elite as 'those who control the international flow of money and information, preside over philanthropic foundations and institutions of higher learning, manage the instruments of cultural production and thus set the terms of public debate.'[9] The meritocracy that forms a new elite, whose members are 'symbolic analysts'[10]- people who specialise in the interpretation and deployment of symbolic information - includes practitioners of economics. It is, perhaps, because academic economists are ensconced in the meritocracy, that their research work takes the structure of power as given. Few see themselves as the favoured few who monopolise positions in education. The growth of complex epistemic communities, nurtured by numerous policy research institutions, in which economists play important roles, are not considered by economists to constitute part of a class, meritocracy or elite with common interests. At best, these institutions are seen to be producing normative analyses (as well as being a source of contract income). At worst, they are seen to be fronts for special interests. But then competing special interests are assumed eventually to cancel one another out.

Conspiracies are the stuff of novels and are not the subject of research. The Sherman Act and the SEC cover the unhealthy phenomenon of collusion, when it occurs, but its practice is assumed to disappear, as a matter of course, as markets become competitive. Unencumbered by such non-quantifiable variables as power and ideology, most academic economists proceed to explore the limits of their value-free experiments in deduction.

Journalists have not been so reticent. They have cheerfully ignored the thin line between positive and normative analysis and produced ideological tracts that have either enthused over or condemned the global system that they see as having replaced the Cold War system. Many can be regarded as tracts that support or attack the interests of the elite.[11] Some commentators, such as Thomas Friedman, have asserted a form of technical determinism, that, in the words of Eichengreen, 'everything we need to know about recent history flows from the microchip.' Everything, from the fall of the Berlin Wall, to the opening of trading regimes, has been inevitable because information technology has made it impossible to sustain totalitarian and autarchic systems.

Wright's historical analysis counters such assertions by showing that there have been few political systems that have granted their subjects broad access to the available information technology. As Wright has pointed out, polities that 'fail to respect this liberating logic tend to get punished with relative poverty. Far from being new, this is to some extent the story of history.'[12]

As was pointed out in Chapter 2, the spread of the Internet in the United States owes much to the regulatory preferences granted by the FCC, while the explosive growth in transactions over the Internet is due, in some part, to Congress's tax concession. Similarly, the highly controversial removal of capital-account restrictions in emerging markets was not, according to Bhagwati, the inevitable result of advances in information technology but rather the outcome of the co-ordinated efforts of US Treasury officials and self-interested Wall Street financial interests.[13] In sum, policy makers, not impersonal technological advances, impose and remove barriers to exchange through markets.

These and other questions are raised in the following section, 'Explaining the Transformations,' in which contesting explanations of transformations or large-scale historical changes are examined.

In the third part of the Chapter, hypotheses with respect to the entry and exit of transport regulation in North America are introduced and evaluated. This discussion builds upon Chapter 1 (in which were introduced the distinct periods of regulatory change in North America's transport sector), and upon Chapter 2, which described the emergence of the global market economy.

In part four, there is an evaluation of the explanations of the means by which the intercourse of communications, trade and finance emerged from within their attenuating regimes to form this interactive and reinforcing market process known as the global market. The methodological implications of parts two, three and four summarised in the concluding part five of this Chapter.

EXPLAINING THE TRANSFORMATIONS

Essentially, the roots of Western Civilisation are considered to be in ancient Greece, in Christian ethics, in Roman law and in Germanic notions of freedom. From these roots emerged practices and institutions which, in combination, have given Western Civilisation its distinctive character. The separation of spiritual from temporal authority, the rule of law and social pluralism have given rise to the protection of private property, a defence against the exercise of arbitrary coercion, and have nurtured a sense of individualism and liberty.

Two-and-a-quarter centuries ago, Adam Smith observed the emerging commercial culture of his day and, on the basis of his observations produced the 'Wealth of Nations' in which he laid the foundation of the just economy, the system of natural liberty and justice that underpins the rules for the economic order. Individuals, subject to natural liberty, promote both economic development and justice. The economic order and its constituent institutions, which are formed by liberated individuals subject to self-restraint and social, not legal constraint, embody justice. The possession of the self-interested notion and the freedom to express it, were the preconditions of the commercial exchange economy. They, in turn, have facilitated the individual's self-determination.

Smith offered an explanation of commercial civilisation. He put forward a theory to explain how economic man interacted with spontaneously created competitive markets. In his argument, he proposed that the introduction of freedom and increasing opulence provided the justification for his advocacy of the promotion of the free market. In his philosophic history, he argued that the breakdown of the old order had led to the emergence of commercialism. Accordingly, natural liberty, which embraced freedom of opinion, the rule of law and commercialism, were equated and mutually reinforcing. As opulence spread among individuals, so the reasoning went, more were free to choose self-interested goals. The system of natural liberty would promote the just society.[14]

Smith argued that the market process, as well as the commercial civilisation that it shapes the product of an evolutionary process. No one planned the market. The market is the result of a fortuitous coincidence of circumstances. According to Smith, economics is the study of self-interested man's interaction with the market process. These two concepts, self - interested motives and the market process, will be examined and used as frameworks within which to place the contending explanations of large-scale historical change.

The socio-biologist, Hayek, grounded his analysis in the work of Smith and Hume. He argued that behaviour is responsive to rules and institutions as well as to heredity and deliberate human intentions. These rules and institutions are the products of social evolution, of unconscious rather than intended human action.[15]   The competitive market is a spontaneous phenomenon. The market is a discovery procedure that cannot inform, in advance, the facts that constitute knowledge and that determine the actions of competitors. By contrast, the evolution of rules predicates the development of libertarian rule. Liberty (or freedom) is not intrinsically of value in promoting the formation of the competitive market, but is an instrument that evolves from custom and common laws that serve, in turn, to enhance progress by facilitating initiative.

Smith's observation relating to the evolutionary nature of the market process and its links with economic and political developments implies that the West's economic development was autonomous.[16] This order went far beyond the exchange of money and goods with a handshake in a corner of the town square. It was the emergence of an order in which a vast and growing range of activities were co-ordinated through a market process. But most important, is the implication that it can only happen once. If so, this has consequences for those who search for historical laws. Historicists have to face the fact that it is not possible to deduce general laws from a single case. Furthermore, if language, morals, law and money are not the product of purposeful human action but of selective evolution that is not guided in a direction by 'laws', then such 'laws' are meaningless. Also implied is a warning to those who have assumed a custodial role with respect to the global economy. Autonomous economic development in one part of the world explains why imitation and coercion rather than indigenous invention have been the chosen routes elsewhere to industrialisation and modernity.[17] Non-western societies may lack the inherent capacity for adaptation of Western societies. These may, perhaps, have been impaired by subjection to the coercive policies of former colonisers. If the market order fails, other orders may not emerge to reconcile society's desires. In sum, the capacity for adaptation in the Western culture, which underpins *laissez-faire* policies, cannot be assumed to emerge spontaneously in Non-western cultures.

To some, this view that the West's development was autonomous is indicative of a narrow and misleading Eurocentrism. The rise of the West, it is alleged, was facilitated by the existence of what was in effect a world economy that flourished on the Eurasian landmass prior to the sixteenth century.[18] The rise of the West in world economic and demographic terms relates to the decline of the East around 1800. The West overtook the East, firstly, by using silver extracted from the American colonies to buy entry into the Asian market and then, by resorting to import substitutions and export promotion on the world market.[19]

This analysis supports Marx's contention that the respective societies of the West were shaped by the forms of their economies and it deploys his Manichean interpretation of events. The villains, however, are identified, not as capitalists, but as Europeans. They are viewed as the ruthless exploiters of a gifted, accomplished, but fatally vulnerable, Asian people.

There is much in this interpretation that is open to criticism. Certainly, during the European Renaissance, Asia, and in particular China, led the West in technological achievement. Francis Bacon identified three inventions - the compass, gunpowder and printing - which were transforming the Europe of his time. All three had originated in China. But while these inventions and this knowledge massively contributed to the furtherance of technological development in Europe, they failed to transform China. Two hundred years later, the supremely transforming innovation was the steam engine, invented by British engineers.

Two points emerge from these observations. The first is that technical application is, unarguably, shaped by social forces. The second, that in the invention-driven, modern European world, people drawn from the masses continually appear on the stage of history, a stage that had hitherto been populated exclusively by monarchs, military commanders and prelates. These newcomers, in ever-increasing numbers, were innovative entrepreneurs whose calling card was the wealth they had accumulated through market transactions.

Those explaining large-scale changes in history are equipped with two further dimensions. One, that factors other than economic forces, factors such as culture, religion and ideology have played, and continue to play, a role in the propulsion of the West. Two, that change is influenced by human agency as well as by structural or institutional transformations. These are dimensions that add to the range of explanations of large-scale historical change. But so too does the dimension of power. The difficulty here is that the form and causal connections of power are the subject of dispute.

The introduction of belief systems and ideology into the game has meant that political power and economic power are not solely responsible for leaving indelible imprints on history. But what has been the relationship between belief systems and ideology, on the one hand and technological and economic development, on the other? Was Max Weber correct in asserting that the tenets of religion actually influenced the course of economic development in the West? Or does the understanding that the singular dynamics of the economy of the West were in motion prior to the Reformation negate this proposition? If there is a connection between the impact of belief systems (including both ideology and religion) and political systems on economic development, what is it? Is there a discernible alignment of ideological, political and economic power that either facilitates or inhibits transforming economic development? Are ideas and ideologies autonomous, spreading because of their inherent persuasiveness alone, or are they believed and propagated because they re-affirm self-interested motives? Are ideas and ideologies independent of structural relationships or are they connected? Does the economy exist independently of other social relationships or is it dependent upon these relationships? Given that the modern transformation is concomitant with human agency, are there links between structures and human agency? Are structures and agents mutually or exclusively constituted?

The fact is that the social sciences are without a comprehensive, refutable hypothesis of the sociology of belief (knowledge).[20] Belief and aims appear to be irreducible factors in the human situation. These are, clearly, thorny issues.[21]

Smith's individualistic mode of explanation of economics was confronted by what became two related approaches. On the one hand, an understanding of human affairs can be acquired by deploying the same methods as those engaged in by physical scientists; and on the other, collective entities, not the individual, should be accorded priority in the explanation of social and economic life. The latter conception consists of versions of utopian political collectivism in which the aims of society are considered to be attained best by conscious, central direction, while, in relation to the former, that of a 'generalised calculus of utility maximising behaviour' explains widespread human behaviour.[22] It is recognised that technical change - by expanding man's calculating capacities - and biology - by influencing the evolution of society - significantly influence human behaviour. Ideology and technical change are explained by changes in prices.

The givens of the neo-classical theory - endowments, technology, preferences and rules – pre-ordain the return of the economy to a unique equilibrium. The inevitable path to equilibrium implies that history is predictable.

In the neo-classical construction, satisfactions, including material satisfactions, are known, measurable and maximised by competitive markets. The gross domestic product (GDP) measures economic performance. Proponents of the neo-classical growth model argue that, in the long term, the rate of population growth, as well as the rate of technological change, affects the rate of growth.[23] Solow estimates that technical progress - changes in the ways of doing things – have accounted for 80 per cent of the long-term rise in US per capita income. Changes in factors of production may affect the level of growth. They may result in temporary deviations from the equilibrium growth path, but they will not affect the equilibrium growth rate.

The neo-classicists' deterministic economic explanation confronts questions concerning the causal role of non-economic variables. Whether, in what form and to what extent are the neo-classical model's exogenous parameters of tastes, technologies, endowments and rule structures to be treated as endogenous? Are tastes and ideology largely responsive to the economic environment, or are they derived from it and do they shift according to the adherence or movements in personal moral codes? Is technological change exogenous, the results of entrepreneurs' intuitive behaviour, or is it largely the response to market forces? Despite the classicists' argument, does the market ante-date the rules and institutions, or is it the other way around? Is the law and are the courts prior to the market?

Institutionalists, whose intellectual roots reach back to the German historical school, deem economic behaviour to be a consequence of 'enculturation', and, hence, can be more fully explained by a description of cultural patterns as reflected in institutions. It is not the maximising individual who is the object of analysis, but the institutions, in which cultural patterns – or models - rather than neo-classical predictive models are developed. The neo-institutionalists, however, retain economic man at the centre of attention. They examine the rules, both formal and institutional, which organise the behaviour of individuals and which are treated as given in the neo-classical models. Changes in such rules are explained as resulting from the aggregation of the responses of rational to shifts in prices and perceived individual costs and benefits.

Prominent neo-institutionalists have been disinclined to recognise that rules antedate the market. North and Thomas, in explaining the growth of Europe over eight hundred years, starting in the year 900, give the prime spot, not to technical change, economies of scale, accumulation of human or physical capital, but to the emergence of efficient economic organisations.[24] The authors 'endogenise' institutions, explaining the emergence of efficient institutions within the neo-classical deductive model in which self-interested individuals undertake decisions in the face of changing ratios of labour. In their model the change in population is the major causal variable. The political, judicial and economic processes function as if they were efficiency creating. Note, however, that this analysis concerns pre-modern Western societies.

Perceived in terms of purposeless motion, the market process has been seen to proceed by conquering space, by reducing space in the form of transport systems, and to diminishing time by increasing the speed of communication. To Marx and Engels, the unleashed drive came from the bourgeoisie who 'cannot exist without constantly revolutionising the instruments of production.'[25] Technology was regarded as a social process and invention was not the result of individual initiative.

For Schumpeter, however, the dynamic disequilibrium was wrought by the innovating entrepreneur. With his creative rather than adaptive responses to opportunities, Schumpeter's entrepreneur is an innovator whose exercise of will changes the course of economic growth and causes the vicissitudes of the capitalist process.[26] The tendency towards equilibrium, although strenuously disputed by Schumpeter, has been hypothesised as being shaped by the capacities of the institutions of society, and, in particular, by the economy and the polity. They provide incentives and opportunities for agents to restore equilibrium within their particular world of activity. Such agents are also described as entrepreneurs.[27] Whether it is a class or an individual that is the agent of change has been of less concern than the resulting 'creative destruction.'

Schumpeter rejected the notion that the competitive market is the core process of the capitalist system. Perfect competition, with firms maximising production, was, to him, a mirage. To Schumpeter, the capitalist engine was driven by new commodities, new technology, new sources of supply and new types of organisation. They disrupt the *status quo*. They threaten the very existence of corporations. These incessantly revolutionising forces destroy old orders and create new ones. This process of 'creative destruction' is the essential fact about capitalism. It is what capitalism consists in, and is the economic environment that every capitalist concern has got to live in.[28]

Schumpeter did not confine his analysis to the forces of transformation, but included the shifts in social and political orders. He postulated that these were brought about primarily by his 'organon', the innovator-entrepreneur. The entrepreneur established 'new combinations' that resulted in new markets, new goods and new methods of production, the conquest of new sources of supply and new organisations of industry. Once introduced, others followed. The clustering of innovations propelled the spins in the business cycle.

Schumpeter saw competition as a discontinuous process. Agents and entrepreneurs are mobilised by the profit motive into a dynamic of moves and counter-moves. The process results, not only in greater economic efficiency, but also in greater innovation. (His, it should be noted, is a view of the competitive process that challenges the hypothesis that consumer welfare increases as a result of cost efficiencies which, allegedly, lead to higher profits, improved technical application, innovation and higher growth.) Schumpeter's – and the wider Austrian school's – counter-argument is that increased profits could be due to market concentration and power. If so, such an outcome indicates an absence of the competitive process and hence a lack of innovation. As has to be expected of activities that apply knowledge, innovations occur abruptly. They are applied during the disequilibria of markets and so contribute to their often-unexpected consequences.

But what are the institutional characteristics that induce innovation? Are technical innovations the result of endogenous processes? Are their forms and applications shaped by market signals? Do these market signals reflect societies' wants, tastes, and performance elevated into ideological form? Arguably, these ideologies and cultural values are not immutable but are, in part, shaped by the environment through the interactive market process.

In pursuit of the answers to such questions, Schumpeter sought to determine whether, in the absence of exogenous shocks – such as wars and institutional change – the economic order of capitalism would evolve or whether capitalism would be destroyed. In 1928, he concluded that the latter eventuality would occur - it would be destroyed.

Capitalism, he argued, whilst economically stable (and becoming ever more stable) creates, by rationalising the human mind, a mentality and a style of life incompatible with its own fundamental conditions, i.e. its motives and social institutions. Capitalism, he said, in the absence of ex-ogenous shocks, would be changed, but not by economic necessity (and probably even at some sacrifice of economic welfare), into an order to which the term 'socialism' might be applied (as a matter of taste or of terminological preference).[29]

This is not so to those who hold to a historicist, materialistic analysis and interpretation. Cultural life is within, rather than outside, the realm of the techno-economic system. The propelling forces of society emerge, not from one's mind, but from one's own involvement in the productive process. They emerge from society, which is shaped by the system of production. The pressure to accumulate capital and the constant search to 'annihilate space through time and reduce turnover time'[30] leads to a succession of time–space compressions. The present age is one of a dramatic social and political transition in the language of communication. It is leading to a compression of time and space horizons and to a preoccupation with 'instantaneity.' In response, cultural forms are searching for spiritual and temporal revolutions.

Cultural critics question the 'sacrifice of nature in facilitating progress.' Innis questioned Smith's notion that the wealth of the commercial society, the extent of the division of labour, is itself limited by the market-widening transport system. Moreover, unlike contemporaries – of whom Schumpeter was one - Innis considers modes of communication, not production and not the belief system, to be the major determinant of the development of cultural empires.[31] Innis observed that the interaction of the forms of media and reality creates bias, which is accentuated through the communications mode. Modern electronic media is 'space biased', disseminating information to all corners. But in penetrating the cultivated preserves of the nation states, the media fragments the citizen's sense of place and community, exciting him to move into the widening space of the growing empire. The properties of the dominant medium shape the concepts of society and facilitate knowledge. Power is knowledge, and power is localised in such a way that it serves particular interests, not the whole population. New media provides political actors with the means of challenging the elites' monopolisation of communication.

Louis Rosetto, founder of 'Wired Magazine,' described the Web as inherently destabilising because:

> It's putting the power of interpretation, the power of getting at reality in the hands of everyone today, not leaving it in the hands of the priesthood or of media that's been telling people for a century what's real and what isn't.[32]

As Innis has pointed out, communicating information can significantly alter the form of information. Not surprisingly, therefore, there has been a continuous struggle for the control of the means of communication. The imperfections in the system of information suggest that random factors have played a significant role in the course of change. They are of such significance that it is open to question whether the emerging, non-market organisations of co-ordination can be viewed as solely or, indeed, even as primarily, the product of a rationalising process - the process that emerged from the drive for gains from trade subject to the constraints of (changing) transaction costs.

Innis, however, did not provide a role for human agency and, as a result, his framework does not fully embrace the evolution of the modern transformation. The neo-classical framework takes the modern transformation as given. It is an ahistorical approach that deploys timeless, taxonomic principles of social structure, functions and institutions. The essence of human nature is in the construction, viz. economic man. He is not time-specific and he is universal. In the ahistoric, neo-classical growth model, population growth and technological change are not explained. Only the rates of population growth and rate of technological change are calculated to affect the long-run rate of growth.

The key characteristics of modern western civilisation over the last three hundred years were described in Chapter 2. It was shown to be the widespread and relentless application of technological innovation. The implicit assertion was that the process of invention, innovation, development and transmission were mutually stimulated and shared within western civilisation. These enabling forces were the products of converging developments in agriculture, metalworking, political, religious and ideological rivalries that facilitated the emergence of the market and stimulated trade and discourse. These were societies tolerant of scientific enquiry. They had the infrastructure to invest in the innovations and the means of securing the property rights of the innovator. Technological innovation was both encouraged and effectively diffused in these societies.

While the exploitation and transmission of technology are social processes, inventions are arguably the result of individual initiatives. The acts of invention have much in common with artistic creations and are difficult to conceptualise in a testable theory. One interpretation is that inventions are the product of *homo sapiens'* adaptability and inquisitiveness. When the appropriate conditions are in place, they occur spontaneously. It has been argued that the history of technological innovation is characterised by evolutionary inter-connectedness.[33] However, this does not preclude the likelihood that the processes of innovation in western culture were enhanced by the adaptation of innovations that originated elsewhere (such as in Asia), neither does it rule out the possibility of there having been revolutionary innovations over the last three centuries that have jolted the course of technical, economic and social evolution.

Whatever the relative weight given to these interpretations, it is contended that invention, innovation and development are the results of both social processes and individual initiatives. Ideas are crucial in the process of invention while their acceptance, application and development are dependent on an enabling social environment.[34]

While to Marx and his followers, technological innovation and adaptation are exclusively social processes in which individual agency plays no role, Baumol accords to entrepreneurship a major role in the growth of both productivity and the *per capita* incomes of industrialised economies. He has explored variations in the emergence of entrepreneurs among societies by observing the allocation between productive activities, such as innovation, and 'largely unproductive activities, such as rent-seeking or organised crime.'[35] On the basis of his comparative historical analysis he confirms:

> ...that it is the set of rules and not the supply of entrepreneurs or the nature of their objectives that undergoes significant changes from one period to another and helps to dictate the ultimate effect on the economy via the allocation of entrepreneurial resources.[36]

In this way, Baumol claims to have verified the endogenous nature of entrepreneurship and its productive and unproductive activities.

In the analyses of others, ideologies play a more active role. For instance, Paulina Borsook claims that the dominant mind-set of the 'digerati' of California's Silicon Valley is libertarianism. Although the government has nurtured the industry with its educational subsidies and contracts, she argues that the digerati's libertarian roots emerged from the counter-culture of the 'sixties and the Reaganism of the 'eighties.[37]

The neo-classical approach involves winding-up the mainspring of economic man, posing a deductive map for his movement and observing his collision with the constraining walls of his world. Ideology, technology and entrepreneurship are beyond the reach of explanation. But to Schumpeter, these are not exogenous, unexplainable factors. They are part of an evolving organism and bear functional relationships with one another. The entrepreneur is the mainspring of economic progress and his innovations are the sparks that, on the one hand, ignite the economic process, but on the other, because of discontinuity, spin the business cycle. The incessant revolution of the economic structure comes from within.

While the overall function of the organism is the maintenance of its own existence, Schumpeter's view is that capitalism is not self-sustaining. It is dying, undergoing the transformation into the new order of socialism. The processes contributing to the transformation includes the corrosive criticism of capitalism by intellectuals and the substitution of bureaucratic management for the opportunistic function of the entrepreneur. These shifts in the social and institutional framework of capitalism undermine the process of accumulation.

Many awkward questions may be posed about Schumpeter's functional relationships. He has, for instance, no satisfactory explanation as to why there are discontinuities in the flow of innovations. Moreover, economic advances appear to have arisen within numerous contexts.[38] In the United States, funded research has been channelled through universities, institutions and smaller, usually entrepreneurial firms. The latter have been further encouraged by the provision of venture capital. The skein of large and small government, non-profit organisations and entrepreneur-driven operations has formed a creative network.[39] The government has nurtured the defence-electronics industry, which formed the substrate for the burgeoning high-tech industry. In short, Schumpeter's alleged conflict between bureaucratic corporative and entrepreneurial activity appears to be simplistic.

The organic conception, with its asserted common origins of modes, may not be linked to their subsequent evolution. His vision evokes the Hegelian device of the unifying inner principle of society, and his notion of decline smacks of *fin-de-siècle* pessimism. Events, fifty years after his predictions were made, would appear to refute his vision of socialism triumphant.

Yet there is much to be said for Schumpeter's approach. The last 150 years are replete with technology-driven investment booms and busts. He described such cycles, acutely, as processes of 'creative destruction.' The railroad boom of the 1880s was followed by the bankruptcies of the 1890s. Railroads exhibited economies of scale, high fixed costs and a perishable service product, freight transport. With many providers, price wars were inevitable and, as inevitably, bankruptcies followed. By contrast, the motor car is a highly differentiable product. By exploiting economies of scale, enforcing high quality standards and engendering continuous manufacturing inno-vations, Ford dominated an industry that, prior to the entry of the Model T in 1908, comprised no fewer than 240 companies. But this dominance was short lived. In the 1920s, Alfred P. Sloan, President of General Motors, carved out a sizeable share of the market by pioneering yearly model changes.

The noted chaotic edges to, and the underlying complexities of economic life suggest that the currently observed fragmentation is a transitory state. The battles between 'old' and 'new' economies are being described as processes of 'creative destruction.'[40] The tailing-off of capital expenditures on new technology, the price cuts by competing firms, the steep fall in technology stocks, the drying up of venture capital and the cuts in research and development are deemed to be the downward side of the new economy's cycle.[41] During this transformation, new products, marketing ideas, financial strategies, innovative salesmanship and constant change will be, as they have been in the past, essential to competitive success. Thomas Friedman observes that Intel's chairman, Andy Grove, took Schumpeter's insight that 'only the paranoid survive' and made it his company's strategy. What he understood was that only the paranoid would remain alert to the possibility that others might create something new that might destroy them. Only those who keep one step ahead will survive.[42]

Alan Greenspan, Chairman of the Federal Reserve Board, has used Schumpeter's insight into the process of 'creative destruction' to explain the contemporary technological transformation. He has likened the current bunching of innovation in information technology and the resulting increasing pace of capital deepening and increased productivity growth to the earlier periods of railroad building and electrification. Both of these bunched periods of innovation 'helped elevate economic growth for a considerable period of time.'[43]

Schumpeter noted that a successful capitalistic economy would nurture freedom of speech and criticism. While he clearly underestimated the intellectual appeal of entrepreneurship and the criticism of government regulation by intellectuals, he was correct about the criticism of 'creative destruction.' During prosperous times, there is also a noticeable contempt among intellectuals for materialism and consumerism, as well as for the open market order that makes them possible. Furthermore, when the economy is growing, intervention is encouraged because it appears to be relatively cheap.[44]

In the longer run, however, institutions and other entities may indeed realign into the predicted socialist order. In North America today, the issues revolve around the effects of limiting individualism by coercing 'represent ivity' based on gender and racial categories and buttressing these orders by imposing forms of political correctness.

Will such limits not only suppress individual creativity but also result in unintended, and hitherto dreaded, backlashes? In general, will the capitalist order collapse from within?

Whatever eventuates, one should not overlook the importance of Schumpeter's insights. More important than his organic conception and prognostications is Schumpeter's delineation of human agency and its relationship to the market process.

The essential differences between Marx and Schumpeter may be summed up as follows:

Where Marx postulated that the irreducible core of the market is the distinctive means of production, Schumpeter holds that the irreducible core is the innovative entrepreneur, a speculator, an opportunist, but also a creator, who, perceives and exploits disequilibria and propels the incessant market process. He transforms the market system by adapting to information generated and co-ordinated through the market process.

More broadly, the market process, in the 'neo-Austrian'[45] view is in a constant state of flux, reflecting, as it does, countless forms of human imagination and interaction. The market is conceived as a spontaneous process, the ends that it serves being the separate ends of the participating individuals. Markets are not perfect when attaining optimum equilibria with full information, but contrive to discover scarce information. Neither equilibria nor desired social and economic outcomes are assured.

This approach also makes two methodological points, namely, that the market process is the essence of the modern transformation and that its history has been primarily shaped by the interaction of the entrepreneur with this process.

The word 'primarily' in the last sentence is, in effect, an amber light, warning that these notions constitute an approach to modern history. They do not constitute, nor do they offer, a complete explanation. This is not possible. Too many constituent elements remain beyond the grasp of deductive theories. Belief is an irreducible factor. The innovative process, which appears to have similarities with the artistic process, has yet to find an encompassing, refutable hypothesis. Predatory theories of the state vie with contractual theories of the state. The limitations of abstractionism are frequently ignored. This is a grievous omission, for abstraction generates a distance from phenomena, which allows verification to masquerade as scientific testing.

EXPLAINING TRANSPORT REGULATION AND DE-REGULATION

Chapter 1 delineated three distinct periods of regulatory change in North America's transport sector: the entry of rail regulation in the late nineteenth century; the introduction of extensive protective regulation in the 1930s; and the exit of regulation in the late 1970s and 1980s. This section introduces and evaluates various hypotheses with respect to the entry and exit of transport regulation.

The first explanation to be examined is the Marxian hypothesis. According to Marxian analysis, contradictions in all forms of capitalist systems lead to over-accumulation. Ensuing crises cannot be avoided. They can merely be contained by means that do not threaten the social order. Controlled deregulation, through managed deflationary policies such as control over the pace of technological and organisational change by buttressing monopolies; the unleashing of creative destruction and the absorption of over accumulation through temporal and spatial displacement, are some of the means deployed by the capitalist system to avert the crisis of over- accumulation. The task is never complete. Accumulation is never fully absorbed.

A mega-thesis is developed. The progressive implantation of capitalism by means of transport and telecommunications infrastructures, trade and direct investment extends the space within which the over-accumulation arises, leading to heightened competitive tension between regimes and nations. Spatial and temporal integration lead to the interconnection of markets, regions and economies. The amplitude and incidence of market crises increase. They, in turn, threaten the securities of space and place. At the nexus of these contradictions, the compression in time-space triggers, not only a crisis of over accumulation, but also cultural and political crises.

The state, according to this hypothesis, deploys regulation to avert a crisis of over-accumulation. The Marxian interpretation of the entry of railroad regulations in the United States proceeds as follows: the railroad barons had attempted to monopolise rail services by containing the over-supply of services by forcing restrictive controls, but their methods were offensive and discriminatory. The state attempted to restore social order by replacing self-regulation with regulation by commission. The spread of regulation into market exchanges, and particularly into public utilities, was reflective of a growing social unease engendered by a sharp compression of time and space during the first decade of the twentieth century. The introduction of protective regulation in the 1930s reflected the severity of the over-production during economically depressed conditions. Similarly, the move to deregulation, some forty years later, reflected an attempt to counter the declining productivity and profits of the mass industrial order.

In evaluating these explanations of regulatory entry and exit, a fundamental tenet of Marxian analysis has to be addressed. It is the assertion that ideas, ideology and institutions do not have an independent existence. They emerge from capitalist society. Clearly, Marxian analysis provides insights as to how circumscribing forces impact on the evolving market process. This illumination, is, however, dimmed by three factors.

One, the evolving market, it can be contended, was shaped by societies that exhibited ideological conceptions of man different from those that were projected through cultural and political processes. Capitalist ideologues accepted, and some justified, the recurring crises of the system. Cartelisation was, in part, legalised in Europe, but unacceptable to the American polity, where anti-trust regulations, protective regulation and corporate concentration characterised the industrial order.

Two, innovation, ideas and ideology, while they may have been harnessed by the entrepreneur have, according to Marxians, no life of their own, for they are determined by the prevailing mode of production. Arguably, there is a reverse causality. Ideas are not passengers, but are the fuel, and entrepreneurial innovation is the engine. Combustion shapes the modes of production and drives the capitalist system. The alleged paranoia of Andy Grove of Intel, for example, powered his entrepreneurial drive that, in its turn, propelled the personal-computing revolution.

Three, this Marxian thesis is underpinned by a theory of government which holds that, whatever the description of the political system - representative democracy or fascist dictatorship - the state's coercive power is wielded exclusively in the interests of one class - the capitalists. This exclusive outcome is challenged by those who assert that the political system is influential in determining the choice of controlling instrument and in the distribution of returns between labour, capital, government and consumers.

The so-called public interest hypothesis implies a polity consisting of individuals whose aim is to achieve a pareto optimum allocation of resources. These aims propel regulatory agencies and governments to economise on transaction and bargaining costs. These processes realise information about individuals' preferences for public goods and externalities.

The public interest hypothesis predicts that regulatory instruments will be deployed because they will result in increases in efficiencies. When faced with a natural monopoly, subject to substantial sunk costs, efficiency conscious regulators will establish maximum rates. Ramsay prices will be introduced where marginal costs are below average costs and entry is difficult. When faced with externalities the regulator will create taxes, subsidies or marketable rights. The symmetry of this theory is that regulation departs when, due to shifts in demand and/or technologies, the market no longer fails. The diminution of scale economies and increases in the mobility of resources renders sunk costs as spent. By closing the gap between price and marginal cost, a convergence of the regulated and deregulated (market) equilibrium will have been affected. Efficiency conscious regulators will voluntarily close up shop and depart.

Such efficient outcomes in terms of allocation suggest that individuals do not have exclusively self-interested motives. If they had, they would have taken the opportunity to coalesce into groups and would have competed for such distributive gains as the 'majoritarian decisions rule' (see below) affords. These ambiguities concerning resource allocation and the distributive implications of regulation are cleared away by a set of Chicago economic theories of government and regulation. In these theories, individuals are deemed to be self-interested and to belong to groups that use political influence to enhance the well-being of their members. However, the motives activating the entry and exit of regulation remain ambiguous. Regulation is regarded as 'the fulcrum upon which contending interests seek to exercise leverage in their pursuit of wealth.'[46]

Stiegler and Friedland were dissatisfied with the hypothesis that the public interest was served by regulation. They showed that the regulation of the rates of the natural monopoly governing the supply of electricity had not resulted in lower rates.[47] Posner's examination indicated that by establishing different price-marginal cost margins, the regulator, in effect, instituted an implicit form of taxation. Producer rents were the sources of subsidies that were directed at selected consumers. Stiegler suggested that wealth was being transformed in the political marketplace.[48] Self-interested politicians supplied the regulation demanded by self-interested producers and consumers. The successful bidder, it was predicted, would be the numerically compact group. Such interests enjoy a comparative advantage in organisation costs. Hence, the compact producer group that enjoys this comparative advantage tends to win the bidding over the dispersed consumer or tax-paying group. However, as individuals and agents are assumed to be self-interested maximisers engaged in a zero-sum distribution game, individual self-interest, not the utility or wealth of the commonweal, will be maximised.

Peltzman considered the implications of a set of restrictive conditions.[49] He showed that a regulator, faced with constant returns to scale and negative externalities, would allocate benefits across the different interest groups. The outcome would be, as predicted by Posner, the emergence of cost-based, cross-subsidisation patterns. There was also an empirical point to this analysis. The persistent existence of such internal cross-subsidisation challenged Stigler's conclusion that the more compact producer interests would be the outright winners. Becker's contribution was to show that competing, rational self-interested agents enhanced the public interest.[50] His argument was that no opportunity should be left unexplored. Competing agents would minimise the dead-weight costs and transform a zero-sum game into a positive-sum game. According to Becker, competition, not the foresight and benevolence of the regulator, serves the public interest.

By contrast with the Chicago school's evolution towards a rationalisation of the public interest hypothesis, is the Brennan-Buchanan 'Leviathan thesis.'[51] This asserts that an interest group does capture the rents. This group goes to the agents with the monopoly of power, but they are not the producers or consumers. They are individual government officials and regulators.

The above sets of economic theories of regulation deduce two main characteristics. The first is that a compact, well-organised group will benefit more from regulation than will diffused groups; and the second, that as the returns from regulation arise from the distribution of wealth, regulatory policy will seek to preserve a politically optimum distribution of rents across the respective coalition. Changes in this equilibrium, including deregulation, arise from two main sources: structural or technological changes shift the rents available for the different coalitions; and, changes in the political market place cause a shift in the power of the different coalitions.

A troubling aspect of a verification exercise is that the characteristics of the regulated entity make it difficult to identify motives, and, therefore, to establish whether regulation was, in the first place, undertaken in the interests of the public. The deduction that the regulator will redistribute rents between the constituencies (by means of internal cross-subsidisation) in effect, implies that the regulator acts in the public interest irrespective of the original, winning motive for regulation. As a consequence, the analyst has to rely on notions of market failure in order to establish the likely motive for regulation. The task is easy when a natural monopoly was thought to exist, as in the case of the early railroads. It is less easy when it is clear that the industry is not a natural monopoly, as was the case with the air carrier and trucking industries.

An alternative hypothesis builds upon Arrow's impossibility theorem.[52] He argued that the general interest is not expressed through the process of representative democracies. He proved that it was not possible to have collective rationality from a set of unchanging individual preferences. The resulting social ordering of feasible alternatives was neither complete nor transitive. The impossibility theorem implied that it was not possible to derive a welfare function possessing consistent properties from the aggregation of individual preferences, as expressed through voting (under a majority rule for instance), even when the preferences of individuals were different (to a small degree), and stable.[53]

There are three implications of the impossibility theorem that are worth noting. One, whatever the voting system in operation, issues of income or distribution cannot be evaluated without undertaking interpersonal comparisons of utility. Two, the inconsistencies characterising the aggregate of individual preferences suggest that notions such as the public interest or the common good possess little that is common or public and probably a lot that expresses the interest of the promoter. By failing to identify the public, the hypothesis that the government promotes the interest of the public is not testable. Three, policies emanating from the democratic political systems are indeterminate. One source of the indeterminacy or instability is majority rule. This type of rule facilitates redistribution from the losers to those with the majority of the votes, the winners. Conversely, it is arguable that a political marketplace that is subject to majority rule results in distributions that find equilibrium, converges towards efficiency and so satisfies the public interest.

The stability, or otherwise, of the political system and the means by which it is disturbed or restored constitutes an alternative hypothesis. This hypothesis is applied to the American system of government. The majoritarian, representative democracy of the United States, it is alleged, has enjoyed stability because agents desire stability and seek to sustain supportive structures. The separation of powers and the various differing constituencies were designed to prevent the conflicting factional interests from dominating the political process and distributing income in their favour at the expense of the common weal.

Ideology has also played a part. The Supreme Court, over which John Marshall presided for the first three decades of the nineteenth century played a crucial role in controlling the encroachments made on private property rights by one faction, state government. The rules that were established were immunised from the political whims of legislatures.[54] It can also be inferred that they were such as to constrain the federal, if not always state governments, from appropriating private property and so promoting regulation as the preferred instrument of federal control. Accordingly, regulation has been a favoured instrument of majoritarian representative governments of the United States.

Some of these notions have been incorporated within the general economic model of maximisation subject to constraints and incentives. The general point is that policies emanate from an environment in which the underlying economic and political incentives impinge on political decision makers. The so-called 'path dependency theory' states that a change - accidental or otherwise - in the set of factor prices in the economy will change the incentive structure and cause a shift along a different policy path. Arrow's impossibility theory has been incorporated in the so-called 'theory of structure-induced .[55]

McKelvey's theory does not state that the political outcome will be, necessarily, chaotic.[56] Instead he focuses on how stability will be restored. The stabilisers are to be found in the decision making processes and in the structures. However, if there are changes in the decision making processes or changes in outcomes triggered by shifts in economic conditions, there is likely to be a shift in policy.

Note that these changes are not necessarily triggered by a shift in preferences. Shifts in preferences or ideologies are ignored in this economic model. Noll has an explanation for this. Economists, he says, ignore explanations based on shifts in ideology because 'they are based on a denial of objective rationality.'[57]

Suppose the change or disturbance is not merely executed by a decision maker but has been caused by an entrepreneur. The implication is that the change is motivated by the perceived accrual of political advantage by Schumpeter's creative (rather than adaptive) entrepreneur. It is a retro-spective, historical explanation as to how regulation or deregulation in a certain sector or industry occurred. Individuals learn rationally and respond discontinuously rather than adaptively. Such an hypothesis is, in effect, an explanation of how a particular random shock - in the shape of a rational political or bureaucratic entrepreneur who acts opportunistically and whose action had sufficient force to destabilise the equilibrium - could have occurred. This leads to a change in policy, in this case a change to regulation or deregulation.

The rational expectation theory provides the basis of another hypothesis, which, in essence, states that if opportunities for reward exist, rational, self-seeking agents would already have acted upon them. This, however, leads to the tautology that no contrary evidence exists because it cannot exist. Those promoting the contending hypothesis purporting to explain the entry and exit of regulation are then placed on the defensive. They are required to disprove that economic relationships are not random, but systematic. The historical analysis involved in such tests is difficult to execute. There is an imprecision involved in locating and measuring rents.[58] There is also a realisation that, although the political marketplace may involve rational actors, the agents in the particular regulated industries - the managers, unions and investors - may act in an adaptive manner.[59]

Proponents of the rational expectations hypothesis also have difficulty in establishing the course of change and in distinguishing the public interest from the special interest motive for change. Proponents have the task of proving the advantages of their interpretation when they simultaneously hold the view that they know, or knew more than the political action, but that the actions in the particular market acted rationally.[60]

In sum, three categories of hypotheses are in contention to explain the arrival, spread and departure of transport regulation: The Marxian hypothesis; economic theories of regulation (including public and special interest hypothesis); and the entrepreneurial hypothesis.

In the late nineteenth century, the railroads of the United States and the railways of Canada were thought to exercise monopoly power in many, if not all markets. This monopoly power existed, in part, because rail companies were natural monopolies. Furthermore, transaction costs were high and certainly much higher than they were a century later when, thanks partly to the use of computerised systems, rail services were largely subject to market regulation.

One interpretation is that the government regulation of entry and the self-regulation of rates led to politically unacceptable rate discrimination over which the over-burdened common law courts were unable to adjudicate. Regulatory commissions were seen as instruments for correcting market failure. Here was scientific government in action, substituting institutional arrangements for the allegedly non-existent competitive market in transport services. By deploying their regulatory power over rates, the commissions were intended to establish structures of rates that would enhance the public interest. However, within a short period of time it became questionable whether the public interest, rather than the interests of the rail carriers, was being enhanced. The question arises because of the nature of the responses of governments to cyclical downturns and the generally permissive entry policy pursued by the regulatory authorities. The resulting excess capacity of rail services spurred company consolidations and requests for the legalisation of rail cartels. The government of the United States exempted the rail cartels from the anti-trust laws, while the government of Canada enhanced the operation of a rail duopoly.

In Canada, railways were regarded as instruments of development to be promoted and protected. Shipper interests were to be guaranteed primarily by statutory rates, not through regulatory commissions.

In exempting the rail cartels from the anti-trust laws, the US government was establishing a precedent. Regulation was not only protecting the shipper but also protecting the railroad companies from intra-rail competition. Later the railroads were to be protected from trucking competition. Marxians could claim such regulatory action confirms their hypothesis, but, over time, it cannot be shown that protective regulation benefited, exclusively, the capitalist rail companies. The longevity of regulation suggests that the benefits of regulation were shared between shippers, management, owners, and regulators.

Trucking and airline enterprises were not regarded as natural monopolies.[61] Rather, they were thought to constitute structurally competitive markets. Legislators, however, were persuaded to regard trucks as a com-petitive threat to rail carriers and air carriers as infants whose survival depended on subventions. During the protracted depression, legislators were informed that the survival of both air and trucking modes was endangered by their seeming tendencies to engage in destructive competition. The pre-vailing philosophy of the New Dealers in Washington, and the liberal administration in Ottawa, led by the energetic C. D. Howe, was to enhance the public interest by restoring failed markets. Fare and entry regulations were to serve the public interest by protecting incumbent carriers from destroying themselves in intra- and inter-modal competition.

The system of protective transport regulation in the respective countries facilitated cartelisation. According to the economic hypothesis, regulators could be expected to preserve a distribution of rents across the respective coalitions of carriers, unions, passengers/shippers and regulators. Technical change or action within the political marketplace could disturb the dis-tribution of rents and result in regulatory reform and deregulation.

The exercises in the verification of the regulatory reform and deregulation in the late 1970s to early 1980s gave a low score to the economic hypothesis.

Only banking deregulation can be claimed for the economic hypothesis. The rents provided by interest rate ceilings were dissipated by non-price competition and eventually destroyed in the late 1970s, following the arrival of competing instruments in the wake of unprecedented increases in market interest rates.   However, the widespread existence and persistence of regulation in the diffused agricultural industry ran counter to the expected characteristics of a regulated industry.   Peltzman argues that deregulatory measures in telecommunications were initiated subsequent to the arrival of technical change but prior to the subsequent erosion in rents.[62]

Examination of the trucking cartels showed that trucking companies and unions enjoyed high rents.[63]   According to the economic hypothesis, deregulation cannot be the result of a dispute among disappointed coalitions of interest. As for the railroads, evidence suggests that the regulators did spread around the spoils most effectively among the respective coalitions. The equilibrium of the 1920s had been disturbed by the advent of trucking competition, which was handled by the regulation of trucks and the introduction of value-of-service rate-making.   Regulatory intervention induced excess capacity and the secular decline in demand reduced the wealth to be distributed, and, with it, the support of the railroads for the regulatory system.   The bankruptcies in the 1970s, according to this explanation, prompted a choice between national ownership or a constrained form of deregulation.[64]

As for the airlines, there are those who claim victory for the economic hypothesis.   The interpretation is that the regulatory system, which redistributed rents from high density to low density routes, encouraged rent dissipation on cost, thereby increasing service rivalry. The result was an increase in dead-weight losses, which made deregulation an increasingly attractive alternative for the major carriers.[65] Levine explains this by arguing that during the period of deregulation in the late 1970s, the rents accruing to carriers and labour increased.[66]

This dispute over rents is a reminder of a point made earlier, namely, the difficulty of measuring, and hence of identifying, changes in the rents accruing to the respective coalitions. There is, furthermore, the point that deregulation - of the financial, transportation and energy sectors - was bunched over a short period of time, 1970 to 1980, and located within a small number of modes and industries. Indeed, in many industries regulation was retained during the brief deregulatory era, while others, such as healthcare, the environment and labour-contracting, experienced an extension of regulation. Alfred Khan, chairman of the CAB between 1970 and 1980, appears to recognise that the deregulation of the railroads and trucking cannot be adequately explained as the response of rational agents adjusting to revealed information. Instead, he explains the spread of deregulation as being due to the 'demonstration effect.'

> He suggests that changes in the economic condition of the industry, together with a macro-economic environment of stagflation, set up conditions for deregulation in the airlines, where there were weak unions and most of the rents had already been dissipated. Deregulation in trucking then followed, partly because the lessons learned from airline deregulation were transferred to trucking by the same political coalition, consisting of (Edward)Kennedy, Ralph Nader, the Consumer Federation of America, Common Cause, the National Association of Manufacturers and the National Federation of Independent Small Businesses.[67]

In stating this, Khan establishes the pivotal event of the deregulation of the civil aviation sector and proffers a path dependence explanation, viz., that the deregulation of the domestic civil aviation industry was accepted politically because it was thought to have a negative impact on inflation. Most interestingly, he implies that the above-mentioned coalition of political entrepreneurs went forward, sniffing for disequilibria, which they found and exploited in the rail, trucking (and telecommunications) sectors.

However, there is another way of describing these events. It could be argued that the coalition of political entrepreneurs led by Senator Edward Kennedy and Senator Cannon, along with Khan and his colleagues at the CAB, were exploiting an unstable industry suffering from exhausted rents. This 'randomness' could be described as the concatenation of politicians on the lookout for a target; the arrival of Khan and his reforming team at the CAB; and the perilous stage of the airline industry cycle. Khan and Levine, the latter an academic with a reputation as a promoter of deregulation, could be characterised as Schumpetarian entrepreneurs or, perhaps, as economists on white horses, fortuitously at the right place at the right time, allied with politicians willing, and able to push for deregulation.

Levine has presented his account of the deregulation process governing the domestic civil aviation industry:

> .... this initially doubtful congressional faction ultimately helped control the legislative process in favour of deregulation, which by then was perceived to be in the public interest. And it did so in the face of die-hard opposition by factions (including the industry) whose positions were undermined by the ultimate transparency of the degree to which their positions were motivated by purely private, rather than 'public interest' considerations of gain and loss. And, on the administrative side, even conceding that chairman Khan and his chief staff aides had relatively little to lose by the diminution of CAB power, these changes were supported by the initially sceptical but ultimately convinced career staff and by members of the board who were prepared to see their own power diminished for the benefit of the public.[68]

This interpretation has to be qualified, for Levine omits a crucial event. Three years prior to Levine's arrival at the CAB, a staff study, headed by a career bureaucrat, J. R. Pulsifer, evaluated the performance of the airline industry and the regulatory agency. The Pulsifer study argued that the latter's exercise of protective regulation was sufficiently detrimental to warrant deregulation.[69]   As the study shows, this influential group of career bureaucrats within the regulatory agency was ideologically opposed to the prevailing notion that regulation protected and sustained the 'public utility' of the civil air transport system. They made recommendations that ran counter to the supposed self-interest of bureaucrats.

Those arguing the Leviathan hypothesis are placed on the back foot. They are obliged to show that bureaucratic authors of this report, rather than the appointed executives who actually executed deregulation, intended to serve their own self-interest.

The staunch defence of protective regulation formed by the notorious iron ring of carriers, politicians and regulators, had been shattered. The initial breach had been made, not by an entrepreneur from the carrier sector, nor by a 'disinterested' academic, but by a regulator at the CAB who was ideologically committed to the merits of the competitive process through unregulated markets. The mobilising agents who activated change were the coalitions of bureaucratic and political entrepreneurs who perceived and acted upon the emerging opportunities. In sum, this exploration of the deregulatory process of the civil aviation industry in the United States confirms the entrepreneurial hypothesis.

The deregulation of the transport sector in Canada, an account of which is given in Chapter 1, Part 4, also confirms the entrepreneurial hypothesis. That account also argued that the deregulation of the United States transport sector had more than a 'demonstration effect' on Canadian political entrepreneurs and the supportive epistemic community. This shift in the 'rules of the game' was seized upon by the political entrepreneurs and converted into supporting evidence in their case for the deregulation of the Canadian transport system. Accordingly, it is argued that the earlier deregulation of the United States transportation (and telecommunications) sectors aroused the interest of Canadian passengers and shippers and prompted them to act. An epistemic community of academic and consumer groups argued that Canadian shippers and passengers could experience the gains then currently enjoyed by American transport consumers, if the government were to launch an extensive programme of regulatory reform.

In sum, an evaluation of the respective interpretations suggests that the entrepreneurial interpretation explains the egress of transport regulation and, in the case of Canada, the spread of protective regulation to trucking and air modes. As for the arrival of transport regulation in the United States, two factors were considered to be important: the rising cost of transacting through the common law courts as against the deemed efficacy of scientific government, and an ideological shift away from complete reliance on *laissez-faire* policies.

EXPLAINING THE GLOBAL MARKET PROCESS

The last part of Chapter 2 outlined the alleged consequences of the contemporary global market process. This process, it is argued, stemmed in large part from three liberating measures: the passage of NAFTA in 1993; the removal of capital-account restrictions in emerging markets; and the WTO's Basic Telecommunications Agreement of 1998. The primary task here is to outline and evaluate the explanations of the means by which the intercourse of trade, investment, finance and communications emerged from within their attenuating regimes to form an allegedly interactive and reinforcing global market process. This enquiry entails setting up an interface between economics and international relations and will feature terms such as 'power', 'regime' and 'hegemon.'

Realists see affairs as they are, not as they should be. They identify power as the primary pursuit of all agents in both the domestic and international arenas. According to structural realists, the state is perceived to have a purpose or purposes and nation states are the spontaneous outgrowth of the activities of self-regarding actors. The complex interdependencies of nation states have been conceptualised in terms of regimes. The international trade, monetary and communications regimes are conceived as multilateral agreements among states whose aim is to regulate national action within these areas. More generally, regimes are seen to be forms of co-operative behaviour in which the regime's structure may either facilitate order and stability or, alternatively, unintentionally generate instability.[70] This is a useful conceptualisation in that it provides a means of describing the task at hand, i.e. to explain the recent opening-up of the international trading, financial and communications regimes.

One version of the stability hypothesis is that the emergence of open and stable international regulatory regimes necessitates the existence of an hegemonic power. Hegemonies are wealthy and powerful states that possess the capability and motivation to create, maintain and enforce the provision of international public goods. Just as the state-supplied public goods of law, justice and defence have facilitated civilised social intercourse, international public goods, such as stable international trading and financial regimes, can be shown to have facilitated international civility and commercial exchange across borders. The openness of the constituent regimes, their maintenance and decay, is explained, not as the product of rational exchange between governments, but in terms of the power of the hegemon relative to its potential rivals. Armed with military might and economic power, the behaviour of the hegemon can be compared with that of the dominant member of a cartel. The dominant member or the leader provides international public goods, by either coercing or bribing regime members. According to the stability hypothesis, hegemonic eras are characterised by open trading systems and stable international financial regimes, while declining hegemonies suffer from protectionism, trade wars, and competitive devaluations.

What is the explanatory power of the stability thesis in relation to US economic policies during the Clinton administration? More specifically, was the emergence of the United States as the undisputed hegemon the primary reason why the Clinton administration entered NAFTA and promoted the Multilateral Agreement on Investment (MAI)? If it is accepted that the collapse of the Soviet empire removed the main (military) rival to the United States, then it could be argued that NAFTA was launched at the very time that the United States became the undisputed hegemon. When negotiations were initiated, however, the US economy was in a recession. As studies have shown, open trade regimes were correlated with periods of prosperity and closures correlated with depressions.[71] While a recession is not a depression, the expected tendency during a recession would be towards the closure of trading regimes. Lipson's study of the GATT regime, however, features a qualification. He argued that the reductions in trade barriers continued during a period when the United States was in economic decline. The reason: the costs of regime maintenance were shared more broadly than when the once-dominant hegemon incurred the costs.[72] Lipson's study is also of interest because it suggests that the perceived relative economic performance of the hegemon could influence the opening or closure of trading regimes.

Paul Krugman has devoted some considerable attention to this issue because, as he has shown, influential analysts had made a dangerous mistake in depicting the US economy as a corporation that was losing to its competitors. Their argument was that US Inc. would start winning only if it were to become more productive and, therefore, more competitive. Krugman argues that they were using the wrong analogy. The United States should not be seen as a corporation. This was a dangerous misconception because it could have lead to policies that closed the trading regime. International trade is not about competition but about mutually beneficial exchange in which productivity increases allow a country to consume more, not to 'beat' competing countries.

In his book, 'Pop Internationalism,' Paul Krugman points out that the Clinton administration was staffed with influential advisors such as Ira Magaziner (Health Plan), Robert Reich (Secretary of Labor), and Jeffrey

Garten (Under-secretary of Commerce for International Aid), all of whom adhered to the view that the economic fate of the United States would be decided by the outcome of a three-way competitive struggle with Japan and Germany. This argument, which all had expounded upon in books that achieved popular readership, clearly supported the institution of trade protectionist policies. However, instead of protectionism and trade wars, the Clinton administration instituted NAFTA and launched a liberal set of policies through the WTO. Krugman's explanation as to why the move to open trade occurred reads thus:

> ...what seems to be happening is that the idea of being an outright protectionist is still unacceptable in polite company; so whatever each author's argument, he always ends up with some more respectable recommendations, such as training or limited industrial policy.[73]

There is another explanation for this outcome, however. This is provided by Eichengreen, who conducted an examination of the correlation between the international monetary system and the rates of growth of the US relative to its trading partners. An overvalued dollar reduces the competitiveness of exports and encourages import penetration.[74] If, as is postulated, US exports are capital intensive, reduced exports will lower the rate of return, the rate of investment and the growth rate. If US exports are knowledge-based and subject to increasing returns, persistent overvaluation will shift comparative advantage in production to foreign producers. The move away from the traditional exports, grounded by diminishing returns towards knowledge-based exports, implies a re-orientation of policy. Rather than considering tariffs and subsidies, attention is given to the strengthening of the national research base, the pooling of resources and the fostering of strategic alliances.[75]

In the terminology of a structural-induced equilibrium theory, these shifts in the structure of the economy reinforced the ideology of the polity that was opposed to protectionism.

By way of comparison, in her explanation of the shift towards free trade in the 1930s, Judith Goldstein argues that political leaders instituted a structure and process of decision making on trade policy that made liberalisation a possibility.[76] Congress did not make tariff decisions but they were the subject of international treaties that were negotiated by the President. Congress could either vote for or against them without amendment. Goldstein also argues that political leaders had adopted the neo-classical school's conception of international trade. Rather than being a zero-sum game, international trade was designed to promote mutually beneficial exchange. Indeed, her line of causation was from a change in ideology to a change in policy. Political leaders had made liberal trade policy a possibility and protectionist policies less likely, because they had adopted structural changes, which, in turn, were the result of a shift towards 'a better economic theory.'

Ideology, in this construction, involves what, in the neo-classical economic model, are termed preferences over policies and institutions. Preferences are derived from a combination of value judgements about social outcomes and positive theories about cause-effect relationships. But, unlike the preferences in the standard economic model, preferences in this construction change because of a change in values and/or because of a rational re-evaluation of alternative theories. There is yet another proposition: that progress in the science of economics itself, as well as improvements in economic education can cause the decision maker to make different and allegedly better decisions, even though the 'facts' and preferences over outcomes do not change.

Krugman was concerned with erroneous 'theories' that had become the 'conventional wisdom' of the power elite. He explained why the crypto-protectionists had pursued other objectives. They were diverted, he said, from enacting policies that would have plunged the US into trade wars by policy entrepreneurs who held to the anti-protectionist ideology.

This, however, is not an explanation as to why the international trading regime opened, but it suggests a reason why protectionism did not take hold.

In this policy-making game, corporations were spectators, not players, though John Cavanagh, author of a joint report of the Institute for Policy Studies and the Interhemispheric Resource Center, thinks otherwise. According to Cavanagh, 'the Clinton administration triggered an acceleration of corporate-led globalisation in all three major areas (trade, investment and finance) of policy making.' This acceleration, in the 1990s 'stems from a disproportionate (and growing) concentration of political power and influence in the hands of global corporations.'[77]

By the early 1990s, a surge of entrepreneurial creative destruction was transforming the United States economy. The fortunes of corporations rose and fell according to the way in which they adapted to constantly changing information technology. Not only was this technology re-ordering business organisations in the United States, it was making possible the transnational organisation of work and of an increasing integration of production within networks. That the potential for such organisations was particularly marked in the enthusiasm of the telecommunications corporations for a multilateral agreement that would open domestic markets is understandable. According to the Office of Telecommunications of the Department of Commerce, the WTO's Basic Telecommunications Agreement signed in 1998 opened up a market valued at $550 billion.[78] Banks and financial institutions were aware that their lending, advising, portfolio and underwriting activities would be more profitable were they to enjoy the freedom to move capital in and out of emerging markets. Manufacturers in the United States and Canada were keenly aware of the lower wage rates in Mexico. A trade agreement would allow them to do what they had, hitherto, been prohibited from doing, namely, to assemble and manufacture products in Mexico at low wage rates and then, free of tariffs and quota, to import them into Canada and the US. Likewise, it was no secret to Mexican and Canadian manufacturers that the US was the largest market in the world. However, the enthusiasm among the Mexican business and political elite started to wear thin following the debt re-structuring of the 1980s and the gradual opening of the economy to trade and investment. The Clinton administration desired to have a politically stable neighbour on the southern border of the US. The election of a committed neo-liberal regime in Mexico in 1988 and the ascendancy of a group of technocrats, known as the *científicos*, set the stage for the extension of the customs union to Mexico.

The competitive dynamics of the US economy has wrought changes to the power elite that C. Wright Mills described forty-five years ago. There has been a re-ordering of power as new, technical industries have replaced smokestack manufacturers. The four largest corporations in the US, in 1956, were General Motors, Standard Oil, Ford Motor and US Steel.[79] The four largest corporations in the US (and in the world), as measured by market value in August 2000, were General Electric, Intel, Cisco Systems and Microsoft.[80]

Business corporations are still the most powerful entities, but for the most part, rule-breaking entrepreneurs have replaced organisational men, who 'must fit in.' The ethos of these corporations is supportive, not of protection, but of free-market competition, and its partner, 'creative destruction.' Their relationships with constituent members of the power elite are also shifting as they become global corporations. They are becoming more interested in protecting their earnings, wherever they are made, than in the defence of the country and its peoples in which, perhaps, a minority of their employees live and work.

Mills argued that the military elite had much in common with the business elite. Today, however, it would appear that these business elites share an ideological outlook with elites in other countries and have more in common with one another than they have with the military elites of their own countries.[81]

The emergence of global enterprises suggests that there is no longer a case for dividing the world between the international and the domestic, but that three new conceptual spheres have emerged, in economic space: supra-regional, national and sub-regional. It is a world that consists of at least three different levels of social organisation: states, national societies and global societies. Exchanges within this global system are triangular, involving state to-state exchanges, firm-to-firm exchanges and state-to-firm negotiating and bargaining. The elites in the respective levels of social organisations conduct these exchanges. At the corporate level, this elite has been described as the 'transnational managerial class.' Exchanges over the desired international regime or economic order are conducted by a constituent of the elites, known as the epistemic communities.

Peter Cowhey predicted the role that epistemic communities would play in opening the international telecommunications regime. These groups had already attacked the legitimacy of the existing domestic regimes. It was then predicted that they would join forces with other communities that were pressing for free trade and then prize open the international telecommunications regime:

> The technology of telecommunications was once conducive to a political bargain built around national telephone monopolies. The international communications regime improved the technical performance of the system while organising an international cartel built around bilateral bargaining and guided by multilateral commercial rules. It fostered an epistemic community devoted to the idea of a 'natural monopoly' for telephone services. Later, the digital technology revolution gave large users of the communications system, newer electronics companies, and would-be providers of enhanced services an incentive to challenge national regulatory systems. Once they succeeded domestically, they sought to extend the reforms to the global level. They had the market power to erode the old regime, and they turned to the organising principle of free trade as a guide for reform. This has introduced the beginnings of an alternative epistemic community for the telecommunications regimes and a new mix of institutional jurisdiction and powers to alter the old regime. More generally, it is setting a precedent for bringing most services under the umbrella of free trade rules, a significant liberalisation of the world economy at a time when many fear the decline of an open economic regime.[82]

Cowhey's prediction of the opening of the telecommunications regime is grounded in the cognitive hypothesis, which by contrast with the hegemonic stability thesis, concentrates, not on structural relationships, but on mobilising agents. These are bureaucratic and political entrepreneurs who perceive and act on emerging opportunities, both micro and macro, and who adopt ideologies that serve to rationalise their expected gains. Motivated by the realisation of the potentialities promised, in particular, by technical change, political entrepreneurs are to be found aligning with those members of the epistemic community whose articulated vision of an alternative order reinforces the assault on the *status quo* regime. The vulnerability of the international regime will be proportionate to the relative importance of the domestic regime under attack.[83] Ideologies, belief systems and knowledge are introduced as explanations of regime change. The cognitive hypothesis is an inductive, *post hoc* approach.

When the article was published in 1990, Peter Cowhey was an academic at the University of California, San Diego. The paper analysed the forces that had brought about the changes in the US domestic regulatory regime and then, in effect, made a prediction as to how the international telecommunications regulatory regime would open up. A little later, he joined the FCC's International Bureau. According to the then Chairman, Reed Hundt, Cowheys and Hundt presented the case for the WTO's treaty on the liberalisation of telecommunications and trade around the world.[84] The analyst had become a policy entrepreneur in the 'game' of opening up the international regime.

Cowhey suggests that technical change brought about structural and price changes that shifted the incentives facing private and governmental actors. Their actions altered the path of development of the telecommunications industry and, indeed, of the whole economy. In other words, the advent of microchip technology made it possible to shift from electrical to digital and optical technologies. As a result, the distinctions between data-processing and communication began to blur. These technical developments led to displacements and convergence, which, in turn, undermined the rationales of public utility regulation and the policing of natural monopolies. However, the regulatory changes were not quite those as predicted by Cowhey.

In its desire to promote the data processing industry, the FCC pursued a policy that differentiated between communication services, that were regulated and data services, which were unregulated. The opponents of a regulated Internet had an exemplar in the deregulated airline industry.[85] The super-highway in information was to be spared from regulation. By the mid-1990s, the unregulated Internet had evolved into a highway upon which broadcast, cable, wire, wireless and satellite 'lanes' were converging. The *Telecommunications Act* of 1996 was intended to introduce competition into a traditionally protected, monopolistic industry.

This has not happened. According to Adam Thierer, the '*1996 Act* allowed the FCC to make an unprecedented power grab and agency bureaucrats were able to impose their own version of industrial policy on an already over-regulated sector.'[86]

Michael Powell was appointed Chairman of the FCC in early 2001. In his first public statement he reflected on the *Telecommunications Act* by stating that deregulation, not government intervention, was the best way to spur competition in telecommunications.[87]

Along with a number of European countries, the FCC auctioned off the airways for wireless communication. George Gilder argued that this was, in effect, a tax on the wireless Internet. What the FCC had done was to make scarce what is inherently abundant, and, in so doing, to subject property rights to the whims of regulators. Wireless developments are being driven out of the United States into Japan, Korea and Finland where there are no such taxes.[88]

In 1998, sixty-nine governments, whose markets accounted for more than 91 per cent of global telecommunications revenue, signed the WTO's treaty on the liberalisation of telecommunications sectors and the trade in telecommunications products. Forty-five countries permitted full foreign ownership control of all telecommunication services and facilities while fifty-eight countries adopted pro-competition regulatory principles. Pekka Tarjanne, Secretary General of ITU, made the argument in support of this multilateral agreement:

> We will never have a global information society until we have a global information economy, and we will never have a global information economy without free trade in telecommunications and information services because telecommunications services are essential to all forms of economic activity.[89]

Tarjanne also implied that most countries had no option but to open their telecommunication markets. Thanks to call-backs and calling cards, no market was truly closed. Furthermore, information and the facilities to process data 'have become a strategic resource as important as land, labour and capital.'[90] It remains to be seen, however, whether countries are willing to see such strategic industries owned and controlled by global, but still foreign, corporations.[91]

In the meantime, the US telecommunications industry showed its opposition to the incursion of Deutsche Telekom, (which is partly government owned), into the US domestic market when it sought US legislators' approval for its purchase of mobile phone company, Voicestream. Similarly, the governments of some European countries have opposed cross-border mergers of telecommunication companies. The European Commission drafted a recommendation to block the merger of WorldCom Inc.'s merger with Sprint Corp. Such conflicts appear to have spurred the consideration of a multilateral organisation that would standardise the treatment of international merger proposals.[92]

In Europe, proposed amendments to the Directive for Electronic Communications could balkanise the European Union's 191 billion Euro telecom market. According to the original plan, the European Commission would be able to review major decisions of individual national regulators. However, a number of national regulators wish to retain these review powers. If passed, the possibility is that, instead of a single set of rules, Europe could revert into being a patchwork of national rules and case law. Similarly, there are proposals to change codes, known as 'Rome II,' that will give preference to the laws in the country of the consumer in cross-border disputes. This is likely to create legal uncertainty for businesses operating over the Internet in Europe.[93]

The apparent opening of the international telecommunications regime contrasts with the attenuated international civil aviation regime. The realisation in the United States that a move towards greater liberalisation in the international air transport regime will require a switch from sovereignty-centred, protectionist ideology indicates the frequently unpredictable influence of such change on the crucial volitional element among the players within a regime. Indeed, a significant factor regarding the evolution of open, liberal regimes, is the failure of epistemic communities either to extend legitimacy to market outcomes or to reduce their commitments to re-distributive justice through coercive government. Criticism is frequently focused on the attempted means of achieving redistribute goals, and not always in a positive acceptance of the outcomes of market liberation.

Jagdish Bhagwati has drawn upon this changing structure and ideology of the power elite to explain the successful promotion of capital account convertibility among emerging markets. He identifies what he calls the 'Wall Street-Treasury complex' as the driving force that prised open the international capital markets. Many national monetary authorities preferred not to allow currency convertibility for current account transactions because, under the Bretton Woods fixed rate regime, the full freedom of capital movement constrained their ability to combat inflation and to deploy counter-cyclical monetary policies. The oil price shocks of the 1970s, followed by the debt crises of the early 1980s, led to a tightening of controls. However, the IMF's policy solution to these crises was to encourage emerging market economies to ease capital controls and to raise interest rates. The free movement of capital, it was argued, would lead to the global integration of financial markets. Capital flows would bring about a convergence of interest rates and lead to a more efficient allocation of resources. The global financial markets would improve domestic policy making by rewarding 'sound' policies and by punishing unsound ones.

Bhagwati's explanation is that the opening of the international capital market regime 'reflects ideology and interests - that is lobbies.' The ideology 'is clearly that of markets.' The self-interested entities are Wall Street financial firms:

> This powerful network, which may aptly, if loosely, be called the Wall Street-Treasury complex, is unable to look much beyond the interests of Wall Street, which it equates with the good of the world. Thus, the IMF has been relentlessly propelled toward embracing the goal of capital account convertibility.[94]

In September 1997, the Interim Committee of the IMF endorsed the move to capital account convertibility for IMF members. This was not the most propitious timing, for the world's capital markets were convulsed as capital flows reversed course, flowing from the plunging emerging markets of South East Asia and Latin America to the safe havens of the US and Europe. Questions started to be asked. Why should the Asian tigers have opened up their financial and capital markets when their savings rates were, in some cases, 30 per cent or more? Was it because of pressure from the Wall Street-Treasury complex? It is alleged that players well connected to this Wall-Street Treasury complex targeted a number of Asian markets, sold their currencies short and so destabilised their exchange rates, asset prices and the prices of goods and services. Those convicted of such manipulation of the US market could be sent to prison. Why, despite the protests from emerging markets, did neither the IMF nor the US Treasury move to dissuade such manipulation by introducing rules and penalties in the international market similar to those operating in the US market?

The hardest hit markets were those that discovered that raising interest rates not only failed to support their currency but that such action precipitated the collapse of their financial sectors. Financial institutions had borrowed too much and made too many imprudent loans to their 'cronies.' Such behaviour was not to be condoned. It was to be punished by letting the market 'deal' with the corporations and financial institutions.

This was not to be so, however, when the Wall Street Treasury complex was threatened, in the fall of 1998, following the default of $13.5 billion of debt by Russia. Long Term Capital Management (LTCM), a hedge fund, faced the prospect of liquidating its $1000 billion in assets. The leverage of LTCM was on a scale every bit as extreme as the debt incurred by Korean semi-conductor manufacturers. However, the banks were not to be punished for their injudicious lending. LTCM was not driven to the wall. William J. McDonough, President of the Federal Reserve Bank of New York, orchestrated LTCM's rescue by fourteen private banks. His fear was that markets would 'possibly cease to function.'[95]

In Washington there had been two schools of thought concerning the transformation of Russia from a communist to a market-driven economy. One of these stressed the importance of introducing the institutional infrastructure necessary for a working market economy, the other recommended shock treatment. This meant the immediate exposure of the Russian economy to market forces. According to Joseph Stiglitz, chief economist at the World Bank between 1996 and 1999, the latter school won the approval of the Treasury Department and the IMF because they made sure 'there was no open debate.' Stiglitz goes on:

The rapid privatisation urged upon Moscow by the IMF and the Treasury Department had allowed a small group of oligarchs to gain control of state assets. The IMF and Treasury had re-jigged Russia's economic incentives, all right, but in the wrong way. By paying insufficient attention to the institutional infrastructures that would allow a market economy to flourish - and by easing the flow of capital in and out of Russia - the IMF and the Treasury had laid the groundwork for the oligarchs' plundering.[96]

The reversal of investment flows out of emerging markets, out of Russia and into Wall Street, contradicted the predictions of those who had claimed that 'immense' benefits would accrue to the global economy as a result of liberating the international capital market regime. There was abundant evidence to show that the only economies to benefit from the free movement of capital and floating exchange rates were the advanced, diversified economies with large and sophisticated financial markets.[97] The experiment with an open regime was over for many of the battered emerging markets. Some introduced capital controls, while others tied their currencies to a major currency through a currency board or adopted a leading currency as their national currency.

These were the responses of governments to what they regarded as financial imperialism. In their view the managers of the international financial regime were the mere poodles of the Wall Street Treasury complex. This was also the view of Stiglitz:

Did America - and the IMF - push policies because we, or they, believed the policies would help East Asia or because we believed they would benefit financial interests in the United States and the advanced industrial world? And if we believed our policies were helping East Asia where was the evidence? As a participant in these debates, I got to see the evidence. There was none.[98]

Stiglitz attempts to explain why, in spite of the recommendations from the leading economists to implement an institutional infrastructure, the IMF and the US Treasury subjected Russia to 'shock therapy', and why the IMF continued with policies of contraction when they were forcing East Asian economies deeper into recession.

According to Stiglitz, the economists of the IMF and the US Treasury held to the universal doctrine that shock therapy works for economies in transition to a market economy. The corollary of this doctrine of neo-classicism is that institutions and history do not matter. He argues that the senior officials of the US Treasury stuck to this shock policy and publicly supported the architects of the disastrous privatisation scheme because 'the Treasury Department is arrogant about its economic analysis and prescriptions.' The Treasury Department is so arrogant about its economic analyses and prescriptions 'that it often keeps tight - much too tight - control over what even the president sees.'

But these are smart people who adhere to the wrong doctrine. By contrast, the IMF, according to Stiglitz, is staffed with inferior economists who apply inferior methods and models. Their policies were reacting to the past and not adjusting to possible future outcomes. As a result, their policies of contraction hastened the demise of the emerging market economies.

Both institutions, however, have one factor in common. They are insulated from what he terms as democratic accountability. The source of their fallibility in this, the world's most powerful democracy, is the 'undemocratic culture of international economic policy making.'

It may be that the advocates of shock therapy have believed their ahistoric doctrine with their construction, economic man, to be superior to institutional alternatives. They may have believed that it was irrelevant that Russia had no effective market for property rights, or that Russian society had not experienced a Protestant reformation. Such a belief is shocking and so is the lack of open debate. Indeed, the manner in which this policy was implemented suggests that we have witnessed, not a group of economists who believed their doctrines to be more important than the lives of millions of people, but a group of functionaries who were mere spectators. They watched while well-placed insiders in Washington, Wall Street and Moscow wrote the rules in a game that was to win them billions.[99]

Stiglitz has stipulated the necessary condition for the application of 'smart' economics. The prescriptions of economists should be subjected to open scrutiny from others who hold differing paradigms and doctrines. Likewise, the institutions of international economic policy making should be transparent and accountable to the international community.

There are others who also recommend such democratic accountability. Their objective, however, is not to see the adoption of smarter economic policies. They wish to reduce the political power and influence of global corporations and to see a drastic reduction in the rate of growth of what the polls say the people do not want: foreign trade and immigration.[100] These objectives, they argue, can be achieved by subjecting the negotiations over international trade, finance and investment regimes to democratic and accountable processes. They would set these democratic forces in motion by removing the president's discretionary power over international trade agreements.

These advocates of democratic accountability are concerned at the loss of jobs in the US, particularly in manufacturing, and the widening gap in remuneration between skilled and unskilled workers. The alleged cause of these disparities is the opening of the trading and investment regimes. To restore the manufacturing base and reduce the disparities, the US system of government should heed the wishes of the people and institute 'fair' trading and investment regimes. This means imposing, on any new trade deal, provisions against child labour and loose environmental standards. However, according to the free traders, this would amount merely to disguised protection for labour unions. This could result in retaliatory measures, and a closing of the trade regime in which all sides would lose. The people should be saved from themselves. They are in error because they have been presented with the wrong diagnosis.

International trade, which was still only about 10 per cent of the GDP of the US in 1993, is neither the main cause of the reduction in the manufacturing sector nor the main reason why the less educated US workers earn declining real wages. The former is primarily caused by the shift in domestic spending away from manufactured goods towards services. The evidence suggests that the growing wage gap has not been caused by factor price equalisation. The rising demand for skilled labour and the fall in demand for unskilled labour has not been caused by a changing mix in response to international trade, but by technical change.[101] In other words, the falling demand for unskilled labour has been caused primarily by changes in production methods not by changes in what is produced.

Indeed, it can be confidently argued that international trade is not the primary cause of the secular rise - or the fall - in the national income of the United States. The primary cause is the advancement and application of technology, which has led to increases in total factor productivity. Between 1992 and 1996, GDP growth averaged 3.2 per cent, while over the period 1996 to 2000, GDP growth averaged 4 per cent and rates of employment reached thirty-year highs. The year of 1996 marks the start of the Internet era during which there has been a bunching of reinforcing technical innovations. These innovations have engendered a steep rise in investments. It is estimated that some 30 per cent of this spurt in growth in GDP is due to spending by companies on their high-technology infrastructures.[102] This includes computers, servers, switching devices and software.[103] These investments have yielded steep gains in productivity and earnings, which, in turn, have spurred further capital deepening and increases in productivity.

There have also been significant changes in monetary and fiscal policy, which have complemented these surges in innovative investments. This cycle of high-tech-led productivity increases has allowed the economy to grow without straining capacity. The Federal Reserve Board's monetary policy has contained inflation by managing the growth of aggregate demand to within these expanding limits of capacity. Concurrently, with astute monetary management, has been the federal government's conversion of chronic deficits into bountiful surpluses. Much of the credit for these surpluses, however, must go to the system of government, with its separation of powers.

The Democratic administration's spending plans were contained by a Republican Party-controlled Congress in 1994.

By contributing to full employment, low inflation and high growth rates, the Federal Reserve Board and Congress have engendered a toleration of free-market competition and the creative destruction that is inherent in this technically-driven transformation. The boom environment has emboldened those who have sought to extend market-driven globalisation. In the end, it did not matter what the theorists had said. NAFTA was passed because US corporations had estimated that their opportunities far exceeded the threat of Mexican competition. Similarly, business interests informed the politicians that the business opportunities in a market of 1.4 billion consumers exceeded, by far, the threat of Chinese competition. Hence, the passage through Congress of the Permanent Normal Trade Relations with China in September 2000. These estimates would have been far less persuasive if, instead of being accompanied with a growing economy, NAFTA had coincided with a recession.[104]

The superior economic growth rate of the United States economy has also demonstrated the ability of competitive market capitalism to raise living standards. The advances in information technology have lowered transaction costs and stimulated an expansion in trans-national market transactions. Expanding markets have increased competition, reduced the effectiveness of most forms of intervention and activated the deregulation of domestic markets and the privatisation of government enterprises. This interactive, market-expanding process has aided the diffusion of technical change and helped to raise living standards. There are, however, limits to this process of globalisation.

It is the elites in the G-7 nations who profess to understand and promote globalisation. The general public in these nations has not been called upon to endorse, through the ballot box, global enhancing trade and monetary policies. Yet some sections within these societies have not been quiescent. They have charged the international financial agencies with operating a credit cartel and with wielding this power to effect economic policies that unfortunately for the inhabitants, have been failures, in part, because they have given out wrong advice. The shock treatment given to Russia displayed an egregiousness that may yet prove fatal to the IMF. Few developed economies have shown a willingness to open their markets to the products of the developing countries. Most importantly, the clients of the financial institutions are governments, and most of these have reneged on their negotiated agreements of 'aid for government austerity and market liberating measures.' The elites in these developing countries have either been unable to deliver their economies into the global system or they have simply continued to advance their interests at the expense of their citizens and the taxpayers of the donor countries.

The IMF-World Bank credit cartel policy of extending loans in return for market reforms has proven to be an expensive failure. Few developing economies have been, or will be drawn into the global market by these means. A number of thinkers have suggested that the governments of these developing countries be taken over and returned to a form of benevolent colonial administration. Others advocate that governments stand aside and encourage global corporations to use their resources to activate a mutually advantageous technological transformation. One such approach suggests that the revolution in bandwidth, via new low-orbit-satellites, will make possible the availability of low-cost mobile phones.[105] Some are advocating the international lending agencies be transformed from a credit cartel into a grant-dispensing agency for G-7 taxpayers' monies. If this proposal is put into operation, the poor in these developing countries will effectively be placed on the welfare rolls of the donor countries.

While many governments appear willing to free their domestic markets in order to attain rising living standards, very few are willing to open all sectors of their economy to global corporations. In refusing to sanction the General Electric-Honeywell merger, the European commissioners were mindful of the interests of their European aerospace manufacturers. The EU (as well as Japan) has shown a reluctance to lowering the walls that protect its farmers. Few countries allow foreigners to own their media companies.[106] The US Congress has shown its opposition to foreign airline carriers amalgamating with US companies or for government-owned tele-communication companies to owning US wireless operators. Similarly, European tele-communications operators have met government resistance to their plans to amalgamate with national enterprises. South American telephone monopolies have been effectively barring US carriers into their markets by setting high charges to use their local networks. Such actions do not auger well for the WTO's Basic Tele-communications Agreement, for it remains to be seen how many nations will be willing to see their tele-communications industries owned and operated by global tele-communications corporations.

Similarly, governments have been willing to lower their tariffs and embrace free trade but few have shown any enthusiasm for common labour markets. Politicians have been alerted to the expected downward effects on the wage rates of the lower skilled workers, their inability to allocate welfare entitlements and the possible balkanisation of their societies. In the near future, the United States and Canada will be confronted with the possibility of forming a common market with Mexico. Likewise, Europe will be grappling with the consequences of expanding the common market from fifteen to twenty-three states. The elite in these countries will be called upon to articulate their notions of nationalism and transnationalism. Does nationalism foster competitiveness? Does this competitiveness lead to international conflict? Can this aggression be subverted by encouraging multiculturalism and multilingualism and will this engender an allegiance to global government, which is, after all, an abstraction above and beyond the nation-state?

Whatever the outcome of these deliberations, there is, as yet, no global government with a global central bank. Instead of one currency managed by such a central bank, there is a tripolar system based on the dollar, yen and the euro. Despite achieving convergence in rates of inflation, the leaders of the respective blocs have insisted upon policies that have resulted in volatile exchange rates that are out of sync with economic fundamentals. Resources have, as a result, been misallocated. Similarly, the liberation of international capital flows has served to distort rather than to enhance the efficient allocation of resources. Bereft of controls, emerging markets have been subjected to speculative attacks that have resulted in damaging dislocations. During these crises, the huge public loans from the IMF have allowed private investors to get their money out. The emerging markets remain vulnerable, because the tripolar system has yet to introduce punitive measures against speculators.

Nor has the tripolar system agreed as to how and when private investors are to be compelled to join government bail-outs of troubled emerging markets. Such inaction confirms that the IMF-US Treasury's priority lies, not with achieving an efficient global allocation of capital, but with sustaining and protecting the profitability of Wall Street's financial institutions.

The aforementioned financial crises indicate the source of the instability of this tripolar system. Markets are now so interdependent that default by Russia can threaten the collapse of the New York stock market. This suggests that the reinforcing increases in high-tech investments, stock markets and exchange rates, could move sharply in reverse as a consequence of a shock anywhere on the globe. That place could, of course, be the United States and the shock could be the slackening of the rate of innovation and a subsequent drop in the growth rate to historic levels. Whether market reverses spin the economy into a recession or merely into a slow-down, the tolerance of the general public for liberated markets and for market-driven globalisation will be sorely tested

According to the path-dependency theory, a change in sector prices will trigger a shift in policy. This shift could be away from market-oriented resource allocation towards the government as a source of security. This could mean the reintroduction of regulations and protectionism. Such measures could, in turn, further depress the US and the global economy.

But what about the elite and the epistemic communities? If faced with the publics' desire for protectionism, will the elite continue to champion global interests and will they staunchly support the free-market and its partner, creative destruction? Will globalisation still be in the economic interest of the elite? Will the impulse of the entrepreneurial culture be sufficiently strong to overwhelm the undoubted opposition both within the United States and other advanced economies to technological dynamism and economic growth? Or will the entrepreneurs of this anti-materialistic movement emulate their libertarian opponents of two decades ago and effect a policy coup?

These questions pose problems for the contending explanations of regulatory change. The deterministic economic hypotheses are based exclusively on the behaviour of self-interested entities facing shifting constraints. There is no place for a shift in ideology among the elite or any other entity or group. By contrast, the cognitive hypothesis invites the consideration of the structure of economic decision making and the establishment of a testable theory of belief in relation to this process.

The limits to such an exercise are also manifest. It is not possible to measure the significance of ideology on events and events upon ideology. Rather, it is asserted that ideas and ideology do help shape events and that whatever the prime source of change, it is strengthened when guided by a belief or ideology.

Two points are worth making. The first is that the influence of ideology in shaping policy and influencing events will be determined by the constitutional structure and the constraints on the exercise of executive power.[107] Second, it is observed that ideology, when in the form of a desired order, is different from a scientific paradigm. The former is not displaced and confined to history when supporters of alternative candidates declare it invalid. The return, in modified form, of mercantilist, anti-materialistic and *laissez-faire* ideologies testifies to the durability of economic paradigms.

METHOD AND CONJECTURES

Central to the above three exercises has been the quest for explanations. The element common to the accepted explanations is a conceptualisation of the individual, not as an automaton or passive entity or as an ideal type, but as a responsive, human entity - an entity that is described as an entrepreneur, who possesses purposefulness, expresses preferences, beliefs, expectations and knowledge. Such human qualities, along with the element of uncertainty, limited knowledge and institutionally-shaped incentives, form the circumstances within which the individual entrepreneur makes decisions, the consequences of which propel the respective bureaucratic, political and market processes.

The deductive theories of individual human nature in which economic man is posited as applying reason to his circumstances, which are known perfectly, have been regarded by one critic, Shackle, as being misguided. He has alleged that they have yielded erroneous results.[108] As the future is unknown, the said economic approach implies that conduct is based on reason applied, not to known circumstances but to those that are unknown and uncertain. Although the individual's conduct is based on subjective expectations about circumstances, reason, according to Shackle, cannot be based solely on uncertainty, nor can the bridge to individual conduct between reason and uncertainty be accomplished by the deployment of probability analysis. Such analysis is not about uncertainty; it is about numbers that convey information. It is an example, according to Shackle, of the conceptual imprecision in economics. Future events, characterised by singularities, disqualify the past as a predictor of the future. There is no instrument that can predict the likelihood of future events.[109]

Shackle's world is a kaleidoscopic one of flux and change, of markets ceaselessly co-ordinating and disseminating information that infringes on human choice and decision making. Man's actions invariably involve the future, but the future is unknowable. While the shape of the future may have its outline generated by individual desires and imaginations, it is known to no one, neither the participants in the markets, nor the individuals in the collectivities. In such a world, it is not only the response of individuals to scarcity that is important, but also their response to uncertainty.

This Austrian explanation of the ensuing processes presents a challenging research agenda. The explanatory agenda includes accounts of how individuals respond to circumstances; how their preferences and beliefs affected their behaviour and how - or whether - co-ordination is assisted and equilibrium restored or extended as a result of individual responsiveness.

The favoured approach is an inductive one. It consists of observing the conjuncture of the past and of the present on the individual interacting with the interconnected bureaucratic, political and market processes. The deployment of *post hoc* observations, however, must limit the interpretation to the particular event rather than to a generalisation. *Post hoc*, the circumstances perceived by the analyst will usually be considerably different from that actually experienced by the entrepreneur at the time of the decision. Successful entrepreneurial politicians, for instance, probably rely on their intuition and foresight rather than their ideological baggage. Yet it is such baggage that, *ex post*, analysts may be tempted to incorrectly attach to the politician at the time of the decision. However, we cannot go very far without a satisfactory explanation of what shapes individual perceptions, preferences, beliefs and ideology.

The distance travelled will, in part, be determined by our understanding of the rhetorical,[110] of how the activists, the academic, bureaucratic and political entrepreneurs, came to believe and act on what persuaded them. Have the activists, 'the players' - the entrepreneurs - been persuaded exclusively by a theory of truth, an epistemology of what they hold? Does the truth take the form of knowledge derived from the scientific test of falsifiable hypotheses? What is the truth that persuades?

Leaving the first question until later, the economist engaged in a modern project can be expected to answer with an emphatic affirmative to the second question. Operating within the public space of the university, seemingly protected from private interests and political interference, and, therefore, immunised from metaphysics and moral precepts of others, the economist is free to apply the crucial falsifying tests within (and now even beyond), the walls of the discipline's traditional empire. As for the third question, this can be addressed by examining the so-called 'Washington Consensus.' In this doctrine, the phrase 'universal convergence' is substituted for the word 'truth.' It is accompanied by the declaration that 'drawn from the body of robust empirical generalisations that form the core of economics,' the market economies subject to macro-economic discipline enjoy superior economic performances over those with attenuated markets and profligate treasuries.[111]

Despite these claims, there are reasons to doubt that economists, let alone the 'laity,' are persuaded, either solely or primarily, by the knowledge (truth) emerging from the scientific process of refutation. Few economic hypotheses lend themselves to such rigorous testing, because they face many uncontrollable variables.[112] Contrasting with the few that have been so tested, are the many that have been subject to verification. Even economists who regard themselves as scientists are inclined to establish truth by offering their beliefs rather than by testing their doubts. Theories subject to verification are accepted for reasons other than their, often patchy, predictive accuracy and these reasons are to do with individual preferences, values and belief. For instance, the recommendation of pricing rules for public entities is reflective of the values and preferences of the advising economist, for, as their wholesale rejection indicates, these rules have not been subject to rigorous tests of consequence (see Chapter 7). Acceptance of the theory that the market generates more efficient outcomes than more coercive orders involves a belief in the complementary value of freedom from coercion as well as the assertion of superior economic consequences.

To know what persuades individuals possessing autonomy is to provide an explanation of their volition, for their action is, in large part, assumed to be shaped by what is persuasive to them. Ideas, theories and ideologies accepted and articulated by influential decision makers are clearly highly persuasive. The above observations and interpretations suggest that individuals, including practitioners of scientific economies, are persuaded to accept ideas, theories and ideologies, neither primarily, nor because, they embody truth derived from axiomatic demonstration.

Addressing the questions as to why a theory is persuasive to economists and other individuals, and why it quickly disseminates, requires more than the consideration of logic, knowledge or truth that it contains or reveals. Consideration must be given to the form of the theory, to the language and style of its presentation to the media through which it is propagated, the attributes, nationality and location of the propagating theorist and school of thought, and the political and social milieu of the receiving communities.[113]

This question has not been answered because the intrinsic merits of ideas, theories or ideologies were not considered to be the major sources of their persuasiveness. Rather, the three exercises of this Chapter reveal that the theories that were persuasive were so because those who deployed them were also persuasive. They were influential groups of bureaucratic and political entrepreneurs who spotted propitious stages of technological and economic development and who fashioned their ideas and theories into a confirmatory ideology for the activist politician.[114]

Although having adopted this approach, it is nevertheless interesting and, perhaps useful, to offer for consideration some selected speculations.

Its style and its exclusion of mathematics can in part, account for the persuasiveness of Keynes's General Theory. The acceptance of Keynesianism within the Anglo-American elite of the time is partly explained by the prestige of his university, Cambridge, his assured position in the establishment of what was then a major power and the access to elite positions afforded his disciples. The dissemination of Milton Friedman's theory of monetarism, likewise, owed something to his skills as a controversialist, a performer on television and to the location of Chicago-trained disciples within the economic elite of a number of Latin American and European countries. John Williamson's 'Washington Consensus' was launched at a time when the Soviet system had collapsed and many developing countries were seeking an alternative economic and political order.[115] The polarised politics, hyper inflation and rise of irrationalist parties in Austria during the immediate aftermath of the First World War, it can be argued, influenced the methodology of the influential logical positivists and the interpretation of Hayek and Schumpeter, in particular, as to the direction of liberal, democratic capitalism. To the logical positivists, the scientist was to be protected from dangerous, irrational politicians, afforded neutral space and high, epistemological status. Arguing from their Austrian experience of popular rule and the damaging redistributions and misallocation of constructivism, Hayek and Schumpeter were decidedly pessimistic as to the prospects of yoking majoritarian, representative democracy to the market economy.

Central to Hayek's epistemological theory, his social theory and his criticism of constructive rationalism, is his concept of the spontaneous order of rules that govern the conduct of individuals. Defined by laws that, in turn, define property and rights, the market process is a spontaneous order. The market process enables individuals to discover knowledge of the economy, of society and of themselves by adapting their behaviour as a result of trial and error. Progress is perceived as evolving from individuals who seek to learn from mistakes, not from conscious, state intervention, for the latter involves the substitution of inferior means of discovery and co-ordination of knowledge, so that the benefits of such solutions are greatly less than the costs.

Conceptualised as a spontaneous, evolving order, this deductive process of refutation cannot be tested by its predictive value, for 'theories' of evolutionary process are not predictive. This is a handicap for those who intend to persuade, or to build a case for change on the prediction of improvement. As the survey of the formulations of the deregulatory economists of the transport sector in the US in Chapter 6 will show, they did not consider that market to be an evolving process. It was a state whose imperfections were examined and outcomes predicted by the reforming economist. Comparing predictions with outcomes, however, served to question the deregulators' assumption of knowledge superior to that possessed and discovered by market participants.

Proponents of rational intervention claim that the market is neither spontaneous nor orderly.[116] Democratic socialists make a projection here in which Hayek is bracketed with proponents of a vulgar version of the free market. To Hayek, the market is not an independent, disembodied process, for it is defined by property and rights that are shaped by an evolving law and enforced by justice. Removing government from the economy will not automatically improve co-ordination. This will be achieved, for the most part, by institutions that facilitate such co-ordination by means of the competitive order, and by individuals solving such problems through institutions that facilitate co-ordination (not through ordered competition aimed at particular goals). Hayek, however, fails to present a means of repairing the damages of the constructive rationalist. He leaves open the possibility of altering institutions (without presenting a set of criteria of evaluation) or of establishing the extent to which the development of legal and political institutions is spontaneous and, therefore, part of the spontaneous order.[117] A consequence of this ambiguity is that Hayek faces attack, not only from socialists, but also from Tories who adhere to Oakeshott's conservatism.[118]

Without the pressure of change, particularly technical change, there would be no economic progress and without the action of opportunistic entrepreneurs the economy would fail to have a co-ordinating market process and would simply regress into stagnating pools of autarchy. To the Austrians, competition between agents in the market process serves to co-ordinate plans. New knowledge, technical progress and intervention seem to tear up plans and combinations and then   disintegrate, only, to amended by the actions of entrepreneurs. The latter, by identifying and acting, facilitate co-ordination and move the process towards equilibrium.[119] Such entrepreneurs are not exclusively calculating, *homo economicus*, but intuitive individuals alert to the opportunities of making a profit (producers), increasing satisfaction (consumers), accruing power (bureaucrats), and achieving power and glory (politicians). Yet, just as these actions are not accounted for by models constructed upon rational, calculating man facing shifting constraints, so the consequences of their actions cannot be assumed to reinforce co-ordination and so restore equilibrium.

Buchanan's model of the bureaucratic Leviathan does not account for the emergence of an iconoclastic deregulator, in the form of Roy Pulsifer, within a regulatory agency, the CAB. Wall Street foreign exchange dealers described Leo Melamed and his colleagues as a bunch of 'crap shooters in pork bellies', when they introduced, in 1971, a public market in foreign currency futures, the International Monetary Market (IMM). Paul Samuelson also, incorrectly, predicted that the first successful futures market in financial instruments would attract neither the worth of governments nor their exchange rates and stock markets.[120] Stephen Littlechild, despite developing an analysis based on an Austrian perspective, declared that Prime Minister Margaret Thatcher's privatisation programme 'was a stroke of political entrepreneurship for which I, like other commentators, was quite unprepared.'[121] Robert Peel astounded his contemporaries by repealing the Corn Laws and launching Britain's free trade movement. He had done the unthinkable; he had put nation before party.[122] Few political analysts of the realist school can account for the emergence of Gorbachev within the Communist Party of the USSR. Nor did many envisage the balkanisation of the Soviet Empire within so short a period of time.

These may have been surprises, but technological innovations, from the railroads to information technology, quickly attracted adherents who endowed them with 'magical' properties. To such Gnostics, these are redemptive technologies that allegedly reveal a truth, which will transform the material world. The technological entrepreneur is endowed with a salvationist's spirit. His endeavours will extend knowledge and freedom.[123] Yet, to those whose activities and lives have been adversely effected, entrepreneurs are not knights on white horses lancing bureaucracy's Leviathans.   They are dangerous ideologues whose lance has shattered the nurturing bureaux and whose reward is ostracisation. The entrepreneur in the market is not a hero in the eyes of those in industries and activities that have been destroyed, but a precursor of Schumpeter's 'perennial gale of creative destruction.' He is depicted as a Mogul or a barbarian horseman of the Apocalypse. To the party man, the trimmer, an activist, reforming politician who shifts the paradigm, is a dangerous dogmatist who destabilises the system by fracturing the accommodating coalitions, forcing consideration of the conflict between individual values and social outcomes. Despite the material rewards, such is the abnegation that few resist the temptation to become respectable, forsaking Hyde for Jekyll, poacher for gamekeeper, wealthy (but benighted) commoner for knight of the realm.

Similarly, the noted inclination of the predatory financial entrepreneur to pen opinions that declare an apostasy in market-driven, entrepreneurial opportunism, is suggestive of the disdain for the fickleness of financial markets and the strength of conformist forces.[124]

These entrepreneurs have operated within markets that have been shaped by societies that have exhibited different ideological conceptions of man. One result has been that there is no single justifying ideology that has served to preserve the crisis-prone capitalist system.

According to liberal philosophers and apologists, the liberal order in Britain emerged, not from man's conscious designs, but from their purposive actions. Individual liberty was to be attained by containing the coercive state. Yet at its apogee, liberal, hegemonic *Pax Britannica* faced the scorn of cultural critics. The preferences of the traditionalists, both discovered and invented, ambushed the advancing, but tainted, acquisitive industrial class.[125] Traditionalists mobilised the power of a central government to douse the spirit and halt the drive of industrial entrepreneurship. In Britain, freedom from the coercive state was not to be enjoyed by industrial entrepreneurs but by gentlemen entrepreneurs of the financial markets.[126] French philosophers dismissed British liberal prudence. Reason was applied to human affairs in the creation, by conscious design, of utopian societies. From *a priori* reasoning, abstract principles were deducted and from these the principles of new economic and political organisations were formulated. These principles were to be applied in pursuit of an ideological version of the future, regardless of the customs or traditions of the society. The capture of elite educational institutions by Saint Simonian thinkers reinforced the strengthening of state authority in France. A strand of scientism that infiltrated into mainstream neo-classical economics in the form of 'engineering' can also be traced to these schools of thought.

In Continental Europe, many societies were involved both in the construction of their nation states and in steering their growing markets. As a result, French thought, not British liberalism, held sway. Particularly influential, were the revolutionaries turned entrepreneurial reformers of the Saint-Simon school of socialism. Through the replication of the *Credit Mobilier*, a deposit and investment institution designed to facilitate industrial and infrastructure investment, Continental capitalism took its distinctive form. Monopoly or finance capitalism, rather than the British type of competitive capitalism, emerged.

These developments coincided with the mid-century public works and railway projects. The Marxist, Hobsbawm, in considering the conversion of Saint Simonians such as the brothers Isaacs and Emile Pereire, P. F. Talbot and F. M. de Lesseps, who built the Suez-Canal, into 'dynamic adventurous entrepreneurs', declared that:

...such men thought in continents and oceans. For them the world was a single unit, bound together by rails of iron and steam engines, because the horizons of business were like their dreams, world-wide. For such men destiny, history, and profit were one and the same thing.[127]

Although the French philosophical notions of the perfectibility of man influenced the polity of the United States, its philosophical roots were grounded in the British liberal tradition. American society had a pre-eminent regard for political and civil rights. Indeed, it was the form that its polity took that was to have profound consequences for the relationship between the state and individual liberty. The majoritarian, representative form of democracy has been shown to have an inherent tendency to interventionist, re-distributive measures.

This tendency of the American political system explains, in large part, why special interest groups have been able to impose constraining, protective economic regulation. The influence of majoritarian rules also explains why a change in such constraining measures and a move towards economic liberalism requires an ideological shift of sufficient force to actually change or remove the majoritarian rules.

Now at issue is whether the various forms of capitalism will co-exist, adapt or merge into the American version of entrepreneurial capitalism. This is known as a system of shareholder value, in which capital is raised through the market and directed towards investors' or owners' objectives. It is by no means certain that this form of capitalism, whether assisted or not, will triumph over the various forms of corporatism that exist in Continental Europe and South East Asia. Nor is it certain that liberal, capitalistic democracies will triumph in the Third World. Globalisation is no longer the undisputed torch-bearer of economic growth and modernisation. The neo-imperialistic policies of the United States government and its Western allies are failing to embed market institutions and freedoms. Discredited one-party states remain in place, while the West's representative democracies creak under the threats to the functions and funding of government.

Whatever the system or systems which will emerge they will be faced with two realities. The first is that global capitalism, as socialism, cannot be effectively guided by a few wise bankers who, instead of planning the economy, fix the rate of interest and establish the money supply. The operations of the financial institutions of the United States and international institutions will come under increasing pressure to democratise. The second reality is the statelessness of the ever-increasingly powerful capital markets. It remains to be seen whether the institutions and regimes that emerge will facilitate an improvement, or activate a degradation, in co-ordinated market activity.

Notes

1.   Bergsten, C.Fred (2000), 'The Backlash Against Globalization,' *Institute for International Economics*, 9 May, p.3.
2.   Lukas, Aaron (2000), *WTO Report Card III Globalization and Developing Countries*, Center for Trade Policy Studies, Cato Institute, 20 June, p.2.
3.   Talbot, Strobe (2000), 'Self-Determination in an Interdependent World,' *Foreign Policy*, **118**(Spring), p.157.
4.   Pfaff, William (2001), 'The Question of Hegemony,' *Foreign Affairs*, **80**(10).
5.   Crossette, Barbara (2000), 'Canada Tries to Define Line Between Human and National Rights,' *The Times*, London, 14 September.
6.   Friedman, Thomas L. (1999), *The Lexus and the Olive Tree*, London: Straus & Giroux.
7.   Parenti, Michael (1995), *Against Empire,* San Francisco: City Light Books, p.15.
8.   Mills, Wright C. (1956), *The Power Elite*, reprinted with a new afterword by Alan Wolfe (2000), NewYork: Oxford University Press.
9.   Lasch, Chrisopher (1996), *The Revolt of the Elites and the Betrayal of Democracy*, London: W.W. Norton, pp, 25-26.
10. Reich, Robert B. (1992), *The Work of Nations, Preparing Ourselves for 21st Century Capitalism,* New York: Simon and Schuster.
11. See for instance Buchanan, Patrick J. (1998), *The Great Betrayal: How American Sovereignty and Social Justice are Being Sacrificed to the Gods of the Global Economy,* London: Little, Brown & Company; Micklethwait, John and Adrian Wooldridge (2000), *Future Perfect: The Challenge and Hidden Promise of Globalization,* London: Crown Business Books.
12. Wright, Robert (2000), *Non Zero. The Logic of Human Destiny*, London: Pantheon Books, p.198.
13. Bhagwati, Jagdish, (1999), 'It's a Small World After All', *The New York Times*, 3 May.
14. Buchanan, James M. (1976), The Justice of Natural Liberty, in Fred. R. Ghahe (ed.), *Adam Smith and the Wealth of Nations,* Boulder, Colorado: Associated University Press, p. 68.
15. Tool, Marc R. (1987), 'Evolutionary Economics,' *Journal of Economic Issues*, **21**(3), p. 958.
16. Hall, John A. (1986), *Powers & Liberties. The Causes and Consequences of the Rise of the West*, Harmondsworth: Pelican Books, p.5.
17. Karl Polanyi argued that the market consisted of anonymous entities, trucking and trading in a social vacuum. In effect, they were disembodied from society. Thanks to the inherent social and political tensions that are aroused, Polanyi argued that this condition was unsustainable. The result was state intervention and an economy that is, in part, embodied in society by the state. Polanyi, Karl (1944), *The Great Transformation,* Boston: Beacon Press.
18. Abu-Lughad, J. (1989), *Before European Hegemony: The World System AD 1250-1350*, London and New York: Oxford University Press.
19. Frank, Andre Gunder (1998), *Re Orient. Global Economy in the Asian Age,* Berkeley and Los Angeles: The University of California Press.
20. Belief is probably a more appropriate term because knowledge implies truth of what is known. Frequently, the sociology of knowledge is concerned with explaining the social causes of beliefs such that they are neither caused, nor related, to the truth of what they describe. See North, Douglas C. (1981), *Structure and Change in Economic History*, London: W. W. Norton & Co., Chapter 5.
21. Giddens, A. (1984), *The Constitution of Society. An Outline of Theory of Structuration*, Cambridge: Polity Press.
22. Becker, G.S. (1976), *The Economic Approach to Human Behaviour,* Chicago: University of Chicago Press, p. 9.
23. Solow, R.M. (1970), *Growth Theory: An Exposition*, Oxford: Oxford University Press.

24. North, Douglas C. and Thomas, Robert (1973), *The Rise of the Western World: A New Economic History,* Cambridge: The University Press.
25. Mark, Karl and Friederich Engels (1872), *The Communist Manifesto,* reprinted (1985), London: Penguin, p.83.
26. Schumpeterian entrepreneurship promotes disequilibrium; Austrian entrepreneurship promotes equilibrium. 'Austrian entrepreneurship stems from the discovery of the existence of profitable discrepancies, gaps and mismatches in knowledge and information that others have not perceived and exploited, and the entrepreneur acts to capitalise upon the opportunity for gain or advantages which that discover presents. These activities increase knowledge about the situation, reduce the general level of uncertainty over time, and promote market processes that help to reduce or eliminate the gap between leaders and followers.'
27. 'No matter what part of a modernising economy is being investigated, we observe that economic conditions change, that each change entails a specific disequilibrium, and that human agents act to regain equilibrium in their domain. What they do is in essence entrepreneurship'. Schultz, Theodor W. (1990), *Restoring Economic Equilibrium,* Oxford: Basil Blackwell, p.23.
28. Schumpeter, Joseph. A. (1950), *Capitalism Socialism and Democracy,* London: George Allen & Unwin, p.83.
29. Schumpeter, Joseph. A. (1928), 'The Instability of Capitalism,' *Economic Journal,* 38*(*September), p.386.
30. Harvey, David (1989), *The Condition of Post-modernity. An Enquiry into the Origin of Cultural Change,* Oxford: Blackwell, pp.306-307.
31. Innis Harold, A. (1951), *The Bias of Communication,* reprinted with an introduction by Paul Hayer and David Crowley (1991), Toronto: University of Toronto Press.
32. Basalla, George. (1988), *The Evolution of Technology,* Cambridge: Cambridge University Press.
33. Barringer, Felicity (2000), 'Old Dogs See Opportunities in New Tricks,' *The New York Times,* 11 December.
34. Buchanan, R. A. (1994), *The Power of the Machine,* London: Penguin Books, p. 39.
35. Baumol,William J. (1990), Enterpreneurships: Production, Unproduction and Destruction,' *Journal of Political Economy,* **89**(5), p.893.
36. Ibid., p. 894.
37. Borsook, Paulina (2000), *Cyberfish. A Critical Romp Through the Terrible Libertarian Culture of High Tech,* London: Public Affairs.
38. Reich, Robert B. (1984), *The Next American Frontier,* Harmondsworth: Penguin, p. 298.
39. Chandler, Alfred D. (1990), *Scale and Scope: The Dynamics of Industrial Capitalism,* Cambridge MA, Belkop Press of Harvard University Press: pp. 605-621.
40. Kessler, Andy (2000), 'Creative Destruction can be Lucrative,' *The Wall Street Journal,* 18 April.
41. Mandel, Michael. J. (2000), *The Coming Internet Depression,* London: Basic Books.
42. Friedman, Thomas, op.cit., p.11.
43. Greenspan, Alan (2000), *Global Economic Integration: Opportunities and Challenges,* The Federal Reserve Board, Jackson Hole, Wyoming, 25 August.
44. Postrel, Virginia (2000), 'It's good times, not bad, that nurture the enemies of the free market,' *The New York Times,* 7 September.
45. There are a number of writers, including von Mises, Polanyi, Shackle as well as Hayek who have contributed to what could be termed 'the Austrian theory of knowledge'. See Kukathas, Chandran (1990), *Hayek and Modern Liberalism,* Oxford: Clarendon Press, pp.103-105.
46. Pelzman, Sam (1976), 'Toward a More General Theory of Regulation,' *The Journal of Law and Economics,* **14**, pp.211-248, at 212.
47. Stigler, George J. and Clair Friedland (1962), 'What can Regulators Regulate? The Case of Electricity,' *Journal of Law and Economics,* **5**(October), pp. 1-16.
48. Stigler, George J. (1971), 'The Theory of Economic Regulation,' *Bell Journal of Economics,* **2,** pp.1-21.

49.   Pelzman, Sam, op.cit.
50.   Becker, Gary S. (1983), 'A Theory of Competition Among Pressure Groups for Political Influence,' *Quarterly Journal of Economics,* **3**(August), pp. 371-400.
51.   Brennan. G. and James M. Buchanan (1984), 'Voter Choice: Evaluating Political Alternations,' *American Behavioral Scientist,* **28**(November/December), pp.185-201.
52.   Arrow, Kenneth J. (1951), *Social Choice and Industrial Values,* London: Wiley.
53.   James Buchanan exposed the 'strange' project of trying to model a community of separate persons teleologically, as if 'social states' could be arranged in an order of ascendancy, and in terms of a maximand. Buchanan, James (1954), 'Social Choice in Voting and the Market,' *Journal of Political Economy,* **62**(August), pp.334-43. Buchanan also differentiates his observation from Arrow, for he charges the latter with not adopting methodological individualism.
54.   Arrow and Black had pointed out the potential for cycles when issues involved redistribution under a majority rule. Members of losing coalitions would have an incentive to join winning coalitions. Separation of powers is one means by which stability can be attained. Black also demonstrated, in his medium voter theorem, the existence of a majority rule equilibrium. Black, D. (1948), 'On the Rationale of Group Decision Marking,' *Journal of Political Economy,* (February), pp.23-24.
55.   Shepsle, Kenneth A. and Barry R. Weingast (1981), 'Structure-Induced Equilibrium and Legislative Choice,' *Public Choice,* **37**, pp.503-520.
56.   McKelvey, Richard D. (1979),'General Conditions for Global Intransitivities in Formal Voting Models,' *Econometrica,* **47,** pp.1085-1111.
57.   Noll, Roger G. (1999), *Telecommunications Reform in Developing Countries,* AEI-Brookings Center for Regulatory Studies, Working Paper 99-10 November, p.6.
58.   See, for instance, Levine, Michael E. (1986-87), 'Airline Competition in Deregulated Markets: Theory, Firm Strategy and Public Policy,' *Yale Journal on Regulation,* **4**(2) pp. 393-494. Levine points out that, unbeknown to him as a deregulator, the airlines had hidden assets from leases on gates and historic leases on hangers. He also argues that, contrary to Pelzman's point, labour enjoyed substantial rents under regulation.
59.   It would appear from the accuracy of the predictions concerning investment in aircraft that the world's airline industry behaves in an adaptive manner, responding to changes in demand, and subject to lead times in aircraft orders. See, Ellison, Anthony P. and E.M. Stafford (1974), *The Dynamics of the Civil Aviation Industry,* Lexington: Lexington Books, DC Heath & Co.
60.   Both Levine and Khan, former deregulators at the CAB, argue that researchers, including themselves, uncovered information about the airline (and other), industries that contributed to their deregulation. They imply that the deregulated airline industry consists of rational actors. Their predictions about the deregulated industry were consequently unable to reveal anything that the rational actors already knew and acted upon. It is arguable, however, that the actors in the airline industry remain adaptive in their reactions. Kahn, Alfred E. (1990), 'Deregulation: Looking Backward and Looking Forward,' *Yale Journal on Regulation,* **7**, pp. 325-334; Levine, Michael E., *Airline Competition,* op.cit.
61.   Keller, Theodore E. (1984), 'Theories of Regulation and the Deregulation Movement,' *Public Choice,* **44**(1), pp.103-145.
62.   Peltzman,S. (1989), 'The Economic Theory of Regulation after a Decade of Deregulation,' *Brookings Papers on Economic Analysis*: *Microeconomics,* Washington: Brookings Institution. p.32
63.   Ibid.pp 24,25.
64.   Keller, Theodore E., op.cit.
65.   Ibid.
66.   Levine, Michael E., *Airline Competition,* op.cit., p 443.
67.   Peltzman, S, *Brookings,* op.cit., p.59. Khan quoted by Peltzman, S.
68.   Levine, Michael E. (1981), 'Revisionism Revised? Airline Deregulation and the Public Interest,' *Law and Contemporary Problems,* **44** (1), p.194.
69.   Civil Aeronautics Board (1975), *Regulatory Reform: Report of the CAB Special Staff Report,* Washington DC.

70. Haggard, Stephen and Beth A. Simons (1987), 'Theories of International Regimes,' *International Organisation*, **41**(3), p.495.
71. McKeown, Timothy J. (1983), 'Hegemonic Stability Theory and 19ᵗʰ Century Tariff Levels in Europe,' *International Organisation*, 37(1), pp.73-91.
72. Lipson, Charles (1982), 'Transformation of Trade. The Sources and Effects of Regime Change,' *International Organisation*, **36**(2), p.42.
73. Krugman, Paul (1998), *Pop Nationalism*, Cambridge, Massachusetts: The MIT Press, p. 83.
74. Eichengreen, Barry (1990), *Elusive Stability. Essays in the History of International Finance 1919-1939*. Cambridge: Cambridge University Press, p.311.
75. Arthur, Brian W. (1990), 'Positive Feedback in the Economy,' *Scientific America*, February, p.98.
76. Goldstein, Judith (1986), 'The Political Economy of Trade : Institutions of Protection,' *American Political Science Review*, 80, pp.161-184.
77. Cavanagh, John 'US Leadership in the Global Economy,' *Foreign Policy in Focus*. http:// www.foreignpolicy-infocus.org/papers/ economy/index.html.
78. Department of Commerce, Office of Telecommunications, WTO, *Q's & A's on the Agreement on Basic Telecommunications Services.* http:// infoserv2.ita.doc.gov/ot
79. Mills, C. Wright, *Power Elite*, p.367.
80. World Business (2000), 'The World's Largest Companies,' *The Wall Street Journal Reports*, 25 September.
81. Mills, C. Wright, op.cit., p.375.
82. Cowhey, Peter F. (1990), 'The International Telecommunications Regime: The Political Roots of Regimes for High Technology,' *International Organisation*, 44(2), pp.198-199.
83. Haggard, Stephen and Beth A. Simons, op.cit., p.510.
84. Hundt, Reed E (2000), *You Say You Want A Revolution*, New Haven and London: Yale University Press, p.203.
85. Gates, Bill (1995), 'Deregulation Essential to Information Highway,' *Business Day*, Johannesburg, 22 June.
86. Thierer, Adam D. (1997), What's Next for Telecommunications Deregulation? *The Heritage Foundation*, Roe Backgrounder, No 1145, p.3.
87. Dreazen, Yochi J. (2001), 'FCC Chairman Signals Change, Plans to Limit U.S Intervention,' *The Wall Street Journal*, 7 February.
88. Gilder, George (2000), 'Internet in the Balance,' *The Wall Street Journal*, 20 October.
89. Tarjanne, Pekka (1997), *Telecommunications and World Development: Forecasts, technologies and services*, I.T.U., Moscow,5February,p.2.www.itu.int/ti/papers/ moscow97/.htm
90. Ibid., p.3.
91. Bussey, Jane (2000), 'Telcom game rigged by Latin monopolies, US phone giants say,' *The Miami Herald*, 11 June.
92. Mitchener, Brandon (2000), US Endorses a Global Approach to Antitrust,' *The Wall Street Journal*, 15 September.
93. Meller, Paul (2001), 'Proposed Law Stirs Concern on Europe E-Commerce,' *The New York Times*, 8 February.
94. Bhagwati, Jagdish (1999), 'Capital Myth,' *Foreign Affairs*, **77**(3), p.11-12.
95. Lowenstein, Roger (2000), *When Genius Failed: The Rise and Fall of Long-Term Capital Management*, London: Random House.
96. Stiglitz, Joseph (2000), 'The Insider,' *The New Republic*, April 17 & 24, pp.58 and 60.
97. Cooper, Richard. N. (1999), 'Should Capital Controls Be Banished?' *Brookings Papers on Economic Activity*, (1), pp.89-142.
98. Stiglitz, Joseph, op.cit., p.60.
99. The House Republican study group produced a report in September entitled, 'Russia's Road to Corruption,' (http://www.policy.house.gov/russia), The looting of Russia has been the subject of a growing number of articles and a number of charges have been made. In September 2000, the Justice Department sought $124 million in damages from Professor Andrei Shleifer, Project Manager J. Hay and two others. They allegedly used the Harvard-

managed US foreign-aid programme, inside information and influence and resources to promote their own personal investments in Russia's nascent capital markets. In the same month, a shareholder lawsuit alleged that the chairman of the Bank of London, profited from Russian laundering activities. Likoudis, Paul (2000), 'How Clinton and Company and the Bankers plundered Russia in the '90s,' *The Wanderer*, 4 May.

100. John Cavanagh quotes from a poll taken at the end of 1999 in which 58% of Americans said that 'foreign trade has been bad for the US economy,' while almost three-quarters responded that immigration 'should not increase, because it will cost US jobs and increase unemployment.' Calmes, Jackie (1999), 'Despite Buoyant Economic Times, Americans Don't Buy Free Trade,' *The Wall Street Journal*, 10 December.

101. Krugman, Paul, op.cit., Chapter 9.

102. Barta, Patrick (2000), 'Analysts say high-tech spending boom is starting to level off and may decline,' *The Wall Street Journal*, 25 September

103. A number of studies suggest that more than half of the increase of recent productivity gains has occurred outside the computer, software and telecommunications sectors. Some of these have come from improvements in manufacturing technologies. See Liesman, Steve (2000), 'Crucial Driver of US productivity gains may be improvements in machine tools,' *The Wall Street Journal*, 28 September, and Jorgenson, Dale W. and Kevin J. Stiroh (2000), 'US Economic Growth at the Industry Level,' *American Economic Review, Papers & Proceedings*, **90**(2), pp.161-167.

104. Thanks to a tight monetary policy, Canada entered a recession in the early nineties. Some blamed this recession on the recently-launched free trade deal with the United States.

105. Gilder, George (2000), *Telecosm: How Infinite Bandwidth Will Revolutionize the World*, NewYork: The Free Press.

106. Rich, Jennifer L. (2000), 'Brazil Weighs Foreign Investment in Media Companies,' *The New York Times*, 28 June.

107. Gilmour, in analysing the success of Margaret Thatcher in pursing her ideology, mentions the potential that a determined Prime Minister enjoys under Britain's constitution of conventions. Gilmour, Ian (1992), *Dancing with Dogma. Britain under Thatcherism*, London: Simon and Schuster, pp.274 and 275.

108. Shackle, G.L.S. (1972), *Epistemics and Economics: A Critique of Economic Doctrines*, Cambridge: Cambridge University Press.

109. Coddington, Alan (1975), 'Creaking Semaphore and Beyond: A Consideration of Shackle's "Epistemics and Economics",' *British Journal of Philosophy*, **26**, pp.151-163.

110. McCloskey, Donald N. (1985), T*he Rhetoric of Economics*, Brighton: Harvester Press.

111. Williamson, John (1993), Democracy and the Washington Consensus, *World Development*, **21**(8), pp.1329-1336, pp.1329, 1330.

112. McClosky, Donald N., op.cit., Chapter I.

113. Spengler, Joseph J. (1970), 'Notes on the International Transmission of Economic Ideas,' *History of Political Economy*, **2**, pp.133-151.

114. Nor has a detailed study of the role of intellectual pressure groups been conducted. Earlier, in Chapter 2, endnote 25, we saw how Milton Friedman identified a group of policy advisers drawn primarily from Columbia University. These, he claims, were influential in shaping the 'liberal' shift that was contained in the New Deal. Later, Friedman offered an explanation for historical turning points: 'It's my impression that you have long cycles of public opinion on the one hand and public behaviour on the other... The case for free markets has been won rhetorically. Everybody now believes in competition, believes in freedom, believes that governments should have a relatively minor role and that markets should be relatively free. That's the rhetoric, and it's reached a peak since the fall of the Berlin Wall. On the other hand, if you look at the practice, in the United States and also most other Western countries, government is more powerful, more extensive, more intrusive now than it was fifty years ago. In that sense we have moved backward and been following the prior socialist trend of opinion. I think we are sort of at the peak of the collectivist way. Over the next twenty, thirty or forty years, the rhetoric - combined with the remarkable effects the Internet is going to have on our lives - will produce a decline in the role of government and a widening of human freedom.'

Stevenson, Richard. W. (1998), 'Just a Bump in Capitalism's Long Road,' *The New York Times*, 22 November. Descriptions of the rise of intellectual coalitions, policy groups and active political movements favouring the liberalisation of markets, monetarism and supply-side economics are dealt within a number of texts. An early study is by Steinfels, while Keegan gives an unsympathetic account of the rise of such groups in the Unites Kingdom, drawing heavily from Blumenthal in his interpretation of developments in the United States. Steinfels, Peter (1979), *The Neo-conservatives*, London: Simon and Schuster; Keegan, William (1993), *The Spectre of Capitalism*, London: Vintage, Chapter 4; Blumenthal, Sidney (1986), *The Rise and Fall of the Counter-Establishment*, London: Time Books.

115. Naím, Moisés (2000), 'Washington Consensus or Washington Confusion?' *Foreign Policy*, **118**(Spring).

116. Keegan, for instance, quotes Polanyi: 'There was nothing natural about *laissez-faire*. Free markets could never have come into being merely by allowing things to take their course... *laissez-faire* itself was enforced by the state.' The point made by Polanyi was that the unregulated market created social instability. Polanyi, however, fails to refute the historical evidence that markets developed incrementally at the edge of political power. Nor does he provide an explanation of the formation of property rights or the means by which groups influenced the state to rope in the disembedded, self-regulating market. Keegan, William, op.cit., p. 40; Polanyi, Karl, op.cit., p. 139; Braudel, Fernand (1982), *The Wheels of Commerce*, London: Collins, pp. 227-228; Jones, E.L. (1981), *The European Miracle,* Cambridge: Cambridge University Press, pp. 89-93 and 102-103; North, Douglas C. (1981), *Structure and Change in Economic History*, op.cit., p. 181.

117. Kukathas, Chandran*, Hayek*, pp. 103-105.

118. 'English Politics escaped the evanescence of imperfection - but that resistance (to rationalist disposition of mind) has now been converted into an ideology. This is the significance of Hayek's *Road to Serfdom* - not the agency of his doctrine, but the fact that it is a doctrine. A plan to resist all planning may be better than the opposite, but it belongs to the same style of politics.' Oakeshott, Michael J. (1994), *Rationalism in Politics and Other Essays*, Indianapolis: Liberty Press, p. 26.

119. Kirzner, I. M. (1973), *Competition and Entrepreneurship,* Chicago: University of Chicago Press.

120. Milton Friedman describes his role in the launch of the IMM. He wrote a memorandum, under the innovators' auspices, explaining the need for such a market that they could use in persuading those in Washington with authority: 'Leo Melamed deserves his lion's share of the credit for seizing the opportunity offered by Nixon's closing the gold window, recognising the importance of taking advantage of that opportunity promptly, and having the courage to do so, despite the risks.' Friedman, Milton (1993), Foreword to *Leo Melamed on the Markets,* London: John Wiley & Sons, Inc., p. xii.

121. Lillechild, S.C. (1986), *The Fallacy of the Mixed Economy. An Austrian Critique of Recent Economic Thinking and Policy*, London: The Institute of Economic Affairs, Hobart Paper, First Edition 1978, p.102.

122. Taylor, A.J.P. (1982), *From Napoleon to the Second International. Essays on Nineteenth-Century Europe*, London: Penguin Books, p.123.

123. Davis, Erik (1999), *Techgnosis: Myth, Magic and Mysticism in the Age of Information,* New York: Crown Publishing Group.

124. Sir James Goldsmith, the late financial entrepreneur, expressed opinions on a wide range of matters. He was particularly scathing as to the merits of free trade, immigration and modern agriculture. Another financier, George Soros, has declared an interest in 'real' investment rather than in currency arbitraging. Ross Perot, while appearing to run for the office of President, argued not only for a reduction in the power of government, but also to close the door on free trade. Goldsmith, James (1995), *The Trap*, London: Macmillan.

125. Wiener, Martin J. (1981), *English Culture and the Decline of the Industrial Spirit, 1930-1980*, London: Penguin Books, Chapter 3.

126. Cain, P. J. and A.G. Hopkins (1993), *British Imperialism: Innovation and Expansion, 1688-1914, and Crisis and Deconstruction, 1914-1990*, London: Longman.

127. Hobsbawm, E. J. (1975), *The Age of Capital, 1848-1875*, London: Abacus, p.74. Note the similarities between Marx and Schumpeter's interpretations. Both deployed the concept of dialectical change and self-created disequilibrium. Schumpeter stressed the conflict between the rational bureaucratic businessman and the vainglorious warrior-entrepreneur, while Marx stressed the struggle between the owning and working classes. See also Heilbroner, Robert L. (1986), *The Worldly Philosophers*, Sixth Edition., London: Simon & Schuster: p.303.

5. Alternatives to Attaining Efficient Resource Allocation through Transport Markets: Origins and Implications

INTRODUCTION

Transport acts as a link between activities separated by space. In moving people and objects, it contributes to the creation of value and income. Produced by a unit of conveyance (vehicle) and a medium (infrastructure) to facilitate movement, transport is a perishable, service input, enabling freight and passengers to be transferred between, as well as within, centres of production. It is also a consumption good, inasmuch as riding, piloting and sailing are pleasurable activities desirable in themselves.

By mobilising the state's coercive power, transport services have been major inputs in the establishment of the public goods of protection, law and justice. Transport has facilitated the administration of government by facilitating the passage of written communication.

Similarly, the transport of private correspondence and the physical movement of people have facilitated social intercourse and engendered a broad sense of social cohesiveness that has contributed to the political discourse of nations.

Numerous combinations of units of conveyance provide transport services with mediums in or on which they move. These range from human porters traversing uncharted terrain to supersonic aircraft taking off, travelling in air space and landing at airports with the assistance of navigational aids. There are five major transport mediums: water, road, rail, air and pipelines. With the exception of railways, which, in rail-tracks, provide the medium, and are the sole transport medium, transport services are provided by buyers who combine seller with self-supplied inputs, such as cars and trucks with roads, aircraft with airports and ships with canals and ports. Vehicles vary according to their specialisation, from the ship and the railway capable of carrying a wide range of goods and passengers, to the pipeline usually carrying oil or gas.

The demand for movement of freight and passengers is derived from decisions made by travellers and firms. These depend, in turn, on the direct satisfaction the trip or movement yields and on their contribution to the production of a third activity, either a visit or a delivery to the productive process at the point of destination. As the demand for a particular trip or movement will depend on the character of the journey, such as for business or non-business, or on the nature (density, fragility, perishability) or the commodity to be shipped, the demand for any particular mode of conveyance will depend on the relative price and characteristics of service, such as speed, comfort and stability offered by the mode and the respective substitutes.

Transport infrastructures are often substantial, both in relation to the markets they combine to serve and, in the case of developing economies, as a share of total national product. They form part of the 'social overhead capital,' a pre-requisite to economic development. Transport infrastructure combines with vehicles to limit, as Adam Smith noted, the division and productivity of labour by determining the extent of the market.[1] But, in turn, transport infrastructures are limited in the extent to which their economics of scale can be exploited by the demand generated by the developing economy.

Because transport demands tend to be characterised by daily and seasonal fluctuations, transport infrastructures have often been designed to accommodate peak demand. Yet, because utilisation falls, for long periods of the day and of the year, far behind capacity, transport infrastructures are characterised by non-rivalry of consumption. In other words, the consumption possibilities of, say, a road or an airport by a vehicle owner do not depend on the consumption of others. Hence, up to the point of congestion, at which point the (customer supplied) vehicle inputs per unit of output depend on the rate at which the infrastructure are utilised, the infrastructures have the properties of a public good.

It is the 'public good' characteristic of under-utilised infrastructure that has been considered to be one of the sources of economies of scale and scope.[2] Bridges, ports, airports, roads, canals and railway tracks have frequently been characterised by scale economies. They are derived from the indivisibility of the under-utilised facility in so far as the total costs of producing a single transport service rise less than proportionately with output. On the assumption that, at a given level of output for a single service the infrastructure is not fully utilised, then its use for the production of more than one service (e.g. rail passenger and freight services) may provide the possibility of (positive) economies of scope. In such a situation, the single agent (e.g. a railway) will be able to produce a given level of output of each product (passenger and freight services) more cheaply than a combination of separate agents (railways) each producing a single product (passengers or freight) at the given output level.

Transport entities that possess economies of scale and scope have the potential to increase their productivity. This is because such a single entity can produce more of different services for less input. But if their prices differentiate sufficiently among locations, shippers and passengers, they may be considered to be engaging in discriminatory action. The characteristic of a public good disappears, however, when the vehicle's inputs per unit of output are shown to depend on the rate at which the infrastructure is utilised. At such a point of utilisation, the traveller in the additional vehicle causes a slowing in the journey time of all vehicles using the infrastructure.

The additional traveller incurs the costs of his slower speed, but not the costs of the aggregate of slower speeds incurred by all other infrastructure users. Congestion is then characterised by a discrepancy between the privately perceived average level of operating and time costs (private costs) to which individual vehicle owners are responsive, and the marginal level of (social) costs which they ignore. Marginal social cost will exceed marginal private cost (i.e. average social cost). As demand of use is assumed to be based on marginal private cost incurred by the vehicle operator, the level of vehicle use will exceed the socially optimum level.

Such observed deviations between social and private costs and prices maintained in excess of marginal costs by the exercise of monopolistic power have elicited two different responses from economists. One is associated with Pigou,[3] the other with Knight and Coase.[4] The Pigouvian approach has been that of an engineer working to an established blueprint, represented as the desired and attainable state of enhancement. Instruments such as regulation, taxes and subsidies are then considered to be the means of correcting for the deviation between the blueprint and the observed working of the (transport) market. The blueprint, however, has been challenged as inappropriate in those markets characterised by free and easy entry and exit - in other words, those subject to the competitive process. In such 'naturally' contestable markets, the recommended choice of instruments is reversed. Deregulation rather than regulation serves to release the competitive process and the attainment of a more efficient order.

Wary of idealised blueprints and sceptical that collectivities will implement efficiency-enhancing instruments, the Knight-Coase approach is positive rather than prescriptive. This approach explains the functioning of the market by examining the underlying systems of legal and morally enforced rights and the location and extent of transaction costs. Prescriptive analysis, however, is encouraged by this approach. In particular, emphasis is placed on the influences acting upon transport markets. Of interest is the influence of defined rights, of the long-evolved process of common law and of the more recent regulatory legislation. In general, emphasis is concentrated on the social arrangement and their influence on the allocation of resources.

This chapter situates the respective transport policy prescriptions by highlighting their conceptual origins. In the next part of the chapter the Pigouvian, or engineering approach to the 'transport problem' is examined. The concept of contestable markets is examined in part three, while parts four and five describe the comparative, neo-institutional approach. This approach is then deployed, in Chapter 7, to explore and evaluate the prescriptive policies forwarded to correct the resource misallocation in the air and water transport systems of North America.

ECONOMIC ENGINEERING

The response associated with Pigou, which shall be dubbed 'economic engineering,'[5] is founded on a formula of rules shown to be necessary for the efficient satisfaction of wants of an economy of self-interested, maximising agents subject to idealised conditions. The deviations are interpreted as denoting resource misallocation. The end objective of economic activity, according to the economic engineer, is the maximisation of the economic welfare of society. A state of efficiency is achieved, as judged by the criterion of Pareto optimality, if no agent's utility can be raised without reducing the utility of any other agent. States of efficiency are Pareto optimal and, as deductions from general equilibrium analysis show, perfectly competitive equilibria for some initial distribution of endowments are Pareto optimal.

Perfectly competitive equilibria are characterised by the equation of price with marginal cost and average cost. Hence, the efficiency rule is deduced. A move towards a more efficient state will be obtained by equating price with marginal cost. Given that at the optimum, price equals marginal cost and average cost, the profit rate is, in effect, a measure of optimum investment. Thus, if the profit rate exceeds the opportunity cost of capital, the investment should be increased. If the profit rate is less, then investment should be reduced. Misallocation, as measured by the extent of congestion and the less than competitive output of a monopoly, can be converted into efficiency of allocation by equating social and private cost[6] and prices and marginal costs respectively. Where the input is perceived to be in the provision of a public good,[7] efficiency can be achieved where real marginal costs are equated with the private plus public demand.

The move to a more efficient state implies an existing equilibrium in which prices do not equate with marginal costs. It is a situation that raises three questions for the economic engineer: What is the cause of the inefficient equilibrium? Would the efficiency pricing rule or a modification lead to increased efficiency? How is the rule to be implemented?

If he perceives that there are interdependencies between agents not accounted for in his calculus; or if production economies are such as to create a single (or few) sellers in a market; and if these lead to inefficient equilibrium, the economic engineer inclines to deploy the concept of economic surplus. This provides him with a means of measuring the welfare effects of deviations from the optimum and it enables him to proceed with equating price with marginal cost. If inefficient equilibrium occurs in sectors not under consideration and is beyond the influence of the economic engineer, the question is raised as to whether the pricing rule should be enforced. Optimality, or efficiency, in the transport sector might require a price greater or less than marginal cost to counter non-attributable inefficiencies in other sectors. This is the second best 'solution'. There are frequently two other factors that act against the acceptance of the unaltered pricing rule. They are the issues of 'revenue adequacy' and of equity.

An enterprise whose prices are set at marginal costs may incur unacceptable financial losses, and it may also not be possible to use fiscal instruments to adjust the distribution of incomes. Such constraints may necessitate the consideration of some form of average, as distinct from marginal cost pricing, and the satisfaction of equity considerations by introducing rates structures that support forms of internal cross-subsidisation.

In those less developed economies in which distorted pricing mechanisms are found, economic scarcity is considered to be inaccurately reflected.[8] Maintenance of the foreign exchange rates at above market levels causes foreign goods, measured in domestic prices, to be too low relative to domestic goods, and exports, also in domestic prices, to be too low. The marginal product of labour will not equate with the wages paid, as many will not produce sufficient to sustain their existence. The result of these and other distortions are patterns of production that are far different from those considered to be socially optimum (efficient). Such are these distortions in a developing economy (compared with a developed market economy) that it is argued that there is a *prima facie* case for the deployment of shadow or accounting prices.[9] Such would be the case not only in financial product prices (as would be usual with the adoption of the pricing rule), but across the board, including labour, capital, imports and exports. Such shadow prices would accurately reflect economic scarcity. With the diagnosis completed, the economic engineer proceeds to recommend an instrument with which to equate prices with marginal (or adjusted incremental) costs.

Instruments such as regulation, subsidies, taxes and accounting prices are compared with the mechanism of the market as a means of accomplishing the desired state of enhanced efficiency. In the developed economies, traditionally, industries or sectors were characterised as either competitive or monopolistic. In the former, static efficient allocation was assumed to be accomplished by the competitive process, in the latter government regulation was often advocated.

This traditional view of markets and the approach to instrument choice has been challenged by the notion of contestability. The proponents of contestability argue that competition for the market constrains behaviour as effectively as would competition within the market. Even if the market is 'occupied' by only one seller, as long as there is free and easy exit, the market will be subject to the competitive process. In 'naturally' contestable markets, the choice of instruments is reversed. Deregulation rather than protective economic regulation serves to release the competitive process and facilitates the attainment of a more efficient equilibrium.

FROM PERFECT COMPETITION TO PERFECTLY CONTESTABLE MARKETS BY WAY OF MARKET FAILURE

The Arrow-Debreu model of competitive general equilibrium reformulated the (Walrasian) system of competitive equilibrium. Under strong assumptions about technology, tastes and producers motivations, the developers of this model proved that a decentralised economy, relying on price signals for market information, could attain competitive equilibrium.[10]

The decentralised economy consists of individual agents divided into households, endowed with goods and entitlements,[11] and firms, acting as agents that convert inputs into outputs. Goods are defined by their physical inter-dependencies. Given these conditions and behaviour as specified, prices are set at equilibrium, market-clearing values. The theory offers no explanation as to how prices are determined.

There is a continuity of equilibrium positions. These depend on the form of the distributions of endowments. The corresponding allocations of these equilibria also possess important properties. They are Pareto optimum and efficient states in that, by allocating goods, no one agent's utility can be raised without reducing the utility of another agent. The equilibrium and the latter efficiency theorem formalise the reasoning of the 'invisible hand,' leading self-interested behaviour to 'serve the common good'. The converse of the efficiency theorem, (also known as the fundamental theorem of welfare economics), is that every Pareto-efficient allocation can be decentralised into a competitive equilibrium. The competitive price system is unbiased, in that no one group, whether capital, labour, or consumers, is favoured.

In a competitive equilibrium, self-seeking agents will equate their marginal costs to given prices. The agent will find that it will not pay to continue to employ extra resources to produce extra output because incremental revenue just covers incremental cost. Consuming units will purchase the good until the value to them of the cost unit consumed equals its price. Given that the value of the particular purchase is that of the service of other goods and services involved in its production (i.e. as marginal costs equal marginal opportunity costs and as price equals marginal cost), the consuming agents, in purchasing the goods until the value to them of the last unit consumed equals the price, will be at the optimum. At this point marginal cost will equate with marginal utility.

The value to society of the last unit of consumption (the marginal utility) will be equal to the value of the inputs used to produce this last unit (the marginal cost). Expressed in different terms, the fundamental theorem implies that for Pareto optimality to exist, it is necessary that marginal private cost should equal marginal social costs for all goods and for all agents.

It does not follow, however, that a competitive equilibrium is socially optimum, for every Pareto optimum state is conditional upon the distribution of endowments. The choice of the social optimum is a public decision, involving the discovery and establishment of the desired distribution of endowments. It is also noteworthy that these theorems hold if there were just a single potential buyer and seller of any goods, for larger numbers pay no explicit role in the equilibrium theory.[12] Consideration of increasingly large finite economies introduces large numbers and price-taking aspects, commonly understood to be perfect competition.

By acting as communicators of dispersed information, markets and prices in such a decentralised economy facilitate mutually beneficial trades by co-ordinating economic activity and in so doing, allocate resources efficiently. Insufficient allocation can occur and the market will 'fail' if there are too few markets, if there is non-competitive behaviour and if there is an absence of equilibrium.

If, instead of all agents being completely informed, information is imperfectly distributed, equilibrium will not exist in the respective markets. Given the self-interested motives of agents, the informed one will be propelled into acting monopolistically. For instance, agents in an industry may know more about their own costs than their competitors. They could be attracted to reduce their prices below average variable costs and so drive out their competitors. Widespread destruction will be followed by an attempt of the surviving agent or agents to sustain prices above cost. The predator's profitability will be short-lived if competitors have ease of entry into the market. The resulting price-cuts will plunge the market into renewed in-stability. Equilibrium will not be achieved.

In the competitive general equilibrium model, all goods are defined as having prices and hence markets. The sum of individual quantities consumed aggregate to the quantities produced and the prices faced by the household equals the producing agents' price. Such goods are termed 'private'. Some markets, however, only have one producing agent. Others are without markets.

Monopoly occurs whenever a single agent can produce the output of the industry at lower costs than two or more agents can. Such sub-additivity[13] exists when the cost of joint production is less than the cost of separate production for any scale or combination of outputs. It is not necessary, therefore, that the monopoly agent with 'the cost advantage' enjoys economies of scale. Indeed, if there is a range of output over which the monopoly agent experiences decreasing returns to scale, a rival agent may be able to produce the level of output corresponding to the lowest point on the average cost curve. The rival agent would be able to undercut the monopoly agent that was attempting to supply the market. This could possibly lead to an unstable equilibrium.[14] Monopoly is, therefore, not the 'natural' outcome of the success of an agent enjoying declining average cost, but rather of cost advantage, which may be a position that is not necessarily sustainable in the face of competition.

Countering this possible 'failure' of unstable equilibrium is the situation where the monopoly agent, enjoying declining average cost, is unable to sustain monopoly profits. Demsetz[15] has indicated that a monopolist's competitive behaviour could be promoted if potential entrants proffered bids to serve the market at a lower price. Such an outcome, triggered by the emergence of monopoly profits, could occur when an agent bids, not to enter competitively into the market, but instead bids for the market.[16]

The workability of competition in markets characterised by increasing returns to scale has been generalised into the concept of contestability,[17] extended to cover multi-product agents and shown to lead, if stringent conditions are satisfied, to socially desirable outcomes. The conditions constituting a contestable market were established to analyse the equilibrium properties of markets in which agents possessed economies of scale of production. It is a requirement of contestability that entrants do not face any discrimination in costs and that an agent can leave the market without impediment. By deploying Stigler's notion of barriers to entry,[18] freedom of entry for an agent is defined as being 'free' of any disadvantage relative to incumbent agents. Hence, production processes characterised by economies of scale are no barrier in that they are assumed to be accessible to entrants and incumbents. Capital is assumed to be saleable or re-saleable without loss. So, assuming an agent can leave without impediment, capital costs, once sunk, imply a cost that must be incurred by an entrant but which does not again have to be incurred by an incumbent.[19] With entry absolutely free and exit absolutely without cost,[20] any perceived opportunity to profit will attract entrants, who, when they have profited, can run so that any equilibrium will be characterised by zero profits. Unlike the perfectly competitive market, with many price-taking agents, the markets characterised by monopoly or oligopolistic agents could be contestable. 'In short, a perfectly competitive market is necessarily perfectly contestable, but no vice versa.'[21]

If the agent produces two or more products and the costs of producing each one are declining, then the agent would be a (natural) monopolist in each of the individual products. If there are positive complementarities (i.e. positive economies of scope) in producing these outputs in that the agent can produce a given level of each output more cheaply than a combination of separate agents (each producing a single product at a given output level), then the combined output level is sub-additive.[22] Possessing the properties of sub-additivity, the profit maximising, multi-product monopolist will be able to sustain its prices if they are set at levels that preclude profitable opportunities to potential entrants. The set of sustainable prices will be established at levels 'they can bear,' i.e. at levels above the marginal cost of producing the products in inverse proportion of their point price elasticity. Such inverse elasticity prices - or Ramsey prices - are also Pareto optimum[23] in that the multi-product monopolist establishes prices at levels that satisfy the financial constraint of breaking even and that maximise the (producer and consumer) welfare.[24] Duopolists and oligopolists are able to immunise themselves from attack from entrants by equating their equilibrium prices with marginal costs. Indeed, in general, agents in contestable market 'must behave ideally in every aspect,' in such a way that there can be no sustained cross-subsidisation nor predatory pricing.[25]

There are agents in contestable markets, however, whose properties are insufficient to sustain equilibrium. As examined earlier, if the cost of supplying a sub-group of consumers is less per unit than the cost of supplying the entire group of consumers, then the agent may find it difficult to sustain prices. Panzar and Willig[26] show that a similar outcome is possible in a multi-product firm characterised by more pronounced product-specific scale economies than economies of scope. Such an agent is vulnerable to a competitor specialising in a single product that is a close substitute to the joint product of the monopolist agent. Baumol has also demonstrated that when there are economies of scale in the production of durable capital, an inter-temporal contestable monopoly will be vulnerable in the long run 'to entry or replacement by rivals whose appearance is inefficient because it wastes valuable social resources.'[27]

The production or consumption of a good may have indirect as well as direct effects in that agents, other than the producing and consuming agents of the good, are influenced in their production and/or consumption. If such externalities are not priced and do not have markets, equilibria will, in general, not be Pareto optimal because the optimising behaviour of agents will lead them to equalise direct (private) and not direct and indirect (social) marginal rates. Self-seeking, competitive agents reveal their preferences through their behaviour in market exchanges. It follows that private goods less costly than the chosen collection must be less appreciated by such agents. The sum of an agent's consumed quantities of a private good equals aggregate production, while each price of the goods consumed by the agent equals the producing agent's price.

By contrast, a public good is one that is characterised by agents' benefits, being independent of the benefit enjoyed by other agents, but directly related to the total availability of the (public) good. The services of a public good are in joint supply, in that if a unit is made available to one agent, it can be made available to other agents at no extra cost.[28] It is also impossible to exclude non-paying agents from consuming. As a result, it is difficult to engage in differential pricing by relating charges to consuming agents' marginal evaluation. It has been shown that a set of differentiated marginal prices summing to marginal cost is required for a Pareto-optimum provision of such a public good.[29] This requires the imposition of rates according to the individual consuming agents' marginal evaluations. Therefore, the task of the supplying agent[30] of the public good is to devise an instrument that will extract, as does the producing agent in a market transaction of a private good,[31] the true preferences and evaluations of the consuming agents. This task is difficult because of the impossibility of exclusion. Note that the supplying agent is attempting to create a separate price for each incidence of consumption of the public good. In effect, the consuming agent is a monopsonist, with no incentive to treat prices as fixed and invariant to his demands. The self-interested consuming agent, aware that he will not be excluded if payment is not made, will hope that some agents will go ahead and pay for their services. Hoping that the service is secured by such payments, the non-paying agents will pile aboard the joy ride. In a decentralised market of many self-seeking agents, the likelihood is that the free-loaders will predominate and the public good will be withdrawn.

The failure of a monopolistic supplier of a public good to sustain the provision of such a good can be seen to lie with two factors, The first: the lack of incentives for the consuming agents to reveal their true preferences; and the second, the large number of agents, many of whom can be expected not to be motivated to signal their marginal valuations of the services of the public good. The inherent characteristic of the public good, namely, the inability to exclude non-payers, constrains the effectiveness of voluntary exchange in inciting agents to show their information.

Market failure can clearly occur because of the existence of 'incentive constraints.'[32] Along with a permutation of asymmetric information and too few markets, this prevalent constraint serves to relegate the welfare economist to an outside position, in that his or her analysis is not based on individual agents' private information. The presence of incentives constraints add to the task of considering alternative mechanisms that will entice agents to share their information.[33] A standard position has been that as market failure is inefficient, all agents can and should, be made better off. The tasks are seen to be those of assessing the feasibility and desirability of instrument (taxes, subsidies, regulation, public ownership, etc.) choices that satisfy the Pareto criterion of improvement.

NEO-INSTITUTIONAL ECONOMICS

Knight, in his 1924 paper,[34] examined Pigou's interpretation of the misallocation of investment resources between industries. In Pigou's example, the misallocation occurred between a poorly surfaced, broad road, and that of a better, but narrower and congested road, subject to increasing costs. Knight's interpretation of Pigou's approach was that 'excessive investment' occurs in increasing cost industries because of 'free enterprise.' Pigou's ideal of allocative efficiency was to be restored by the imposition of a tax on the rising cost, narrow and congested road, causing the number of trucks to be reduced to the point 'where ordinary cost (i.e. vehicle operating costs) plus the tax, became equal to the cost on the constant cost road, assumed to be left tax free.'[35]

Knight's interpretation of Pigou's approach is summarised in the following passage:

> ... the assumptions diverge in essential respects from the facts of real economic situations. The most essential feature of a competitive condition is reversed, the feature namely, of the private ownership of the factors practically significant for production. If the roads are assumed to be subject to private appropriation and exploitation, precisely the ideal situation which would be established by the imaginary tax will be brought about through the operation of ordinary economic motives.[36]

Knight's comments on the posing of an ideal and the attempts to deploy instruments to achieve this ideal are contained in the following:

> That free enterprise is not a perfectly ideal system of social organisation is a proposition not to be gainsaid and nothing is further from the aims of the present writer than to set up the contention that it is. But in his opinion the weakness and failures of the system lie outside the field of the mechanics of exchange under the theoretical condition of perfect competition. It is probable that all efforts to prove a continued bias in the workings of competition as such, along the lines followed by Professor Pigou and Graham, are doomed to failure.
> The correct form of the problem of general criticism referred to at the outset of this

paper is, therefore, that of bringing these lurking assumptions above the threshold into the realm of the explicit, and of contesting them with the facts of life - the conditions under which competitive dealings are actually carried on.[37]

According to Knight, the problem was not that a competitive market system failed to allocate resources efficiently. The problem was the absence of a competitive market. In the provision of those transport services in which there was a bifurcation of the decision making process between vehicle and infrastructure owners, the misallocation of resources was not the product of a failed competitive market, but rather of the failure of self-interested owners to internalise their costly or beneficial interactions. This failure was due to an absence of defined property rights. The result was an inability of owners to engage in the competitive market process.

An agent's rights over assets are multi-dimensional and include the powers to consume and generate income. Exercising such power involves exchange. When rights are perfectly delineated and enforced by the coercive power of the state, as is implicitly assumed in the Walrasian general equilibrium model, prices are sufficient to secure efficient allocation. The value of such perfectly designed and enforced rights can be measured by the net present value of the rights income agents would be willing to expend to obtain the right.

An implication of Coase's insight[38] is that if all rights are freely transferable and the cost of transacting is zero, agents will find, by means of voluntary transactions, the highest value use of the rights, no matter what the initial partitioning. As Coase also indicated,[39] because of the high transaction costs involved in exchanging and in the enforcement of ownership, rights are rarely, if ever, fully delineated. The assignment of rights is costly, so that the partitioning of rights by the state could have consequences for their efficient allocation. When transaction costs are positive, numerous activities emerge to influence exchange by providing margins which participating agents in the exchange can adjust. These margins are other than quantity and price. Agents motivated by self-interest can be expected to maximise the value of their (attenuated) rights by optimising at these margins and, in so doing, minimising the dissipation created.[40]

The costs involved in the exchange and enforcement of their rights are the reason why agents fail to internalise costs, because it is costly to exchange and enforce rights. Take, for example, a market where congestion is generated in the use of an infrastructure. Users dissipate resources of time (queuing) in maximising the value of their right of use. The reason why vehicle users who suffer congestion are unable to make effective payments or bribes to other vehicle users to limit their travel is because of the high transaction costs generated by the system of rights. The owners (usually governments) of many infrastructures often do not have (or choose not to exercise) the right to exclude vehicles from enjoying their communal right to the infrastructure. Access is on a first-come-first-served basis. Under such a communal rights system, those who do not pay vehicle users to take alternative routes cannot be excluded from the use of the infrastructure. By creating a free-rider problem, the system of communal rights eases transaction costs, which, in turn, serve to thwart transactions that are mutually advantageous. Similarly, consumers do not actually combine and bribe a monopolist transport supplier to pursue the pricing policies of competitive firms by equating price with marginal cost. The reason is that the cost of combining numerous consumers and the costs of enforcement are far from zero.

Although high transaction costs can preclude such outcomes, maximising agents are assumed to make adjustments that minimise the potential loss in the value of their rights that constraints can cause. When all transactions that are mutually advantageous have been undertaken, the market will be in equilibrium, and, by definition, Pareto efficient.[41]

Equilibria at each margin will denote a market in equilibrium. In the case of an infrastructure, margins at which equilibria could be attained are in waiting time, vehicle movements, journey time and type of vehicle.[42] Regulation of a competitive market often to a number of margins in quality, so that in equilibrium, the marginal value of increased quality is equated with the associated increase in cost.[43]

At such Pareto-efficient equilibria, costly interaction exists. In the case of inherently competitive industries subject to price regulation, the possibility exists of congestion, excess capacity and severe competition. The economic engineer compares these equilibria with the simulated optimal equilibria based on assumed zero transaction costs and then measures the extent of the resource misallocation. The neo-institutionalist, however, does not use positive transaction costs to measure misallocation. Rather, they are identified as influencing the location of the equilibria. Optimality is a function of the total set of property rights. The optimum *status quo* is deemed to have been attained after all gainful, voluntary exchange has taken place. Individual preferences, expressed through gainful trade, are determinants of change, not the judgements of a social welfare function. Hence, changes in instruments or in the institutional framework are unambiguously[44] acceptable only if they satisfy the Pareto criterion.

For social policy, the fundamental issue reduces to this. At any given moment there is a legally sanctioned structure of property rights in existence. Thus, if the prevailing structure is to be modified by social action designed to reduce or eliminate the effects of an externality, taxes must be imposed on those who will gain from the proposed legal change, and compensation must be paid to those who will suffer capital loss or loss of satisfaction as a result of the new law. Presumably, agreement of the terms of the tax-compensation scheme can be reached through a political process, but the basic mechanism is one of 'trade'. In principle, an individual (A) seeking to modify the behaviour of another individual (B) (who is generating an externality) can engage in trade with the latter and then, both can move to preferred positions on a 'contract curve' where Pareto equilibrium holds.[45] Under such a normative rule, individuals could and, no doubt, would invest resources in market and political activity in order to achieve change that would be in their interests.[46] In effect, this would mean that change, including fundamental 'institutional'[47] change, could be bought by the highest bidder. Such a normative bias is disputable. The approach, however, by extending the notion of self-interest beyond economic agents to political, bureaucratic and legal agents involved in the decision process, leads to an interesting question. Does the resolution of conflicting interests result in the unerring commitment to the economic engineer's allocative efficiency?

COMPARATIVE INSTITUTIONAL APPROACH

The market, the firm, and the legal system are social arrangements that have influenced, sometimes unintentionally, the allocation of resources. The allocation of resources to and within the transport sector and its constituent entities has involved three arrangements, within which order has been established. They are by means of private negotiation, by the establishment of liability adjudicated by courts and by regulatory agencies. Promoted by the promise of gains in allocative efficiency - but often implying, rather than stating explicitly that allocative efficiency should be the goal of policy - recommended changes to these three arrangements have often been preceded by posing the perceived imperfect working of the *status quo* arrangement with an implicit perfect or near perfect alternative. This takes the form of government regulatory intervention.

There is an alternative. It is that the substitution of the unregulated market will generate 'optimum' outcomes. The former, in which the proposed policy of government intervention would work perfectly, has been dubbed, by Demsetz, the 'Nirvana' approach.[48] The latter has been described by Eisenberg as the 'Heavenly Market Fallacy.'[49]

Coase, who recognised that 'we are choosing between social arrangements which are all more or less failures,'[50] rejected comparisons of actual, imperfectly working arrangements with idealised arrangements that assumed cost-less exchange. They were misleading and, instead, he suggested that:

A better approach would seem to be to start our analysis with a situation approximating that which actually exists, to examine the effects of a proposed policy change and to attempt to decide whether the new situation would be, in total, better or worse than the original one. In this way, conclusions for policy would have some relevance to the actual situation.[51]

The approach of Coase suggests three tasks: first, to undertake a critical consideration of those formulations that deploy maximising agents; second, to identify deviations between private and social products; and third, thereafter to propose measures to correct such deficiencies.

Given that agents maximise their utility functions subject to constraints,[52] efficient outcomes follow logically, for all agents are rational maximisers equating efficiently at all margins. By the assumption of these models, all arrangements are efficient and are, therefore, not differentiable except with the deployment of an extraneous social welfare function.

Identifying divergences between private and social product and bridging the divergences between private and social product, and removing the deficiencies by deploying instruments such as taxes, subsidies and regulation, in Coase's words 'diverts attention from those other changes in the system which are inevitably associated with the corrective measure, changes which may well produce more harm than the original deficiency.'[53]

A positive aspect of interest group pressure is that they have, on occasion, exposed the limitations of the chosen instrument of correction.[54] One of the frequently overlooked factors is the cost of administering the instrument of correction. This should be included in the calculus. The decision rule should then be to deploy the instrument only so long as the marginal costs of control are less than the marginal costs of the externality plus the marginal damage cost of the externality. Coase does not argue for the consideration of selected margins, but recommends the comparison of (practical) arrangements of institutions. Instead, he says

...the choice between different social arrangements for the solution of economic problems should be carried out in broader terms than this and that the total effect of these arrangements in all spheres of life should be taken into account.[55]

This approach has been endorsed, retrospectively, by a proponent and administrator of the deregulation of the interstate civil aviation carriers in the United States:

...the full benefits of airline deregulation have not been enjoyed. ...(T)he cause stems from the failure of the Civil Aeronautics Board to treat interrelated elements. We did a partial equilibrium analysis, deregulating the rate-and-route- authority that we had within the CAB, without fully addressing such policy issues as airport capacity and air traffic control. We did not initiate an airport plan that aligned well with the new freedom for rates and routes.

I think this lack of system wide perspective was a strategic error... In sum, officials must look at the whole problem as opposed to just looking at the problem that was within the CAB domain.[56]

The approach of the comparative institutional analysis established by Knight and Coase (and pursued by adherents of the public choice, property rights and economics of law 'schools' that constitute the neo-institutional approach) has contributed to the exposure of the unattainable optimum of the economic engineer and elucidated the misjudgement of the piecemeal engineering implied in the above statement. Possessing the core notions that normative rules are not established by extraneous social welfare functions, but from the revealed choice of individuals through voluntary exchange and that through such unconstrained exchange, individuals are best able to maximise their gain, the neo-institutional approach presents an alternative, normative standard. More significantly, this approach offers the possibility of subjecting to refutation a set of hypotheses concerning the relations of rights to efficient outcomes and of observing the implications for economically efficient outcomes of self-centred agent's exchanges within political and economic markets.

The approach is generalised in the hypothesis concerning self-interested individual agents trading for gain, facing ownership rights and incentives, and subject to transaction, information and policing costs. Being self- interested, agents consider whether it is in their interest, given the transaction costs, to trade or to own rights. Agents can be expected to appropriate rights whenever the perceived accrued benefits exceed the costs of defining, negotiating, policing and enforcing the rights. Private ownership and the right of use and sale are necessary to assure deployment by the user to whom it is most valuable, while incompatible uses can be accounted for if properties are owned and can be traded. The choice of institutional arrangements emerges from an order of private agents' ownership of rights, their voluntary use and exchange and whose calculus minimises social costs.

Cost-minimisation achieved by individual voluntary trade, is, however, not an 'objective' criterion to be used in determining whether decisions should be made through one order or the other. For there is, within each *status quo* set of property rights, determinants of what are costs, who have to incur costs and who is financially able to express their will in trading. There is, in effect, an implicit social welfare function. The Austrian conception of the competitive market adds a further qualification to the evaluation of any proposed change in arrangements. Can the individuals that, for example, comprise government acquire and apply knowledge effectively in the form of intervention that exceeds the efficiency of the unrestricted exchange through the market? Does the intervention lessen the incentives of private and public sector individuals to expand effort in the discovery, creation and exchange of valuable information?[57]

The rejection of the claims of some adherents of neo-institutionalism to freedom from externally imposed values does not impair the potential of the neo-institutional approaches.   This approach directs attention to the differentiation between the normative and the positive and illuminates the often implicitly idealised order that the proposal's instruments purport to attain. By illustrating the influence of political and legal institutions on the order within which activities are undertaken, the neo-institutionalists caution against generalisations within and between systems of governance. The resulting methodological implication is that a cautious, case study approach is recommended, with defined entities confined to a specific time and system of governance. Such an approach is conducted in Chapter 6.

Notes

1.   Smith, Adam (1776), *The Wealth of Nations,* Books I-III, reprinted with an introduction by A.S. Skinner (1986), London: Penguin Classics, pp.121-122.
2.   Elizabeth. E. and Friedland, Ann, F (1982), 'Market Structure and Multi- product Industries, *Journal of Economic Literature* (20 September), p.1026.
3.   Pigou, A.C. (1912), *The Economics of Welfare*, London: Macmillan.
4.   The approach is linked with a number of scholars associated with the Departments of Law and Economics at the University of Chicago, and including, as well as Knight and Coase, Buchanan, Demsetz and Stigler. The approach deploys much more that is common to the public choice-property rights literature that has emerged from Universities other than Chicago.
5.   This approach has been so described by Sen, A.K. (1987), *On Ethics and Economics*, Oxford: Basil Blackwell, p.4.
6.   When the physical capacity of a system is fixed, production-scheduling problems may occur as a result of delay in use caused by the (random) arrival of service. Problems are of three kinds. One, there is the issue of the optimal use of the facility. How many customers should be served if the additional customer (marginal user) imposes external effects (configuration in the form of costs and value of time foregone) on all other customers (users)? Two, what are the effects of an absence (or presence) of a toll on the characteristics of the service demanded and provided? Three, if the physical capacity can be expanded 'in the long run,' how much should be expanded to achieve economic efficiency? Emphasis has centred on the first question, arising as it does with respect to runway and terminals in airports, roads, docking facilities in a port and many other non-transport infrastructures. The 'answer' that will achieve an efficient use of the congested facility is in the form of a 'tax' or toll equal to the marginal cost. It is suggested that this will internalise the external cost (congestion), and in so doing, individual users will make decisions that will lead to a socially efficient balance between congestion and use. The appropriate toll may be negligible during off-peak periods, but may be a multiple of the prevailing toll during the peak. Accordingly, such peak-load congestion tolls shift the demand so that less capacity is required for given demand, as more use can be made of a given capacity. The resulting revenue provides a measure of the benefits that would accrue from additional capacity. This potential policy, however, may have to be modified in the light of other external benefits accruing from the use of the facility, such as uncorrected departures from optimal conditions elsewhere in the economy. Such

deviations question whether the 'optimal congestion' toll is a second-best allocation. More significantly, a toll instituted to promote short-run efficient utilisation will not necessarily generate revenue so as to equate with the cost of capacity expansion. If the entity is government owned, the revenue may not be applied optimally to expansion and, instead, may find its way into the general exchequer, or congestion may be pitched at monopolistic levels. The overcharging would then lead to sub-optimal expansion. Lave, Lester B. and Joseph S. De Salvo (1968), 'Congestion, Tolls, and the Economic Capacity of a Waterway,' *Journal of Political Economy,* **78,** pp.375-391.

7. Thayer, for instance, considers '...the historic and contemporary roles of (US), airlines as public utilities, instruments of foreign policy, reserve military forces, and private businesses,' and regrets the treatment of the carriers under the 1978 *Airline Deregulation Act* as private business. He offers the suggestion that they 'must be rearranged into a co-ordinated system which somehow abolishes head-to-head competition'. Thayer, Frederick, C. (1982), 'Airline Regulation, The Case for a "Public Utility" Approach,' *The Logistics and Transportation Review,* **18**(3), pp.221, 221 and 230.

8. Little, Ian. M.D. and James A. Mirrlees (1968), *Manual of Industrial Project Analysis in Developing Countries, Social Cost Benefit Analysis,* **Vol.2,** Paris, Development Centre of the Organisation for Economic Co-operation and Development, pp.31-37.

9. Ibid., p.37.

10. Hahn, F. (1980), 'General Equilibrium Theory,' *The Public Interest,* Special Issue, pp.123-129.

11. The household's 'basket of goods' includes its stock of leisure which it can supply as labour to firms.

12. Roberts, J. (1989), 'Perfectly and Imperfectly Competitive Markets,' in Eatwell, John, Milgate, Murray and Peter Newman (eds), *The New Palgrave. Allocation, Information and Markets,* New York and London: W.W. Norton, pp.231-240.

13. Faulhaber, Gerald. R. (1975), 'Cross-subsidisation, Pricing in Public Enterprise,' *American Economic Review,* **5**(December), pp.966-977.

14. Faulhaber obtains unstable prices as a result of an empty core of a co-operative game among the agents.

15. Demsetz, H. (1968), 'Why Regulate Utilities?' *Journal of Law and Economics,* **11**(October), pp.55-65.

16. Demsetz acknowledged Sir Edwin Chadwick's paper, published in the *Journal of the Royal Statistical Society* in 1859, concerning the distinction, of which the railways were used as an example, of 'competition for the field' as distinct from 'competition within the field'. See also Ekelund, Robert, Jr. and Edward Price, III (1979), 'Sir Edward Chadwick on Competition and the Social Control of Industry Railroads,' *History of Political Economy,* **11** (2), pp.213-239.

17. Willig, Robert D. (1990), 'What can markets control?' *Perspectives on Postal Service Issues,* Roger Sherman (ed), Washington DC; and Baumol, William, J. Panzar and Robert Willig (1982), *Contestable Markets and the Theory of Industrial Structure,* San Diego, CA: Harcourt Brace Jovanovich, Chapter 10.

18. 'A barrier to entry may be defined as a cost of producing (at some or every level of output), which must be borne by a firm which seeks to enter an industry but is not borne by firms already in the industry'. G. Stigler (1968), *The Organisation of Industry,* Homewood: Richard D. Irwin, p.67.

19. According to Bailey and Friedlander, 'The conditions required for perfect contestability. are demanding. They involve easy access to the market on equal terms for new entrants and old incumbents. They demand that durable capital goods be easily transferable by second-hand sale or alternative deployment that recoups their cost. They require that industry-specific human capital should not be market-specific but should be transferable from market to market to avoid large personnel costs for hitting and running. They demand that price reductions not be matched immediately but instead that there be a delay before incumbents can meet an entrant's price'. Bailey, Elizabeth E. and Anne F. Friedlander (1982), 'Market Structure and Multi-Product Industries,' *Journal of Economic Literature,* **20,** pp.1024-1048, at 1041.

20. Baumol, William J. (1982), 'Contestable Markets, An uprising in the Theory of Industry Structures,' *American Economic Review*, **72**(1), pp.1-15, at 3.

21. ibid., p.4.

22. Baumol, William J. (1977), 'On the Proper Cost Test for Natural Monopoly in a Multi-Product Industry,' *American Economic Review*, **67**(5), pp.809-822.

23. Baumol, William J. Bailey, Elizabeth E. and Robert D. Willig (1977), 'Weak Invisible Hand Theorems on the Sustainability of Multi-Product Natural Monopoly,' *American Economic Review*, **67** (3), pp.350-365.

24. It has been shown that where firms set quantity as against price sustainability, the sufficient conditions are easier to satisfy than if price is sustainable. However, it has also been found that the 'quantity sustainable equilibrium' is not related to any welfare-maximising equilibrium. See Brock, William and Jose Scheinkman (1981), 'Free Entry and Sustainability of Natural Monopoly,' *Centre for Math: Studies in Business and Economics*, Report 8118, University of Chicago.

25. Baumol, William, Panzar, J. and Robert Willig, *Contestable Markets*, op.cit., p.2.

26. Panzar, John. C. and Willig R.D. (1977), 'Free Entry and the Sustainability of Natural Monopoly,' *Bell Journal of Economics*, **8**(1), pp.1-22.

27. Faulhaber, Gerald R., op.cit., p.3.

28. Head, J.G. (1974), *Public Goods and Public Welfare*, Durham NC: Duke University Press, pp.77.

29. Ibid., pp.70-73.

30. The perfectly competitive market is not capable of establishing marginal prices, which differentiate (discriminate), between different consumers of a given product. Hence, consideration is given as to whether the monopoly of one producing agent may produce the needed differentiated prices.

31. Assuming that there is no asymmetry of information between buyer and seller.

32. Note that: 'The impossibility of withholding some part of the benefit of an activity from those who do not pay is of course precisely the definition of the neo-classical concept of external economies. The impossibility of exclusion, which characterises a public good, is such that when one individual consumes a unit of service, an identical quality service unit is consumed by all other individuals without payment'. Head, J.G. op.cit., p.81.

33. Meyerson, Robert. B. (1989), *Mechanism Design*, in Eatwell, John, Millgate, Murray and Peter Newman (eds), *The New Palgrave. Allocation, Information and Markets*, New York and London: W.W.Norton, p.191-206 at 201.

34. Knight, F.H. (1924), 'Some Fallacies in the Interpretation of Social Cost,' *Quarterly Journal of Economics*, **38**, pp.582-606.

35. ibid., p.585.

36. ibid., pp.586-587.

37. ibid., p.605.

38. The 'Coase Theorem' is implied in Coase, Ronald H. (1960), 'The Problem of Social Cost,' *Journal of Law and Economics*, **3**(1), pp.1-44, and was also alluded to in Coase, Ronald H. (1959), 'The Federal Communications Commissioners Commission,' *Journal of Law and Economics*, **2**(1), pp.1-40.

39. Coase, Ronald. H. (1988), *The Firm, the Market, the Law*, Chicago: University of Chicago Press, p.15.

40. Cheung, Steven N.S. (1976), 'A Theory of Price Control,' *Journal of Law and Economics*, **17** (1), pp.53-71.

41. Eggertsson, Thrainn (1990), *Economic Behaviour and Institutions*. Cambridge: Cambridge University Press, pp.24-25.

42. Barzel, Yoram (1984), *Economic Analysis of Property Rights*, Cambridge: Cambridge University Press, Chapter 2.

43. Douglas, George W. and James C. Miller III (1974), *Economic Regulation of Domestic Air Transport. Theory and Policy*, Washington DC: The Brookings Institution.

44. Goldberg has pointed out that the public choice and property rights schools, both of which stress the importance of the institutional framework, of incentives and constraints on all agents, economic, political and legal, and of the effects of transaction costs on allocation,

have also, in common, a normative bias. The public choice-property rights (PC PR), approach is based on two notions. First, the complexity of the institutional framework is such that we can only analyse changes, not make *de novo* comparisons. Second, individuals will be able to attain gains from trade through voluntary exchange. Goldberg, Victor. P. (1980), 'Public Choice-Property Rights,' in Samuels, Warren J. (ed), *The Methodology of Economic Thought*, Transaction Books, p.403.

45. Furubotn, Eirik G. and Pejovich Svetozar (1972), 'Property Rights and Economic Theory: A survey of Recent Literature,' *Journal of Economic Literature*, **8**(4), p.1142.

46. 'Public Choice Analysis - the application of the theoretical method and techniques of modern economics to the study of political processes - is conceived to be about institutional reform, and improvements in the *rules* under which political processes operate. This perspective requires that we shift attention away from the analysis of policy choice by existing agents within existing rules, and towards the examination of alternative set of rules.' Brennan, G. and. Buchanan, James M. (1988), 'Is Public Choice Immoral? The Case for the Noble Lie,' *Virginia Law Review,* **17** (Feb-May), pp.179-189, 179 at 187.

47. '...although we do not believe that narrow self-interest is the *sole* motive of political agents, or that it is necessarily as relevant a motive in political as in market settings, we certainly believe it to be a significant motive. This differentiates our approach from the alternative model, implicit in conventional welfare economics and widespread in conventional political science that political agents can be satisfactorily modelled or motivated solely to promote the `public interest,' somehow conceived. That model we, along with all our public choice colleagues, categorically reject.' ibid., p.181.

48. Demsetz, Harold (1969), 'Information and Efficiency, Another Viewpoint,' *Journal of Economics,* **12** (1), pp.1-22.

49. Eisenberg, Melvin A. (1989), 'The Structure of Corporation Law,' *Columbia Law Review,* **89** (7), p.1525.

50. Coase, Ronald. A. (1964), 'The Regulated Industries-Discussion,' *American Economic Review*, Papers and Proceedings, pp.194-195.

51. Coase, Ronald A., 'Problem of social cost,' op.cit., p.43.

52. If transaction costs are zero and all agents are fully informed, as is often assumed in the 'perfectly competitive model,' there is no rationale for arrangements such as the firm and the use of such a 'model' as a comparison with reality.

53. Coase, Ronald A., op.cit., 'Problem of social cost,' p.43.

54. Wolfe, Charles. Jr. (1979), 'A Theory of Non-market Failure, Framework for Implementation Analysis,' *Journal of Law and Economics*, **22** (1), pp.107-140.

55. Coase, Ronald A. op.cit., 'Problem of social cost'. p.43.

56. Comments by Elizabeth. E. Bailey, in Morrison, Steven A. and Clifford Winston (1989), 'Enhancing the Performance of the Deregulated Air Transportation System,' *Brookings Paper on Economic Activity, Microeconomics*, Washington DC: Brookings Institution, pp.61 and 113.

57. De Bow, Michael, E. (1991), 'Markets, Government Intervention, and the Role of Information. An "Austrian School" Perspective with an Application to Merger Regulation,' *George Mason University Law Review*, **14**(1), pp.31-98.

6. Deregulation as Economic Engineering

Economists, unlike scientists, are rarely able to conduct controlled experiments. But one event - the deregulation of the US domestic civil aviation industry in 1978 – has provided economists with an approximation of a controlled laboratory experiment.

For over two decades, the airline industry has been free of government control over prices, entry and exit, but has been subject to anti-trust laws and safety regulations. The infrastructure of the airline industry has also remained under government regulation. As long as fifteen years after the economic deregulation of the airline industry, a Congressional Commission could still point out that '...virtually everything an airline does - from pushing off the gate and taking off and landing airplanes, to selecting and changing flight paths, can be done only with the prior approval of a federal air traffic controller.'[1]

This influence of the federal government over the operating efficiency of the airline industry has grown with the passage of time. Air traffic has increased and the allocation of rights for the use of infrastructure has become critical. Initially, however, individuals who attempted to evaluate the effects of deregulation of the airline industry in isolation recognised that they could not completely separate such consequences from those that would have occurred had the industry remained subject to regulation. Most researchers approached this methodological hurdle by comparing conditions before deregulation with those obtained during and after it. They interpreted the changes in long-run efficiency benefits as being due to what Winston has called 'basic theoretical ideas':

> ...an industry's adjustment to deregulation will, in theory, be shaped by intensified competition and increased operating freedoms that will cause the industry to become more technologically advanced, to adopt more efficient operating and marketing practices, and to respond more effectively to external shocks.[2]

Winston recognises that the predictions made prior to the deregulatory process were mostly guided by static models that assumed that carrier operations and technology would not be significantly affected by the removal of protective economic regulation. Furthermore, two decades ago, the underlying technical characteristics of the industry were still not well understood. The empirical evidence supported the assumption that returns to scale, whatever the output measure used, were constant (beyond the smallest trunk carrier). The share of the market held by the incumbent carriers, after the removal of the protective regulation, would be indeterminate. It might expand or contract. If there were economies of scope, but no economies of scale in the production of short-haul and long-haul services, carriers that joined forces to produce services would gain a larger share of the market than those specialising in one type of route.

Individual carriers would provide the predicted increase in the range of quality of service and fares following deregulation. These carriers would specialise in one type of route and possibly one quality of service, and the range of services, qualities and fares would be provided by a number of carriers.[3]

The form and extent of economies of scale and scope could be expected to determine whether there were advantages to size in city-pair markets, over carriers' entire networks or in producing one, two or more products. In the longer run, the question was whether adjustment towards the underlying technical conditions would be reached by the advent of new, competing carriers or, alternatively, if there were too many trunk carriers, by financial failures of some and the merger of others. If there were such economies or economies of operation density, and if the number of carriers that could profitably compete were to be less than the number of the 'original' pre-deregulation trunks, then competition would eventually have resulted in the elimination of the excess carriers. The competitive process on the routes with too many carriers could have resulted in short-run excess capacity and temporarily very low fares. Some of the losing carriers would go bankrupt and disappear. Others would become carriers in different markets.

Under CAB regulation, carriers were assigned linear routes. Competition, however, forced carriers to make better utilisation of their fleets. One strategy, pioneered by Delta and replicated by other former trunk carriers, was to form a network of spokes feeding flights into and out of hub airports. Aircraft not only carried passengers bound for hub cities but also for hundreds of other destinations reachable from the hub. As a result, carriers were able to multiply the services they offered passengers. Carriers entered and some, such as Eastern and Braniff, exited. Although there was a high mortality rate for start-up carriers, new entrants accounted for 18 per cent of the market in 1996.[4] Despite impediments, there was a spate of mergers in the mid-eighties.[5]

Acquisition of federally-certified airlines must be approved by the Department of Transportation. In terms of the *Federal Aviation Act* of 1958, the department is required to use 'public interest' criteria in evaluating mergers. These criteria include the 'need to encourage fair wages and equitable working conditions for air carriers.'

Unlike most other private sector industries, the airline industry is heavily unionised. Seniority plays a large part in determining the type of aircraft and the routes pilots fly. For a pilot, losing a job means re-starting at the bottom of the rung elsewhere. As a consequence, pilots are highly sensitive to and critical of decisions about routes and mergers. This means acquiring airlines make substantial concessions to employees in order to secure merger approval. The leveraged and debt-financed mergers were estimated to have added about $2 billion a year to the industry's debt service. This accounted for some 60 per cent of the reported aggregate losses in 1990 to 1992.[6]

Over these two deregulatory decades there have been substantial changes in telecommunication and computer technologies. The airlines' equipment cycle continued to spin. The western economies oscillated, while the price of oil gyrated. All of these factors influenced carrier behaviour and the industry's performance, but none has been as significant as what happened on 19 June 1971. On that date Herbert Kelleher founded Southwest Airlines.

From its base at Love Field in Dallas operating 3 Boeing 737s, the carrier started its service to the Texas triangle of Dallas, San Antonio and Houston. Over the past thirty years, the carrier has been unwavering in the execution of its initial strategy. Southwest has deployed a homogeneous fleet of aircraft; has kept to a point-to-point route structure serving secondary, less congested airports. It has insisted on 'on-time' schedules. It serves no food, save for nuts and coffee and it shows no movies. But it offers low fares with a peak-off-peak structure, and it has continued to use direct booking. By utilising aircraft to the maximum and keeping costs at least 50 per cent below the majors, the strategy has given rise to the so-called 'Southwest effect': driving down competitive fares by 10 to 50 per cent. Twenty-nine years later, Southwest is the nation's seventh-largest airline, carrying 63.7 million passengers to 57 cities in the US. It has earned $625.2 million. Unlike most of the majors, which grew primarily by merging, Southwest transformed itself and, in the process, the entire airline industry.

Thanks to the hub-and-spoke systems that require a larger fleet of aeroplanes to serve many locations, extensive (and expensive) gate staff and concentrated operations during 'bank' periods, unproductive time had increased for the major operators. Most ominously, aircraft and flying staff utilisation could not match those attained by point-to-point operators such as Southwest and its imitators. A study by a Merrill Lynch & Co., in 1993, revealed that Southwest's pilots were approximately 40 per cent more productive than United's.[7] Airlines were charged with engaging in destructive competition.[8] In the fall of 1993, Robert Crandall, Chairman and CEO of American Airlines, admitted that his carrier had become a dinosaur on account of its low productivity. He blamed the work rules of the unions and the high benefits received by union members for the problem and threatened to sell American Airlines unless productivity was raised to match that of competitors.[9]

The early 1990s were propitious for re-negotiation of union agreements. Carriers were losing billions of dollars annually and the unions knew that workers faced substantial lay-offs. Employees, in return for salary and benefit cuts and changes in work rules, traded for stocks and seats on the company boards at Trans World Airlines and Northwest Airlines. In 1994, United negotiated an employee stock-ownership plan. The two largest unions - the Air Line Pilots Association and the International Association of Machinists and Aerospace workers - and a group of non-union salaried employees agreed to wage cuts and work-rule changes in return for a $4.9 billion loan to buy 55 per cent of UAL's stock. The stock was distributed to the employees in their retirement accounts over seven years. The salaried employees and the two unions received three of the twelve seats on the board. United's pilots ended up with 46 per cent of the stock, machinists 37 per cent and salaried non-union employees 17 per cent. Flight attendants were not part of the plan.[10] United also cancelled orders for new aircraft, contracted out maintenance and sold its flight kitchens.

In 1998, Donald Carty, who had taken over from Crandall, stated that AMR would concentrate on its core business. They intended to sell off their ground handling business, fixed base operations for private aircraft and their telemarketing and reservation concerns.[11]

Hub-and-spoke carriers also changed their strategy. They formed alliances with regional carriers that served as feeders to the hubs. The latter operated under lower wage structures and, initially, used turboprop aircraft. Then, in 1997, Bombardier introduced a 50-seat and a 70-seat version of its Canadair Regional jet. Embraer (Empresa Brasileira de Aeronautica) followed with its 50-seat RJ-145 and Fairchild Dornier with its 32-seat 328 JET. Variants followed with configurations of 44 seats, 55 seats and 70 seats.

The direct operating costs per seat-mile of these regional jets are significantly lower than that of comparably sized turboprops for routes longer than 400 miles. This has given a boost to regional carriers, which added smaller cities and more frequent services to the spokes of the hubs. Most significantly, the regional jets offer carriers the potential to replicate Southwest's strategy of offering point-to-point service with a much smaller size of aircraft than the 110-189-seat Boeing 737.

Comair was the first commuter airline in North America to fly a regional jet. The carrier now has a fleet of 110 fifty-seat regional jets. Flying under the name Delta Connection, Delta, the nation's third largest carrier, has been able to expand its point-to-point operations by using Comair's regional jets rather than deploying its larger jets. US Airways operates a similar system with its subsidiary, Metrojet, while United operates Shuttle By United.[12]

In 1975, at the Kennedy Oversight CAB Hearings, Professor William Jordan compared the actual performance of CAB-regulated airlines with the performance of those airlines not regulated by the CAB, primarily those operating in Texas and California. He predicted that without CAB regulation there would be between 100 to 200 or more airlines in the United States operating 3 to 4 planes each.[13]

Roy Pulsifer, a former CAB regulator, writing in April 1982, identified Southwest Airlines as the prototype operation that would sweep all before it. He estimated that Southwest's point-to-point operations, specialised equipment and flexible labour rules would yield 'soft' productivity gains in excess of 50 per cent over those of the older carriers.[14]

In a 1998 study, Morrison and Winston estimated that, since deregulation, competition supplied by incumbent carriers had accounted for 18 per cent of the savings from lower real fares. They further estimated that competition supplied by Southwest Airlines had accounted for 31 per cent of the savings, competition from other new entrants 10 per cent of the savings and that improvements in carriers' operating efficiencies had accounted for 41 per cent of the savings.[15]

With the benefit of hindsight, it has become clear that the operational and technical advances that were stimulated by deregulation were the accelerated development of hub-and-spoke networks and the development of networks of complex computers that facilitated yield management. The hub-and-spoke networks allowed carriers to exploit economies of traffic density. enabling carriers to operate larger, more efficient aircraft and to disperse fixed costs over more passengers. Yield management has meant that supply could be pitted against current demand, allowing the carrier to assign different prices to an airline seat that was previously sold at a fixed price.

A second organisational advance might also be noted, but it is open to debate as to whether it is a response to regulation rather than to deregulation. International airline alliances allow carriers to extend their networks overseas without operating additional flights. In so doing, they can side-step restrictions on international services codified in various bilateral agreements. By co-ordinating flight schedules and ensuing gate proximity at connecting airports, the partners in the alliance can offer the passenger greater convenience. Immunity from anti-trust laws means alliance partners can also engage in co-operative pricing of interline trips.

Winston has estimated that average airline industry load factors increased from around 52 per cent for the decade preceding deregulation to approximately 62 per cent since deregulation. Real costs per revenue-ton-mile have declined by at least 25 per cent, while industry profits have been volatile.[16]

Bruckner and Whalen have estimated that alliance partners charge interline fares that are approximately 25 per cent below those charged by non-allied carriers.[17] Morrison and Winston, in a 1995 study, estimated that the annual savings to passengers came to $12.4 billion, while the value of savings in time per annum to passengers aggregated to $10.3 billion.[18]

ATTAINING ALLOCATIVE EFFICIENCY

Professional economists who acted as advisers and deregulatory activists within regulatory agencies at the time of the removal,[19] of protective regulation of interstate transport carriers[20] in the United States, have, through their statements and writings, shed light on their perceptions of the concept of the market and on how it would work under deregulatory conditions. Their conceptions of the market are of interest because of their participation in the formulation and the placement of deregulatory policies. The overwhelming majority of these participating economists regarded the competitive market as a means of attaining allocative efficiency.[21]

The candidate industries for deregulation were those that, if deregulated, were thought to satisfy the conditions of 'workable' competition. Stated differently, they approximated 'workable' contestability. They included industries that, although subject to scale economies, were not regarded as natural monopolies. In such cases, ease of entry would equilibrate prices with marginal costs. According to Bailey and Baumol, 'the railroad industry is more contestable than has been traditionally acknowledged, because there is a strong competitive pressure from other modes of transportation - such as trucking - on the rates charged for shipment of a wide variety of commodities.'[22]

Other highly contestable industries were trucking 'the most contestable of the economy's industries with the possible exception of barge transportation,'[23] and the airline industry, which presented a 'particularly close approximation to contestability.'[24]

It is noteworthy that the notions of contestability were refined during the period of deregulation by economists who were either directly involved or who had actively participated in the debate. The timing is of significance. Those proposing regulatory change were burdened with the 'proof' of improvement. The proponents of contestable markets, by contrast, were free, if they wished, to observe those workings of the deregulated markets that refuted their expectations of 'workable contestability.'

Alfred Kahn, head of the Civil Aeronautics Board (1977-1978), writing at the time of the enactment of the *Airline Deregulation Act* in the fall of 1978, idealised workable competition.[25]   He believed that the deregulated airline industry, despite expected short-run adjustment problems caused largely by the protective regulatory regime and by the separate and diverse ownership of airports, would work. His view was that it might not achieve 'first best' allocative efficiency, but it would achieve an acceptable 'second best' approximation.

Twelve years later, he argued that 'second best' had been achieved. 'Market concentration, route-by-route, has definitely declined, on average, in markets of all sizes and dimensions.'[26] There had been 'increased sensitivity of air fares to the effects on cost of length of trip and traffic density, and of transportation rates generally to the differences between peak and off-peak and front and back haul.'[27] While 'the removal of regulatory restrictions and the pressures of competition have yielded marked increases in productivity'[28] and 'all of this has occurred with no evident sacrifice of safety.'[29]   A disclaimer, 'the performance of even a single industry is multi-faceted, and never susceptible to a definitive evaluation,' prefaced these evaluations.[30]

Bailey and Baumol, postulating an idealised, contestable market, one that achieves allocative efficiency, examined the attributes of a 'workable' as distinct from 'perfectly' contestable market. According to the authors, the critical issue that determines workability is the magnitude of sunk costs, not the entry lag, for 'if sunk costs are small but not zero, the discipline exercised by the threat of potential entry remains potent.'[31]

There are also methodological problems concerning the concept of markets and potential competition in the contestable hypothesis. It implies that markets are separable, and that the suppliers to them are subjected to observable, varying degrees of competitive threat. If, to some degree, all markets, however defined, can be viewed as being subject to some potential competition, the 'test' for perfect or 'degrees' of imperfect contestability cannot be open to refutation. The exercise resolves into the verification of the existence of potential competition.[32]   This process of verification is usually attempted by declaring that the candidate market either meets or fails to meet the technological and demands conditions for contestable markets.[33] It was a process, however, that was shown to be vulnerable to the charge that those entities wishing their markets to be deregulated produced evidence that verified 'a permissive regulatory posture.'[34] Opponents of deregulation also engaged in the verification process, 'proving' by means of empirical evidence, that the deregulated markets were not perfectly competitive markets. They proceeded to describe the deviations in the predictions of the contestability thesis and offered explanations by way of supplementary concepts.[35]

Michael Levine, an early proponent of the contestability hypothesis, has examined the deregulated airline market in the United States. He observes a number of marked deviations between market performance and the predictions of those, including himself, who held that the airline market satisfied the condition for (almost) perfect contestability:

> 'These deviations - mergers, vertical integration, hub domination, complex fare structures and frequent flyer programmes, the role of travel agents, the use made of computer reservation systems, the use of limited airport slots and gates, predation and new entrant fatalities - cannot adequately be explained by the traditional models of airline competition.'[36]

Levine, along with most others, did not predict the horizontal and vertical mergers. These, to Levine, seemed to be due to economies of scale in conveying information to consumers concerning service offerings in the market place, economies of scope that allowed the exploitation of principal-agent conflicts, and production indivisibilities in city-pair markets that influenced the control of discount pricing.[37] Hub-and-spoke route systems emerged rather than the predicted linear route structures primarily because 'hubbing' is a way of 'overcoming production indivisibilities so as to allow frequent jet service in many city-pair markets when traffic density would not otherwise support it.'[38]

Frequent-flyer programmes tied customers by rewarding them in non-linear ways, creating economies of scale and demand and economies of scope, since selecting a carrier with a range of destinations from a city will make it easier for business travellers to earn rewards because they can be earned on trips to more destinations. For would-be new entrants, having neither presence in the market nor a choice of options, frequent-flyer programmes constitute an obstacle to entry. Computer reservation systems facilitated market intelligence. Carriers are able to manipulate market signals and their relationship with the travel agents.[39] Levine recognises that contestability theory has been refuted in that predation has occurred.

The evidence of such deviations from the allocative efficiencies predicted by the proponents of contestability theory, prompted Levine to reconsider the neo-classical model. In particular, he examined the assumptions about information and the nature of the firm. He also reformulated his conception of the air transportation system. It was characterised by 'network effects, which appear both as economies of scope and as revenue returns to scope, information economies of scale, and production indivisibilities for individual city-pair flows.'[40] His paradigm shift, covering the concepts of information, the firm as a substitute for the market, and agency-principal, involves consideration of the production of information and the role of transactions in coping with constraints. These concepts 'explain a great deal about otherwise puzzling aspects of airline competition.'[41]

Not only were the participants in the market able to sift and transmit information by deploying more powerful computer systems, but the emerging networks were deemed to be largely beneficial to the consumer. They were the result, in some cases, of impediments to contestability.[42] His prescriptions for improvement, accordingly, became more circumspect. In many cases, he declined to recommend the elimination of restrictions to contestability. Recognising that the deregulated market '...has made the airline system very much better, in particular ways which have surprised us all, while also recognising that those improvements have been bought at the expense of a new set of problems, at least a few of which may be amenable to correction.'[43]

In sum, Levine implied that the analysis of the imperfectly regulated domestic civil aviation industry was largely correct, but that the imperfections of the deregulated market were not predicted. He argued that deregulation is superior in that it produces, thanks to the creation of incentives, the more efficient satisfaction of consumer requirements.[44]

MARKET POWER AND THE DEREGULATED AIRLINE INDUSTRY

Some analysts questioned the motives of the carriers and asked whether they were exercising market power. By restricting the choices of passengers and charging them higher prices, the carriers were increasing their surpluses but reducing consumers' surpluses and, therefore, their welfare. Although postulating a distinction between competitive advantages 'that occur naturally' and those 'that result from institutions created by the airlines,' some neo-classical analysts claimed to evaluate the loss of benefits to the consumer resulting from the exercise of such market power, as against the benefits that might accrue from the concentrated operations of the carriers. According to these analysts, among the 'competitive advantages' created by the airlines were: the frequent flyer programme; the reward systems for travel agents that pay bonuses when the agent books more travel with one airline to the exclusion of other computer reservation systems; and dominance generated by large scale operations at congested airports. Instead of advocating the deployment of anti-trust legislation, they have proceeded with the apparently positive enquiry of establishing 'more clearly the sources of market power in the airline industry.'[45]

The dominance of major carriers at congested airports was at the centre of a controversy during the next decade. There were two issues. One, whether the possession of scarce rights on terminal gates and landing slots was an incentive for carriers to merge; and two, whether the carriers possessing these rights used them to maximise their surpluses by limiting consumer choices and charging them higher prices. These alleged reductions in consumers' welfare were deemed to be the result of profit-maximising carriers responding to the incentives and constraints that they faced. The government, however, owns and operates the aviation infrastructure, establishes the incentives and constraints and so is, in part, responsible for the allegedly diminution in consumer benefits.

Unlike the privately-owned utility networks, the airside infrastructure and the air traffic control (atc) network are government-owned. Furthermore, carriers pay the market value for all their inputs except for the use of runways and the atc system. Airports and the atc system are not paid for directly by fees charged to the carriers. When traffic increases the airport's revenues and those of the atc do not. Capital expenditures of the airports are funded, in part, from revenue bonds and, in part, by federal grants. In exchange for grants, the airports sign 20-year grant agreements with the Federal Aviation Administration (FAA). The latter have generally eschewed innovative pricing structures and have favoured or 'grandfathered' slot allocations and congestion 'rationing.' When faced with rising demand, the Department of Transportation has had to request funds from Congress in order to undertake capital investment and employ more controllers. The following prediction was made in 1984:

> The failure to signal through the price mechanism the true economic value of peak hour departure and landing slots, as well as the atc system, constitutes the most important institutional flaw in the air transportation system at this time.[46]

The National Civil Aviation Review Commission argued that the atc system should be managed and funded as a commercial enterprise. The Commission recommended the creation of a performance-based organisation to take over the FAA's atc functions funded by cost-based user fees. The Clinton administration introduced legislation, in April 1998, to implement this approach.

Others have recommended the privatisation of both the airports and the atc systems. The reasoning is that privately-owned entities facing competition would have the incentive to minimise costs and to improve high-quality service. Prices would be equated with costs, while capacity would respond to demand. In effect, the task of deregulating commercial aviation would be completed. Whereas regulating aviation infrastructure impedes airline performance, a privatised and competitive system would, its promoters claim, complements airline competition and enhance the well-being of the consumer.[47]

The deregulation and privatisation of the infrastructure of the aviation industry has yet to take place. The existing system is seen by some as affording to carriers, market power which, when exercised, is not in the public's interest. One such instance in which market power was considered a threat, concerned the alliance between American Airlines and British Airways. These carriers applied for anti-trust immunity to engage in co-operative pricing. The Department of Transportation refused the request. Over the non-stop routes, between US gateway cities such as New York and Chicago, and London-Heathrow, the two carriers controlled most of the traffic. The fear was that the carriers would use this market power to set higher prices in these gateway-to-gateway markets.[48]

In January 1998, Northwest Airlines and Continental Airlines agreed to a 'virtual merger.' Northwest bought a 14 per cent stake in Continental that carried a 54 per cent voting interest in Continental. Route schedules and frequent-flyer programmes were to be spliced, but employees, managers and aircraft were to wear separate colours. Shortly after, AMC Corporation announced a link-up with US Airways. UAL Corporation, which controls United, aimed to team with Delta Airlines. The agreements were designed to extend each airline's reach and make each of the carriers more attractive to big corporate buyers of tickets. Such proposals raised questions as to whether the major carriers were using their market clout and deep pockets to crush new competition at hub airports. A single carrier dominated most major hubs.

In spite of the galvanising effect of the entry of Southwest into Baltimore, MD, Providence, RI, Manchester, NH, into several cities in Florida and into the New York market in 1999 (via MacArthur Airport on Long Island), a number of cities, including Rochester, NY, complained that the dominant carrier repelled low fare competition and was charging excessively high fares. Such fares were inhibiting the development of business.

The Department of Transportation threatened to issue guidelines on predatory pricing and other anti-competitive practices.

In early 1999, two US Senators drafted a bill that defined a variety of common practices as anti-competitive. Fourteen passenger airlines responded by agreeing to a 'customer service commitment.' Their intention was to head-off the pending legislation. Ten months after the 'virtual merger' of Northwest with Continental, the Justice Department charged that the deal would lead to higher ticket prices and diminished service for more than four million passengers travelling on seven routes dominated by the two carriers. Then, in May 1999, the Justice Department sought, in Federal court in Wichita, an injunction barring American Airlines from reducing fares below cost and increasing flights as part of an effort to stifle competition.

The case was brought under Section 2 of the *Sherman Anti-Trust Act*. The Justice Department accused American Airlines of using its dominance of the Dallas-Fort Worth International Airport to prevent weaker competitors from gaining entry there in the mid-1990s. The allegation was that American Airlines had raised fares and reduced services to Wichita, Kansas City, Long Beach and Colorado Springs. The carriers involved were Vanguard Airlines, Sun Jet International and Western Pacific.

The US District Judge threw out the Justice Department's anti-trust case against the AMR Corp. in April 2001, four weeks before the case was scheduled to go to trial in a federal court.

On 6 November 2000, Northwest and Continental announced a tentative settlement in which Continental agreed to buy back, for $450 million, the controlling interest held by Northwest. The deal was endorsed by the Justice Department. The airlines agreed to extend their marketing alliance under which they co-ordinate schedules and combine frequent-flyer programmes until 2025.[49]

In January 2001, Rodney Slater, the departing Secretary of Transportation, released three reports. One of the reports found that passengers who take short flights from an airline's hub where there is no low-fare carrier, pay 54 per cent more, on average, than passengers in comparable markets served by a low-fare competitor. A report, authored by Clinton V. Oster and John S. Strong, found that 'predatory practices may have occurred in the past and are a recurring possibility in the US domestic airline industry.'[50]

In May 2000, United Airlines announced its proposed $4.3 billion acquisition of US Airways. The latter carrier agreed to sell most of its operations at Washington's Ronald Reagan National Airport to Robert L. Johnson, the founder of Black Entertainment Television and a US Airways director. The new regional carrier would be known as DC Air. In January 2001, American Airways started negotiations to acquire Trans World Airlines, the nation's eighth largest carrier and agreed to purchase significant assets from US Airways. This move was calculated to ease the concerns raised by the Justice Department over United's proposed purchase of US Airways. Similarly, American Airways wished to purchase a piece of the Boston-New York-Washington shuttle and 49 per cent of DC Air. At the start of 2001, United accounted for 19 per cent of the domestic market and American for 17 per cent. (The mergers were called off, however, in July 2001.)

At a Senate Judiciary anti-trust subcommittee hearing, the chief executive of Air Tran Holdings Inc. testified that his carrier would ask the Transportation Department to redistribute slots at Washington Reagan International Airport that are controlled by United, American, US Air and TWA. Such a decision was necessary to guarantee competition, he said.

Officials of Delta Air Lines and Continental Airline stated that they preferred to remain independent, but that if United and American were to merge, they would be at a competitive disadvantage. The argument was that carriers with the most extensive networks are best able to control their costs, secure lucrative deals with corporations for business travellers and obtain the most revenue from their seats. Gordon Bethune, of Continental, said that the proposed mergers would 'create a cartel that will marginalise smaller competitors like Continental.'[51]

Alfred Kahn testified that the deals were 'troublesome' and 'threatened the effectiveness of competition' in the industry. However, the current anti-trust laws 'should clearly be sufficient' to deal with the matter.[52] Michael Levine stated that that the mergers would be the final shake-out among the Big 4 (Eastern, TWA, American and United) of the regulated era. The mergers would mark the end of the 'arms race' to dominate the country and would represent a failure of the deregulatory movement:

> Once the East Coast is divided in the way that this deal proposes to divide it, I believe that Delta and Northwest and Continental will not be able to construct a network that will be comparable...these airlines (American and United) expect to get revenue premiums-that is, monopoly profits-from customers.[53]

Others, by contrast, questioned the *status quo* of competition in the industry, the motives for the mergers and the diminution of competition that allegedly would ensue. TWA was on the verge of bankruptcy for the third time in a decade, while US Airways had a weak regional network.[54]

ClydeV. Prestowitz, Jr., testified before the House Aviation Subcommittee on 15 June 2000. He contended that the force behind the mergers was not to acquire greater market power to be exercised at the expense of consumers. On the contrary, he said, carriers seek to capture the network effects. When two carriers combine, the resulting network is larger than the individual ones it replaces. Travellers on the larger network are able to reach more destinations without switching airlines. Research by the Economic Strategy Institute and GKMG Consulting Services showed that not only is travelling on a single airline more convenient in terms of connection times and frequent-flyer miles, it is also cheaper. Moreover, combining airline networks would actually increase competition because 'connectivity' would increase. According to Prestowitz, the accrual of network effects by merging would enhance, not detract from, consumers' welfare.

Indeed, Prestowitz regards current and future mergers and airline alliances, as responses to domestic deregulation and the opportunities in the global marketplace. The carriers, he argues,

> ...seek seamless national and international service, so that they can depart from one destination, and arrive at another, without the complications of booking on multiple airlines, possessing multiple tickets, conducting multiple baggage check-ins, and having frequent-flyer benefits distributed among multiple programs.[55]

SUMMARY AND CONJECTURES

Twenty years after the airlines were freed from protective economic regulation, the number of domestic travellers moving over their routes has more than doubled. Most of these travellers have moved over hub-and-spoke networks that provide improved access over seamless national and international routes. Moreover, 80 per cent of those passengers paid less than they would have done under government regulation[56].

Significant portions of these lower fares and increased growths in traffic can be credited to the entry into interstate markets of the low-fare, no-frills, point-to-point services pioneered and developed by Southwest Airlines. The success of these operations have spurred further technical innovations. The regional jet offers the prospect of new markets for point-to-point services served by much smaller and quieter aircraft than the Boeing 737. Similarly, with cumulative expenditures of $180 million, NASA has encouraged competition among private companies to design the engines, wings, guidance systems and safety protections for much smaller aircraft. There is now the prospect of quiet, safe and fuel-efficient jets offering air taxi services on short-haul routes serving instead of the present fifty congested airports, some five thousand public-use landing facilities. Thanks to government support and entrepreneurial endeavours, the rigidity in the present system, involving the mass of travellers routed through a small number of hubs, and the elite moving in corporate jets, could be broken.[57]

This is an industry that has developed, and continues to develop innovations in aircraft and service patterns. In so doing, the carriers and manufacturers have responded to the market and continue to meet the needs of their customers. This is a dynamic market process, characterised by disequilibria that are continually disturbed by opportunistic entrepreneurs seeking greater profits. This dynamic, competitive market process is not characterised by allocative efficiency. Over the long run, prices have not equated with marginal costs but, as the studies of the industry have shown, productivity has risen considerably.

Most of these studies explain these gains in productivity as being due to the removal of protective regulation. The continuation of such regulation would, according to their reasoning, have thwarted innovations in equipment, computer technology and service patterns. Entry barriers would have prevented carriers from developing their networks, while exit restrictions would have prevented them from shedding their excess capacity. Price regulation would have delayed the deployment of computer capabilities and so would have retarded the emergence of yield management.

This exercise, however, is not a counter-factual analysis. The changes in service quality, prices and costs cannot be attributable exclusively to the behaviour of competitive agents in a deregulated market. This is because, to 'net-out' these effects, the analyst would need to know how service quality, prices and costs would actually have changed had the industry remained regulated for the past twenty years. In place of actual outcomes, the analyst has to simulate changes in quality, price, and (retarded) innovations of an imaginary regulatory regime. The question is 'What does the analyst base these simulations upon?'

The answer is that the analyst qualifies, but rarely makes explicit, the ability of the regulator to make decisions. In effect, the analyst places a low probability on regulators making at least as good a decision regarding prices, operations, networks, investments and mergers as those of the carriers' managers.

This evaluation is not based on the assumption that the regulators are inherently inferior to their private sector counterparts, but it is assumed that government regulators face weaker incentives than the carrier manager in discovering and developing useful and profitable information.

This is not to say that the private sector manager does not make mistakes, or that the regulator has no successes. What it does say - or imply - is that a mistake made by the manager will be punished, while a mistake made by a government regulator will not have the same painful consequences. Similarly, the private sector manager will be afforded greater rewards than the government employee when achieving success. In sum, the analyst is asserting that profit-motivated managers in a competitive market are more efficient than government regulators in discovering and using information.

Some analysts, such as Winston, have attempted to compare the performance of the deregulated industry against a set of conditions under which 'maximum efficiency' will be attained. These are the neo-classical textbook conditions of static equilibrium under which prices are equated with costs. But as the twenty-year-old history of the deregulated industry shows, this bench-mark has little value. The competitive process resembles, not the theoretical construction of the textbooks, but a messy series of 'monopolising acts'[58] in which large, competitive carriers monopolise their respective hubs. They are innovative and successful. At issue is, not so much whether the major carriers are engaging in predatory pricing, but whether restricting the entry of competing carriers has enabled them to attain their present size and power. A more revealing line of enquiry would be to explore the extent to which this process of monopolistic competition has been shaped by government regulation of aviation.

Despite their implied assumptions as to the fallibility of government regulators, some neo-classical economists have accused the carriers of anti-competitive behaviour. There is some inconsistency here. At issue is, not the application of the perfectly competitive model to measure resource misallocation, although this has dubious value, but whether government anti-trust officials should be considered to be superior to government regulators. Do they have the incentives to inform themselves sufficiently to construct a shadow market to use in comparing the *status quo* with the welfare outcomes of government intervention? Or, putting it differently, are the anti-trust decision makers more likely to be perfect planners than the former regulators of the airline industry?

Notes

1. The National Commission to Ensure a Strong and Competitive Airline Industry, quoted by Kahn, Alfred, E. (1993), 'Change, Challenge, and Competition: A Review of the Airline Commission Report,' *Regulation*, 16(3), p.1.
    http://www.cato.org/pubs/ regulation/ reg16n3d.html.
2. Winston, Clifford (1998), 'U.S. Industry Adjustment to Economic Deregulation,' *Journal of Economic Perspectives*, 12(3), Summer, p.92.
3. Ellison, Anthony P. (1982), 'The Structural Change of the Airline Industry following Deregulation,' *Transportation Journal*, 21(3), pp.58-69.
4. Robson, John E. (1998), 'Airline Deregulation. Twenty Years of Success and Counting,' *Regulation*, 21(2), p.20.
5. In 1979, Pan American World Airlines purchased National Airlines; in 1985, United purchased Pan Am's Pacific routes and People Express acquired Frontier Airlines; in 1986, Delta bought Western Airlines, Northwest Airlines bought Republican Airlines, Trans World Airlines acquired Ozark Airlines, Texas Air Corp bought Eastern Airlines and People Express; in 1987, American bought AirCal, US Air bought Pacific Southwest Airlines and Piedmont Aviation; in 1991, Delta bought Pan Am's European operations ; in 1994, Southwest Airlines acquired Morris Air; in 1998, American Bought Reno Air. See Carey, Susan (2001), 'With TWA, American Plots Course to Avoid Airline-Merger Pitfalls,' *The Wall Street Journal*, April, 20.
6. Kahn, Alfred E., 'Change, Challenge and Competition,' op.cit., p.6.
7. Weintraub, Richard M. (1993), 'The Airline's No-Frills, Low-Fare Formula Pays Off', *The Washington Post*, 12 September.
8. ' ...I must concede that the industry has demonstrated a more severe and chronic susceptibility to destructive competition than I, along with the other enthusiastic proponents of deregulation, was prepared to concede or predict: namely, tendencies to overly exuberant, competitive expansions of capacity in periods of growing demand, quite possibly attributable to the familiar 'S-curve' phenomenon-the tendency for market shares to increase disproportionately with more intensive scheduling-combined with outward immobility of capital and other inelasticities of supply in the face of decelerated expansion or declines in demand.' Kahn, Alfred E., 'Change, Challenge and Competition,' op.cit., p.5
9. Solomon, Stephen.D. (1993), 'Jurassic Park notwithstanding, the dinosaurs are gone. American Airlines: Going, Going...?' *The New York Times Magazine*, 5 September.
10. Zuckerman, Lawrence (2001), 'Divided, an Airline Stumbles,' *The New York Times*, 14 March.
11. McCartney, Scott (1998), 'AMR Plans to Auction Three of Its Units to Focus on American Airline Business,' *The Wall Street Journal*, 30 September.
12. Zuckerman, Laurence (1999), 'Discounted Fares Arriving in East,' *The New York Times*, 3 February.
13. United States Senate (1975), 'Oversight of Civil Aeronautics Board Practices and Procedures,' hearings before the Subcommittee on Administrative Practice and Procedure of the Committee on the Judiciary, prepared statement of Dr. William A. Jordan, p.479.
14. Pulsifer, Roy (1982), 'Deregulation Implications for Technology,' *Airfinance Journal*, 17(14), April, p.14.

15. Winston, Clifford (1998), 'US Industry Adjustment to Economic Deregulation,' *Journal of Economic Perspectives*, 12(3), p.101.
16. ibid., table 1, p.93.
17. Bruckner, Jan and W. Tom Whalen (2000), 'The Price Effects of Interline Airline Alliances,' *Journal of Law & Economics*, 43(October), p.42.
18. Morrison, Steven A. and Clifford Winston (1995), *The Evolution of the Airline Industry*, Washington DC: Brookings.
19. Prominent among the group were: Alfred Kahn, head of the Civil Aeronautics Board (1977-78); Michael Levine, General Director, International and Domestic Aviation at the CAB; Darius Gaskins Jr, Chairman, Interstate Commerce Commission; G. Douglas, ICC, and Elizabeth E. Bailey, member, CAB.
20. Among the major deregulatory legislation were: *The Railway Revitalization and Reform Act*, (4R. Act), 1976, *Airline Deregulation Act* 1978, *Motor Carrier Act* 1980 and *The Staggers Rail Act* of 1980.
21. Boudreaux and Ellig explore the similarities and differences of the pro-deregulation economists and policy makers with respect to industrial organisation theory, 'Chicago' anti-trust theories, contestable market theories and 'market process' economists who see 'most all regulatory agencies as principal barriers to entrepreneurial innovation.' Boudreaux, Donald J. and Ellig, Jerome (1992), 'Beneficent Bias: The loss against regulating Airline Computerised Reservation System,' *Journal of Air Law and Commerce*, 57(3), p.570.
22. Bailey, Elizabeth E. and William J. Baumol (1984), 'Deregulation and the Theory of Contestable Markets,' *Yale Journal on Regulation*, 1(2), p.125.
23. ibid., p.133.
24. ibid., p.128.
25. 'The economic principals we - my fellow commissioners or board members and I - have been applying are easy to characterise: that economic efficiency requires prices for goods and services to be set equal to their marginal social opportunity cost (that is, the cost of society of the resources that are used to produce additional quantities - resources that will therefore be freed for other uses if and or buyers restrain their demands), and that wherever it is technologically feasible, competition is the best way to achieve this result, as well or to ensure the optimum rate of innovations and the greatest degree of managerial efficiency - X efficiency, as economists now put it.' Kahn, Alfred E. (1978), 'Applying Economics to an Imperfect World. Regulation,' *AEI Journal on Government and Society*, (Nov/Dec), p.17.
26. Kahn, Alfred E. (1990), 'Deregulation: Looking Backward and Looking Forward,' *Yale Journal on Regulation*, 7(2), p.341.
27. ibid., p.343.
28. ibid., p.344.
29. ibid., p.344.
30. ibid., p.340.
31. Bailey, Elizabeth E. and William J. Baumol, p.123.
32. Tests of markets for contestability, 'do not have a direct measure of potential competition, and thus they attempt to infer the influence of potential competitors on the basis of the effect that actual competitors have on their efficiency measures.' Morrison, Steven. A. and Winston, Clifford (1987), 'Empirical Implications and Tests of the Contestability Hypothesis,' *Journal of Law and Economics*, 30(1), p.56.
33. Bailey and Baumol, writing in 1984 during the early years of deregulation, verified that trucks and those parts of the rail industry deemed contestable by the deregulatory legislation met the technological and demand conditions. 'But it is unlikely that perfect contestability (in airlines), will be achieved over the short run since changes in labour contracts and fleet configuration cannot be carried out quickly.' Bailey Elizabeth E. and William J. Baumol, p.131.

34.   'Understandably, the theory was well received by firms in a variety of industries seeking to
      be deregulated. Surprisingly, in a few cases, the theory has also captured the imagination
      of permissive regulators seeking to relinquish their duties during the transition, despite the
      fact that the relevant markets could hardly be labelled perfectly contestable.' Meyer, John
      R. and William B. Tye (1988), 'Workable Competition in Industries Undergoing a
      Transition to Deregulation: A Contractual Equilibrium Approach,' *Yale Journal on
      Regulation*, **5**(2), Summer, pp.284, 285. '
      Some of the "new" analysis was sponsored, directly or indirectly, by large U.S. companies
      (for example IBM and AT & T), which were resisting antitrust challenges. For AT & T,
      William, J. Baumol, Robert. D. Willig, Paul. W. MacAvoy, John. C. Panzar, and perhaps
      25 other scholars at leading departments provided research, new concepts, and direct
      testimony. Their contestability and sustainability ideas were an attempt to oust the
      traditional concepts of monopoly and competitive impacts.' Shepherd, William. G. (1990),
      'Potential Competition versus Actual Competition,' *Administrative Law Review*, **42**(1),
      p.18 and footnote 46.
35.   A critic of deregulation, Paul. S. Dempsey, has posed the ideal of market efficiency, which
      he then proceeds to 'prove' has not been attained in deregulated markets as was predicted
      by the proponents of deregulation. An illustration of his methodological approach is as
      follows: 'The trouble is, transportation is simply not the ideal model of perfect competition
      that many proponents of deregulation insists it was. There appear to be significant
      economies of scale and scope and economic barriers to entry in railroad, airline, and
      less-than-truck load motor carrier industries. Widespread bankruptcies and mergers have
      reduced the number of competitors in each mode to the point that major oligopolies now
      exist. The theory of contestable markets, which poses that if a monopolist or oligopolist
      begins to earn supra-competitive profits, new competitive interest, or the threat thereof, will
      restore pricing competition appears not to be sustained by the empirical evidence.'
      Dempsey, Paul (1988), 'The Empirical Results of Deregulation: A Decade later, and the Band
      Played On,' *Transportation Law Journal*, **17**(1), p.35. See also Dempsey, Paul (1982),
      'Interstate Trucking: The Collision of Textbook Theory and Empirical Reality,' *Transportation
      Law Journal*, **20**(2), p.192; Dempsey, Paul (1990), 'Airline Deregulation and Laissez-faire
      Mythology: Economic Theory in Turbulence,' *The Journal of Air Law and Commerce*, **56**(2),
      Winter, pp.305-412.
36.   Levine, Michael E. (1987), 'Airline Competition in Deregulated Markets: Theory, Firm
      Strategy and Public Policy,' *Yale Journal on Regulation*, **4**(2), Spring, p.408.
37.   ibid., p.425.
38.   ibid., p.441.
39.   ibid., pp.460-461.
40.   ibid., p.468.
41.   ibid., p.422.
42.   '.. many of the major impediments to contestability described here stem from forces that
      produce real economic benefits to the public. To eliminate them in the name of enhancing
      'contestability' would do the public more harm than good. And another important impediment
      to contestability - the profitability of predatory practices - is a disease common to many markets
      in which information is important, and for which there is no known treatment with acceptable
      side effects,' ibid., p.482.
43.   ibid., p.493.
44.   ibid., p.481.
45.   Borenstein, Sevrin (1989), 'Hubs and high fares: dominance and market power in the US airline
      industry,' *Rand Journal of Economics*, **20**(3), pp.344, at 344.
46.   Pulsifer, Roy (1984), 'Airports under Deregulation: Congestion, Saturation and New
      Technology,' *Transportation Research Circular*, 286, November, p.12.
47.   Poole, Jr., Robert W. and Viggo Butler (1999), 'Airline Deregulation: The Unfinished
      Revolution,' *Regulation*, **22**(1),.
48.   Brueckner, Jan and W. Tom Whalen, op.cit., p.542.
49.   Zucherman, Laurence (2000), '2 Airlines Make Deal in Attempt to End Their Antitrust
      Trial,' *The New York Times*, November 7.

50. Bloomberg News Service (2001), 'Airline Targeted', *The Miami Herald*, 17 January.
51. Power, Stephan (2001), 'Airline Mergers Could Continue, Executives Say,' *The Wall Street Journal*, 8 February.
52. Wald, Mathew (2001), 'Hearing on an Airline Merger Raises Wider Concerns,' *The New York Times*, 2 February.
53. ibid.
54. Prestowitz, Clyde V. (2001), 'Fewer Airlines, More Choices,' *The Wall Street Journal*, January 12.
55. Testimony of Clyde V. Prestowitz, Jr. before the US House of Representatives Aviation Subcommittee of the Committee on Transportation and Infrastructure, Thursday, 15 June 2000. http:// www.econstrat.org/cvptestav.htm p.2.
56. Postrel, Virginia (2000), 'Don't blame deregulation for airline problems, blame not enough deregulation,' *The New York Times*, 5 October.
57. Fallows, James (2001), 'Freedom of the Skies,' *The Atlantic Monthly*, **287**(6), pp.37-49
58. Armentano Dominick T. (1999), *Antitrust: The Case for Repeal*, Auburn, Ala.: Mises Institute.

7. The FAA and the US Domestic Civil Aviation System

In the year 2000, more than twice the number of passengers boarded flights in the United States than in 1978, the year in which the domestic airline industry was deregulated. But as the number of passengers increased, so did the levels of public dissatisfaction about flight delays and lost economic productivity. President Clinton, echoing the 'widespread passenger frustration and anger' revealed alarming figures showing a system that was all too frequently in gridlock. Flight delays had increased by more than 58 per cent between 1995-2000, while cancellations rose by 68 per cent over the same period.[1] During the four summer months of 2000, over 160,000 flights were delayed, on average by 45 minutes each.

The constituent parts of the industry started to point fingers at each other, while some interest groups, representing smaller cities that had lost connections to the major centres, blamed airline deregulation for their woes.

However, the malfunctions in the system were more probably due to the failure of the organisation responsible for operating the aviation infrastructure, the Federal Aviation Administration (FAA), to adapt to rapidly changing conditions, than to any other factor.

The FAA resides within the Department of Transportation (DOT). The controllers employed in the air traffic control system (atc), which accounts for 45 per cent of the FAA's budget, decide on the type of services that are to be provided and on the facilities needed to perform these services. The US commercial airports are, almost without exception, operated and owned either by the state or by individual municipalities. By contrast with the carriers, therefore, the air spaces and airports have not been deregulated and privatised, but have remained subject to the central planning dictates of government agencies.

As the 'National Commission to Ensure a Strong and Competitive Airline Industry' (a creation of the US Congress) has stated: 'In the history of American business there has never been a major commercial industry whose minute-by-minute operating efficiency was capped by the daily operating efficiency of the federal government except for the airlines.'[2]

The 1958 *Federal Aviation Act* established the FAA and created a range of obligations for the agency: promoting civil aviation while regulating safety; implementing plans to control noise effects of civil aviation and developing and operating a system of air traffic control for both commercial and military navigation.

Criticism of the system of management of the aviation structure has centred on three sets of issues. The first is the conflict between incompatible goals, in particular the inability of the FAA to satisfy its 'dual mandate' of promoting civil aviation and safety. Secondly, the inappropriateness of the instruments used by the FAA, such as rationing air and airport space, to achieve its goals; and thirdly, the effects of federal operating guidelines on the increasing inefficiency of the FAA, in general, and on the atc in particular.

Critics of the FAA's safety operations have claimed that the agency took too long to attend to safety issues and that there was a shortage of qualified investigators to enforce the safety regulations. Some have gone further, and argued that the FAA should be completely restructured. In their view, the goal should no longer be to promote commercial civil aviation but, instead, to concentrate on 'keeping the public safe in planes.'[3] The crash of Valujet Flight 592 in the Florida Everglades in May 1996 ignited a debate in the mass media over the possible role FAA short comings had played in the tragedy.

In October of that same year, Congress amended the *Federal Aviation Act*. The FAA was no longer charged with 'promoting' civil aviation, but several provisions emphasising safety were added in the wording of the Act.

The most acceptable form of airport expansion in the major metropolitan regions is to build new airports away from the centre. The other viable alternative is to make improvements incremental, in such a way as to make more efficient use of existing facilities, and to increase flights by improving the air traffic control system.

For over thirty years (since 1969) airport traffic congestion has been dealt with by using a crude form of rationing. The FAA divided the limited capacity at the busiest airports into three bundles of slots for schedule, commuter and general aviation operators and then allocated them administratively.[4] Similarly, for over thirty years, three airport systems, LaGuardia, Kennedy; National and Dallas's Love Field, have had in place so-called 'perimeter rules.' These rules were designed to protect operations at the respective airport systems. They limited the distance or the specific states to which non-stop service could be provided to and from the metro area's close-in airport.[5]

Despite rapidly increasing congestion, there has been no significant expansion of US airports over the past thirty years. The Department of Transportation states that over the period 1995 to 1992, only three new runways have been put into service at the twenty-eight largest airports. Most communities have failed to enact zoning regulations that might have prevented residential and commercial development from encroaching on airport borders.

Moreover, environmental awareness has grown along with the need for airport expansion. Between 1992 and 1998, Congress cut, by nearly half-a-billion dollars, the Federal funding of airport capital development. Policy makers started to consider a wide range of financing options, from increased passenger charges, to be levied by airports, to the privatisation of public airports.

In 1996, Congress passed the *Federal Aviation Reauthorization Act*. The Act provides for a comprehensive review of the FAA and authorises a pilot privatisation program. A twenty-one member National Civil Aviation Review Commission was established. Among its responsibilities is a duty to propose comprehensive legislation to overhaul the FAA, including the existing system for financing airport capital development. Faced with widely divergent estimates of the capital required to develop the airport system and in the absence of reliable data, the Commission has declared that there is 'no independent means of estimating airport capital (development) requirements.'[6]

The FAA's atc system has remained virtually unchanged over the period of airline deregulation. Ground-based navigation beacons and radar systems divide the 3.5 million square miles of airspace over the continental US into highways. By 2000, some 20,000 scheduled flights a day were being dispatched single-file, separated by a minimum distance of 5 miles horizontally and 1,000 feet vertically. Since the 1981 air traffic controllers' strike, the FAA from its System Command Centre in Virginia has operated, with the compliance of the carriers, a nation-wide form of traffic rationing. 'Flow control', as this system is called, which began as an emergency measure to cope with the shortage of controllers, now effectively limits the number of landings and take-offs at all major airports in an attempt to control congestion and to make provision for weather conditions.

The airlines have laid the blame for the rising costs of delays at the feet of the FAA's atc system. The weather has also been held responsible. Gordon Bethune, Chairman of Continental Airlines, has claimed that US carriers could save $200 million a year with 'just a lousy 1 per cent improvement in air-traffic-control efficiency.'[7]   The National Air Traffic Controllers Association, however, holds the airlines responsible for over-scheduling at peak-hours and the state governments for their failure to expand airports.

Some analysts have blamed the system of control and ownership of the air transportation infrastructure. Airports and the atc system remain government-owned and -controlled and are consequently 'mired in bureaucratic corporate cultures and non-commercial, anti-competitive ways of operating.'[8] Langhborne Bond, FAA administrator (1977 to 1981), claimed that the problem was that the agency had only two goals, ensuring safety and 'getting its program fully funded regardless of the outcome. They see no connection between funding and outcome.'[9]

The General Accounting Office has estimated the FAA's Advanced Automated System, which was the centre-piece of the agency's $12 billion plan to modernise the atc, entailed a waste of $2.8 billion.[10]   Most atc computer equipment is over twenty years old.[11]   Procurement policies have become counter-productive by driving costs up and reducing organisational effectiveness. Congressional funding is unpredictable and makes long-range planning very difficult.[12]   The new technology used in the centralised weather service, introduced in the winter of 1999/2000, lacked crucial data on the height of the storm clouds, data typically found on weather RADA used by television news stations and pilots.[13]

Robert W. Poole Jr. and Viggo Butler argue that a number of technical advances, such as the global positioning system (gps) and the precision runway monitor (prm), 'have been held back by the FAA's bureaucratic corporate culture and convoluted funding system.'[14]   Global positioning systems offer significant improvements in the capacity of single runways, while the prm is a new type of secondary radar that permits simultaneous bad weather operations on parallel runways spaced 3,400 feet apart. The authors estimate that the deployment of such technology could expand the hourly capacity of congested airports by as much as 50 per cent. They, and others, have also argued for the implementation of the so-called 'free flight' concept. Thanks to new technology, aircraft navigation and tracking has become more precise. Pilots operating under the free flight system would not have to request a clearance from the atc but would merely have to advise of their chosen flight-paths and altitudes.

In 1994, the Clinton administration introduced a bill to corporatise the atc, but despite support from the National Civil Aviation Review Commission, the initiative languished in Committee. In 1996, Congress ordered the FAA to assign costs to each of its services. The FAA replied that such estimates would be delivered in 2002. (In the meantime, Canada's commercial airlines bought the air navigation system from the federal government in 1996. NavCanada, as the new entity is called, is a not-for-profit company.)

Through the auspices of the Reason Public Policy Institute, Poole and Butler have advocated the shifting of the atc out of the FAA and into a new, non-profit corporation that would operate the system as a business. Most significantly, the authors have advocated that atc funding should be shifted from general revenues to user fees, a change that would allow major modernisation to be funded by long-term revenue bonds.[15]   However, the incoming Secretary of Transportation in the Bush administration, Norman

Mineta, has said that privatisation will only become an option once the FAA gets its cost accounting system in place.[16]

Early in 2000, Congress formed a five-member air traffic control oversight committee, mandated to supervise management of the atc. The Committee hired a chief operating officer for the atc. The FAA's operating budget over the following three years was increased from $10 billion to $40 billion. The FAA was also ordered by Congress to spend the money it had raised from ticket taxes exclusively on aviation-related projects. In December 2000, President Clinton appointed the five members of the Committee and instructed the FAA to merge all of its air traffic functions into a single entity called the Air Traffic Organisation. Furthermore, the Committee was instructed to explore changes in rules and regulations that would be needed to facilitate the implementation of congestion pricing at the nation's busiest airports.[17]

Earlier, the Clinton administration had tried and had failed, in the words of Joseph Stiglitz (member of the Council of Economic Advisers, to 1993 to 1995, Chairman,1995 to 1997), to implement 'an effective set of reforms that included user fees more closely reflecting market prices.'[18] According to Stiglitz, the owners of corporate jets and small planes had successfully lobbied against the measures.

The year 2000 also marked the termination of the thirty-year-old slot allocation system at the nation's most congested airports. In many cases, low-cost-low-fare carriers had been unable to buy, lease or swap to obtain slots and were effectively shut out. Smaller cities that relied on such services protested at their exclusion from the major airports.

The Department of Transportation took the view that slot allocations had become obsolete. Their removal, it was thought, would increase competition and expand service to smaller cities. In March 1999, the House Transportation and Infrastructure Committee introduced a provision to lift all limits on slots on flights at La Guardia, Kennedy and O'Hare by March 2000. Washington Reagan was to get twenty-four new flights a day.

Because there was opposition from residents, in airport neighbourhoods who complained of the likely increases in noise, Congress settled on keeping slot limits at O'Hare until July 2002 and at La Guardia and Kennedy until 2007. However, operators of regional jets could offer unlimited service to smaller cities. Moreover, carriers are free to schedule flights at any time they choose, and with few exceptions, the FAA has no control over scheduling.

It turned out that the small, but strategically located, La Guardia airport was to experience the brunt of the carriers' response. Airlines requested and were granted clearance for 608 new daily flights. They added 300 new flights to La Guardia's roster that was already heavily loaded with 1,000 flights a day. As a consequence, the airport was to become responsible for one-quarter of all delayed flights during 2000.

On 19 September 2000, the Port Authority of New York declared a moratorium on new flights during peak hours at La Guardia, it scaled back the number of flights that already had been added and proposed the adoption of a lottery system to determine which airlines would get the rest. On 8 November 2000, the FAA allowed just half of the nearly 300 new flights added since March 2000, and it effectively approved the new cap of approximately 1200 daily flights that will be in place until September 2001. In December 2000, the FAA held a lottery of 159 daily flights for regional jet operators and carriers that are new to La Guardia.[19] These were regarded as emergency measures. Consequently, the Port Authority agreed to work on long-term solutions which they were to present to the FAA for their consideration. The Port Authority is thought to be considering user fees and or some other form of congestion pricing.[20]

At the start of the summer season the FAA outlined a 10-year air traffic control modernisation plan that aimed to increase the system's capacity by a third. Reliance on satellite navigation systems will be phased -in, and so altering the control tower to-cockpit dynamic. Pilots will have the power to plot their own flight paths instead of being confined to existing airways established by ground-based radar systems. The estimated cost was $11.5 billion. As this plan was announced Boeing unveiled their outlined proposal. It would take data from computers already in the cockpits of airliners, containing information on the plane's position and flight plan, and send them to controllers.[21] In the same week the Port Authority of New York and New Jersey proposed congestion pricing for La Guardia. Air carrier organisations opposed these proposals. They argued that peak charges would mean higher fares. In the same week the Port Authority of New York and New Jersey proposed congestion pricing at La Guardia.[22]

These proposed congestion prices are a reminder of the analytical work of economists that stretches back some three decades. For the most part, they have been concerned with devising policies to correct the market failures of congestion, safety and noise pollution. Analysts have argued that carriers have been denied access because incumbent carriers have controlled airport landside gates and airside slots and because there has been attenuation in the supply of airspace.   These restrictions reflected proprietary restrictions activated primarily by the desire to reduce liability for noise damage. The problems of misallocation were accordingly exacerbated by the growth in demand engendered by deregulation. Deeming the restrictions on carriers' entry into a market to be an undesirable attenuation of the market's contestability, analysts have focused on how, efficiently, to allocate resources among the carriers and how to use, and efficiently and rationally to expand, the resources of landside airports and the airspace above airports.

These neo-classical analysts assert that the competitive process uses a set of given information on prices and costs to arrive at equilibrium. Furthermore, this information can be effectively accumulated and deployed by the planners in the respective government agencies.

Unfortunately these agencies have so far failed to adopt the neo-classicists' prescriptions to repair the market failures.   As the above commentary reveals, others have observed the inefficiencies of the FAA.

Their analysis exposes the difficulty planners have experienced in collecting data, making rational decisions and transmitting those decisions when deprived of a pricing system. These critics infer that decisions and responsibility cannot be successfully left to individuals who are not owners or are not in some way directly interested in the means of production under their charge. Faced with these failures of government, a number of policy makers have advocated the privatisation of the constituent elements of the air transportation infrastructure.

The next part of this chapter outlines the complex legal, administrative and ownership structures of the civil aviation system in the United States and summarises the interpretations of the perceived market failures and resulting resource misallocation. Consideration is then given, in the following part, to the policies put forward by the proponents of various plans for allocative efficiency. The third part of the chapter examines the explicit and implied idealised system behind these policies and attempts to identify the implications of these policies for institutional change and redirected resource allocation. The fourth part examines explanations as to why the government has failed to make the most efficient use of its air transportation infrastructure.

ALLOCATING AIRPORT LANDSIDE AND AIRSPACE RESOURCES

Air transit in the United States is controlled exclusively by the federal government. This control is founded on Congress's recognition that the public has a basic right to air transit. The declaration that such travel is a right of national sovereignty is expressed through the *Federal Aviation Act* of 1938. The Act entrusted power to the Federal Aviation Agency (FAA) and the Civil Aeronautics Board (CAB). The latter, under the *Civil Aeronautics Act* of 1938, was empowered to select carriers for routes not already served by incumbents, and hence entry into the industry and to regulate the rates carriers could charge. In 1966, Congress established the Department of Transportation and re-named the FAA the Federal Aviation Administration.

The FAA's responsibilities are: to regulate the use of the navigable airspace, operate a national system of air traffic control, to certify airmen, aeroplanes and (certain) airports for commercial use and to promote air safety. These responsibilities are to be primarily executed through the promulgation of Federal Aviation regulations.

Of particular interest are the agency's functions with respect to the provision of airport and airway navigation facilities and traffic control, and to the administration of the airport-airway programmes. These functions emerged from the 1970 *Airport and Airway Development Act* and the 1970 *Airport and Airway Revenue Act.* The former established expenditure guidelines,[23] the latter an Airport and Airway Trust Fund into which amounts equivalent to those collected from the various user charges were to be transferred, at least quarterly, from the general fund of the Treasury.

The user charges included a tax on commercial air carriers, a head tax on international departures and fuel taxes.[24] In terms of the *Aviation Safety and Capital Expansion Act* of 1990, Congress authorised airports to collect the Passenger Facility Charge. These are charges on each passenger who travels through an airport. Funds from this source accounted for $1.113 billion in airport capital development in 1996.[25]

According to the Declaration of Policy, the Secretary of Transportation was to consider the promotion and development of safety, civil aeronautics, the operation of a common system of air traffic control and navigation. In addition, he was charged with 'the control of the use of the navigable airspace of the United States and the regulation of both civil and military operations in such airspace in the interests of safety and efficiency of both.'[26]

Conceptually, the supply of navigable airspace[27] may be increased by expanding airports, lengthening runways, changing the types of aircraft flying over an area and by changing flight patterns. Demand is influenced by the structure and levels of prices (tolls, taxes) established for the use of the airspace and complimentary landside facilities. The military, and private individuals and corporations own the aircraft using the navigable airspace. Most airports are owned and operated by non-federal entities. Via its investment in airport development through the airport development programme, the FAA has an influence on airport capacity. But constitutional provisions[28] constrain the level and structure of rates that may be charged for airport and navigable airspace. By protecting the rights of those on the ground and of the environment in general,[29] federal laws and zoning ordinances may serve to constrain the expansion of capacity. They also add to the number of federal government agencies influencing the supply, rates and allocation of navigable airspace. These include the Department of Defence, the Department of Justice, the Department of Transport, the Office of Management and Budget, and Congressional members and Committees. As a result, the FAA has had difficulty in specifying its policy objectives.'[30]

As aviation activity increased, congestion at some airports became a problem. However, the arrival of noisy aircraft brought home to the FAA the adverse implications of a lack of clearly defined and exchangeable property rights in airspace resources. Exchange and adjustments at the margins could not readily resolve the conflict of incompatible uses of airspace around airports. Voluntarily reducing flights, introducing sound-proofing, and re-locating activities, were not seen to be maximising the joint value of aviation and near-airport urban activities. There were no defined and exchangeable property rights in airspace resources. Transaction costs were high and. adjustments faced substantial constraints. As a result, the problem was simplified. Aircraft noise was defined as a diseconomy (or negative externality). Noise was a pollutant, causing damage to the passive user of a pacific environment. In such a sector of high transaction costs and asset specificity, the location of liability was to have substantial implications for the form (and level of efficiency) of airspace resource allocation.

In 1962, the Supreme Court established that the individual airport proprietors were solely responsible for the unwanted externality of aviation noise.[31] All relevant levels of government, air carriers, and airport proprietors, in other words the agents supplying and using navigable airspace, were deemed to be collectively responsible for aviation noise-abatement. According to one analyst, the unfortunate consequence 'is that the liability for aviation noise has been partially disconnected from the responsibility for aviation noise-abatement.'[32]

Aviation noise-abatement has been influenced by two legal issues: that of liability (who pays for it), and that of pre-emption (who can regulate.)[33] In 1968, Congress amended the *Federal Aviation Act*. It was authorised to regulate 'aircraft noise and sonic boom' and to assure that standards 'were consistent with the highest degree of safety, economically reasonable, technologically practicable and appropriate for the particular type of aircraft, aircraft engine, appliance, or certificate to which it would apply.'[34] The FAA proceeded to establish noise emissions standards, by means of regulations known as FAR 36 Standards,[35] for individual aircraft rather than attempting to reduce ambient noise levels. The *Noise Control Act* of 1972 amended the *Federal Aviation Act* by adding 'protection to the public health and welfare' to the statement of purpose. More particularly, the Environmental Protection Agency (EPA) was directed to engage in the rule-making process to reduce aviation noise. The FAA, however, retained ultimate responsibility for aircraft (as distinct from airport) noise reduction, while the 'primary responsibility for control of noise rested with State and local governments.'[36] As proprietors of airports, local governmental entities could establish requirements and issue regulations respecting permissible ambient noise levels.[37]

Thirty-five years ago, in *Griggs v. Allegheny County,* the Supreme Court located proprietary liability for noise with the airport proprietor. The reasoning of the Court was that airport managements were able to exercise decisions as to where and how to build and to extend airport facilities. In so doing, they were able to lower airport noise levels. The airport proprietor was faced with the full social costs of noise. In an attempt to lower such costs, the proprietor could conceivably consider changes in airport orientation, including regulation of flight procedures and operations to disperse the sources of noise, condemnation of land or easements surrounding the airport. In cases where the proprietor was the municipality, regulatory adjustments in property, use could be encouraged to minimise the noise emission on activities or persons or uses of property.[38]

In undertaking such action, the proprietor faced substantial constraints. For instance, taking up easements surrounding airports was difficult because of the cost of land acquisition. The build-up of population surrounding airports meant substantial, and highly contentious, residential relocations. An alternative was to use zoning ordinances to ensure land use compatible with flight paths. A frequently encountered difficulty has been that no single entity has possessed the authority to enact zoning ordinances that encased the entire airport area. The application of the doctrine of non-conforming uses to municipal zoning regulations has meant the prohibition of changes to existing activities of land use in the vicinity of the airport.[39] In other cases, property owners subject to noise pollution have deployed the notion, embodied in the principle of inverse condemnation, that private property cannot be taken from public use without just compensation.[40] In *Causby v. United States,*[41] the court held that the passage of aircraft through the airspace could constitute the taking of an easement. This was when they were so close to the ground as to interfere with the use and enjoyment of the underlying land.

Damages have been awarded but compensation has been limited to those cases in which there has been an actual invasion of the airspace above the land. Hence, owners whose property did not lie beneath the flight path did not receive compensation. However, the courts in those states whose constitutions require compensation for a taking or damage, have made a different interpretation. Noise and vibration without an over-flight is considered to be a taking.[42]

Soon after the passage of *Griggs*, the deployment of the jet engine by carriers and increasingly larger and noisier aircraft threw into doubt the reasoning that the airport proprietor was 'responsible' for aviation noise. Although liable for airport noise, the airport proprietor was, in many cases, unable to impose controls on the operation of aircraft. Many were met with pre-emption under the 'Supremacy Clause' whereby the proposed restrictions were deemed to impose undue burdens on commerce among the states.[43] Those proprietors with long term contracts with carriers had difficulty in shifting the incidence of noise liability costs directly on to the air carriers.

Airport proprietors who decided to reduce their exposure to liability turned to the promotion of noise-abatement programmes. These programmes have mostly involved the following measures: institution of night-time operating restrictions, jet bans, the use of preferential runways and limiting the number of aircraft operations.[44]

The legal arrangement of single liability (but shared responsibility) for aircraft noise, in which the FAA has responsibility for aircraft noise control and airport capacity enhancement, has been held responsible for encouraging, rather than resolving, conflicts over airport noise. This has led to the misuse and misallocation of navigable airspace[45] and to a balkanisation of the national air transportation system.[46]

The federal agency has been accused of failing to take the lead in reducing airport noise. The alleged reason is that the courts might find the federal agency liable for airport noise damage. As a consequence, through the FAA's FAR 36 standards, the federal agency has attempted to control aircraft noise 'at source' by stipulating quieter engines.

Retrofitting has been an expensive exercise.[47] Because carriers have been given few incentives to re-deploy noisy jets away from such airports, there has probably not been corresponding reductions in noise levels at congested and noisy airports. Airport proprietors have attempted to lower their liability. They have done this by restricting the types of aircraft that may be used, the hours an aircraft may be operated and the volume of traffic that may be processed. They have combined with the FAA's source controls to make adjustments at the margins. But these measures have resulted in higher than needed direct costs (costs to carriers of retrofitting or replacing aircraft to meet FAR 36 standards) and indirect costs. The latter have discouraged more useful interventions and delayed needed airport expansions.[48] Morrison, *et al.* estimate that the present discounted benefits of the mandated elimination of Stage II aircraft, which were reflected in higher property values for homeowners, fell $5 billion short of the legislation's cost to the carriers, reflected in the reduced economic life of their capital stock.[49]

The pricing system for airside and landside airport services evolved from practices developed as far back as the 1940s, when air carrier airports passed from private into public control. Airport fees are subject to the Commerce Clause. They must not discriminate between interstate and intrastate flights, and must not be 'excessive in relation to costs incurred by the taxing authorities.' Federal law restricts all fees of domestic airports to a 'reasonable level.'[50] The *Airport and Airway Improvement Act* requires, as a precondition of approval of a development project, that the airport be administered in a manner that 'fosters competition, preventing unfair methods of competition, maintaining essential air transportation, and preventing unjust and discriminatory practices.'[51]

In general, the public authorities that regulate airports have established rates and fees designed to maximise net revenue. Landing area costs are deducted from any 'excess' revenue for the non-landing area. The residual costs are then calculated to make up the revenue deficiency.[52] These costs are allocated among users in a variety of ways: flat rate per 1000 pounds aircraft landing weight; rate per actual or schedule landing and no landing fees. The first method is most common at the larger airports and rates do not usually vary by time of day. Such rate schedules are in line with the practice in the rest of the world, where take-off weight (rather than landing weight) is usually the basis of assessment.

Airports receive Federal funds primarily for airside improvements, most of which are derived from the Aviation Trust Fund. The Fund receives taxes raised nationally, while the airports are either within a political sub-division or a separate entity, resulting in transfers from the national to the entity of the political sub-division. User fees are usually pitched at the average cost of providing the facilities. Landside facilities are often subject to long-term leases, reflecting the financial requirements of the bond instrument used to finance the airport.

The misallocation of airport slots is perceived as having sprung from the failure of the governments, as owners of the airports, to deploy the price mechanism to match demand with supply. From the resulting first-come-first-served method of allocating slots, the average cost pricing system of charging landing fees according to weight and the institutional arrangement whereby 'capacity is always to be matched to "need" and need is determined independently of price.'[53]

The landing weight based charges are wasteful:

> ... the present system does not permit maximising the value of landing rights to users in general. Present landing fees are undifferentiated by time and based on weight, and passenger demand at today's similarly undifferentiated fare structures is subject to heavy peaking. As a result, a maximising airline schedules as many flights as possible at peak hours. Since the airline will only experience the average, rather than the marginal, delay, measuring the cost to the line of adding the schedule against the incremental revenue will yield a more favourable result than would be the case if the costs to all users were taken into account.[54]

Levine, in his 1969 article, outlined the course of the misallocation of resources. These were caused not only by inappropriate so-called cost recovery average cost pricing, but by the 'lack of provision in the system for the assignment of property rights in the use of the airport.

Levine goes on to state:

> For it is the inability of any of the participants to adjust his behaviour so as to maximise the total value of use that creates problems of inefficient use. First-come first-served rights to use the airport vested in the public collectively prevent a high-value user from negotiating with the airport owner or other holder of landing rights so as to buy the right to arrange his use so as to maximise his utility. Without the ability to gain exclusive use of some part of operating capacity for some period of time, all the efforts of the high-value user to limit delay by limiting his output will be thwarted by a lower-value user taking his place. But if the higher-value user could establish his status as such by manifesting a willingness to pay the higher price for the uncongested use of the airport, then society would benefit. Users of the airport, and society would benefit by obtaining a greater total value from resources invested in airports.[55]

The perceived problem with the ownership structure of landside property rights was that incumbent carriers owned them outright. Furthermore, carriers possessing long-term leases were unprepared to sub-lease their property rights at terms that could be met by the new entrants. The argument was that the prices of the rights were not reflected in the exchange prices. Carriers who were willing to pay the most money for them could not obtain them.

CORRECTING FOR MISALLOCATION

The property rights order in the US domestic civil aviation system can be characterised as a non-exchangeable use of airspace by carriers and a first-come-first-served allocation of slots. The length of airport-carrier contracts has influenced landside property rights. Slots have been subjected to average cost pricing. The airport proprietor is liable for noise damage, while carriers have been subjected to 'noise source' equipment controls.[56] These have formed a set of incentives and constraints that have led to an expensive misallocation of resources. Three distinctive corrections have emerged. Each claims to improve the allocation of resources in this sector.

One, recommendations have been made to create and distribute exchangeable property rights in airside and noise slots and to deploy regulatory intervention to ease exchange of airport landside rights. Two, by contrast, the engineering or Pigouvian approach proposes to equate private and social costs of pollution and congestion. This is to be arranged by means of tolls and taxes, and by a re-organisation of institutional structures so as to unleash forces complimentary to the sustained attainment of the equations of allocative efficiency. Three, a radical restructuring of agents' objectives and shifting property rights is proposed. This is to be achieved by re-locating liability and then co-ordinating the resulting institutions to achieve the desired trade-offs between allocative efficiency and 'social' objectives.

As for this first set of proposals, theory became actual policy in 1986. An FAA rule permitted carriers to sell slots, at four of the high-density airports, for any consideration.[57] The so-called 'buy-sell' rule 'grandfathered' the carriers holding slots on 16 December 1985, permitting them to buy, sell, trade or lease slots beginning on 1 April 1986.

Internal slot transfers were restricted. Along with 5 per cent of total slots, which were to be allocated by lottery, were those slots that became available under the 'use it or lose it' provision. They were also to be distributed by lottery. The FAA argued that the buy-sell provisions would encourage the exchange of slots towards their highest value use. This was to be achieved by providing an incentive for a carrier to 'liquidate a slot at a price higher than the value to the using carrier' and 'to acquire a slot at a price, which will permit a return on investment higher than the next preferable investment alternative.'[58]

In the case of landside property rights, sub-leasing was 'impractical' as a means of permitting access. This was because of high incumbent utilisation of existing space or because of exorbitant rates for sub-leases.[59] The remedy was to allow open access to other competing airlines upon fair and reasonable terms.[60] The 1983 Airport Access Report suggested buying out the incumbent and then 'reallocating leased spaces.'[61] In the meanwhile, the federal government, under the 1982 *Federal Aviation Act*, mandated non-discriminatory access to terminal facilities.[62]

Critics of the regulation of noise externalities have advocated the formation of noise pollution rights and their sale or allocation in the manner in which slots were allocated under the buy and sell rule. By allocating rights according to the age and noisiness of the carrier's fleet, noisy fleets would be given fewer slots. An incentive would be created for carriers to substitute quieter aircraft.[63] Rather than the micro-management under FAR 36 standards, carriers would be rewarded for reducing noise emissions by being able to sell the emissions they do not need to others having difficulty meeting the limits. As in rights to pollute the air, a noise pollution allowance futures contract could be envisaged that would allow carriers to shift the risk of price changes in allowances to investors.

The second, Pigouvian approach has also been promoted as a means to promote the more efficient using navigational air space. A fee is imposed on each unit of noise pollution. This gives the noise-maker an incentive to control the noise up to the point where further control would cost more than the charges it would save.[64]

The system, proposed by Nierenberg, is one in which:

> ...airlines would be required to pay take-off and landing fees in proportion to the amount of noise emitted. Imposition of noise changes at airports, as recommended in this article, would give airlines an incentive to reduce their own noise since reduced noise would mean lower charges. (Alternatively, rebates from present take-off and landing fees for quieter aircraft and operations would create similar incentives to reduce noise exposure).[65]

Nierenberg's proposed airport noise charge scheme establishes damage-related (rather than compliance-related) at the 'appropriate' level, in terms of the costs and benefits of noise-abatement, so as to 'achieve the optimum balance between costs and noise reduction benefits.' [66]

The Department of Transportation, in its 1983 Airport Access Report, proposed a system of direct changes varying according to aircraft noise levels and time of day of operations.[67] In the same report, the Department of Justice proposed that the cost of noise should be identified and passed on to airport users, arguing that this provided a more appropriate incentive than the current federal noise restrictions.[68]

Morrison, *et al.* considered a Pigouvian noise tax. Their estimate of the net welfare gain to society from imposing an efficient noise tax based on mark-ups between the private and social marginal costs of aeroplane use was $0.013 billion or a present discounted welfare gain of $0.184 billion. The authors point out that air travel behaviour is highly inelastic to changes in costs of aeroplane noise 'which suggests that an efficient noise tax (or permit) would be unlikely to influence traveller and carrier behaviour in ways that would reduce aeroplane noise.'[69] Instead, the authors recommend that air carriers or airports should have adopted the option to pay homeowners for the right to fly Stage II aeroplanes.

A distinguished panel of analysts has advocated congestion charges.[70] The appropriate, allocatively efficient pricing structure has been restated by Morrison and Winston:

> Each take-off and landing imposes costs on other users in the form of delay. For runway use to be optimal, users must be charged fees that reflect the (external) costs that they impose on others and on the airport authority. These are called marginal cost fees. In the long run, capacity should be added until the extra cost of the added capacity equals the attendant reduction in delay costs. This is the basis for optimal runway investment.[71]

Levine contends that his recommended pricing system would have results similar to those that would have emerged had rights been assigned to the airport operators.[72] Park and Carlin have pointed out the similarity between the allocative results of their pricing system and one obtained by issuing property rights. These would be freely traded among airport users and could be issued for particular hours in proportion to current use. The number of slots for each hour could be chosen to approximate the efficient number. The free market in slots would then allocate them to the highest-value users.[73]

The third approach is distinctly different. The failure of 'the system' to define public interest, the lack of transparency in accountability and the 'absence of co-operative planning and leadership' prompts Creswell to introduce eight policy principles 'which with a consensus and understanding can grow.'[74] Among these principles is one in which 'all affected groups must actively co-operate in formulating and supporting actions to increase fairness, efficiency and accountability.'[75]

To reduce the resulting imbalances, Creswell proposes the adoption of three principles of good government. The first is that 'the responsibility of government and the private sector to promote the general welfare of its citizens (the quality of life),'; the second, that 'disproportionately placed burdens on private property will be avoided (private); and the third, that interested agents should strive to compensate noise impacted property owners when fairness dictates.'[76] Implementation of these principles necessitates a new statutory approach in which 'self-interest should be discouraged.'[77] A further policy principle is that substantiation and procedural standards for airport area land use planning should be introduced to reduce 'inconsistency, inequity and inefficiency.'[78] Furthermore, Creswell advocates 'legislation to spread liability', and the inclusion of 'provisions for just compensation to impacted property owners.'[79]

PERFECT AND IMPERFECT ALLOCATION

These policy analysts hold in common an understanding that the spontaneous bargaining between agents through markets and the courts has failed. However, the property rights framework offers insights into the analysis of market failures. In congested air transport markets, the cost of time spent in the queue (plus landing fees) represents the cost to the carrier of establishing the property right (the slot). However, other methods of allocation have been deployed such as the committee, which allocates exchangeable slots. The explanation for this system of allocation is that agents and, in particular, the carriers, had exhausted the lowest cost methods available to them to attain that which regulation places in the 'public domain.' As the value of traveller's time rose, resources lost in queuing rose to levels sufficient to cause the supplier (the federal and local government proprietors) to delineate and to market the right. In creating marketable exchangeable rights they were relieved of the responsibility and costs of monitoring committee rationing schemes.[80]

The emerging property rights in airspace, however, have been influenced by another externality, that of noise pollution. Unlike congestion, in which the whole group loses more or less the same in time and costs and in which there can be assumed to be legal symmetry of intentions between the participants, the noisy do ill to those passive entities who merely wish to enjoy quietness. Such asymmetry has caused some to question the ethics of accepting voluntary exchange within such a property rights structure. They object to the sound polluter bribing the victims to desist.[81] The definition of property rights has been shaped by the placement for the liability for noise pollution with the airport proprietors.[82] Their exchanges have been influenced by the imposition of restrictive zoning standards and prohibitions. Placing liability on the airports and deploying equipment abatement controls has probably meant suffering the loss associated with a sub-optimally small amount of manageable airspace to secure environmental gains. The alternatives were to incur the costs of either non-liability of aviation agents, higher cost abatement policies or a cessation of the voluntary exchange in the market.

An efficient arrangement would be one that allocated rights and liabilities in such a way as to minimise the sum of the costs of noise damage, and of avoiding noise damage. When transaction costs are low, the maximising legal process would require the parties to transact in the market, and when they are high, parties would be encouraged to use the courts to shift resources to their more valuable use. In the latter situation, the 'correct' initial assignment of rights would be important, for high transaction costs would preclude the use of market transactions in correcting a mistaken initial assignment.

Nierenberg would appear not to have such a perception of the 'efficient' arrangement. He is critical of the legal process as a means of reducing airport noise (not as a means of attaining an efficient net resource cost). He observes that among the means of recovering for airport noise damages under traditional tort theories, inverse condemnation suits have achieved the most success over the other remedies (trespass and nuisance), but 'the slowness of the court system and difficulties of success limit the practicality of even this remedy.'[83]

Creswell does not directly mention such transaction costs, but refers to the lack of definition of property rights (uncertainty about the nature of the 'property interest' damaged by the aviation activity) and the liability system that creates incentives for victims to exaggerate the claims of injury. The common law liability system is such that it 'impair(s) rather than enhance(s) its ability to financially resolve disputes between an airport and its neighbours.'[84]

Nierenberg, however, fails to compare the *status quo* with his policy, for in 'the authors opinion, noise charges are less costly, at least as effective, and ultimately less burdensome to administer than other alternatives.'[85] Creswell presents a radical reorientation of institutions, exhorting them to forsake self for the public interest, implying that policies will emerge without cost from the reorganised entities that will establish an appropriate trade-off between allocative efficiency and 'quality of life.'

An 'efficiency analysis' of airport landslide gates has considered the element of sunk costs in such installations and the consequences of incumbent carriers deterring competing entrants. As the need to sink costs cannot be regulated away, one approach has recommended simulating contestability by encouraging the government to interfere to ensure equal access to the sunk facility (the gates). Another approach assumes even more improbable conditions. It envisages the situation as if the costs had yet to be sunk, in which freely contracting carriers reach a contractual equilibrium with the delineated, competitively assigned capacity of the airport. The complementarity of the 'surrogate contestability' approach[86] with the contractual equilibrium approach[87] is that both see contracts as the means of achieving contestability. They do this by constraining the incumbent's foreclosure of entry.[88] The two approaches, however, differ in their interpretation of reality. The adherents of equitable (enhanced contestability) policies emphasise the prohibitively high transaction costs of contracting and exchanging property rights to portions of sunk airport investment,[89] while the proponents of the contractual equilibrium approach discovered, ten years after the deregulation of the interstate carriers, that gate space bottlenecks no longer existed.[90]

Borenstein has explored, but has not found, a theoretical justification for the notion that a competitive market allocation of operating licenses, such as airport slots, will be put to their 'surplus maximising use.'[91] The implication is that the imprecise partitioning of the property rights (slot indivisibility) and the heterogeneity of productive technology will remain and will continue to constrain the movement towards the (social) potential.[92] Borenstein estimates that the allocation of licenses by the market towards their highest valued use[93] diverges from the potentially social optimum by a factor of ten. Thanks to the expected continued rigidity and hence divergence, tampering with the market allocation would be futile.[94] Instead, he requires that the assertion that the market's allocation of licenses is the most efficient be 'justified' by means of empirical comparison with alternative, non-market allocations. Even so, Borenstein is confident that the market allocation of licenses will achieve a more efficient outcome than the former method of allocating by airport committee.

Morrison and Winston quote Borenstein's argument that the market allocation of slots 'will not assure efficiency.'[95] They also argue that to privatise airports and to permit monopoly pricing practices would generate net benefits that would be 'lower than currently.'[96] They advocate the replacement of the current aircraft weight-based landing fees with marginal cost landing fees, including the aircraft's contribution to congestion. Their estimates are that this will generate $3.8 billion in annual net benefits (mostly time savings).[97] A further $7.2 billion in annual net benefits would result from undertaking 'efficient' investment in runway capacity:

> Efficient pricing along or in combination with efficient investment would significantly reduce the strain on airport capacity, eliminate the perceived need to limit flight operation, and postpone the expensive construction of new airports.[98]

Under the current revenue constraints and weight-related landing fees, an airside that is uncongested is characterised by marginal costs that are zero. Landing fees, which are proportional to total flight costs, exceed marginal costs, but as congestion increases, marginal costs run up and exceed landing fees, until landing fees fail to cover the congestion externality during the more congested periods. Morrison and Winston propose a form of social marginal cost pricing, which includes marginal airport cost plus marginal congestion cost, but excludes other externalities such as noise and pollution. Congestion, consumer (airline) surplus plus producer (airport) surplus is maximised when landing fees are equated with marginal congestion costs. If runway capacity is subject to constant return to scale, optimal pricing and investment will generate airport revenue equal to runway cost. Calculating the optimum capacity involves equating the extra cost of runway capacity with the savings in delay cost to all users during all periods.

The authors did not minimise the problems involved in making the requisite estimates. They were also aware that 'optimal' marginal congestion pricing would involve very substantial landing fee increases for commercial, commuter, international carriers and general aviation operators. Only cargo carriers, who tend, under the current system, to use heavy aircraft at off-peak hours, were expected to experience lower tolls. Realising that such outcomes are unlikely to win carrier support for a change in the current aircraft weight based tolls, the authors show that if optimum tolls and optimum investment are simultaneously introduced, such 'redistributional' implications of toll changes between the five carrier groups will be minimised. The authors argue that the welfare gains to a long-suffering public are self-evident.

Furthermore, they encourage the government to remove the legislative impediments to marginal congestion pricing and to ease the restrictions on runway expansion. Funding would be linked with investment decisions. Potential losers would be bought off by compensating them. This virtuous set of changes would maximise welfare by establishing optimum congestion tolls and optimum investment.

There is an asymmetry as to behaviour within Morrison and Winston's Nirvana approach. Implicit in their set of proposals is that agents will not respond to technical and market changes. By contrast, institutions are expected to change considerably. They are expected to facilitate optimum public utility pricing and investment policies.

MARKET FAILURE AND GOVERNMENT FAILURE

Over the last thirty years, numerous authors have advocated optimum congestion tolls.[99] Most have argued that their introduction would enhance the general welfare. The federal government also has an interest in encouraging the introduction of fees related to user and congestion costs, for such measures would lower their outlays on grants.[100] Despite these apparent incentives, most airport authorities have shown a resistance to implementing optimum pricing policies. Those experiments with pricing schedules that have been made, at New York and Boston for example,[101] have been made by multi-purpose port authorities. The vast majority of airports charge non-aeronautical service 'at market,' and aeronautical services on a cost recovery basis. They have been disinclined to introduce peak load, marginal congestion tolls.

One reason for this disinclination is possibly that marginal congestion, peak load tolls are seen by airport operators to be inefficient and that they can be made effective only by incurring heavy transaction costs.[102] Another possible reason is that, given the structure of ownership, operation and regulation of airports, there is little incentive for airport owners to introduce such toll structures. While some airports are owned and operated by the same public entity, the larger commercial airports have defined, legally binding agreements with private companies, the airline carriers. They specify how the responsibilities, and the risks of airport operation, are to be shared between the two parties. It is the distinctive public-private characteristic of the major commercial airports that distinguishes their financial operation and objectives from those entities that are either wholly public or private enterprises.[103]

The constraints of contracts and statutory regulations are significant. The reason is that the airport operator and airline carriers can be expected to maximise their returns and minimise their costs. Neither agent can be expected to adopt tolls and rates that purport to maximise efficiency and social welfare unless regulated to do so. Regulations, as mentioned earlier, impose equity on rate structures. They do not necessarily induce efficiency. Agents within these entities are adaptive to changing conditions and constraints. The advent of deregulation, the uncertainty of carrier presence and the importance of demand to sustain revenue rather than contracts have led to contract re-negotiations. They are contracts with shorter and more flexible terms. They are also moving more towards the compensation method and away from the residual method. The reason is that, under the former contracts, if surpluses on non-aviation activities are achieved, they can lead to reduced carrier rates.[104]

Morrison and Winston imply that agents are not adaptive and that, through market transactions, they cannot be relied upon to take externalities into account. The accommodation of externalities is to come from changes in federal regulations, statutes and funding. The authors, however, fail to show that such institutional engineering will produce a constellation of interests that will be receptive to implementing a structure incorporating congestion tolls, neither do they show that toll revenue will be allocated exclusively to airport capacity expansion. Moreover, they fail to demonstrate how capacity expansion, if constrained by finances rather than the regulation of competing demands for navigational airspace, will be undertaken.

By the end of the decade Winston had undergone an apostasy. Government failure, not market failure was the source of the transport 'problems':

> By repeatedly failing to enact efficient policies to correct market failures and by rigidly pursuing policies that have undermined the efficiency of every transportation mode and the welfare of most users - especially those with the lowest incomes - policy makers have assured that pervasive government failures are compromising the performance of the US transportation sector far more than market failures.[105]

Winston presents four reasons why government has not only failed to correct for market failures but has exacerbated the problems. The federal government, he says, has addressed socially costly spill-overs such as congestion, noise, pollution and accidents 'often without considering how the market will respond to such transportation spill-overs.'[106] Moreover, government pursues inefficient transportation policies because policymakers respond 'more to political forces than to market forces.'[107] Thirdly, 'the flying public's appreciation of efficient take-off and landing fees would be mild at best,' and finally,

Government simply lacks the appropriate economic incentives and faces too many practical and political constraints on its use of labour, acquisition of technology, and so on, to implement even rough approximations of efficient airport charges. (Imagine the battles it would take just to reach a consensus on an estimate for the value of passengers' time).[108]

Winston might also have added a fifth reason: a failure to recognise the legal limits placed on price structures that included congestion prices. These will continue to be ruled out for being 'discriminatory.'

Winston argues that privatising airports and the atc system could eliminate the observable failures of government. A privatised system would 'allow innovation and state-of-the-art technology to flourish free of government interference.'[109] These would emerge from private airports that faced competitive discipline from users and alternative facilities. The failure of government to operate an efficient atc is well documented. Jamie Lynn Treanor quotes the findings of one study which shows that the privatisation of the atc system would generate savings of 30 to 40 per cent over the present government-owned and operated system. 'At the heart of these privatisation plans is competition. Competition drives the private sector and breeds efficiency. Injecting competition into the air traffic control arena may be the answer that management of the congested airways needs.'[110]

Winston's proposals come with a rider. As part of the privatisation contract airports would be required to include a cost-based noise tax. This provision would then allow the inefficient noise controls to be rescinded. However, have Winston and the other neo-classicists learnt 'enough' of the externalities to construct a shadow market? Winston recognises that government planners labour under a shortage of information and are handicapped by a lack of incentives.

Will the information he and other economists discover be in any way 'superior' to that discovered and used by the discredited government planners? In this case is not the neo-classical economist acting as a planner? Furthermore, will this information be superior to the information discovered and acted upon by competing entities in the market? After all, Winston now recognises that such a process would usher in a more efficient and technically sophisticated aviation infrastructure sector, one that would complement the dynamic, deregulated carrier sector.

Notes

1. Sharkey, Joe (2000), 'Clinton Sees His Future: Long Lines In Airports,' *The New York Times*, 10 December.
2. Kahn, Alfred E. (1993), 'Change, Challenge, and Competition: A review of the Airline Commission Report,' *Regulation*, **16**(3), p.1. http://www.cato.org/pubs/Regulation/reg-16n3d.html

3.   Carlisle, Lea Ann (2001), 'The FAA v. The NTSB,' *The Journal of Air Law and Commerce*, **66**(2), Spring, p.66.
4.   The FAA, in response to air traffic delays, issued, on a trial basis, Amendment No. 93-13, effective 27 April 1969, which designated O'Hare, Kennedy, La Guardia, Washington National and Newark Airports as high density airports and prescribed special air traffic rules. This was known as the 'high density rule.' The rule established quota on the number of instrument flight rule movements per hour that would be accepted at those airports and allocated the hourly reservations among the designated classes of users: air carriers, scheduled air taxis and general aviation operators. The rule was made permanent in October 1973. In conjunction with the rule the carriers formed committees for each class of user, the purpose of which was to schedule their operations. The committees were granted immunity from the anti-trust laws. In 1985, the Department of Transportation began to allow slot re-sales at O'Hare, Kennedy, La Guardia and Washington National. Existing slots as of 16 December 1985 were 'grandfathered'. In 1986, the Department of Transportation also retained around 5 percent of the slots at O'Hare, National and LaGuardia, and distributed them by lottery to non-incumbent carriers.
5.   Gilbreath, Robert B. and Paul C. Watler (2000), 'Perimeter Rules, Proprietary Powers, and the Airline Deregulation Act: A Tale of Two Cities and two Airports,' *Journal of Air Law and Commerce*, **66**(1), Winter.
6.   Rowley, Chrisopher R. (1998), 'Financing Airport Capital Development: The Aviation Industry's Greatest Challenge,' The *Journal of Air Law and Commerce*, **63**(3), February-March, p.612.
7.   Carley, William M. (1999), 'FAA Sparks Criticism With Efforts to Speed Traffic at Airports,' *The Wall Street Journal*, 9 September.
8.   Poole, Robert W. Jr. (1999) and Viggo Butler, 'Airline Deregulation: The Unfinished Revolution,' *Regulation*, **22**(1), p.51.
9.   Wald, Mathew L. (2001), 'Experts Back Privatizing Flight Control,' *The New York Times*, 23 February.
10. Zuckerman, Laurence and Mathew L. Wald (2000), 'Crisis for Air Traffic System: More Passengers, 'More Delays,' *The New York Times*, September 5.
11. Treanor, Janie Lynn (1998), 'Privatization v. Corporatization of the Federal Aviation Administration:Revamping Air Traffic Control,' The *Journal of Air Law and Commerce*, **63**(3), February-March, p.637.
12. ibid, p.642
13. McCartney, Scott (2000), 'Efforts to Ease Delays In Summer Air Travel Also Produce Snarls,' *The Wall Street Journal*, 14 September.
14. Poole and Butler, op cit., p.48.
15. RPPI, National Think Tank Unveils Comprehensive Air Traffic Reform Blueprint, 22 February, 2001. http://www.rppi.org/022201.html
16. Wald, Mathew L. (2001), 'Transportation Chief Supports Fees to Ease Airport Crowding,' *The New York Times*, 14 March.
17. Zuckerman, Laurence (2000), 'New Panel Will Try to Solve Air Traffic Snarls,' *The New York Times*, 7 December.
18. Stiglitz, Joseph (1998), 'The Private Uses of Public Interests: Incentives and Institutions,' *Journal of Economic Perspectives*, **12**(2), Spring, p.11.
19. Brannigan, Martha (2000), 'How the Government Turned La Guardia Into a Fliers' Nightmare,' *The Wall Street Journal*, 4 December.
20. Editorial (2001), 'Ending Gridlock at La Guardia,' *The New York Times*, 9 April.
21. Phillips. Don (2001), 'FAA to Outline 10-Year Plan to Modernise', *The Washington Post*, 4 June.
22. Newsday (2001), 'Airlines oppose Plan to Raise La Guardia Fees,' *The Miami Herald*, 7 June
23. Under Section 18 (18), conditions were attached to federal aid: 'the airport operator or owner will maintain a fee and rental structures for the facilities and services being provided the airport users which will make the airport as self-sustaining as possible under the

circumstances existing at that particular airport, taking into account such factors as the volume of traffic and economy of collection.'

24.   'Since 1971, the Fund has been controversial, Congress arguing that the fund is primarily an account for capital projects to assure adequate aviation system capacity, while Administrations have argued that the Fund should help finance all aviation programs, including FAA operations. Consequently the Fund has become, alternately a capital account and a user-pay system. In 1981, for instance, user taxes were no longer placed into the Trust Fund. They were placed in the General Fund.' Creswell, Lyn Lloyd (1990), 'Airport Policy in the United States: The Need for Accountability, Planning and Leadership,' *Transportation Law Journal*, 19(1, 1,) footnote 259, p.81.

25.   Rowley, Christopher R. (1998), 'Financing Airport Capital Development', op.cit., p.63.

26.   *Federal Aviation Act* of 1958, Sec. 103. (1992).

27.   'Airspace' capacity refers to the number of aircraft movements that the airport and the supporting air traffic control system can accommodate in say an hour.

28.   In the Evansville case, the Supreme Court subjected airport fees to the Commerce Clause restraints. Specifically, airport fees must: not discriminate between interstate and interstate flights; reflect a fair, if imperfect, approximation of the use of facilities for whose benefits they are imposed; and not be excessive in relation to costs incurred by the taxing authorities. The Commerce Clause is not violated if the airport fees imposed are 'reasonable and are fixed according to some uniform, fair and practical standard.' (1972). 405. U.S.: p.717.

29.   Neuhoff, Tom Jr. (1992), 'Obstacles to Increasing Airspace: Jumping through Environmental Law Hoops, '*The Journal of Air Law and Commerce*, 58(1),Fall, p.221.

30.   Creswell, Lyn Lloyd, 'Airport Policy,' op.cit., p.53.

31.   In *Griggs* versus *Allegheny County* the Supreme Court found the airport proprietor (Greater Pittsburgh Airport) alone liable for airport noise damage. The finding was that the airport proprietor was held to have taken an 'air easement in the constitutional sense'. The reasoning was that as the airport proprietor owns the land on which the airport operates, he ultimately has control over who comes on to the land. Hence, the airport proprietor must bear the burden. (1962). 369. U.S.: p.84.

32.   Yost, Nicholas C. (1977), 'Aircraft Noise. Liability and Regulation,' *Trial*, 13(9), September, p.34.

33.   Werlich, John. M. and Krinsky, Richard P.(1981-1982), 'The Aviation Noise-abatement Controversy: Magnificent Laws, Noisy Machines, and the Legal Liability Shuffle,' *Loyola of Los Angeles Law Review*. 15(1), p.70.

34.   49 U.S.C. 1431. (b) (i) (1970).

35.   The initial FAR 36 regulations, established in 1969, prescribed maximum noise levels for newly-designed commercial jet aircraft heavier than 75,000 pounds. Failure to meet the standard meant the certificates of air-worthiness were to be denied. All new aircraft of older design sold after 31 December 1974, were subject to the original FAR 36 standard. In 1976 the FAA required jets in service to comply with FAR 36 standards by means of 'retrofit' (i.e. replacement). The timetable was set so that the entire commercial fleet would meet prescribed standards by 1985. Stricter noise standards, by means of amendments to FAR 36 regulations, were established in 1977 to be applied to the projected next generation of jets. Aircraft, which were certified prior to the publication of the 1969 standard, became known as 'Stage 1' aircraft. 'Stage 2' aircraft are those that met the 1969 standard, while those adopting the stricter 1977 standard are known as 'Stage 3' aircraft. Boeing 707 is a Stage I aircraft, the Boeing 7-27 and DC-9 are Stage II aircraft. As technology progressed the full elimination of Stage II aircraft from all US airports by the end of 1999 was mandated by the 1990 *Airport Noise and Capacity Act*. See Creswell, Lyn Lloyd, 'Airport Policy,' op.cit., p.56. 'While this Stage 1 aircraft ban greatly reduced the noise emissions of individual aircraft operations, the increase in aviation activity occurring after the deregulation of the airline industry eroded much of the advantage. Today, Congress is under pressure from airport neighbours who claim noise levels have increased and want a ban of Stage 2 aircraft'.

36.   ibid., 4901 (a) (3).

37. The rationale for permitting airport proprietors to exercise noise controls was outlined in the Air Transport Association of America versus Crotti. 389. F. Supp.58 (N.D. Cal. 1975)
38. R.A.G.Jr. (1975). 'Shifting Aircraft Noise Liability to the Federal Government,' *Virginia Law Review*, **61**(6), October, p.1299.
39. Magee, Steven H. (1996), 'Protecting Land Around Airports: Avoiding Regulatory Taking Claims By Comprehensive Planning and Zoning, '*The Journal of Air Law and Commerce*, **62**(2), November - December.
40. Patterson, Stephen E. (1970-71),'The Airport Noise Cases: Condemnation by Nuisance and Beyond,' *Wake Forest Law Review*, **7**(2) pp.271-296.
41. 328. U.S. 256 (1946)
42. Vittek, Joseph F. (1972), 'Airport Noise Control - Can Communities Live Without It? '*The Journal of Air Law and Commerce*, **38**(1), pp.93, 494. This phase "a taking' has specific meaning in law. It refers to the 'Takings Clause' which prohibits the government from forcing the individual from bearing alone the public takings.
43. ibid., p.495.
44. Werlich, John M. and Richard Krimsky, 'Aviation Noise,'op.cit., p.98.
45. The US. Department of Transportation (1976), Aviation Noise-abatement Policy 21, outlines actions the airport proprietor can take, and which include: establish landing fees based on aircraft noise characteristics or time of day of operations; schedule engine run-ups at times of least annoyance; locate areas where aircraft engines are serviced or run-up so as to cause least annoyance. The policy also outlines actions the airport proprietor can propose to local government, with financial assistance from the FAA, proposals that can be made for FAA consideration and implementation and actions that can be complemented after the airport user, the general public and the FAA have had an opportunity to review and advise.
46. '...when either many airport neighbours are uncompensated for, or must live with, high levels of aircraft noise; or the airport and the national air transport system must accept severe restrictions on operations in the face of growing community, regional and national need for aviation services .' Creswell, Airport, op.cit., pp.87-88.Nierenberg, Roy A. (1978), 'Incentives versus Regulation: The Case for Airport Noise Charges,' *The George Mason University Law Review*, **2**(2), Winter, pp.167-175.
47. The gradual replacement of the stock of jets by less noisy aircraft could be seen, however, as a result of the noise regulation.
48. 'Indirect costs of noise control regulation may show up in the inhibition of valuable activities. Noise curfews for example, the proposed 9:30 p.m. curfew at Washington's National Airport - may disrupt travel plans as well as prohibit otherwise lucrative flights. Hence, it represents a 'loss' to would be passengers and to the airlines. In addition, regulation proposed in Illinois which would forbid airport expansion unless noise controls goals were achieved, could lead to crowding at air terminals if noise control measures are delayed, or if a rapid expansion of air service (eg. through lower air fares) were to increase noise exposure and terminal usage above predicted levels,' ibid., p.183.
49. Morrison, Steven A., Clifford Winston and Tara Watson (1999), 'Fundamental Flaws of Social Regulation: The Case of Airplane Noise,' *The Journal of Law and Economics*, **42**(2), October.
50. 49, U.S.C. Sec. 1513 (b), (1976).
51. ibid., p2202(a)(5)
52. This is the so-called 'residual cost' approach, under which the airlines guarantee an airport's solvency by agreeing to pay all costs not covered by income from non-airline-related activities. An alternative method is the 'compensatory' approach, under which the airlines are charged the actual costs of the facilities and services they use. See a CBO study (April 1984), *Financing US Airports in the 1980s*, Congress of the United States, Chapter II. For an early analysis of airports as public entities and in which the mentioned cost approaches were developed, see Bollinger, Lynn. L., Allan Passen, Robert E. McElfrigh, (1946),'*Terminal Airport Financing and Management*,' Boston: Graduate School of Business Administration, Harvard University.

53. Levine's multi-part pricing system, with its facilities user charges based on the runway used and time of day, set 'to whatever level of delay the FAA might regard as appropriate' (at 103), is 'demand pricing', users paying according to their perceived benefits 'would produce results similar to assigning property rights to the airport operator. The operator could maximise the value of his investment and would be guided in making new investment by the demands of consumers' p.104. Levine, Michael E. (1969), 'Landing Fees and the Airport Congestion Problem,' *Journal of Law and Economics*, **12**(1), p.87.

54. ibid., p.91.

55. ibid., p.100.

56. Airlines have been given incentives to carry out noise reduction changes. 'If anything, the present regulatory system encourages airlines to oppose noise reduction since the airlines benefit from regulatory delay. It has also led them to advocate in essence a public subsidy to help pay for compliance with mandated 'source' standards'. Nierenberg, Roy A., 'Incentives versus Regulation,' op.cit., p.169.

57. FAR Amendment 93-49, 50 Fed. Reg. 552, 180 (1985). For a discussion of the formation of this rule, and for an analysis of the operation of other allocative devices, including scheduling committees and administrative regulation, see Hardaway, Robert. M. (1986), 'The FAA 'Buy Sell' Slot Rule. Airline Deregulation at the Crossroads,' *The Journal of Air Law and Commerce*, **52**(1,1), Fall.

58. Hardaway, Robert. M. (1986), 'The FAA "Buy Sell" Slot Rule,' op.cit., p.8.

59. ibid., p.49.

60. Hardaway argues that '...the misallocation effects of oligopoly pricing may be reduced, however, by vigorous enforcement of the anti-trust laws when it appears that market power is being used to deny entry for anti-competitive purposes.' Hardaway, Robert. (1991), 'Economics of Airport Regulation,' *Transportation Law Journal*, **20**(1), p.56. Bailey and Baumol also argue for 'equity policies' as surrogates for contestability: 'If the facility is privately owned, the government requires that all firms seeking to use the facility be given access to it, that the access price be reasonable, and that all users be charged the same price. If the sunk facility is in the hands of a local public authority, then the authority is encouraged not to discriminate among private users in its access policies.' Bailey, Elizabeth, E. and Baumol. William J. (1984), 'Deregulation and the Theory of Contestable Markets,' *Yale Journal on Regulation*, **1**(2), p.124.

61. Report of the Airport Task Force. Hearing Before the Subcommittee on Investigation and Oversight of the Committee on Public Works and Transportation, 98th Congress, 1st Session, 1, (1983), p.93.

62. '...Any interested person may apply to the Secretary of Transportation, under regulations prescribed by him, for such recommendation and certification with respect to any landing area or air navigation facility proposed to be established, constructed, altered, repaired, maintained or operated by, or in the interests of, such persons. There shall be no exclusive right for the use of any landing area or air navigation facility upon which Federal funds have been expended.' *Federal Aviation Act*, 49 U.S.C. App.1349 (a) (1982).

63. Bailey, Elizabeth E. and William J. Baumol, 'Contestable Markets,'op.cit., p.169.

64. Bell, Robert B. and Lisa. M. Bell (1980), 'Airport Noise: Legal Developments and Economic Alternatives,' *Ecology Law Quarterly*, **8**(4), pp.607-645.

65. Nierenberg, Roy A., 'Incentives versus Regulation', op.cit., p.169

66. ibid., p.185.

67. Airport Task Force, op.cit., p.55.

68. ibid., pp.63-64.

69. Morrison, Steven A. and Clifford Winston, 'Fundamental Flaws of Social Regulation,' p.739.

70. For earlier marginal cost pricing proposals see Levine, Michael R., 'Landing Fees,' op.cit., pp.102-3. See also Carlin, A and R.E. Park (1970), 'Marginal Cost Pricing of Airport Runway Capacity,' *American Economic Review, Papers and Proceedings*, 60(May), pp.310-319.

71. Morrison, Steven A and Clifford Winston, (1989), 'Enhancing the Performance of the Deregulated Air Transportation System,' *Brookings Papers on Economic Activity. Microeconomics*, Washington. Brookings Institution, pp.61 and 85. The authors go on to

state on p.85: 'To calculate marginal cost fees and optimal capacity and to evaluate their effects, we need an airport cost function including both capital costs and operating costs, a delay function expressing the relationship between runway use and delay, and a set of airport user demand functions.' And on p.97: 'Optimal pricing can be easily implemented, but severe distributional issues arise because optimal pricing results in higher landing fees and a net loss to those passengers whose valuation of delay savings does not offset the higher fares they will have to pay. We argue that some compensation can be made and that remaining political opposition can be overcome, but the latter will require the federal government to take a strong leadership role.

72.   Levine, Michael R., 'Landing Fees,' op.cit., p.100.
73.   Carlin, A and R.E. Park, op.cit.,'Marginal Cost Pricing,' p.318
74.   Creswell, Lyn Lloyd, op.cit.,'Airport Policy,' pp.83-84.
75.   ibid., p.84.
76.   ibid., p.89.
77.   ibid., p.92.
78.   ibid., p.96.
79.   ibid.
80.   Barzel, Yoram (1974), 'A Theory of Rationing by Waiting,' *Journal of Law and Economics*, **17**(1), p.73-96. See Hardaway, Robert, 'Economics of Airport Regulation,' op.cit., pp.17-19, for a discussion of the emerging recognition of the value of slots but the difficulties in establishing them as legal rights.
81.   Rothenberg, Jerome (1970), 'The Economics of Congestion and Pollution: An Integrated View,' *American Economic Review*, Papers and Proceedings, **60**(May), pp.114-121.
82.   '...in general, liability placement does affect the allocation of resources, even abstracting from income effects and transaction costs. For liability not to matter, the externality must take a special form. It must be the case that B's marginal cost is invariant with respect to A's output and also that the external marginal cost (imposed by A on B) is invariant with respect to B's output. Whether or not these conditions hold is an empirical matter and cannot be determined *a priori* in any general sense. This is a severely delimiting qualifications to the Coasian result.' Dick, Daniel. T. (1976), 'The Voluntary Approach to Externality Problems: A Survey of the Critics,' *Journal of Environmental Economics and Management*, **2**(1), pp.185-195, at 191.
83.   Nierenberg, Roy A., 'Incentives versus Regulation,' op.cit., p.179.
84.   Creswell, Lyn Lloyd, 'Airport Policy,' op.cit., p.31.
85.   Nierberg, Roy A. 'Incentives versus Regulation,' p.179.
86.   Bailey, Elizabeth E and William J. Baumol, 'Contestable Markets,' op.cit., p.115.
87.   Meyer, John. R. and Tye. William, B. (1988), 'Toward Achieving Workable Competition in Industries Undergoing a Transition to Deregulation: A Contractual Equilibrium Approach,' *Yale Journal on Regulation*, **5**(2), Summer, pp.273-297.
88.   'Regulation, long term contracts, or other impediments can slow the response of incumbents to entry. Moreover, a new firm can forestall retaliation by entering into contracts, before it actually opens for business, with customers it lures from incumbents'. Bailey, Elizabeth E and William J. Baumol, 'Contestable Markets', op.cit., p.115.
89.   ibid., p.131, where the bottleneck aspect is stressed. Note, however, the revised views of Bailey, who wrote on airline deregulation in 1992. She goes on to describe the benefit to consumers of hubs, central reservation systems, yield management systems, which, under the contestability approach, would have been seen as barriers to entry: 'The new core capabilities airlines have adopted since deregulation have proved to be powerful tools for efficiency as well as for industry concentration. Benefits are so inter-linked with technology that new rules to address the structural imperfections associated with hub-and-spoke route systems as well as price management and computer reservation systems would necessarily increase costs.' Bailey, Elizabeth. E. (1992), 'Airline Deregulation. Confronting the Paradoxes,' *Regulation*, **15**(2), Summer, p.25.
90.   'As a result of either forced divestiture or increased flexibility over time, gate space is generally not considered to be a barrier to entry in the airline industries, although some exceptions remain.' Meyer, John. R. and William B. Tye, 'Toward Achieving Workable Competition,' op.cit., p.276.

91. Borenstein, Sevrin (1988), 'On the Efficiency of Competitive Markets for Operating Licenses,' *Quarterly Journal of Economics*, **103**, pp.356-385.

92. ibid., pp.374-375.

93. Borenstein does acknowledge that the buy/sell programme at Chicago O'Hare airport is causing slots to move to users who would produce the 'most transportation with them', ibid., at p.377.

94. If, as expected by Borenstein, different carriers would continue to deploy different technologies in different markets, regulating the slots among carriers over routes that are contestable 'would not be effective in controlling inefficient use of these licenses'. ibid., pp.378-9.

95. Morrison, Steven A. and Clifford Winston, 'Enhancing Performance,' op.cit., p.98.

96. ibid., endnote 78.

97. ibid., p.84.

98. ibid.

99. As well as those mentioned in the text see: Grampp, William D. (1968), 'An Economic Remedy for Airport Congestion: The Case for Flexible Pricing,' *Business Horizons*, **2**(October), pp.21-30; Minasian, Jora. A and Ross D. Eckert (1960), 'The Economics of Airport Use, Congestion and Safety,' *California Management Review*, **2** (Spring), pp.11-24; Warford, Jeremy. J. (1971), 'Public Policy toward General Aviation,' *Studies in the Regulation of Economic.*, The Brookings Institution, Washington.DC; Abouchar, Alan (1970), 'Air Transport Demand, Congestion Costs, and the Theory of Optimal Airport Use,' *Canadian Journal of Economics*, **3**(3), pp.463-475;Little, I.M.D. and K.M. McLeod (1972), 'The New Pricing Policy for British Airports Authority,' *Journal of Transport Economics and Policy.* **6**(2), May: pp.101-115; Walters A. A. (1978), 'Airports - an Economic Survey,' *Journal of Transport Economics and Policy*, **12**(May), pp.125-158; Morrison, Steven. A. (1987), 'The Equity and Efficiency of Runway Pricing,' *Journal of Public Economics*, **34**(October), pp.45-60; Borins, Sandford F. (1982), 'The Effects of non-optimal pricing and investment policies for transportation facilities,' *Transportation Research*, **16B**, pp.19-29; Creager, Stephan. E. (1983), 'Airline deregulation and airport regulation,' *Yale Law Journal*, **93**(2), pp.319-339.

100. Morrison Steven A and Clifford Winston, 'Enhancing Performance,' op.cit., pp.87-88. The study suggests that removing federal grants would encourage airports to introduce peak-load pricing. This argument appears to be based on the notion that the federal government would 'encourage' airport managers to impose viable fees. More significantly, general aviation airports, which set minimal fees, would be forced to charge revenue-generating tolls.

101. At most airports peak-hour charges are prevented by long term contracts between management and airlines. Massport and the Port Authority of New York and New Jersey are entities that enjoy some independence from local and state entities, and both have introduced forms of peak load pricing at their airports. In the case of Logan International Airport, however, the peak-load system was opposed by the DOT on the grounds that it was discriminatory. As a result, peak pricing at Logan was applied only to general aviation carriers.

102. The extent to which changes in tolls are passed on to consumers depends on the actual and potential competition in the respective markets the carriers serve. As a percentage of total operating costs of the larger airport, these increases would be small when divided among the number of passengers. For the commuter carriers the higher landing fees at peak hours translates into higher increases in cost per passenger on small rather than on large aircraft. This was one reason for the DOT arguing in the Massport case that the landing fees at Logan were discriminatory. Morrison Steven A and Clifford Winston, 'Enhancing the Performance,' op.cit., p.119. In order to present the passenger with the peak charge, it has been recommended that the landing fees should be imposed as a direct tax on the price of the passenger ticket, proceeds going to the airport authority, ibid., at p.130. Such a tax, however, would not only be resented by the carriers, it would probably be ruled as unjust and discriminatory.

103. Costs at FAA operated airports are recouped by levying landing fees and terminal charges; capital developments are financed through Congressional appropriations. Port authorities, which are legally chartered institutions with the status of a public corporation, operate some twenty- per cent of the US, large commercial airports. Thanks to their power to issue their own debt, and revenues drawn from toll bridges and marine terminals, port authorities exercise

considerable independence from state and local governments. Airport or aviation authorities, with a smaller revenue base then port authorities, have similar independencies, operating approximately one-eighth of the large (and a quarter of the medium) airports. Alaska, Connecticut, Hawaii and Maryland operate state run airports, managed by state departments of transportation. Half of the large commercial airports are operated by municipal or county governments, typically owned and run as a department of the city or county, reporting to city or county council directions. The city of Indianapolis has contracted with a private operator to manage the Indianapolis airport system. CBO, Financing US Airports, 15-18.

104. ibid., pp.36-37. Under the compensatory approach, the airport operator assumes the major financial risk of running the airport and charges the airline fees and rental rates so as to recover the actual costs of the facilities and services that they use.

105. Winston, Clifford (1999), 'You Can't Get There from Here: Government Failure in US Transportation,' *Brookings Review*, **17**(3), Summer, p.37.

106. ibid., p.43.

107. ibid., p.45.

108. ibid., pp.45-46.

109. ibid., p.37.

110. Treanor, Janie Lynn.,'Privatization v. Corporatization,' op.cit., p.634.

8. The Organisational Re-design of Canada's Aviation Infrastructure

With fewer than thirty million people occupying one fifteenth of the planet's landmass, Canada has been heavily reliant on transport systems to forge its widely dispersed regional communities into an inter-provincial common market and nation state. Much of the 12 per cent of GDP spent on building Canada's transport system has passed through the public portals. Until the late 1980s, the federal government owned the dominant domestic air carrier, the air navigational system and the airports, and it managed them through a central planning agency located within Transport Canada.

By the end of the following decade, however, the air navigational system had been privatised and the federal government had devolved the operation of the airports onto local authorities. Privatisation, deregulation, commercialisation and contracting-out amounted to a complete re-design of Canada's aviation infrastructure. The replacement of the system of co-ordination by command and control with a decentralised, competitive system, entailing market incentives, was a response to the constraints of government deficits - the over-elaborate government-run system had cost the public too much money.

Moreover, from the mid-eighties onwards, priorities had shifted away from pork-barrel politics. The advent of NAFTA demanded an efficient transportation system for North American exporters and importers alike.

CANADA'S CENTRALLY-PLANNED AVIATION INFRA-STRUCTURE

As a major provider of long-distance passenger transportation for more than fifty years, the state-owned domestic civil aviation operation, by facilitating east-west social intercourse over long distances, had assisted greatly in the consolidation of the Canadian confederation. Aviation infrastructure was, moreover, an attractive investment. Airports and navigation systems engendered a sense of modernity that rubbed off on other federal institutions of government and, thanks to purchases made in the immediate post-war period, the federal government owned and ran most of the nation's public airports.[1]

In Canada, aeronautics also falls under federal jurisdiction, regardless of whether an airport is owned by the federal government or by a provincial or municipal authority.[2]   Therefore, matters such as airworthiness, air navigation, and standards applicable to the construction and maintenance of runways are managed under federal jurisdiction.

Transport Canada, a Federal Department, operated the most important public, commercial airports in Canada. A division within the Department engaged in system-wide planning and forecasting, while management was conducted through the Ottawa-based headquarters, which controlled regional and local offices.

The operation was extensive by any measure. In fact, the federal government of Canada was responsible for the largest air programme outside the (former) Communist world. At the start of the 1990s, it owned and operated over 220 airports, with an airport infrastructure valued (excluding land values) at about $10 billion. Annual revenues amounted to some $800 million and it employed 4,000 people.[3]

Funding, particularly during the growth and construction period of the early 1970s, was by government appropriation. Unlike the situation at most major US airports, air carriers played no role in financing airport operations or investments.

In 1969, the self-supporting Airports and Ground Services Revolving Fund was established to finance the operation and development of certain maturing airports. After the *National Transportation Act* [4] was introduced in 1967, the Department strove to devise a policy that would satisfy the legislature's objective of recovering a share of the costs of providing the infrastructure for air transport.

The reason for this financial directive was that government subsidies in Canada (as in the United States) had begun to burgeon. This happened, in part, because of the gap that was opening up between regulated prices and the actual costs of providing transport infrastructure. Research showed that all modes were being subsidised in Canada. In 1973, according to Oum, 'taxpayers carried 17.08 per cent of the cost of air transportation; 27.1 per cent of the cost of marine transportation and 5.65 per cent of the cost of road transportation.'[5] (In the United States, by way of comparison, in 1984, federal subsidies as a percentage of total programme costs made up 23 per cent of the cost of civilian aviation services, 100 per cent of deep-draft ports and harbours and 91 per cent of inland waterways.)[6]

Bird, an observer of the phase of airport development in Canada in the early 1970s, identified the over-investment in aviation infrastructure as being due to the failure of Transport Canada to deploy an effective pricing system[7].

However, he offered no reasons for his conclusions. Feldman and Milch, also observers of this era of airport development, postulated that the system of governance should 'provide effective and equitable solutions'[8] and, in this respect, the system did not pass their test. There was a failure to balance the consequences of aircraft noise and land-taking against the contributions made by air transports with regard to the mobility of goods and services.

The planners' rejection of cost-based pricing, and their advocacy of capacity expansion for future needs, was a reflection of aviation interests, not of efficient and economical operation.[9] Unwilling to incur full user costs, the aviation industry successfully pressured the planners in the Department to shift the incidence of costs on to the Federal Treasury. Future planning was conducted without the aid of the pricing system, but in the full confidence that the Treasury would accommodate all over-expenditure. Excluded from consideration were the urban dwellers' concerns over noise and property values.[10] Choices of location and land use, however, were, greatly influenced by the political process, the decisions illustrating that: '...the airport system was not understood within the context of an urban system, nor even consistently within the framework of a national airport system.'[11]

Planning eventually came down to earth for political reasons,[12] and with rational planning the erroneous expectations that the planners had cherished for the future came under scrutiny. Airport capacity was greatly in excess of needs at such airports as Mirabel and Montreal, and inadequate at others like Toronto and Vancouver. These imbalances and inconsistencies were due, according to Feldman and Milch, to intra-agency conflict, but they were also the result of the opportunism of government officers who, when faced with opportunities to acquire land, obviated conflict either by buying up affected land, or, alternatively, by attempting to exclude critics from the planning process. The resulting unequal treatment of the provinces not only discredited the process of central planning but also discredited the confederate system of governance.

The Canadian federal government has been able (as few public airport proprietors in the United States have been), to exercise control over land acquisition and its management. As a result, the Canadian government has bought sizeable areas of 'noise lands' at considerable expense. But, while it may be argued that the potential costs of damages have been minimised through the policy of land acquisition, there are strong reasons for thinking that those affected by aircraft noise have not been treated equally fairly. The same charges have, in fact, been levelled in the case of the very different domestic civil aviation system in operation in the United States.

Both systems had another unfortunate characteristic in common: the absence of pricing structures that approximate user costs.

To neo-classical economists the substantial and 'unbalanced' recovery of infrastructure costs - or, to put it differently - of unbalanced subsidies, causes the misallocation of resources. Services that are provided free discourage conservation. When freight rates deviate from costs, the average freight costs to society increase. As freight costs are components of most other commodity costs, 'distorted' freight rates create distortions in other prices.

Having identified the resource misallocation, the task of the economic engineer is to infer the optimum allocation. Most have deployed technical variations of the comparative cost approach. The costs of providing transport services are defined as a function of shipment distance. The higher cost mode is then adjusted to account for the inventory costs to shippers of the slower average transit time and larger sizes of lots. Comparisons of the adjusted high cost mode to the lower cost mode are made, and, according to Levin:

> An 'optimal' allocation is inferred on the assumption that the best cost mode should carry all the traffic over the range of its cost advantage. Within a given mileage block, the welfare loss is simply the quantity actually transported by the high cost mode times the differences between the rate paid to the highest cost carrier and the marginal cost of the low cost carrier. Summing over mileage blocks, one obtains the total welfare loss from rate regulation.[13]

Instead of using a linear approximation of the dead weight loss of consumer surplus by measuring the area of the (Harberger's) welfare triangle, Oum considers modal cost price elasticities and a translog cost function to account for the non-linearity of the demand curve. He estimated the efficiency losses for inter-city passenger and freight flows in Canada some quarter a century ago to have been $200 million.[14]

THE BREAKDOWN OF OTTAWA'S HEGEMONY

As the manager of airport infrastructures, the Department of Transport was charged by the Government with the task of recovering a fair proportion of the total costs of the airports.[15] This responsibility was re-affirmed in the 1987 *National Transportation Act* (NTA).[16] According to the NTA, economy and efficiency can be achieved in the air transport sector by intra-modal competition and by the recovery of '...a fair proportion of the total real costs of the resources, facilities and services provided to that carrier or mode of transportation at public expense.'[17] Six statutes, and their pursuant regulations, specify the powers, duties and functions of the Minister with respect to the Department's airports.[18] Of these, the Cabinet, under the 1983 *Aeronautics Act,* authorises the Minister of Transport to impose charges 'for the use of ... any (other) facility or service provided by or on behalf of the

Minister at any aerodrome.' In addition, paragraph 13(a) of the *Financial Administration Act* empowers the Cabinet, on the recommendation of Treasury Board, to prescribe by regulation, fees and charges for services. Paragraph 13(b) enables Cabinet, again on the recommendation of the Treasury Board, to authorise Ministers to prescribe user fees and charges with respect to their departmental programmes, 'notwithstanding the provisions of any other act.'

The Department's response to its this legislation was fourfold. First, in terms of a cost recovery policy it attempted to identify costs and specify revenues to be raised from users; second, the Airports Authority (within Transport Canada) was changed, 'from a public service to a public enterprise organisation.'[19] Building upon the measures in the November 1984 Economic Statement, the May 1985 Budget outlined a Deficit Reduction Program. Transport Canada subsequently entered into an Agreement on Deficit Reduction Principles with the Treasury Board (a central agency of government), covering the period 1985 to 1991. Hence, the third response was the establishment of a target of financial self-sufficiency. Fourthly, the Department launched an 'airports devolution policy.'

The cost recovery policy and the self-sufficiency targets were interdependent of each other. The rates and fees established within the framework of the cost recovery policy determined, in part, the generation of revenue and hence influenced current financial performance. By affecting demand and revenue, such rates influenced investment decisions and, therefore, future supply and financial performance. By influencing demand and the future supply of services, and, in part, by determining revenues, such rates and fees decided the net costs of the airport system borne by the 'stakeholders' i.e. the commercial airlines, passengers, local concessionaires and commercial operators who operate businesses at airport facilities.

In December 1978, the Department had issued a 'General Policy on Cost Recovery-Air Program.' The costs to be recovered included: direct operation and maintenance expenses; indirect expenses; depreciation; and interest on the undepreciated value of capital assets. The International and National airports groups were to be 'subject to full cost recovery.' Regional airports, it stated, 'will be subjected to gradually increasing recovery of costs with the objective of achieving full recovery.' The costs of developing remote airports would be borne by the government.

Subsequent to the 1987 changes to the NTA, the Department revised the 1978 Cost Recovery Policy. The 'Proposed New Cost Recovery Guidelines and Policies' presented draft guidelines and policies upon which the Department proposed to rely in increasing the recovery of the cost of its Air and Marine Facilities and Services.[20] (A revised draft was completed at the end of 1989.)

The reformulated cost recovery policies were launched in 1987. In the meanwhile, the 1978 'General Policy on Cost Recovery' provided the policy framework. There was a problem with the cost base, for there had been a failure to distinguish between costs attributable to providing services to the users, and the costs of other non-transport objectives. There was also a failure to identify clearly users of the system (and the costs that were properly recoverable from users), and those that were properly borne by the taxpayers. In calculating depreciation, and the imputed cost of capital, the method adopted was to value assets at their historical rather than at their replacement cost.[21]

Three regulations promulgated under the *Aeronautics Act* of 1985 pertained to charges for facilities and services provided by Department of Transport airports: a) Air Services Fee Regulations; b) Airport Ground Transportation Fees Regulations; and c) Airport Vehicle Parking Charges Regulations.

Through the Air Service Fee Regulations, the Minister established fees for landing, terminal, loading bridges, passenger transfer vehicles and (aircraft parking) fees at all Transport Canada operated airports. These landing and terminal fees were based on the methodology of 'residual costing' outlined in the 1978 General Policy on Cost Recovery. The costs included operations and maintenance (on a cash basis), overheads, depreciation and imputed interest, less allowance for state and military aircraft.

Deducted from the estimated costs were revenues from concessions, rentals, and other charges (including fuel concessions).[22] The difference between costs and revenues was the 'shortfall' and was the 'target' sum to be recovered from air carrier users of the airports. (Note that movements in total costs and movements in revenue earned from concessions, determined this shortfall.) The difference measured by the 'shortfall' was the cost base upon which landing and terminal fees were determined.

The policy did not specify what percentage of the shortfall should be covered from aircraft operations. In practice, the level of fees tended to be determined, not by the size of the shortfall, but by the strength of the resistance to rate increases offered by the carriers.

The method outlined above of establishing national landing and terminal fees was formulated in the 1986/87 financial year. Prior to that year, revenues contributed by the Air Transportation Tax (att) were, along with commercial revenues, deducted from net costs. (The att on travel within the jurisdiction of the Canadian tax laws is an *ad valorem* tax, imposed on the value of the tickets sold. Outside this jurisdiction, the tax is a specific sum. Customs & Excise collect the tax). Eighty-six per cent of the revenues from the att were allocated to the airports. The number of passengers enplaned and deplaned at the 23 airports in the Revolving Fund were then aggregated and expressed as a percentage of all enplaned and deplaned passengers. It was this percentage of the sum allocated to airports that was added to commercial revenues and subtracted from the total costs of the 23 airports, that produced the estimated 'shortfall.'

Such a procedure was possible because the 1978 General Policy did not expressly specify how revenues from the att should be deployed in the residual costing method. The Senior Management Committee of the relevant division in Transport Canada (CADA) changed the procedure in 1986, so that the att revenue items would be treated as a 'below the line item.'

The calculation of landing fees was based on the maximum permissible take-off weight, and was payable by all jet and turbo-prop aircraft, including helicopters, at all airports. There were no landing fees for piston engine aircraft.

An investigation into which 'user' group was paying for the airport system revealed that passengers, through the att, and Government appropriations contributed over 60 per cent of the total capital and operating costs in 1988/89. Commercial revenues accounted for 18 per cent and the airlines for 20 percent. Such shifting of the incidence of the costs was possible because the NTA referred to carriers bearing a 'fair proportion of the total costs'. It was silent as to whether passengers should be considered a 'mode of transportation.'

As to the formulation of rates, the Minister of Transport had authority over eight categories of user fees, rentals and permits. To change the level and structure of these fees required changes in regulations. The system was a cumbersome, but appropriate method for a public utility, but not for an enterprise that had adopted a commercial objective. The system lacked flexibility and revenue was being lost.

The high overheads of the centralised planning system, and the provision of facilities and services without the same 'bottom line' consideration or the requirement to repay capital obtained through Parliamentary appropriations, would appear to be the major reason why the costs of operating Revolving Fund Airports exceeded those of similar selected US airports.[23]

Although the fees charged to aircraft users purported to be based on average, system-wide costs, they were, in fact, established at levels that were unrelated to the costs of airport usage. Aircraft user fees were uniformly applied across airports and over time of day, so that they did not vary with usage of the airport. There were no peak charges at congested times.

As a result of uniform fees, lower cost airports were under-utilised, while higher cost airports were over-utilised. The result was a wasteful rationing of time in the form of queuing at the congested airports. Revenue failed to measure wants, so that reliance was placed on controversial physical measures of congestion to determine investment priorities. Such a policy, in which costs did not reflect replacement costs and fees that did not reflect costs of usage, resulted in weak signals influencing investment decisions.

Airport capacity resided at the wrong locations. Not only had the user fees failed to prove adequate investment signals, they had also raised insufficient revenue to cover costs. This meant that that a disproportionate share of the costs of airport infrastructure was borne by the air passenger, who paid the hefty air transportation tax, and the general taxpayer, who was called upon to meet the growing financial shortfalls of the airport programme.

Under the 'Agreement on Deficit Reduction Principles' entered into between the Department and the Treasury Board, the Department planned to reduce net expenditure by $1.2 billion over the six-year period 1985 to 1991. The operating deficit of the system in 1988/9 dropped to $205 million, from $456 million in 1984/5. By excluding the att, however, the operating deficit showed a modest improvement, dropping from $649 million in 1984/5 to $544 million in 1988/9. The 'Major Federal Airports Programme', furthermore, had not achieved its stated objective of financial self-sufficiency.

Transport Canada, by then a public enterprise organisation, considered alternative management options for Canadian airports. A task force on airport management had been established in 1977. In 1979, the task force recommended that the major airports be placed under an 'airport authority', which would be a Crown Corporation. In 1986, a second task force on airport management was formed. It delivered its report in 1986. In 'A Future Framework for the Management of Airports in Canada,' the Minister announced, on 9 April 1987, an airport policy whereby local airport authorities (LAA) could assume direct management of federal airports. The LAAs were intended to be independent business entities created under federal, provincial or municipal legislation, to manage and operate a local airport system and associated business enterprises. Each LAA was comprised of a Board of Directors of Canadian citizens representing local business and community interests.

The stated policy consisted of two elements. First, discussions were to open concerning ownership. Second, airport managements were to stress the commercial potential while at the same time being responsive to local interests.[24]

The airport transfer programme envisaged that a new ownership structure would induce changes in the financial objective, operation and pricing systems. But the changes were slow in coming, because, while statements of intent had been signed, the number of actual transfers was insignificant. More significantly, the hegemonic position of Transport Canada, with its centralised planning role and cross-subsidisation of airports had been undermined by deregulation. As a result, the carriers made increasing use of Toronto and Vancouver as hubs. Growing financial shortfalls showed that uniformity of rates did not make financial sense.

The two major airports became detached from the system. The third terminal and associated parking facilities at Toronto's Pearson's International was financed and operated, not by Transport Canada, but by a private consortium. Pearson and Vancouver also dealt with their congestion problems by operating systems of schedule co-ordination. The 'New Cost Recovery Policy' also initiated a more market-oriented approach to pricing, arguing for peak-period changing at major airports and associated air navigation facilities.[25] In place of the 'residual approach' to cost recovery, the Recovery Policy encouraged a compensatory approach.[26]

COMMERCIALISATION

The incoming Liberal government in 1993 was committed to lowering the debt to GDP ratio. In a policy paper, 'New Directions for Transportation in Canada', the federal government noted that Canadian taxpayers were directly subsidising the Canadian transportation system at a cost of $1.6 billion. Taking into account indirect subsidies, the total cost to the taxpayer was $2.3 billion. Much of the system was over-built. Ninety-four per cent of all air passengers and cargo used only 26 of 726 operational airports.

In the 1994 budget, Transport Canada was instructed to review the 'potential for commercialisation of its major activities.' Two initiatives were launched within the aviation sector. They were the National Airports Policy (NAP) and the commercialisation of the air navigation system.

Under the NAP, the federal government retained its regulatory powers, but changed its status from that of owner and operator to that of owner and landlord. The avowed aim of this re-design of the airport system was to shift the cost of running Canada's airports from the shoulders of taxpayers onto those who actually used the facilities.

The 26 airports identified as part of the National Airports System (NAS) were leased to what were called 'Canadian Airport Authorities' (CAAs). Agreements with the existing local airport authorities were, accordingly, adjusted to comply with the terms of the contracts with the CAAs. They, in turn, were made responsible for financial and operational management. The regulations governing the setting of fees and charges in parking, general terminal services and ground transportation were transferred to the respective CAA. It was expected that giving such control to the CAAs would make them more responsive to local market conditions and to help them to become financially self-sufficient (in relation to operating and capital costs) within a five year period starting in April 1995.

The CAAs are not-for-profit corporations headed by boards of directors, whose members are nominated from among functionaries at various different levels of government as well as by other interested organisations such as labour unions. The federal government elects up to three directors.

Some analysts feared that the CAAs were constituted in a way that would limit both their incentives and the ability of their managements to become more efficient.[27]   The non-profit objective was thought to be capable of attenuating their market power, so that 'monopoly rents' would be dissipated. However, experience has shown that some have responded well to the opportunities afforded them and have moved quickly to develop their market opportunities.   The larger airports have also changed over to the compensatory method of accounting.

While CAAs were seen as the answer to the problems posed by major airports, regional and local airports serving scheduled passenger traffic, but handling fewer than 20,000 passengers each year, were offered to provincial and local governments, airport commissions, private businesses and other interests. The new owners were free to establish ownership and management arrangements that matched the interests of their communities.

From the beginning of April 1995, the federal government undertook to remove its operating subsidies from these airports over a five years period. In the place of subsidies, an 'Airport Capital Assistance Programme' was instituted to provide financial assistance for safety-related airside capital projects.   These projects were to be partly cross-subsidised from the lease revenue from NAS airports.

Canada's air navigation system (ans) continues to provide air traffic control, flight information services, airport advisory services and navigational aids.   They are provided through area control centres, air traffic control towers, flight service stations, a national radar system and communications system.

In the 1994/5 forecast of expenditure for Transport Canada's Aviation budget, some $710 million were allocated for the ans. An estimated $544 million of the ans' revenue came from the air transportation tax on air travellers, with $41 million coming from other sources. The ans employed 6,000 personnel at headquarters, in six regional offices and at numerous sites across the country.

Contained in Transport Canada's policy, mentioned above, was an outline of its modernisation programme which envisaged the introduction of a $600-million Canadian Automated Air Traffic Control System (CAATS) by 1998.[28]

McFetridge has argued that the impact of the government's austerity programme was the prime reason why Transport Canada had failed to successfully operate the ans. 'Government wage and staffing ceilings and procurement postponements limited the ability of the air navigation system to maintain service and improve quality at a time when increasing demands were being placed on it.'[29]

There appears to have been an exhaustive debate within the government over the organisational forms for the air traffic control system (atc). The role of the competitive market process in ensuring efficiency, responsiveness and innovation in the provision of air navigational services was limited.[30] The air navigation system was a natural monopoly. Efficiency would not be enhanced by having competing systems within the same geographical area. There were also problems of having contractors compete for the right to operate a (natural) monopoly system owned by the government. It was conceivable to have regional companies competing along their market boundaries. But this alternative threw up two issues. One, whether the government welcomed the emergence of different charges in different regions, and two, the play of incentives on a monopoly with a secure franchise. Regional companies with monopoly franchises would not have an incentive to engage in innovative rivalry. A government-protected monopoly could not be expected to be innovative. Hence, the best that could be expected from any of the realistic alternative arrangements was a reduction in the inefficiencies associated with an unrestrained monopoly and a more responsive system.

Transport Canada and the Treasury Board would be subject to regulation, while the users (the carriers) favoured a model that had been adopted in New Zealand, namely a private non-profit corporation.[31] This was the organisational form that was finally adopted. The rationale for this compromise between privatisation and government-ownership was that this organisational form could effectively provide the essential services of a natural monopoly. Because the proposed new corporation would be subject to user representation, it not expected to exploit its monopoly power and so need not be subject to regulation. Hence there was the prospect of avoiding the inefficiencies associated with the regulation of a monopoly. This arrangement could also be described as an unregulated monopoly of an essential service that has no close substitutes.

Following the instruction to study the commercialisation of the ans, Transport Canada opened consultations in 1994 with user groups, unions and other interested groups. The 1996 *Civil Air Navigation Services Commercialisation Act* provided the legal means of transferring the ans from Transport Canada to the non-profit organisation, NavCanada, that was established in 1995 under Part II of the *Canada Corporations Act*.

NavCanada paid $1.5 billion for the transfer of the air navigation system in October 1996. The new owner offered Transport Canada employees working in the ans equivalent working conditions and benefits and current collective agreements continued to apply.

NavCanada is a non-share-capital or non-profit corporation. It was intended that it would operate on a cost-recoverable basis, including any debt-serving costs. The corporation is free to introduce user charges to cover operating costs. It has the right to seize aircraft if necessary in order to defray delinquent user charges. The air transportation tax (att) was to be phased out over two years, during which time the federal government would provide transitional payments to NavCanada to cover anticipated att revenues.

NavCanada has members rather than shareholders and they are divided into voting and non-voting members. The former includes commercial air carriers, business aircraft operators, representatives of NavCanada employees and the federal government. The 15-member board of directors is composed of representatives of the voting members. Commercial air carriers have appointed four members, the federal government three, two have been appointed by the unions and one by the business aircraft owners. These ten members, in turn, have selected four more board members who are not permitted to be stakeholders. The fourteen then appointed a Chairman.

NavCanada is 100 per cent financed by debt. This debt takes the form of revenue bonds such as those used to finance many public projects in the United States. Note that the users bear the financial risk entailed by liability for the risky stream of user charges. The effects of this ownership structure on the risk-taking behaviour of NavCanada have yet to be realised. Similarly, it remains to be seen whether the oversight powers of some of the directors will be sufficient to ensure the efficient delivery of navigational services.

Immediately after taking over air traffic control, NavCanada entered into a $486 million contract with Hughes Aircraft of Canada to supply CAATS. When it comes into operation in 2002, this system promises to combine radar and flight data on one computer screen and an automated flight-data processing on a national basis.

In the meantime, Toronto's Lester B. Pearson International Airport provides a showcase of the system, with controllers using touch-screen computers to track and manoeuvre 1,400 planes a day.

Many of the new systems are conducted in-house and reflect the ability of NavCanada to pay competitively and to earn a predictable revenue stream.[32] On 1 November 1998, the Air Traffic Tax (att) was rescinded. Air traffic control was thereafter funded from air navigation fees levied on aircraft operators. Charges are differentiated between the provision of services in relation to the landing and take-off of aircraft and the provision of services in relation to aircraft in flight. They reflect a 'reasonable allocation of the costs of providing the services in those circumstances.'[33] Surplus revenue made in the year ended August 2000 totalled $1.75 million. This surplus must, however, be ploughed back into the corporation.

NavCanada has introduced significant changes. In the first two years, it invested more than $250 million in a programme aimed at improving safety and technology. Three new control towers were installed over three years. NavCanada has also laid off a large number of administrative workers, cutting the payroll from 6,300 to 5,200 and there have been protracted negotiations with the unions over flexible working hours and higher pay. A programme was launched to train 200 air traffic controllers over the first three years of operation.

NavCanada has won the applause of many US critics of the FAA. They ignore the less than enthusiastic response NavCanada gets from the unions in Canada and charges that NavCanada favours Air Canada. Typically, US enthusiasts argue that the Canadian system 'has significantly reduced the federal deficit, replaced ageing equipment, and lowered prices for consumers.'[34] Others point to the responsiveness of the organisation, summed up in the words of a senior NavCanada official: 'The company sought to run the system for the benefit of the users, instead of the convenience of the government.'[35]

Notes

1. McNairn, Colin H. (1969), 'Transportation, Communication and the Constitution: The Scope of Federal Jurisdiction,' *The Canadian Bar Review*, **68**(3), September, pp.354-410. McNairn, Colin H. (1971), 'Aeronautics and the Constitution,' *The Canadian Bar Review*, **69**(3), September, pp.411-445.
2. CAN. REV. STAT. C. N-17. (1970).
3   Office of the Auditor General (1990), 'Airports Comprehensive Audit, 1989-90, Financial Self- Sufficiency Project Report,' 1 February.
4   The 1967 *National Transportation Act* contained an objective and a number of related implementation principles from which the cost recovery policy was derived. The object was to achieve: 'An economic efficient and adequate transportation system' (which), 'is most likely to be achieved when each mode of transport so far as practical, (should), bear(s), a fair proportion of the real costs of the resources, facilities and sources provided that mode of transport at public expense. 'The transport system is also: 'An efficient instrument of support for the achievement of national and regional social and economic objectives, and provides accessibility and equity of treatment for users.'
5. Oum, Tae (1982), 'Efficiency Losses from the unbalanced recovery of the cost of transport infrastructure in Canada,' *The Logistics and Transportation Review*, **18**(1), p.7.
6. Congressional Budget Office (1983), *Charging for Federal Services*, Congress of the United States, US Printing Office (December), Washington DC, Table 1, p.4.
7. 'The present policy, with landing fees based primarily on weight, together with the regulation of air fares which limits competitive pricing, virtually generates inefficient use of airport facilities, peak-hour congestion, and the consequence continual 'need' for more and better airports, 'Bird, Richard, M. (1976), *Charging for Public Services. A New Look at an Old Idea*, Toronto: Canadian Tax Papers No, 59, Canadian Tax Foundation, p.81.

8.   Feldman, Elliot J. and Jerome Milch (1983), *The Politics of Canadian Airport Development, Lessons for Federalism*, Duke University Centre for Commonwealth and Comparative Studies, Durham, NC: Duke Press Policy Studies, No. 47, p.27.
9.   ibid., p.29.
10. ibid., p.46.
11. ibid., p.41.
12. The failure to adjust technical analysis in a political context converted transport planners into apologists for government policies. The expropriation of 96,000 acres of land for Mirabel was justified by air transport planners as a technical solution to problems of noise and urban development, yet the decision stemmed from political conflict with the Province of Quebec. Shelves of studies produced by Transport to justify both the need for a new airport in Toronto and the selection of Pickering Township as the site could not erase the political origins of the project. But the Vancouver proposal was the most egregious case of the use of technical arguments to obscure political decision making. The runway project was created by Transport to justify the expropriation of land on Sea Island, and Transport officials seized any available technical argument to gain approval for the plan.' ibid., p.45.
13. Levin, Richard C. (1978), 'Allocation in Surface Freight Transportation, Does Rate Regulation Matter?' *The Bell Journal of Economics*, Spring, p.19.
14. Oum, Tae, op cit.
15. In December 1978, the Canadian Air Transport Authority (CATA) issued a General Policy on Cost Recovery - Air Program. The policy stated the principles issued in a 1975 policy, and then applied its objectives. International and National Airports '...are subject to full cost recovery, except for costs to be assumed by the Government (which costs are separately identified), for the implementation of any expressly stated Government policy requiring depreciation from the objective of commercial viability.' Regional airports '...will be subject to gradually increasing recovery of costs with the objective of achieving full cost recovery.' As regards development and remote airports, '...the degree of recovery, will reflect Government objectives.' Cost recovery was to be achieved by specifying three revenue sources along with a statement of the residual costing approach:
     1) Concessions, rentals and charges for specific services and facilities paid by aeronautical and non-aeronautical sources.
     2) Any share of the Air Transportation Tax revenue to be allocated.
     3) Landing fee and general terminal fee revenue to the extent that this is a shortfall between the total revenue from (i), and (ii), and cost recovery goals. 'The time frame to achieve cost recovery goals will be related to the stated goals of the Government, with consideration to be given to the economic impact on the air industry, ICAO recommendations will also be considered, 'Costs' were defined as: 'comprising direct operation and maintenance expenses, indirect expenses, depreciation and interest on the un-deregulated value of capital assets,'
16. 2nd Session, 333rd Parliament, 35-36, Elizabeth II, 1986-87.
17. The NTA also recognises that transport can have a major impact on regional and economic development. Regional economic objections should be considered. 'Transportation is recognised as a key to regional economic development and commercial viability of transportation links is balanced with regional economic development objectives in order that the potential economic strengths of each region may be realised.'
18. These statutes are: *The Aeronautics Act, The Department of Transport Act, Government Property Traffic Act, Public Lands Grants Act, Financial Administrative Act and The National Transportation Act.*
19. The Department, in December 1986, initiated a development model for managing airports under the Transport Canada Airports Authority Model (TCAAM). The study, completed in February 1988, made a number of recommendations and concluded that the change from public service to a public enterprise organisation was attainable.
20. Transport Canada (1990), 'Proposed New Cost Recovery Policy, phase II', Discussion Paper, April, TP10041.
21. Office of Auditor General, (1990), 'Airports Comprehensive Audit, 1989-1990,' Legislative Mandate, March. Draft, (A.P. Ellison, Consultant).

22. Through the Air Ground Transportation Traffic Fare Regulation, the Minister promulgates, under the *Aeronautics Act*, permit fees to sponsors of taxicabs, limousines, bus and courtesy vehicles of the airport. Through the Airport Vehicle Parking Charges Regulation, the Minister establishes charges for (auto), parking services at areas available to the general public provided by Transport Canada airports. Under Air Terminal Building Space Rentals (AK-32-10-100), airport space rentals are formulated. The policy applies to the determination of space rentals changed to tenants paying fixed annual rates for space occupied in the air terminal building. The air terminal building space rentals apply to the aircraft operators. They pay the rents for their ticket counter, baggage-handling, VIP lounges, etc. Non-aircraft operators who use space for their concessions - such as auto rentals, restaurants, news-stands, etc. - are charged concession rates that are negotiated with the airport marketing branches and are often determined by a process of bidding. Unlike the aircraft operator, whose space rental is explicit, the market determined communal rates presumably include the implicit space rental. According to the Real Property Policy, pursuant to Section 5 of the *Financial Administration Act*, rents of public land are to be set at market rates. Hence, whether the renter of public land is a carrier or a concessionaire, rents are set at market levels.

23. Office of the Auditor General (1986), Annual Report, General Summary, pp.13-50.

24. Suchard, Derek (1988), 'Communities Lining up to take over Airports,' *Air Transport Management,* May/June, pp.5-7.

25. Office of the Auditor General, Airports Comprehensive Audit, op.cit., p.28.

26. ibid., p.214.

27. Hirshhorn, Ron (1995), 'The Governance of Nonprofits,' in Ronald J. Daniels and Randall Morck (eds), *Corporate Decision Making in Canada*, Calgary: University of Calgary Press.

28. Transport Canada (1994), 'Canada's Air Navigation System,' http://www.tc.gc.ca/airports/nap/english/p3.htm

29. McFetridge, D. G. (1997), *The Economics of Privatization*, C. D. Howe Institute Benefactors Lecture, Toronto, 22 October, p.60.

30. ibid., p.58.

31. Airways Corporation of New Zealand became the first fully commercial air traffic control organisation. In 1993, Germany turned its air traffic control system into a government corporation. See Treanor, Janie Lynn (1998), 'Privatization v. Corporatization of the Federal Administration. Revamping Air Traffic Control,' *Journal of Air Law and Commerce*, **63**(3), February-March, pp.655-663. In March. 2001, the British government announced the privatization of the National Air Traffic Control Services (NATS). A consortium of airline companies (British Airways, Virgin Atlantic, British Midland, easyJet, Monarch. Britannia and Airtours), will pay the government about $1. 15 billion for 46 per cent of NATS and, in return, promise to invest in new systems over the next seven years. The 5,500 employees will each be given shares while the government will retain a 49 per cent stake and appoint several directors to the board. The arrangement has been described as a not-for-commercial-return corporation. Webster, Ben (2001), 'Airlines buy control of air traffic', *The Times*, London, 28 March.

32. Wald, Mathew L. (1999), 'Canada's Private Control Towers,' *The New York Times*, 23 October.

33. NavCanada (2000), 'Customer Guide to Charges,' service@navcanada.ca, p.2

34. Treanor, Janie Lynn, op.cit., note 32, p.659.

35. Wald, Mathew L. op.cit.

9. The Reality of Nirvana

While special interests do often dominate over the general interests and while seeming near-Pareto improvements are often resisted, these failures do not undo the great achievements of the public sector, from mass education to a cleaner environment. These features should focus our attention on re-examining both how and what the government should do.

Making government processes more open, transparent, and democratic, with more participation and more efforts at consensus formation is likely to result not only in a process that is fairer but one with outcomes that are more likely to be accord with the general interests.[1]

Joseph Stiglitz

According to the neo-classical paradigm, the economic problem is one of allocating scarce means among alternative ends. Economic transport problems merely form a sub-set of the economic problem. To resolve such problems as are peculiar, if not singular, to transport, scarcity emerging from transport activity is examined and choices are recommended.[2]

Problems in transport activity invariably result from congestion externalities associated with peak usage of a unit of conveyance on a medium in which, or upon which, to move.   The prescriptions are invariably Pigouvian, and their promoters usually stress that they are welfare-enhancing (Paretian). They are Pigouvian in that tax, subsidy and regulatory instruments are recommended as the means of equating output, costs and prices with the 'engineering' economists' ideal or optimum order. And they are Paretian (or near-Paretian) in that these changes will, it is thought, make some individuals better off without making others worse off.

Although the neo-classical paradigm is widely upheld, it is under assault in some quarters. Questions have been asked as to the 'givens' of the neo-classical paradigm. A contending paradigm has even started to take shape, one that does not seek the attainment of an ideal or optimum arrangement but that poses, instead, questions about the form of the organisation and institutions within which the transport services are provided. Why do these institutions change? Why are particular policy instruments applied by the agencies involved?

These questions recognise that economic organisations are largely defined by their systems of property rights and that the allocation of resources is, in turn, influenced by changes in the structure of rules, which. are established by the state and reflect the preferences of those who wield the power of the state. Accordingly, positive theories of the supply of public services, including transport services, in commercial, developed economies require positive behavioural theories of representative government.

It is from such conceptualisations that, it is hoped, a series of answers will be discovered, not only as to why transport undertakings are traditionally located within the public sector, and how they have been supplied, but also why many of them have been deregulated and privatised.

The methodological framework, within which many of these hypotheses are tested, and the prescriptions evaluated, is known as the 'comparative neo-institutional approach.'

The neo-institutional, as contrasted with the neo-classical construction, is distinguished by two normative and two methodological features.

Firstly, the normative rules are not established by extraneous social welfare functions, but from the revealed choices of individuals. Through such constrained exchanges, individuals are best able to maximise their gains. The neo-classical construction of the individual facing the market is an ideal rather than a description of reality.

On the other hand, by contrast with the implicit prescriptions of such economic engineering, the neo-institutional construction offers the possibility of subjecting to refutation a given set of hypotheses.

The neo-institutional approach is built upon a framework consisting of formal and informal constraints as well as systems of enforcement. These constraints define the opportunities available to active agents and also determine the structure of exchange, the deployment of technology and the cost of transacting. They also include the costs incurred in the protection, transfer and capture of property rights.

Rights are never 'perfectly' specified, because transaction costs are positive. Hence, some properties will be in the public, and some in private domain. When such 'commodities' are provided at zero price and made available on a first-come-first-served basis, the time spent in the queue will be conceived as the price of 'acquisition.'

Transport infrastructures are characterised by indivisibilities and public good characteristics up to that point of utilisation at which point congestion occurs. There are two issues of resource allocation: one is the allocation of resources to the transport infrastructure, and the other the allocation of the infrastructure capacity to users of vehicles. If the infrastructure is not congested, the relevant question is 'What level of pricing will generate sufficient revenue to pay for the infrastructure?'

However, once they become congested, the challenge is to devise a method - preferably a set of prices - that will locate the infrastructure's scarce capacity among vehicle users. Frequently, the infrastructures have been encased in organisations, often owned by governments and operated by their agencies, in which the rights of operation of carriers and vehicle operators are often on a first-come-first-served basis.

As publicly-owned agencies without exchangeable property rights, transport utilities are usually operated according to commands and controls. Over time, these agencies have been instructed by economic engineers to impose pricing rules in place of mechanisms that encourage agents to share their information.

While the competitive market process is propelled by human wants and results in a series of co-ordinating prices, the prices imposed by planners invert this process. The prices they set are expressly designed to influence the behaviour of individuals. The neo-classical planner tries to equate user prices with the marginal social costs of using the infrastructure. Planners readily substitute their notions of users' needs for users' wants. As a result, the prices they establish do not necessarily equate to either cost or value. As such, they cannot inform investment decisions. By attempting to modify behaviour they invariably alter incentives. This often leads to perverse outcomes.

The central proposition of both the neo-institutional and the neo-classical models is that free exchange directs resources to their highest valued use. The legal process creates entitlement and exchange includes transaction costs.

The transaction cost approach builds upon these three observations. It asserts that the initial allocation of legal entitlements does not matter from an efficiency perspective, if not from an income distribution perspective, as long as the transaction costs of exchange are nil. This interpretation predicts that externality problems affecting small numbers of entities will have efficient solutions because the entities will be faced with low transaction costs. These will not inhibit the successful negotiation and enforcement of agreements. If one takes, for example, the first-come-first-served property rights structure, one finds that as the value of passenger time rises, resources lost in queuing will rise to levels sufficient to cause suppliers to delineate and market the right. It will be 'worth' incurring the transaction costs of partitioning and exchanging rights when there are few entities involved.

Transaction costs are also used in the 'explanation' of the substitution of regulatory commission for legislative and common law courts. The substitution of commissions with mandatory power over roles for common laws courts, was made because they were deemed to be more efficient and to facilitate non-equitable exchanges. The existing tariffs were too complex to be dealt with on a case-by-case basis, while monopoly carriers exploited their bargaining power over individual shippers and passengers.

Transaction and information costs, however, are frequently difficult to specify and to measure. Tautologies are often forwarded whose 'truth' is established by giving a broad interpretation to the notion of transaction costs. In the small numbers case, 'strategic' bargaining behaviour is often left unexplained. Transaction costs are used as an 'explanation' of an anomaly in an exercise not of positive enquiry, but of rationalisation, in which the premises of the underlying approach are implicitly accepted rather than tested.

Such methodological shortcomings place limitations on the explanatory power of the neo-institutional approach. The spread and retreat of the public utility concept is a case in point. These concepts were initially derived from the conceptualisation of early transport modes and applied, in the late nineteenth and early twentieth centuries to the whole range of modern transport modes and then to other non-transport industries. The spread and then the retreat of these concepts was propelled by ideological fervour, and as such, can only be rationalised.[3] The shift away from *laissez-faire*, voluntary exchanges conducted through common law courts, to the reconciliation of public interest with public regulation, involves, in this approach, the acceptance of an exogenous, unexplained, ideological shift.

The intervention of ideology, however, removes the implicit determination of the economic approach, for, while agents may be expected to maximise at all available margins, it is not inevitable that such action will cause the adoption of the most efficient institutional framework.

Despite this limitation, however, the neo-classical core has great explanatory potential. The assumed efficacy of the common law process can be tested. It has the potential to illuminate the effects of differing orderings of rights on incentives, and, in turn, on performance. Attention is directed to the differentiation between the normative and the positive and, in so doing, exposes the, often implicit, idealised order which the sponsors of the proposed instruments purport to obtain.

Where there are obstacles to spontaneous, private solutions to externalities, is efficacy determined by the common law process of balancing costs against benefit or is it determined by the identity of the one who is deemed to have 'caused' the nuisance?

The neo-classical core of the neo-institutional model posits the direction of change. By adopting rigid pricing and avoiding investment risk; by substituting a reward and punishment that differs from the accrual or loss of material reward for voluntary exchanging of information, and by separating reward and distribution of income from performance, public agencies fail to use the information that is contained in market prices. What are crucially lacking are the incentives to innovate and to perform in a manner that lowers costs and increases productivity. The prediction is that the public agency will be characterised by rigidity, stagnation and revenue deficits and the public interest will not be served.

This set of disincentives is found in the FAA and it adversely influenced the services of airports and the air navigation systems when operated by Transport Canada. It is no exaggeration to describe these as Soviet-style transport systems. Scarce economic services are under-produced and rationed by inefficient queuing, while the *nomenklatura's* empires compete with each other. The citizens are allegedly mollified by the provision of taxpayer-subsidised public transport while the elite have access to private jets and limousines. (A similar segregation is practised in education. The elite espouse the provision of tax-funded public schools while sending their children to private schools.)

Faced with this Soviet-style democratic centralism, Joseph Stiglitz' proffered solution, quoted at the head of this chapter, is to introduce *glasnost* or openness. Stiglitz writes of the failure to introduce near-Pareto improvements to the civil aviation industry. Accordingly, one can assume he would advocate more openness in the civil aviation sector. Presumably he would recommend privatisation and deregulation to open the sector to the efficient information system of the competitive market. One doubts, however, whether he would recommend the opening up of the allegedly 'successful' public education system of the masses to the competitive market process.

The neo-classical core predicts the movement towards separable, exchangeable, privately-owned rights and private financial objectives of the supplying entity. What are of interest, are the shifts in constraints which appear to trigger such changes; of the adaptability of entities towards (or away) from such changes; and the reasons for the successful implementations, or otherwise, of the engineering prescriptions.

Chapter 7 described the centrally-directed civil aviation infrastructure of the United States. It exemplifies those failures of government planning that are exacerbating rather than compensating for alleged market failures. The growing frustration of the users of the system, coupled with the apparent improved performance of the contracted-out, not-for-profit air navigation system of neighbouring Canada may trigger a re-design of the organisational structure of the US aviation sector. The ten-year air traffic control modernisation plan, announced in June 2001, is just that but it was not accompanied with a re-design of the FAA along the lines of, say, NavCanada. Accordingly there is no guarantee that the estimated $10 billion of expenditure will not be wasted.

It should be noted that for a decade prior to the formation of NavCanada, the federal government had launched a transport costing exercise that separated out the costs of operating the airports and the air navigation system. The FAA has yet to execute such an exercise. Indeed, over the last fifteen years, the Canadians have experimented with their institutions, selling off government enterprises that were allegedly natural monopolies and contracting with non-governmental organisations for the supply of services that had been the preserve of government departments. In some sense, this re-design of their institutions resembled the process of comparison recommended by the neo-institutionalists.[4] Note, however, that NavCanada is a government legislated monopoly. As it is without rivals we should not expect this protected natural monopoly to be innovative.

Chapter 8 suggests that the constraint that has shifted and triggered changes in the policies, rights structure and ownership of government-owned and regulated infrastructure entities in Canada were their substantial operating deficits. The Canadian economy could not sustain the profligate and degenerate system of centralised democracy. Two factors were at play: one was the considered need to lower government deficits to remain competitive in the newly-opened North American market, and the second was the response to pressure from the WTO to eliminate non-tariff barriers. Canadian governments were faced with distancing themselves from enterprises or organisations that served as instruments of industrial or regional policy. As a consequence of these changes, the incentive structure changed and that change caused a shift from taxpayers' subsidies towards user-pay systems and from services provided by government departments to new non-profit organisations

The neo-institutional approach redirects enquiry from the neo-classical framework of cause and solution: away from the notion of the 'transport problem' and its remedy. Faced with the Pigouvian engineers' recom-mendation to impose taxes on the identified perpetrator of a nuisance, so as to equate the social cost of the nuisance, neo-institutionalists ask why the rules of common law failed to internalise social costs.

Their questioning leads to a consideration of the costs involved in the delineation, exchange and enforcement of the relevant rights and the effects these transaction costs have had on the internalisation of costs by the respective agents. Although high transaction costs can preclude efficient outcomes, agents are assumed to adjust their behaviour so as to maximise the potential loss in value of their rights that constraints can cause. Positive transaction costs are identified as influencing the location of equilibria and not as a measure of inefficient misallocation. The neo-institutionalist seeks to use exchange through the common law to minimise transaction costs rather than to try to eliminate them with corrective instruments.

As the survey of the United States domestic civil aviation sector suggested (see Chapter 7), the inherent characteristics of this sector, the number of agents, the transaction and bargaining costs, made correction for noise nuisance through private exchange extremely costly. Such a process of correction, however, was not assisted by the constitutional system, which allocated liability and responsibility. Exchanging through the courts was so very expensive that other margins of adjustment were more attractive. Coercive, Pigouvian solutions, not the lubricating of exchanges through the common law courts, were offered as means of reducing the costly dissipation of resources. The proffered solutions reflected, however, not only the inherent characteristics of the sector, but also the picture that is seen within the ideological frame, that seeks the cause, identifies the culprit, measures waste and imposes corrective measures.

The central core of the neo-institutional paradigm is the efficacy of market exchange. Given the existence of separable and transferable rights, it is posited that competitive markets, provide incentives for agents to discover and respond to dispersed information of value. Information is contained in prices. The process of voluntary exchange serves to discover and to co-ordinate information, revenue and costs, inciting individual responses. The discoverer and exploiter of this diffused information and the dynamic, driving force of this competitive market process is the risk-taking entrepreneur. His endeavours will not result in a neat equation of price with marginal cost, neither of price with social marginal cost, but more than likely will result in a volatile ride of short-lived monopoly profits, followed by excess capacity and losses. The competitive process of attempting to monopolise means that monopolies are unstable. Newer, more efficient innovations will break in to the sector, resulting in some new monopoly. This so-called 'serial monopoly' is one in which consumers' perception of quality and value determines market share. Along the way, quality will have been increased and costs will have been lowered.

US airline carriers have built up responsive networks that provide value through interconnecting services. They have pioneered differential, time-of-the-day pricing schemes that are of such sophistication that they have been copied by corporations in the restaurant, hotel and movie sectors. Moreover, such invention leaves the apologists for the antiquated pricing structures of government-operated airports and air navigation systems without an excuse. Rather, such atrophy confirms the deleterious effects of intervening in price determination by substituting individual planners' prices, separating prices from income and substituting command and control incentives of administrative orders. Such measures predictably lessen the incentives of individuals to expand effort on the discovery, creation and exchange of information. There is an important distinction between monopolies that can be replaced by more successful ones, such as US airlines, and those that are sustained by state coercion, such as the US air traffic control system. The airlines are shaped by a competitive market process that transmits knowledge. The monopolising airlines are the successful discoverers of this knowledge.

By contrast, the monopoly air traffic control system stifles the discovery process and the development of knowledge.

There is an important distinction between monopolies that can be replaced, such as the US airlines, and those that that are protected from competition by the state, such as the US air traffic control system and NavCanada. The monopoly airlines are the successful discovers of knowledge in their market. Even so, the state does not work to maintain their position. They operate under the threat that they could be replaced by a more successful carrier. Similarly Lockheed Martin Corp. and Raytheon Corp., which are in competition with Boeing Co. to supply the FAA with satellite-based technology are successful discoverers of knowledge. Indeed, Boeing officials have entered this market because they fear that their sales of aircraft will be 'strangled by air-traffic gridlock.'[5] These innovative proposals did not come from the FAA. Indeed it can be argued that the monopoly air traffic control systems stifle the discovery process and extinguish the development of knowledge.

Despite these observable 'lessons' the view of the economic engineer has frequently prevailed. The forms of incentives in the institution that is to enact the correct rules are ignored. Aware of the dead-weight effects on markets from which funds are raised to invest in, and to finance, the deficits of the 'public' and externality creating transport services, the economic engineer has extended the blueprint by reasoning in reverse. The desired fiscal regime is stipulated - one whose tax incidence falls on final consumers; it is defined as that which does least damage to the regime that achieves 'productive efficiency.' This is a competitive economy in which externalities are corrected.[6]

According to these engineers the 'correct' allocative decisions about whether, as well as by what means, to take a journey would, accordingly, be made. The deficiency, however, of this vision is in legitimising the assumption that the effect of the implemented regime on the fiscus can be measured and assessed. The case studies of comparative institutions throw into doubt such assessments. They illustrate the difficulties of assessing the incentives and the effects on the operation and responses of institutions.

The concurrent rise in deficits, with increasing public resistance to raising general taxes, has led to consideration of raising revenues for public entities from the private capital markets. The shifts to such sources of finance have ushered in revenue-generating pricing schedules, the 'ability to pay' rather than the first-come-first-served basic of allocating rights of use. On the supply side, institutional changes have been introduced, aimed at reducing costs. They have led to shifts in the ownership and exchangeable rights in the supplying entities.[7] Although participation is frequently partial, the incentive to at least break-even is established. The desire to incite user response by means of applying pricing techniques is established.[8] The critical point has been made that these hybrid entities are not inclined to enhance resource allocation.[9] This 'incorrect' pricing will, however, pale into insignificance, for, by equating the revenue raised from tolls with their direct collection costs, the new entities will be responding promptly to their challenges in a manner that is distinctly more promising than their inflexible predecessors.

In triggering shifts in the structure of transport institutions, operating deficits also highlight another factor: the conspicuous failure of Pigouvian engineering. Despite the widespread adoption of their paradigm, the re-commended re-arrangements and objectives have rarely, if ever, been adopted. When changes in the direction of these policies have been made, they have been promoted, not on the promise of improved resource allocation, but on the prediction of improved financial operating performances. It is argued, by some, that failure is explainable by the lack of reality in the assumptions of the Pigouvian approach.

By promising gains in allocative efficiency, Pigouvian recommendations have proceeded by posing the perceived imperfect working of the *status quo* arrangement with an implicit or near-perfect alternative. Usually, two assumptions accompanied the prescriptions. Although it was often assumed that there was a tight attenuation in the response of agents to changes in market parameters, there was, also, confidence in a substantial institutional accommodation, which would facilitate optimum public utility pricing and investment policies.

There was also, frequently, a failure to appreciate what in the physical sciences is known as the Heisenberg principle. This principle argues that the conduct of an experiment inevitably changes the environment within which the phenomenon under consideration occurs. Pigouvian deregulators of the U.S. domestic civil aviation industry failed to predict the effect of deregulation upon the behaviour of carriers because they were unaware of the precise form and content, of such changes. Such information is available, however, only after the deregulatory measure are implemented. This methodological weakness is not patched up by *ex post* rationalisation.

Neither, indeed, can the Pigouvian engineers claim that the deregulation of the domestic U.S. civil aviation industry sprang exclusively from their promotion of the promised benefits.

Behind these, and most other changes, was an ideological shift among influential players within the polity. Just as the earlier shift in ideology had created the political machinery for market intervention and, in so doing, left no market, however well-functioning and immune from intervention, so the ideological shift towards the market order threatened regulatory systems that were functioning well with deregulation and privatisation.

Notes

1. Stiglitz, Joseph (1998), 'The Private Uses of Public Interests: Incentives and Institutions,' *Journal of Economic Perspectives*,**12**(2), Spring, p.21
2. Winston, Clifford (1985), 'Conceptual Developments in the Economics of Transportation: An interpretative Survey,' *Journal of Economic Literature*, **23**(March), pp.57-94.
3. A belief prevailing in the age of Hale (the seventeenth century) was that the public interest could best be promoted by grants of privilege to private individuals and corporations. Later, the resulting monopolies were less favourably received. At the time of the legal search for Hale's statement (*De Partibus*), the eighth decade of the nineteenth century, legal scholars in the United States were responding to the increasing appeal for legislative restraint of monopolistic practices. From this scholarship emerged formalised notions of public utility and common carriage. The government, deeming an activity to be affected with the public interest, imposed regulation protective of the 'natural' monopoly, rendering it benign by establishing non-discriminatory pricing structures at levels that afforded owners 'fair return on a fair value.' Common carriers were identified by being imposed upon by the legal duty to serve the entire public, prohibited from practicing discrimination, and incurring strict liability. See, Basedow, Jurgen (1983), 'Common Carriers Continuity and Disintegration in US Transportation Law,' *Transportation Law Journal*, **13**(1), pp.2-42.
4. McFetridge,D.G. (1997), 'The Economics of Privatization,' C. D. Howe Institute, Benefactors Lecture, Toronto, 22 October.
5. Lunsford, J. Lynn and Martha Brannigan (2001), 'FAA,Boeing, in Air-Traffic Plans, Stress Satellites,' *The Wall Street Journal*, 7 July.
6. Newbery, David. M. (1990), 'Pricing and Congestion: Economic Principles Relevant to Pricing Roads,' *Oxford Review of Economic Policy, **6**(2), Summer,: pp. 22-38.
7. 'National networks of major roads in France, Italy, Spain, and Japan and a few bridges in the United Kingdom, Portugal and other European countries have been built though toll financing. Several of these countries have granted toll motorway concessions to private groups to construct and operate toll roads. The United States has almost 8,000 km of toll facilities. Direct toll financing of motorway construction, maintenance and operation takes the form of a concession granted to an autonomous agency. By gathering together motorway construction expertise in such fields as finance, management, construction, maintenance and operations within a single multi-disciplinary structure, significant productivity gains are achieved. This serves as a permanent spur to innovation, especially structures and provides a firm and homogeneous base for assistance to industrialising countries wishing to try out toll-financing.' OECD (1987), 'Toll Financing and Private Sector Involvement in Road Infrastructure Development,' *Report Prepared for an IECD Scientific Export Group*, Paris, France, pp.12, 50.
8. 'Electronic transponders – a device installed on the bottom of vehicles that can be electronically detached by equipment placed in the road – already exist that can measure road use and allow billing use subsequently, as for telephone use.'
9. Johansen, Frieda. (1989), 'Toll Road Characteristics and Toll Road Experience in Selected South East Asia Countries,' *Transportation Research, A,* **23**A(6), pp.463-466.

10. A Classical Modernist

We must somehow escape on the one hand from our obsession with the moment
and on the other hand from our obsession of history. In freeing ourselves from
time and attempting a balance between the demands of time and space we can
develop conditions favourable to an interest in culture.

H. A. Innis[1]

The eighteenth century was a time when, economic intercourse having
dissolved into chaos, and social life, free of despots, having been plunged
into anarchy, the social philosophers of the Enlightenment sought to
illuminate the innate harmonies of the evolving markets and expound on the
economic and political rights required to sustain a desirable liberal order.

Yet, until this day, the reinforcing institutions that should underpin a
liberal order, namely, dynamic unregulated markets and a democratic polity,
are still not wholeheartedly embraced or universally endorsed.

Understandably, some societies remain steeped in traditions that are
antipathetic to liberalism. The rejection of the liberal order, on the part of
even those societies within which the notions of a liberal order were first
perceived and formulated, suggests that there is no end in sight to the eternal
debate about the nature of the good in social life. In the main, it seems, there
are differing views on what it means to be human.

Classical economists have outlined the implications of making choices for
self-centred man, largely in a state of ignorance and seeming chaos. Later
proponents of the liberal philosophy contributed to modernity by expounding
on materialism and the beneficial consequences of extending to man the
freedom to exercise this side of his nature. They also condemned attempts to
establish and to maintain a materialistic existence by erecting structures that
might constrain man's freedom. Whether or not these structures were
grounded in the self-centred or altruistic side of his nature was irrelevant.
They were restrictions on his freedom, and were condemned.

These ideas have been fiercely contested. Explaining the unintended, and
not always non-beneficial, consequences for society of purposeful individual
actions motivated primarily, if not exclusively, by (theologically)
contemptible self-interest, has not been easy. Neither has it been readily
accepted that circumstances may explain, if not excuse, morally

reprehensible intentions and actions. Those who have materialistic ends in view have not been granted unconditional absolution for the morally dubious means employed to attain them. Not everyone is convinced that the market, by encouraging rather than eliminating greed through open competition, leaves enough room for the employment of the noble virtues in the pursuit of non-materialistic endeavours.

Neither have the Judaeo-Christian traditions found, either in their sacred texts or in their interpretations of human history, support for the secular belief in the perfectibility of man through his own agency. Some, if not all of these unintended consequences, are rejected by the guardians of morality in those societies from which the impulse to shape the surging market has evolved.

The market process, in permeating traditional societies, in transforming domestic into international markets, and mass-industrial into knowledge-based, post-industrial societies, expands spatially, detaching the individual from his communal references of family, town, region and country. Isolated, the individual is finally exposed to the vicissitudes of global market forces. The realisation that, while the chaos of the past may, in retrospect, be seen as having been, essentially, harmonious, the future is decidedly chaotic, and that the impersonal forces of nature operating through the market do not assure the best of all possible outcomes, has drained authority away from institutional leaders and they have been unable to re-shape the global market's international institutions.

Economics, in locating freedom as a teleological concept and then failing to provide the increasingly isolated individual with an ethical compass, exposes the exercise of freedom to the fragile causation of material gain. This is a narrow, potentially self-destructive notion of freedom, for the resentment of the unfulfilled and unsuccessful could unfold in regressive movements that result in freedom's tight attenuation.

Freedom, in this conception, is not related to the deemed good and true in human nature, but to the unworthy.

There has also been a failure to emphasise the distinction made by the eighteenth century classicists. Self-interest, the pursuit of our wants, which may be altruistic, is not distinguished from selfishness, the exclusive pursuit of pleasure.

To sustain the harvest of the global market and to protect it from both ethical outrage within its originating societies and violent resistance from threatened communities, will require the leaders of institutions and organisations of every kind to fill the ethical void by relating the search for the good to the pursuit of the truly human.

The assertion that the good society consists of individuals striving to break these social and natural constraints by freely exchanging through a technologically enhanced market process, is one that is resolutely resisted. Rather than allowing the market to regulate social interaction, some argue that it is the market that should be contained by the power and influence of the society.

This enquiry has been confined within the practice of economics and it has been instrumental in nature. As such, the exercise is 'modern,' for implicit to modernity is a pursuit of purpose, leading to instrumental end-means. Such critiques, however, form part of this enquiry, in that challenges have been issued to a practitioner of political and transport economics - the author – for the purpose of eliciting a methodological response.

One source of these challenges has been identified as post-enlightenment realists or simply as post-modernists. (Such descriptions are borrowed from sociology, central to whose theoretical constructions are explanations of the processes of modernisation and post-modernisation.)

Generalising, it can be said that post-modernists contest the teleology of modernism, meaning that the present, the contemporary world, is the culmination of history. Rather, they argue that there is no proof of a continuum along the line from the past, through the present and into the future.

Post-structuralists, on the other hand, do not lay emphasis on the way societies are divided by the relationships to production. Instead, they seek to discover how the divisions in society are shaped by rhetoric and representative forms. This exploration elevates discourse over structure and questions the demarcation of science from art.

The analyses of post-modernists have thrown doubt on modernity's project in economics, and, in particular, on the supposed objectivity of economic practitioners. Economics, so the argument goes, does not enjoy observer status outside society, culture and history. The lines, carefully constructed in positive economics between observer and observed, knowledge and interpretation, text and author, and between explanation and understanding, are regarded as artificial. In turn, power is added to the blows directed at economics from within the discipline, by practitioners who are more appropriately described as anti-modernists. They are particularly critical of scientism and its domination of economic method.

Efforts to promote an understanding of the market process have been made, in recent times, by a number of prominent intellectual figures. In the late 1950s, Hayek identified certain intellectual trends that were, in his judgement, undermining 'the belief in liberty throughout the world.'[2] His response to this threat was to devise a defence of liberal principles, principles of which economists were to be the guardians. Economists were to be made aware that 'no human mind can comprehend all the knowledge, which guides the action of society' and that the impersonal market process utilises more information than any single individual or group of individuals can possibly comprehend at any one time. Accordingly, economists were to be placed in 'constant opposition to the ambitions of other specialists who demand powers of control because they feel that their particular knowledge is not given sufficient consideration.'[3]

Another approach, that of James Buchanan, is characterised by the selection of developments that prefigure contemporary concerns and the promotion of the views of neglected pioneers of the methodology which he espouses. Buchanan is, appropriately, described as a Whig and as a classical revivalist. He has been prompted to launch an onslaught on scientism by the 'dry rot of postulated perfection,' the aridity of economic and social engineering and the degenerate processes of zero sum re-distribution politics, all of which have been enshrined as basic tenets of majoritarian constitutions. To this revivalist, economics is about exchange rather than choice.[4]

Lester Thurow has turned his attention towards the 'prevailing intellectual mode in economics', the equilibrium price-auction analysis. Writing in the early 1980s, Thurow detected a worldwide trend towards fundamentalism. In his view, 'the return to the equilibrium price auction model in economics represents a parallel development - a desire for psychological certainty in a world that is, in the last instance, uncertain.'[5] Thurow has charted the spectacular predictive failures of the price-auction model and has exposed the weak policy designs of its proponents as well as their inability to control events. Following upon these demonstrations, he asks why there have been no dramatic declarations of apostasy.

Writing in the mid-1980s, McCloskey, noted that anti-modern arguments have 'not extended far into economics, and not into neo-classical economics at all.'[6]

Such observations could be made of another methodology under threat - that of the Marxists. The fall of Eastern European Communist states may have buried Communism as a political practice and plunged societies that were never modern into post-modern chaos, but it has not stopped the practice of Marxian analysis, with its economic reductionism, teleological historicism and class analysis.[7] This provides yet another example of the axiom that action influences thought, and thought action, the connections between belief and speculation, and decisions and policy, remain elusive.

But there is still silence on the question of how preferences and ideology are formed. Human behaviour is patently mutable, not immutable, shaped partly by society, so the quest to emulate seventeenth century astrology, with its mathematical laws of nature, is futile. Individuals are creative, adaptive, and are not automata.

Moreover, the concept of the maximising individual, subject to known constraints, leaves out the alertness of individuals to the call of opportunity for self-advancement or the advancement of self-interest. The market is not a thing, a mechanism, but it is a process, propelled along an unpredictable path by entrepreneurs alert to the possibilities emerging from disequilibria. Through the competitive process, knowledge is discovered and co-ordinated. But knowledge can never be predicted.

The economic man of the neo-classical approach retains the characteristics bestowed on him by the Enlightenment. He remains a passive, ahistorical figure. By contrast with him, Schumpeter's entrepreneur is the *élan vital,* the vital spirit beyond the immediate system - the spark of the spontaneous order. The neo-classical approach mutely consigns entrepreneurship (and the weather) to unexplained 'external' forces and, instead, optimises the 'disturbed' equilibrium.

If one holds to Nietzsche's conception of creativity as emerging from the chaos of strife and overcoming, then the restoration of equilibrium and the ensuing rationalising of society staunches the wellsprings of creativity. Expressions of humanity can only be restored by rejecting future certainties and by willing the destruction of the pacific, rationalised order by championing self-assertion.

Contemporary ideologies of an 'entrepreneurial bourgeoisie' that assign entrepreneurs the role of gently destroying statism and creating society and culture by discovering wants and materialising them with their technical and managerial innovations, are clearly not fascist. Their methods are not the same. Their conception is of motion without goal or content. Man's will is not imposed.

In our examination of the contrasting explanations of the surging global market of the post-industrial order, the neo-classical approach scored badly. The seemingly stochastic processes were not explained, but they overwhelmed the calibrated, deterministic process. The direction and shape of the market process is not reducible exclusively to its economic substructure, but the changing outcomes of colliding ideas and technologies carried by alert entrepreneurs facing and interacting with institutions. To the eighteenth century scientist, the wonder must be that the technical application of knowledge 'of nature' has far outstripped the accumulation of undisputed knowledge of human behaviour. To the contemporary economist, there is amazement at how technology has enhanced the discovery and the co-ordination, but not the prediction, of knowledge by the market process.

The approach adopted throughout the present work implies that individuals adapt themselves to material conditions both within and with institutions. This approach is evolutionary in its conception. It is also fundamentally modern, if not 'positivist' in its methodology. There should be no smugness or noisy trumpeting. On the contrary, world systems, initiated by the processes of the global market, do not contain the summation of the universal history of humanity. Rather, what is recognised, is that the will of individuals is expressed through the market. This will is converted into drives that are expressions of the attempted mastery by individuals over their material environment.

Modern economics has formulated this adaptive process in terms of scarcity; of unlimited wants and limited resources. It has offered idealised solutions, detailed with precision engineering. As Chapters 6 to 9 indicated, the engineering approach has been rejected in favour of exploring the consequence of Smith's notion of exchange, of arbitrage, rather than of choice. An appropriate description of this approach would be 'classical modern.'

If economic engineers have failed to adjust human behaviour by imposing their idealised orders on society it would also be true to say that those who would influence the conditions of choice have also, largely, been unsuccessful. Nonetheless, the persistence of direct, coercive restraints on human behaviour, implemented through legal instruments, suggests that society, acting through the political process, still believes in modifying behaviour and so influencing outcomes.

And what of the role of the economist in government service? It is a question that, in light of the above observations, deserves attention here.

To begin, few, if any economists, are employed as advisers to the 'Prince,' guardians of market freedom, opponents of misguided, interventionist professionals. Those who have retained their distance from governments, who have not, as it were, swilled from the trough, have best accomplished their tasks with true professionalism. So it is plain that, in its pursuit of the consequences of self-interested behaviour of individuals in government, public choice analysis is more effectively accomplished by those outside, than by those inside government. Because organisations are understandably intolerant of those who undermine confidence and morale by exposing the supposed real, self-centred motives of their members (and contrasting them with publicly stated objectives), the whistle has to be blown by a referee, not by one of the players.

Economists employed in government are nothing other than public servants employed to work to an agenda devised by government. They are, of necessity, acquiescent as to ends. In their methods they emulate engineers, as unconcerned with seeking and satisfying the common weal as are jobbing lawyers with the pursuit of justice for its own sake. Just as few of them would be employed as business engineers if they proclaimed the future to be uncertain rather than risky, few would retain their government positions if they were to express doubt as to their information, theories and predicted outcomes.

The work of Shackle on subjectivism exposes the limits of the objective elements in the knowledge with which economic engineers work with and adds a dose of skepticism to their claims to manage economic phenomena. He also explains why their forecasts invariably go awry. According to Shackle, all possible alternative action are initially presented to the minds of individuals.[8] There is no other possible source. The corollary is that human events, including, of course, economic events, are inherently unpredictable, for it is not possible, even with modern computational devices, to centralise all this knowledge in the head (or heads) of forecaster(s) or planner(s).

And yet, the regulatory revolutionaries, whose ideas have undermined regulatory regimes, sprang not from the cluster of academic laureates clinging to the neutral high ground, but from the seemingly desiccated practitioners of economic and legal engineering caught within the impenetrable cages of government. It is possible that ambition and the hope of fame and glory may have motivated their acts of regulatory vandalism. If so, most will have been disappointed. Instead of travelling along elevated career paths, many find themselves in the *culs-de-sac* constructed by their former colleagues presumably to contain them. Few have received recognition. No one has seriously envisaged bureaucrats as having a positive influence on the fate of capitalism. Perhaps the 'self-made businessman,' but certainly not with the desk-bound functionary whose perceived expertise is vested in the skill of writing reports and submissions in various tones of grey. The notion of an active, deregulating bureaucrat is nothing short of a 'logical' impossibility.

Knowing this, were their destructive acts reflective of their acute sense of professional futility, self-disgust and awareness of theirs, and others' loss of freedom?

Whatever the case, their actions in initiating a regulatory revolution firmly rebuts, owing the very nature of their work and the positions they occupied, the notion that they were automatons. Certainly, they were functionaries involved in functional work but more significant were their ideals, and their determination to act in accordance with those principles. In so doing, they decisively refuted the assertion that the material is always prior to the non-material. What eventually transpired was, emphatically, a result of their actions.

They did more than offer a riposte to the determinists. The bureaucrats, the 'no name' academics and the defiant initiatives of the party politicians, whether conscious or not, led in the direction of greater economic freedom. The regulatory breech, the obstacle overcome, the rupture identified by Braudel, in effect, heralded a new phase.[9] In Braudel's borrowed metaphor, transport's 'precession,' its slow movement, was not towards the meridian, but towards liberation. Over the *longue durée*, the continuous pressure of individual exchange re-shaped the institutions, working through and around the obstacles that had constrained movement and the complementary market process. The 'becoming process' of the instant was discernible, the process in which, through the market exchange process, the ideals of freedom and self-realisation were approached, but, because they are ideals, never attained. The deregulation of transport advanced the market process. A crucial, ideological battle was won for economic liberation.

This construction suggests that by conscious, rational as well as by unconscious processes, individuals, exchanging through the market process, alter the institutions and establish the conditions necessary for the enhancement of the market process. Indeed, the very concentration of the process on the instant may have prompted bureaucrats to set this process free and to replace coercion by government.

More controversial is the proposition that at the culmination, long-run effects of such striving through the market process lead in the direction of greater individual freedom and responsibility. This is not to say, however, that subjection to the instant results necessarily in individual happiness. Economic liberals have been cautious in their endorsements, perhaps because this proposition implies the final causes of a teleology. The sceptic will ask what final causes could govern the *ad hoc* changes?

If the historical process is adaptive and evolutionary, then it cannot be directed towards a predetermined end. Indeed, if the concept of modernity is dissociated from its European origins and conceived in revolutionary terms operating within a neutral spatio-temporal sphere, it no longer labours under the notion of a complete state of modernity, of a goal after which post-modern developments emerge.

Those who hold to a cosmic teleology argue that nature does nothing in vain. Some suggest that the gradual process of evolution should be directed by final causes, culminating in the production of man. But there are also those who challenge the notion that evolution is progressive, moving from lower to higher forms. Rather, they might argue, human existence is nothing but an historical accident, the product of natural selection that blindly adapted to shifting local conditions, and so is without direction.

The enlightened Scots, in particular, Adam Smith developed an evolutionary, as distinct from a creationist, approach to social phenomena. The propensity to 'truck and barter' was the consequence of a 'necessary though very slow and gradual' process. Ferguson, another Scot, asserted that institutions were the result of human action but were not the product of the execution of human design. Hume argued that institutions and constitutions slowly evolved and were not the result of a sudden creation by an individual or group. This evolutionary process was ultimately the product of innumerable and usually intelligent initiatives, which were not consciously co-ordinated.

Spencer's conception was that civilisation was not artificial, but of a piece of nature 'with the unfolding of a flower.' All dynamic systems, social and biological, had a tendency to grow more concentrated and heterogeneous as they evolve. To Spencer's internal Law of Evolution, others have added the external mechanism of selection and combined them in the science of complexity, of adaptive, dynamic systems. From such endeavours has come the cry for 'universal truth' or, less grandly, for a 'deep theory of order' in biology.[10]

The debate continues as to whether the history of mankind can be set apart from the rest of nature, or whether it is a continuation of nature's evolutionary transformation. It would seem that the crux of the issue turns on the will and choice of man.

Culture is not inherited via genes, with the result that it becomes a primary factor in human evolution and in the continuation of the further evolution of life on this planet. Not surprisingly, biologists join social scientists, economic practitioners and philosophers in longing to see meaning, to comprehend the whole in a world-picture, in *Zeitgeist*. The picture of the world that has been held up to view in this book has been one of competition through the market process leading to increased choices and so to the liberation of the individual. Only one of the significant parts of the picture has been highlighted. Described in the conceptual language of biology, transport's punctuated trajectory towards liberation has been charted.

Contention has arisen over the points of punctuation, of the regulation and deregulation of transport modes and infrastructure. It is contended that regulation produced results that were unintended by, and possibly contrary, to the wishes of those whose actions constituted the operation of the mechanism. Deregulation cannot, as yet, be so evaluated. It is tentatively suggested that individual action, though intended, will lead to significant but unintended outcomes.

Hayek expected economists to be guardians of economic freedom, shielding the decision-makers from the siren calls of economic and social engineers. They were to convince decision makers by their reasoning, of the consequences of coercion. Unexpectedly, to many, it was within the ranks of the economic and social engineers that the contemporary liberation process discussed in this book was set in motion.

The re-entry on stage of the economic engineer calls for a final reprise of the questions asked and addressed in this book.

The first point to reiterate is that because he or she is an employee of government or business, the non-academic economist is an engineer, valued, primarily, for technical skill. The second point is that the neo-classical approach is inadequate to the tasks set the economic engineer, and, with the passage of time, it is apparent that expertise in institutional organisations, human motivations and finance has, in practice, been substituted for the neo-classical approach. Although many of the neo-classicists are placed deep in academia's protective grove, the emerging heterodoxy suggests growing divisions. Their expressions of pessimism as to the transforming economic order are reflective, perhaps, of the declining prestige of neo-classicism.

The third point is that the neo-classical approach incorrectly interprets the issues at stake in the transport sector. As an economist in this field, the writer feels comfortable as a classical modernist, addressing issues not of choice, but of exchange, through a comparative institutional approach.

The fourth point emerges from the excursions into comparative explanations of transformations. Economic engineers are set tasks that are conducted during 'timeless snapshots.' Functional relationships are iden-tified and measured. It is an approach that is quite inappropriate when examining what appears to be a characteristic of the contemporary transformation of market economics: the time-space convergence, of the expansion of interaction over space and its contraction over time. This convergence is shifting the relations between the constituent entities of the economic and social systems, and from these shifts are emerging a variety of means of 'binding' time and space.[11] Confined to taking snap-shots and in ignoring history, economists are relying on the neo-institutionalists to represent their discipline in an area of enquiry that is led by disciplines of the social sciences that do not disdain the integration and synthesis of approaches. In the meanwhile, those practitioners who have convinced their employers that their skills can outperform the randomness of a dart thrower, will join countless others in escaping to worlds of experience - into entertainment, science fiction, histories of various kinds, where the immediate moment is not of the essence.

Notes

1. Innis, Harold A. (1951), *The Bias of Communication*, reprinted with an introduction by Paul Heyer and David Crowley (1991), Toronto: University of Toronto Press, p. 90.
2. Hayek, F.A. (1960), *The Constitution of Liberty*, London: Routledge, p.4.
3. ibid.
4. 'The behavioural paradigm central to economics is that of the trader whose Smithean propensity to truck and barter locates and creates opportunities for mutual gains. This paradigm is contrasted with that of the maximising engineer who allocates scarce resources among alternatives. As several of these essays in this volume have suggested, the maximisation paradigm is the fatal methodological flaw in modern economics.' Buchanan, James M. (1979), *What Should Economists Do?* Indianapolis: Liberty Press, p.281.
5. Thurow, Lester C. (1983), *Dangerous Currents, The State of Economics*, New York: Vintage Books, p.xix.

6. McCloskey, Donald (1986), *The Rhetoric of Economics*, Brighton, Sussex: Harvester, p.7.
7. *After the End of History*, London: Collins and Brown. Articles Published in 'History Today', between 1991 and 1992, introduced by Alan Ryan.
8. Shackle, G.L.S (1979), *Imagination and the Nature of Choice,* Edinburgh: Edinburgh University Press.
9. Braudel, Fernand (1980), *On History*, Chicago: University of Chicago Press, p.88.
10. Lewin, Roger (1993), *Complexity: Life at the Edge of Chaos*, New York: Macmillan Publishing Co., p.43.
11. Giddens, Anthony (1987), *A Contemporary Critique of Historical Materialism*, **1**, Berkeley and Los Angeles: University of California Press, p.30.

Bibliography

Abu-Lughad, J. (1989), *Before European Hegemony: The World System AD 1250-1350*, London and New York: Oxford University Press.

Aitken, H. G. J. (ed) (1959), *The State and Economic Growth*, New York: Social Science Research Council.

Anderson, Perry (1992), *A Zone of Engagement*, London: Verso.

Armentano, Dominick T. (1999), *Antitrust: The Case for Repeal*, Auburn, Ala.: Mises Institute.

Arrow, Kenneth J. (1951), *Social Choice and Industrial Values*, London: Wiley.

Barzel, Yoram (1984), *Economic Analysis of Property Rights,* Cambridge University Press.

Basalla, George (1988), *The Evolution of Technology*, Cambridge University Press.

Baumol, William, J. Panzar and Robert Willig (1982), *Contestable Markets and the Theory of Industrial Structure*, San Diego, CA: Harcourt Brace Jovanovich.

Becker, G.S. (1976), *The Economic Approach to Human Behaviour,* University of Chicago Press.

Berners-Lee, Tim (1999), *The Original Design and Ultimate Destiny of the World Wide Web by Its Inventor*, San Francisco: HarperSanFrancisco.

Bird, Richard, M. (1976), *Charging for Public Services. A New Look at an Old Idea,* Toronto: Canadian Tax Papers No, 59, Canadian Tax Foundation.

Blumenthal, Sidney (1986), *The Rise and Fall of the Counter-Establishment*, London: Time Books.

Borsook, Paulina (2000), *Cyberfish. A Critical Romp Through the Terrible Libertarian Culture of High Tech*, London: Public Affairs.

Braudel, Fernand (1980), *On History*, The University of Chicago Press.

Braudel, Fernand (1982), *The Wheels of Commerce*, London: Collins.

Buchanan, James M. (1979), *What Should Economists Do?* Indianapolis: Liberty Press.

Buchanan, Patrick J. (1998), *The Great Betrayal: How American Sovereignty and Social Justice are Being Sacrificed to the Gods of the Global Economy,* London: Little, Brown & Company.

Buchanan, R. A. (1994), *The Power of the Machine*, London: Penguin Books.

Cain, J. and A.G. Hopkins (1993), *British Imperialism: Innovation and Expansion, 1688-1914, and Crisis and Deconstruction, 1914-1990*, London: Longman.

Campbell, A. E. (1971), *America Comes of Age, The Era of Theodore Roosevelt*, London: Library of the 20th Century.

Chandler, Alfred D. (1990), *Scale and Scope: The Dynamics of Industrial Capitalism*, Cambridge MA, Belkop Press of Harvard University Press.

Ching, Bin (1962), *The Law of International Air Transport,* London: Stevens & Sons.

Civil Aeronautics Board (1975), *Regulatory Reform: Report of the CAB Special Staff Report*, Washington DC.

Coase, Ronald. H. (1988), *The Firm, the Market, the Law,* University of Chicago Press.

Congressional Budget Office (1983), *Charging for Federal Services*, Congress of the United States, US Printing Office (December), Washington DC.

Corbett, David (1965), *Politics and the Airlines*, London: George Allen & Unwin, Ltd.

Currie, A.W. (1976), *Canadian Transportation Economics*, University of Toronto Press.

Darling, Howard J. (1974), 'Transport Policy in Canada: The Struggle of Ideologies versus Realities,' in K. W. Studnicki-Gizbert (ed), *Issues in Canadian Transport Policy*, Toronto:

Davis, Erik (1999), *Techgnosis: Myth, Magic and Mysticism in the Age of Information,* New York: Crown Publishing Group.

Douglas, George W. and James C. Miller III (1974), *Economic Regulation of Domestic Air Transport. Theory and Policy*, Washington DC: The Brookings Institution.

Eggertsson, Thrainn (1990), *Economic Behaviour and Institutions*, Cambridge University Press.

Eichengreen, Barry (1990), *Elusive Stability. Essays in the History of International Finance 1919-1939.* Cambridge University Press.

Ekelund, Robert B. Jr. and Hebert, Robert F. (1990), *A History of Economic Theory* New York: McGraw-Hill.

Ellison, Anthony P. and E.M. Stafford (1974), *The Dynamics of the Civil Aviation Industry,* Lexington: Lexington Books, DC Heath & Co.

European Commission, Brussels (1990), *A Common Market in Services*, DGXV-Internal Market and Financial Services.

Feldman, Elliot J. and Jerome Milch (1983), *The Politics of Canadian Airport Development, Lessons for Federalism*, Duke University Centre for Commonwealth and Comparative Studies, Durham, NC: Duke Press Policy Studies, No. 47.

Commonwealth and Comparative Studies, Durham, NC: Duke Press Policy Studies, No. 47.

Fogel, Robert (1964), *Railroads and American Economic Growth: Essays in Econometric History,* Baltimore: The Johns Hopkins Press.

Frank, Andre Gunder (1998), *ReOrient. Global Economy in the Asian Age,* Berkeley and Los Angeles: The University of California Press.

Fred R. Ghahe (ed.), *Adam Smith and the Wealth of Nations,* Boulder, Colorado: Associated University Press.

Friedman, Milton (1993), Foreword to *Leo Melamed on the Markets,* London: John Wiley & Sons, Inc.

Friedman, Milton and Rose Freidman (1981), *Free to Choose. A Personal Statement,* New York: Avon Books.

Friedman, Milton and Rose Friedman (1984), *The Tyranny of the Status quo,* Harmondsworth, Middlesex: Penguin Books.

Friedman, Thomas L. (1999), *The Lexus and the Olive Tree,* London: Straus & Giroux.

Gallman, R. E. (1966), 'Gross National Product in the United States, 1834-1909,' in *Output, Employment and Productivity in the United States after 1800,* National Bureau of Economic Research.

Gellner, Ernest (1991), *Plough, Sword and Book. The Structure of Human History,* London: Paladin. Grafton Books.

Giddens, A. (1984), *The Constitution of Society. An Outline of Theory of Structuration,* Cambridge: Polity Press.

Giddens, Anthony (1987), *A Contemporary Critique of Historical Materialism,* **1,** Berkley and Los Angeles: University of California Press.

Gilder, George (2000), *Telecosm: How Infinite Bandwidth Will Revolutionize the World,* NewYork: The Free Press.

Gilmour, Ian (1992), *Dancing with Dogma. Britain under Thatcherism,* London: Simon and Schuster.

Goldsmith, James (1995), *The Trap,* London: Macmillan.

Golub, Stephen S. (1999), *Labor Costs and International Trade,* Washington D.C: American Enterprise Institute.

Gorz, A. (1989), *Critique of Economic Reaso,* London: Verso.

Gray, John (1998), *False Dawn: The Delusions of Global Capitalism,* London: Grante.

Hadley, Arthur T. (1888), *Railroad Transportation. Its History and its Laws,* New York and London: Putnam.

Hall, John A. (1986), *Powers & Liberties. The Causes and Consequences of the Rise of the West,* Harmondsworth: Pelican Books.

Hamouta, O. F. and B. Price. (1991), *Verification in Economics,* London: Routledge.

Harvey, David (1989), *The Condition of Post-modernity. An Enquiry into the Origin of Cultura. Change,* Oxford: Blackwell.

Hayek, F. A. (1955), *The Counter Revolution of Science. Studies on the Abuse of Reason,* London: Collier-Macmillan.

Hayek, F.A. (1960), The *Constitution of Liberty,* London: Routledge.

Head, J.G. (1974), *Public Goods and Public Welfare,* Durham NC: Duke University Press.

Heilbroner, Robert L. (1986), *The Worldly Philosophers,* Sixth Edition, London: Simon & Schuster

Hicks, John R. (1979), *Causality in Economics,* New York: Basic Books.

Hobsbawm, E. J. (1975), *The Age of Capital, 1848-1875,* London: Abacus.

Hundt, Reed E. (2000), *You Say You Want a Revolution,* New Haven & London: Yale University Press.

Huntington, Samuel P. (1997), *The Clash of Civilisations and the Remaking of World Order,* London: Touchstone Books.

Innis, Harold A. (1951), *The Bias of Communication,* reprinted with an introduction by Paul Heyer David Crowley (1991), Toronto: University of Toronto Press.

International Telecommunication Union (1997), *World Telecommunication Development Report 1996/7. Trade in telecommunications,* Geneva, February.

Jones, E.L. (1981), *The European Miracle,* Cambridge University Press.

Kauffman, Stuart (1987), in Philip W. Anderson, Kenneth J. Arrow and David Pires (eds), *The Economy as an Evolving Complex System,* Santa Fe Institute Studies in the Science of Complexity, **5,** Redwood City, CA.

Keegan, William (1993), *The Spectre of Capitalism,* London: Vintage.

Kenneth J. Arrow and David Pires (eds), *The Economy as an Evolving Complex System,* Santa Fe Institute Studies in the Science of Complexity, **5,** Redwood City, CA.

Keynes, John M. (1936), *The General Theory of Employment, Interest and Money,* reprinted (1961), London: Macmillan.

Kirzner, I. M. (1973), *Competition and Entrepreneurship,* Chicago: University of Chicago Press.

Krugman, Paul (1998), *Pop Nationalism,* Cambridge, Massachusetts: The MIT Press.

Krugman, Paul (1999), *The Return of Depression Economics,* New York: W.W.Norton.

Kukathas, Chandran (1990), *Hayek and Modern Liberalism,* Oxford: Clarendon Press.

Lasch, Chrisopher (1996), *The Revolt of the Elites and the Betrayal of Democracy,* London: W.W. Norton.

Laux, J. K. and M. A. Molot (1988), *State Capitalism: Public Enterprise in Canada*, Ithica: Cornell University Press.

Lewin, Roger (1993), *Complexity. Life at the Edge of Chaos*, New York: Macmillan Publishing Co.

Lillechild, S.C. (1986), *The Fallacy of the Mixed Economy. An Austrian Critique of Recent Economic Thinking and Policy*, London: The Institute of Economic Affairs, Hobart Paper, First Edition 1978.

Little, Ian. M.D. and James A. Mirrlees (1968), *Manual of Industrial Project Analysis in Developing Countries, Social Cost Benefit Analysis, Vol. 1,2* Paris, Development Centre of the Organisation for Economic Co-operation and Development.

Lowenstein, Roger (2000), *When Genius Failed: The Rise and Fall of Long-Term Capital Management*, London: Random House.

Lukas, Aaron (2000), *WTO Report Card III Globalisation and Developing Countries*, Center for Trade Policy Studies, Cato Institute, 20 June.

Mahan, Alfred Thayer (1890), *The Influence of Sea Power upon History, 1660-1783*, reprinted with an introduction by Louis M. Hacker (1961), New York: Hill and Wang.

Mandel, Michael. J. (2000), *The Coming Internet Depression*, London: Basic Books.

Marx, Karl and Friedrich Engels (1872), *The Communist Manifesto*, translated by Samuel Moore (1888), reprinted, with an introduction and notes by A.J.P. Taylor (1985), London: Penguin Classics.

McCartney, Scott (1999), *The Triumphs and Tragedies of the World's First Computer*, New York: Walker &Walker Company.

McCloskey, Donald (1986), *The Rhetoric of Economics*, Brighton, Sussex: Harvester.

McFetridge, D. G. (1997), *The Economics of Privatization*, Toronto: C. D. Howe Institute Benefactors Lecture.

Meyerson, Robert. B. (1989), *Mechanism Design*, in Eatwell, John, Murray Millgate, and Peter Newman (eds), *The New Palgrave. Allocation, Information and Markets,* New York and London: W.W.Norton.

Micklethwait, John and Adrian Wooldridge (2000), *Future Perfect: The Challenge and Hidden Promise of Globalisation,* London: Crown Business Books.

Mills, Wright C. (1956), *The Power Elite*, reprinted with a new afterword by Alan Wolfe (2000), NewYork: Oxford University Press.

Noll, Roger G. (1999), *Telecommunications Reform in Developing Countries*, AEI-Brookings Center for Regulatory Studies, Working Paper 99-10, November.

North, Douglas C. (1981), *Structure and Change in Economic History*, London: W. W. Norton & Co.

North, Douglas C. and Thomas, Robert (1973), *The Rise of the Western World: A New Economic History*, Cambridge: The University Press.

Oakeshott, Michael J. (1994), *Rationalism in Politics and Other Essays*, Indianapolis: Liberty Press.

Parenti, Michael (1995), *Against Empire,* San Francisco: City Light Books.

Peltzman, S. (1989), *The Economic Theory of Regulation after a Decade of Deregulation*, Brookings Papers: Macroeconomics, Washington: Brookings Institution.

Pigou, A.C. (1912), *The Economics of Welfare*, London: Macmillan.

Polanyi, Karl (1944), *The Great Transformation*, Boston: Beacon Press, reprinted in paperback edition with a forward by Robert M. MacIver (1975).

Reich, Robert B. (1984), *The Next American Frontier*, Harmondsworth: Penguin.

Reich, Robert B. (1992), *The Work of Nations, Preparing Ourselves for 21st Century Capitalism,* New York: Simon and Schuster.

Risk, R.C.B. (1981), 'The Law and the Economy in Mid-Nineteenth Century

Schultz, Theodore W. (1990), *Restoring Economic Equilibrium*, Oxford: Basil Blackwell.

Schumpeter, J. A. (1911), *The Theory of Economic Development. An Inquiry into Projects, Capital, Credit, Interest, and the Business Cycle*, translated by R.Opie (1965), London and New York: Oxford University Press, 1961.

Schumpeter, Joseph. A. (1950), *Capitalism Socialism and Democracy*, London: George Allen & Unwin.

Sen, A.K. (1987), *On Ethics and Economics*, Oxford: Basil Blackwell.

Shackle, G.L.S (1979), *Imagination and the Nature of Choice*, Edinburgh, Edinburgh University Press.

Shackle, G.L.S. (1972), *Epistemics and Economics: A Critique of Economic Doctrines,* Cambridge University Press.

Smith, Adam (1776), *The Wealth of Nations,* Books I-III, reprinted with an introduction by A.S. Skinner (1986), London: Penguin Classics.

Solow, R.M. (1970), *Growth Theory: An Exposition*, Oxford University Press.

Soros, George (1994), *The Alchemy of Finance*, New York: John Wiley & Sons, Inc.

Steinfels, Peter (1979), *The Neo-conservatives*, London: Simon and Schuster.

Stigler, G. (1968), *The Organisation of Industry,* Homewood: Richard D. Irwin.

Tarjanne, Pekka (1997), *Telecommunications and World Development: Forecasts, technologies and services*, I.T.U., Moscow, 5 February.

Taylor, A.J.P. (1982), *From Napoleon to the Second International. Essays on Nineteenth-Century Europe*, London: Penguin Books.

Taylor, George (1951), *The Transportation Revolution 1815-1860*, New York: Rinehart.

Thurow, Lester C. (1983), *Dangerous Current. The State of Economics*, New York: Vintage Books.

Waldorf, Mitchell M. (1993), *The Emerging Science at the Edge of Order and Chao*, New York: Simon and Schuster.

Weber, Max (1920-21), *The Protestant Ethic and the Spirit of Capitalism*, reprinted, London: Unwin Paperbacks.

Wiener, Martin J. (1981), *English Culture and the Decline of the Industrial Spirit, 1930-1980*, London: Penguin Books.

Wilgus, W.J. (1937), *The Railway Inter-Relations of the United States and Canada*, Newhaven: Yale University Press.

Williamson, John (2000), *A Guide to The Reports*, Washington DC: Institute for International Economics.

Williamson, John (ed.), (1990) *Latin American Adjustment: How Much Has Happened?* Washington Institute for International Economics.

World Bank (1999), *Global Development Finance 1999*, Washington DC.

World Bank (2000), *Global Development Finance 2000*, Washington D.C.

Wright, Robert (2000), *Non Zero. The Logic of Human Destiny*, New York: Pantheon Books.

Journals

Administrative Law Review
Air Transport Management
Airfinance Journal
American Economic Review,
American Economic Review, Papers & Proceedings
American Political Science Review
Annuals of Air and Space Law
Brookings Paper on Economic Activity, Microeconomics
Brookings Review
Business Day
Business Week
Business Horizons
California Management Review
Columbia Law Review
Econometrica
Foreign Affairs
Foreign Policy in Focus
George Mason University Law Review
History of Political Economy
Law and Contemporary Problems
Logistics and Transportation Review
Perspectives on Postal Service Issues
Political Studies,
Public Choice
Quarterly Journal of Economics
Regulation
Regulatory Reporter
The American Review of Canadian Studies
The Atlantic Monthly
The Bell Journal of Economics
The Canadian Bar Review
The Canadian Historical Review
The Financial Times
The Financial Times Weekend

The Johannesburg Star
The Journal of Air Law and Commerce
The Journal of Canadian Studies
The Journal of Economic History
The Journal of Economic Issues
The Journal of Economic Liberation
The Journal of Economic Literature
The Journal of Economic Perspectives
The Journal of Economics
The Journal of Environmental Economics and Management
The Journal of Land and Public Utility Economics
The Journal of Law and Economics
The Journal of Political Economy
The Journal of Transport and Economic Policy
The Journal of Transportation Law, Logistics and Policy
The Logistics and Transportation Review
The Loyola of Los Angeles Law Review
The Methodology of Economic Thought
The Miami Herald
The New Republic
The New York Times
The New York Times Magazine
The Public Interest
The South African Journal of Economics
The Wall Street Journal
The Wall Street Journal Reports
The Wanderer
Transport Practitioner's Journal
Transportation Journal
Transportation Law Journal
Transportation Law Review
Transportation Research
Transportation Research Circular
University of Toronto Law Journal
Virginia Law Review
Yale Journal on Regulation
Yale Law Journal

Index